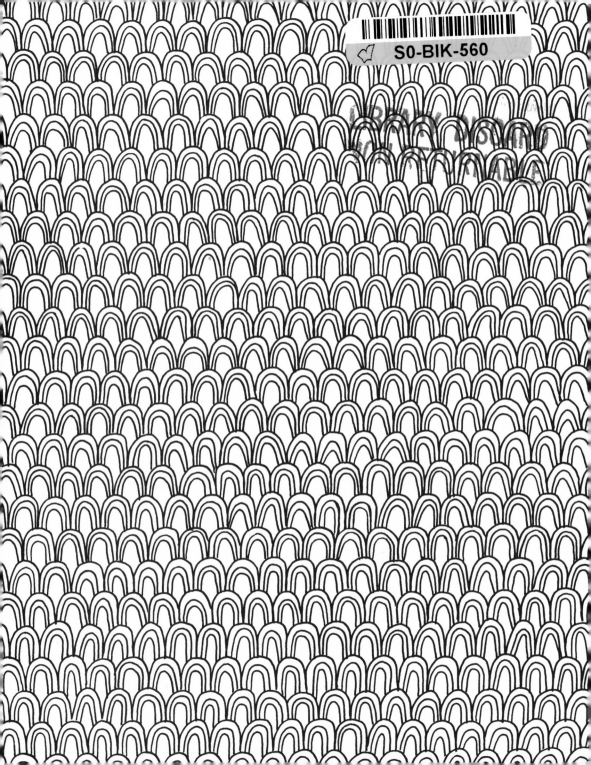

Production assistance by Ted May
Proof reading by Ellen Lindner
Published by Revival House Press

www.revivalhousepress.com
Enquiries: davenuss@revivalhousepress.com

First U.S. edition, September 2015

Printed in the United States

Dedicated with big heart love to Ted May.

Thanks so much to Dave Nuss, Rina Ayuyang, John P, Frank, Nick Abadzis, all my Kates, John Dunning, Fortenski, Heather, Ellen Lindner, Alex and Linda Calvo. Thanks to all the readers and reviewers who supported the book.
Thanks and love to Jeannie and Paul and Veronica.
In fond memory of Dylan Williams who helped so much with the first issue.

MARDOU
SKY IN STEREO

REVIVAL
HOUSE
PRESS

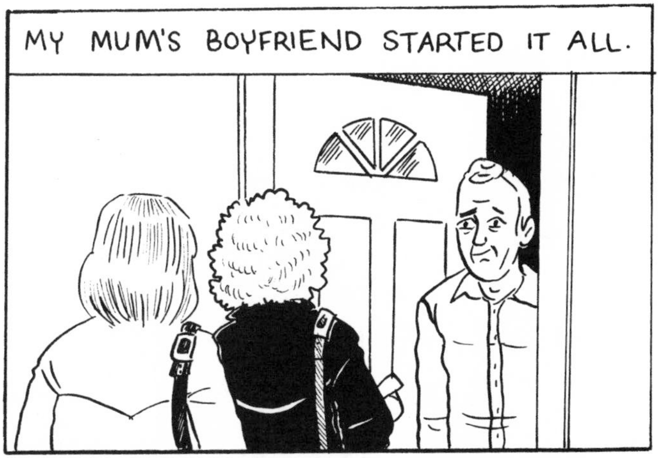
MY MUM'S BOYFRIEND STARTED IT ALL.

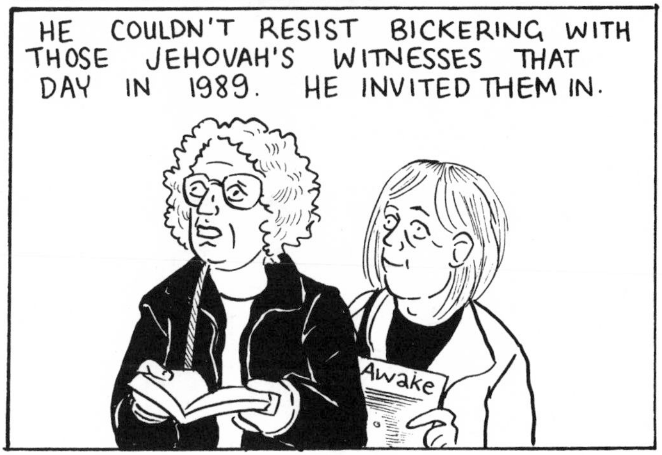
HE COULDN'T RESIST BICKERING WITH THOSE JEHOVAH'S WITNESSES THAT DAY IN 1989. HE INVITED THEM IN.
Awake

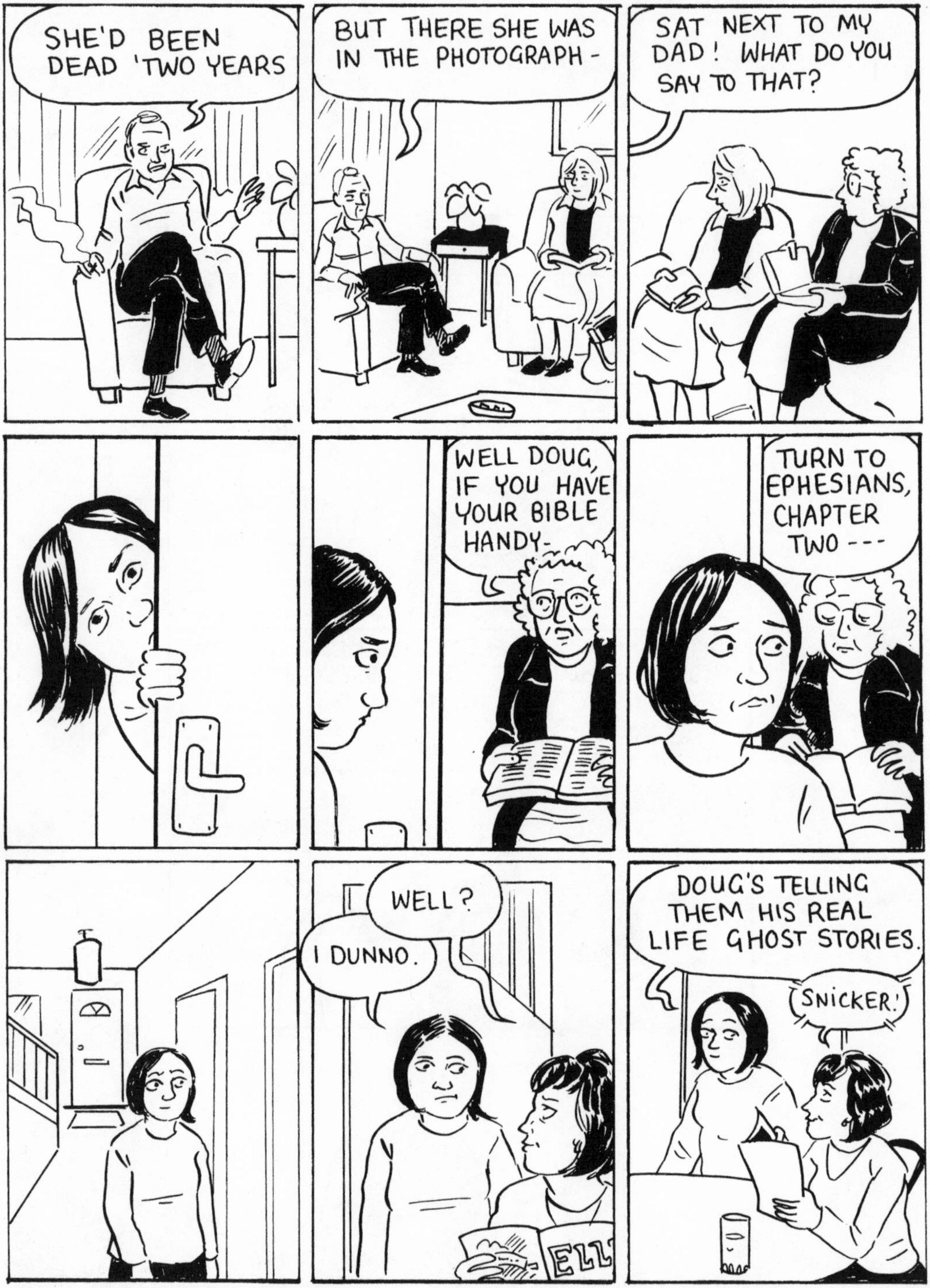
SHE'D BEEN DEAD 'TWO YEARS
BUT THERE SHE WAS IN THE PHOTOGRAPH -
SAT NEXT TO MY DAD! WHAT DO YOU SAY TO THAT?
WELL DOUG, IF YOU HAVE YOUR BIBLE HANDY-
TURN TO EPHESIANS, CHAPTER TWO ---
WELL?
I DUNNO.
DOUG'S TELLING THEM HIS REAL LIFE GHOST STORIES.
SNICKER!
ELL

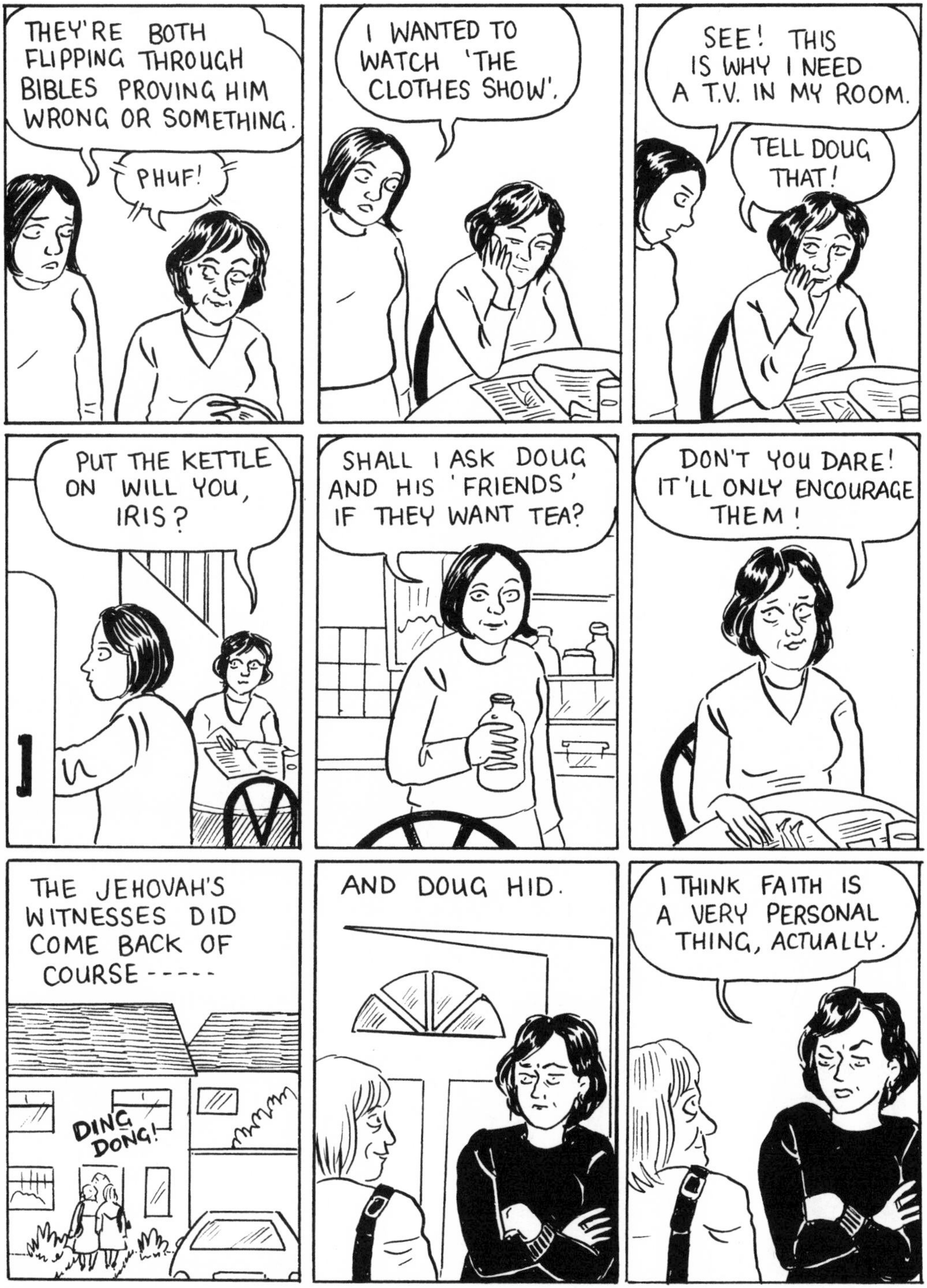
THEY'RE BOTH FLIPPING THROUGH BIBLES PROVING HIM WRONG OR SOMETHING.
PHUF!
I WANTED TO WATCH 'THE CLOTHES SHOW'.
SEE! THIS IS WHY I NEED A T.V. IN MY ROOM.
TELL DOUG THAT!
PUT THE KETTLE ON WILL YOU, IRIS?
SHALL I ASK DOUG AND HIS 'FRIENDS' IF THEY WANT TEA?
DON'T YOU DARE! IT'LL ONLY ENCOURAGE THEM!
THE JEHOVAH'S WITNESSES DID COME BACK OF COURSE -----
DING DONG!
AND DOUG HID.
I THINK FAITH IS A VERY PERSONAL THING, ACTUALLY.

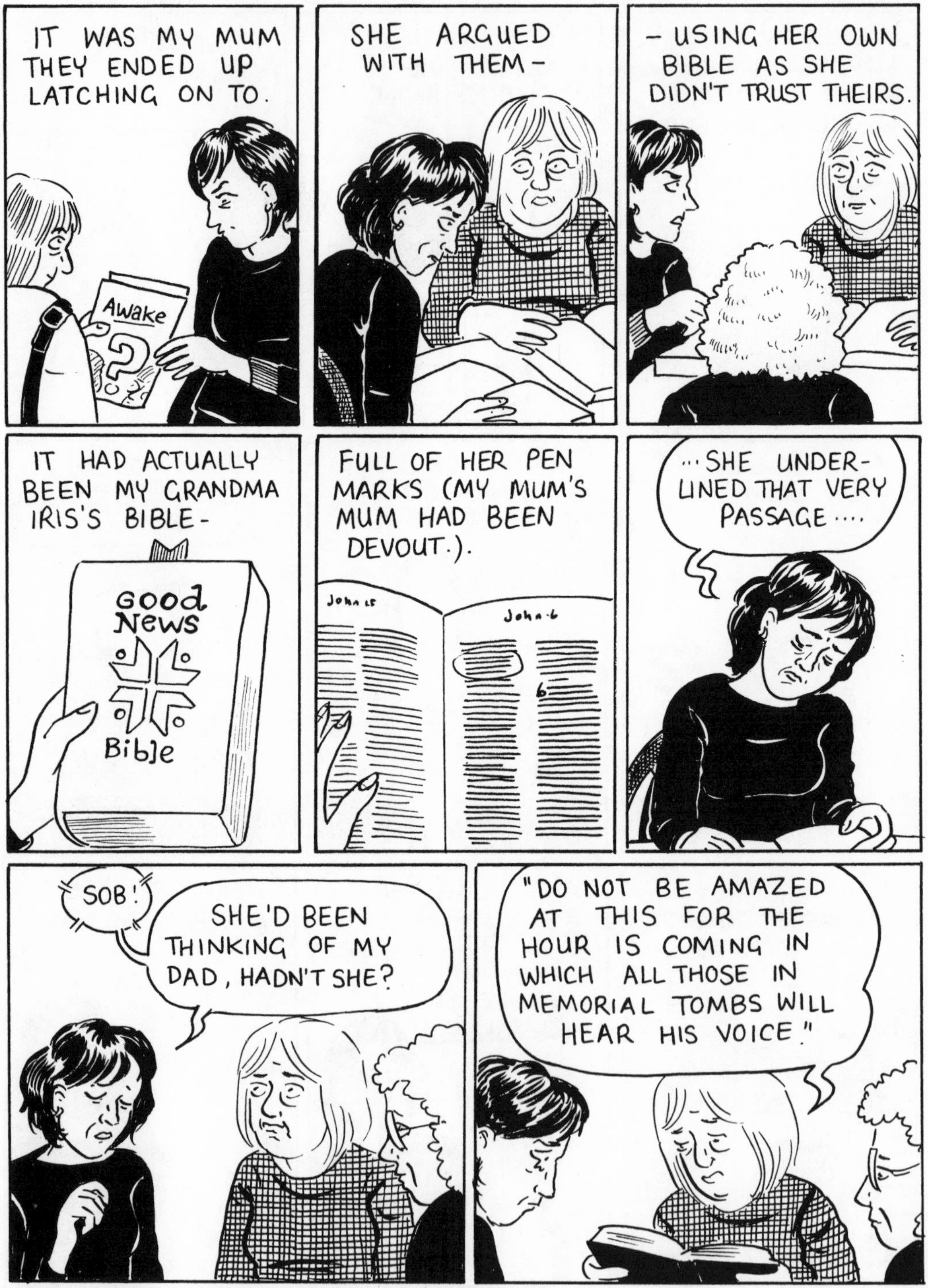
IT WAS MY MUM THEY ENDED UP LATCHING ON TO.
Awake
SHE ARGUED WITH THEM -
- USING HER OWN BIBLE AS SHE DIDN'T TRUST THEIRS.
IT HAD ACTUALLY BEEN MY GRANDMA IRIS'S BIBLE -
Good News Bible
FULL OF HER PEN MARKS (MY MUM'S MUM HAD BEEN DEVOUT.).
...SHE UNDER-LINED THAT VERY PASSAGE....
SOB!
SHE'D BEEN THINKING OF MY DAD, HADN'T SHE?
"DO NOT BE AMAZED AT THIS FOR THE HOUR IS COMING IN WHICH ALL THOSE IN MEMORIAL TOMBS WILL HEAR HIS VOICE."

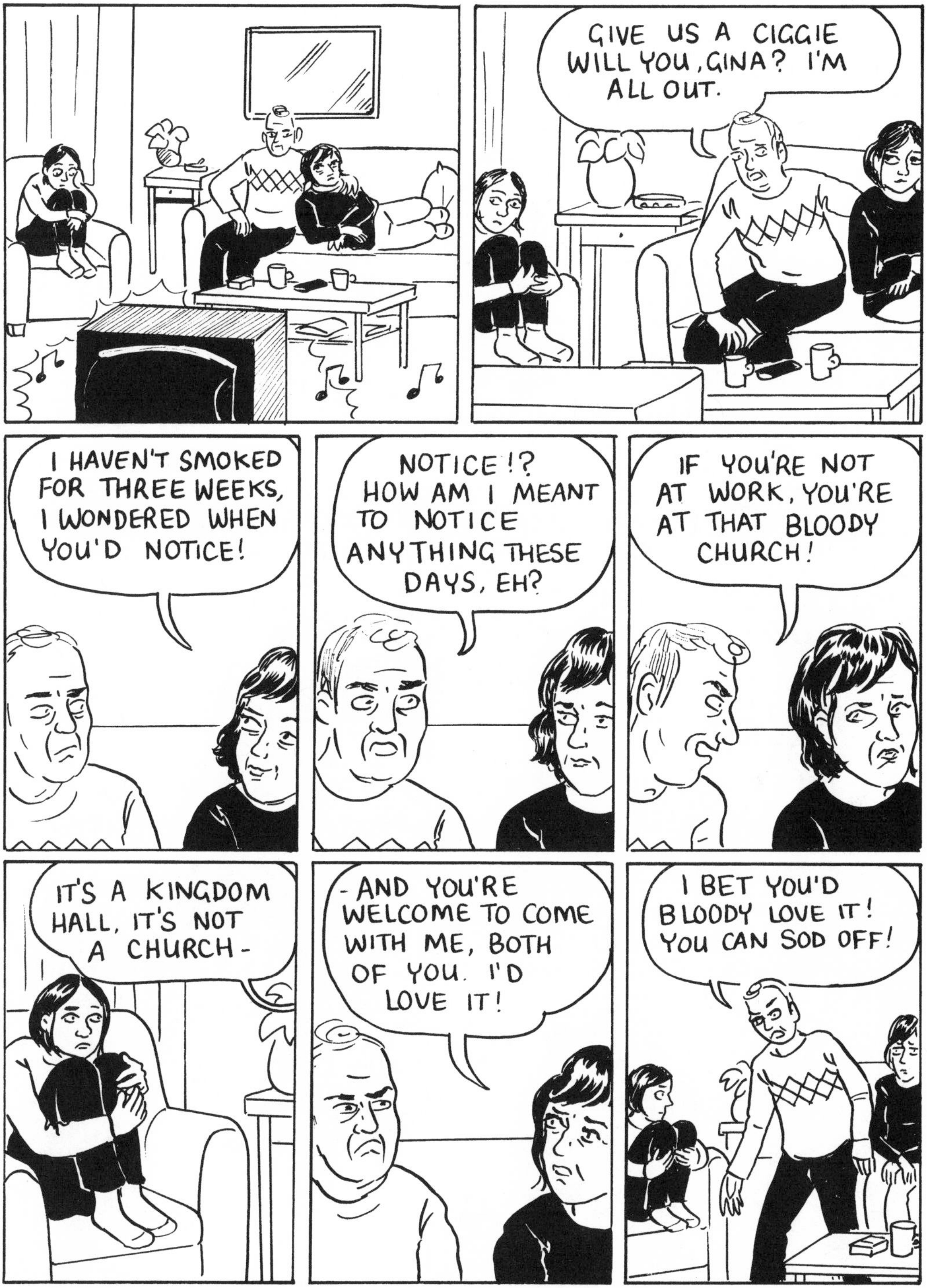
GIVE US A CIGGIE WILL YOU, GINA? I'M ALL OUT.
I HAVEN'T SMOKED FOR THREE WEEKS, I WONDERED WHEN YOU'D NOTICE!
NOTICE!? HOW AM I MEANT TO NOTICE ANYTHING THESE DAYS, EH?
IF YOU'RE NOT AT WORK, YOU'RE AT THAT BLOODY CHURCH!
IT'S A KINGDOM HALL, IT'S NOT A CHURCH-
-AND YOU'RE WELCOME TO COME WITH ME, BOTH OF YOU. I'D LOVE IT!
I BET YOU'D BLOODY LOVE IT! YOU CAN SOD OFF!

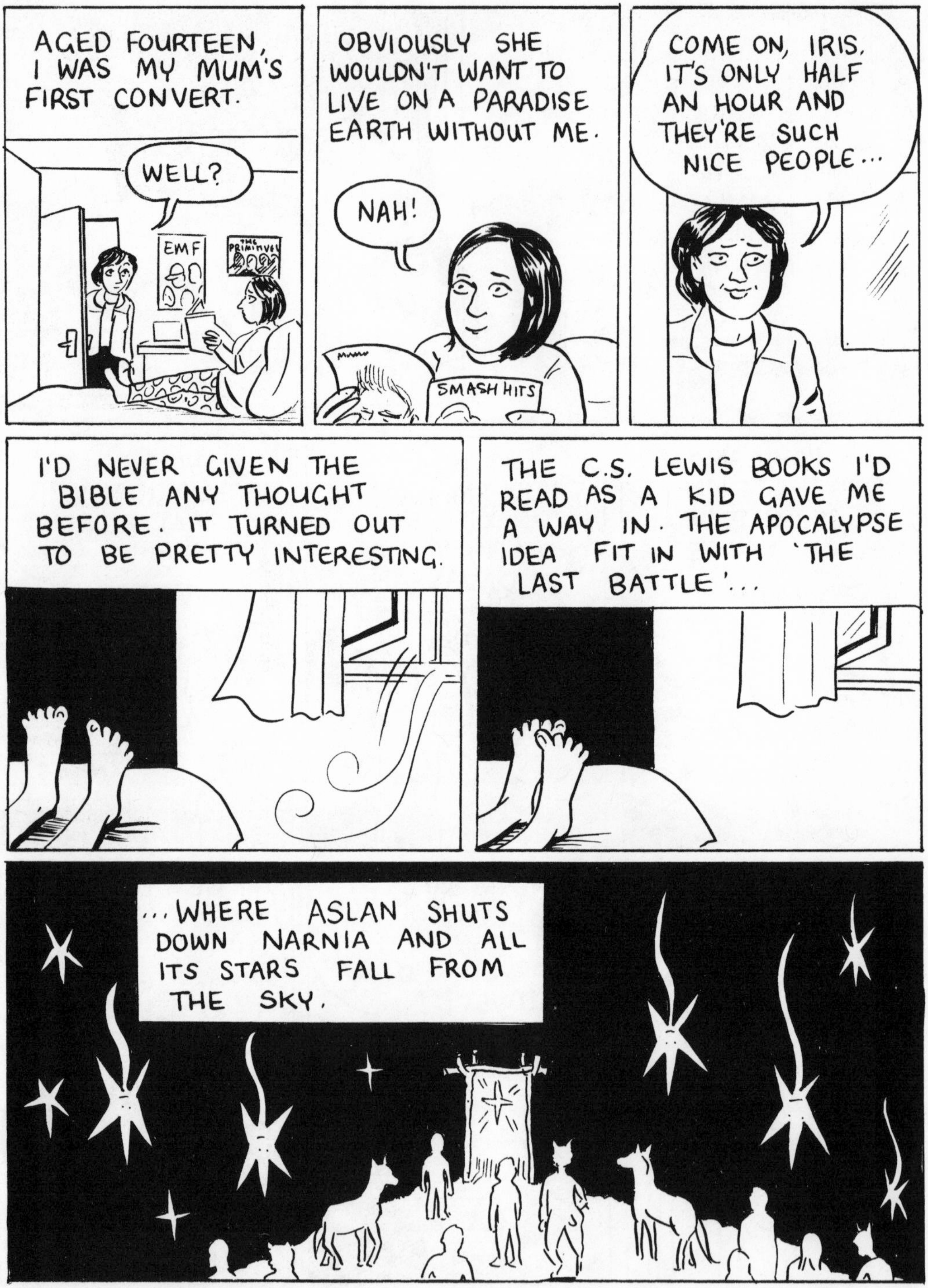
AGED FOURTEEN, I WAS MY MUM'S FIRST CONVERT.
WELL?
EMF
THE PRIMITIVES
OBVIOUSLY SHE WOULDN'T WANT TO LIVE ON A PARADISE EARTH WITHOUT ME.
NAH!
SMASH HITS
COME ON, IRIS. IT'S ONLY HALF AN HOUR AND THEY'RE SUCH NICE PEOPLE...
I'D NEVER GIVEN THE BIBLE ANY THOUGHT BEFORE. IT TURNED OUT TO BE PRETTY INTERESTING.
THE C.S. LEWIS BOOKS I'D READ AS A KID GAVE ME A WAY IN. THE APOCALYPSE IDEA FIT IN WITH 'THE LAST BATTLE'...
...WHERE ASLAN SHUTS DOWN NARNIA AND ALL ITS STARS FALL FROM THE SKY.

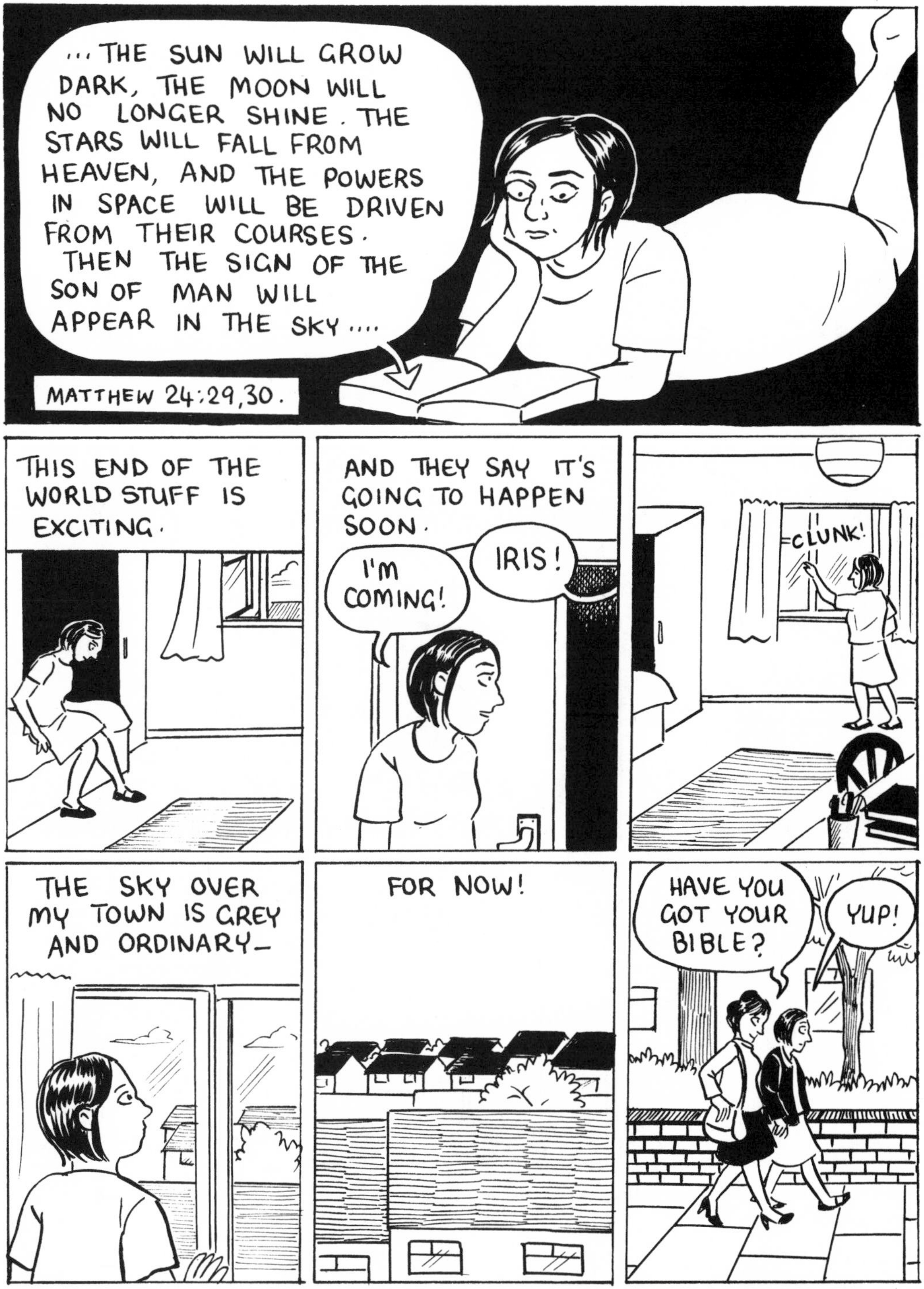
...THE SUN WILL GROW DARK, THE MOON WILL NO LONGER SHINE. THE STARS WILL FALL FROM HEAVEN, AND THE POWERS IN SPACE WILL BE DRIVEN FROM THEIR COURSES. THEN THE SIGN OF THE SON OF MAN WILL APPEAR IN THE SKY....
MATTHEW 24:29,30.
THIS END OF THE WORLD STUFF IS EXCITING.
AND THEY SAY IT'S GOING TO HAPPEN SOON.
IRIS!
I'M COMING!
CLUNK!
THE SKY OVER MY TOWN IS GREY AND ORDINARY—
FOR NOW!
HAVE YOU GOT YOUR BIBLE?
YUP!

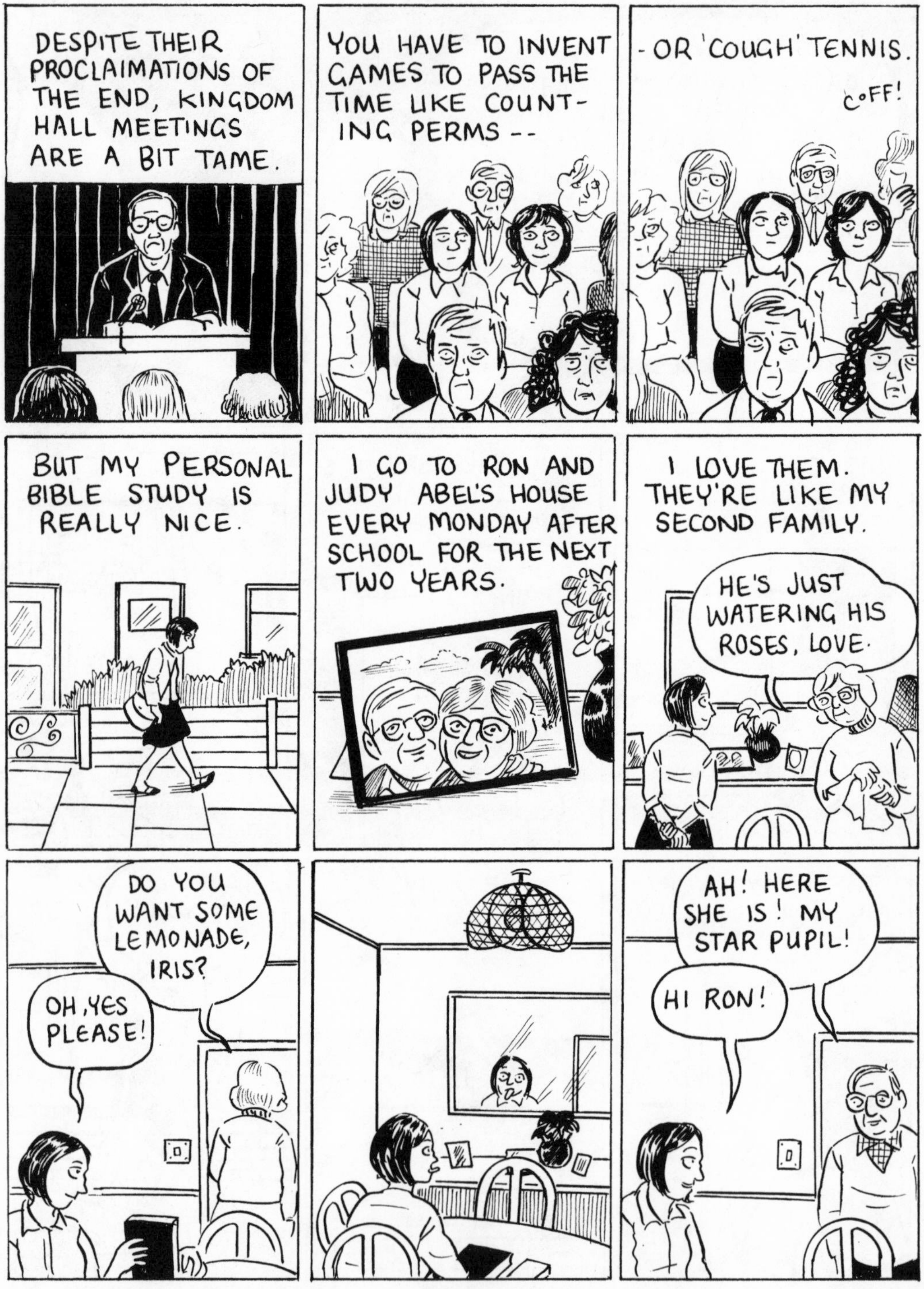
DESPITE THEIR PROCLAIMATIONS OF THE END, KINGDOM HALL MEETINGS ARE A BIT TAME.
YOU HAVE TO INVENT GAMES TO PASS THE TIME LIKE COUNTING PERMS --
- OR 'COUGH' TENNIS.
COFF!
BUT MY PERSONAL BIBLE STUDY IS REALLY NICE.
I GO TO RON AND JUDY ABEL'S HOUSE EVERY MONDAY AFTER SCHOOL FOR THE NEXT TWO YEARS.
I LOVE THEM. THEY'RE LIKE MY SECOND FAMILY.
HE'S JUST WATERING HIS ROSES, LOVE.
DO YOU WANT SOME LEMONADE, IRIS?
OH, YES PLEASE!
AH! HERE SHE IS! MY STAR PUPIL!
HI RON!

IF YOU TWO CAN MANAGE WITHOUT ME, I'VE GOT A TON OF LAUNDRY, RON?

YES, LOVE.

SO, WHERE DID WE GET TO LAST WEEK?

THE DEAD SEA SCROLLS.

OH YES.

I PRETTY MUCH FEEL LIKE A HYPOCRITE MOST OF THE TIME.

LET US PRAY. JEHOVAH IN HEAVEN —

I'M PRETTY SURE I'M NOT GOING TO BE A JEHOVAH'S WITNESS, REALLY....

I HAVEN'T TOLD ANYONE AT SCHOOL ABOUT ALL THIS.

I MEAN, IT'S OKAY FOR RON AND JUDY AND MY MUM ....

THANKS, RON! BYE!

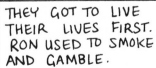

THEY GOT TO LIVE THEIR LIVES FIRST. RON USED TO SMOKE AND GAMBLE.

HE WAS A JOURN-ALIST. I COULDN'T DO THAT JOB NOW IF I BECAME A JEHOVAH'S WITNESS.

IT'S TOO WORLDLY, RON SAID.

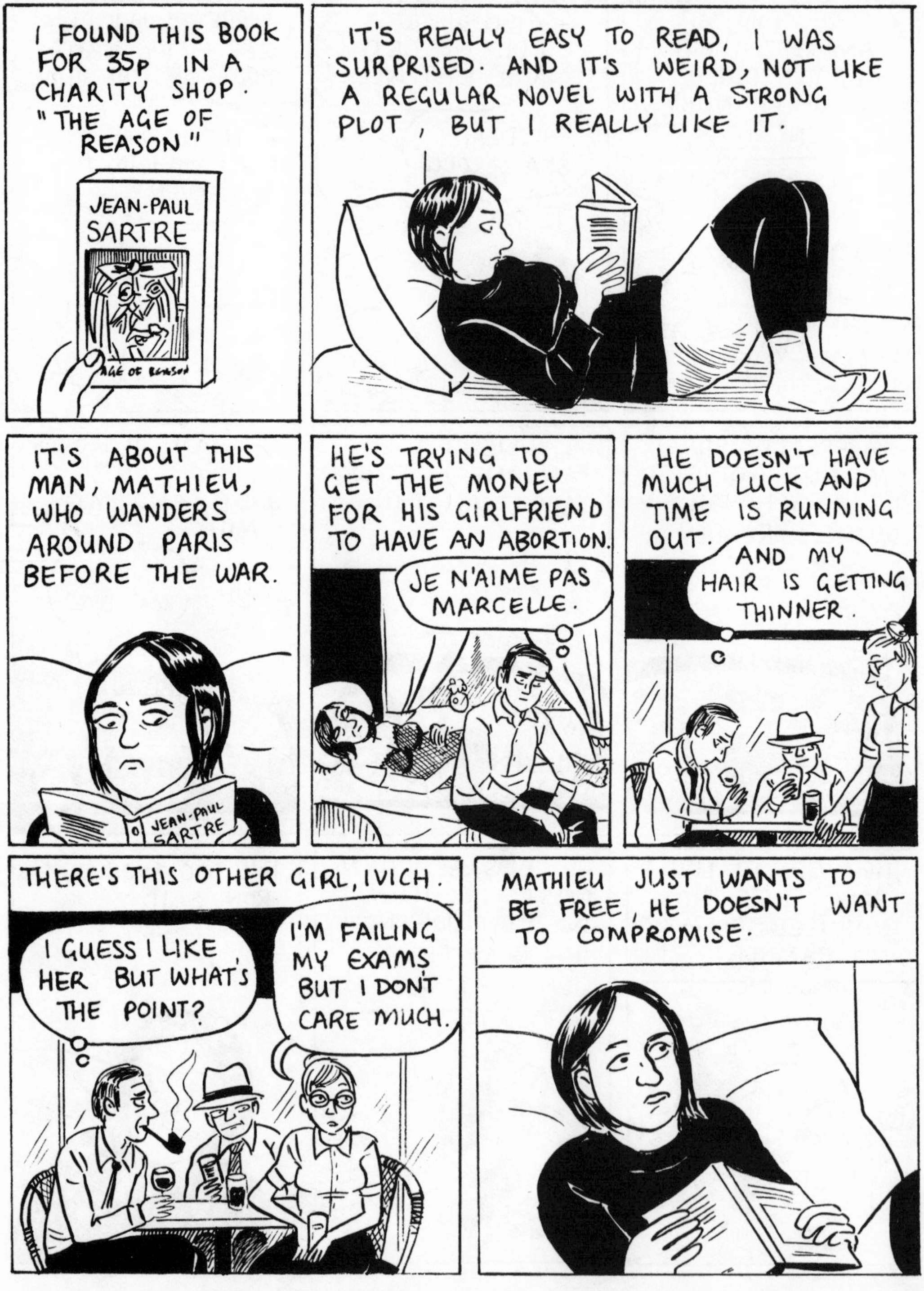
I FOUND THIS BOOK FOR 35p IN A CHARITY SHOP. "THE AGE OF REASON"
JEAN-PAUL SARTRE
AGE OF REASON
IT'S REALLY EASY TO READ, I WAS SURPRISED. AND IT'S WEIRD, NOT LIKE A REGULAR NOVEL WITH A STRONG PLOT, BUT I REALLY LIKE IT.
IT'S ABOUT THIS MAN, MATHIEU, WHO WANDERS AROUND PARIS BEFORE THE WAR.
JEAN-PAUL SARTRE
HE'S TRYING TO GET THE MONEY FOR HIS GIRLFRIEND TO HAVE AN ABORTION.
JE N'AIME PAS MARCELLE.
HE DOESN'T HAVE MUCH LUCK AND TIME IS RUNNING OUT.
AND MY HAIR IS GETTING THINNER.
THERE'S THIS OTHER GIRL, IVICH.
I GUESS I LIKE HER BUT WHAT'S THE POINT?
I'M FAILING MY EXAMS BUT I DON'T CARE MUCH.
MATHIEU JUST WANTS TO BE FREE, HE DOESN'T WANT TO COMPROMISE.

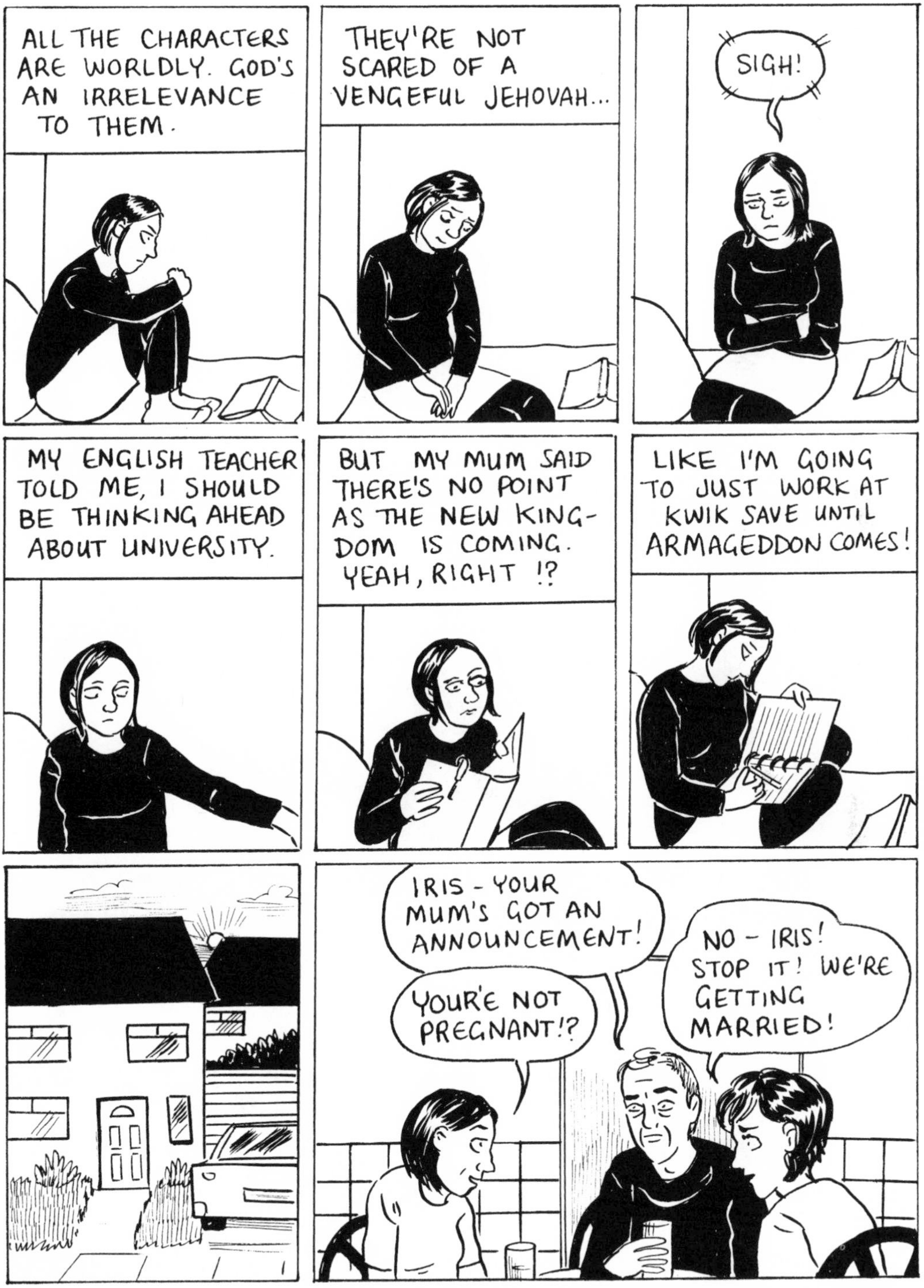
ALL THE CHARACTERS ARE WORLDLY. GOD'S AN IRRELEVANCE TO THEM.
THEY'RE NOT SCARED OF A VENGEFUL JEHOVAH...
SIGH!
MY ENGLISH TEACHER TOLD ME, I SHOULD BE THINKING AHEAD ABOUT UNIVERSITY.
BUT MY MUM SAID THERE'S NO POINT AS THE NEW KING-DOM IS COMING. YEAH, RIGHT !?
LIKE I'M GOING TO JUST WORK AT KWIK SAVE UNTIL ARMAGEDDON COMES!
IRIS - YOUR MUM'S GOT AN ANNOUNCEMENT!
YOUR'E NOT PREGNANT!?
NO - IRIS! STOP IT! WE'RE GETTING MARRIED!

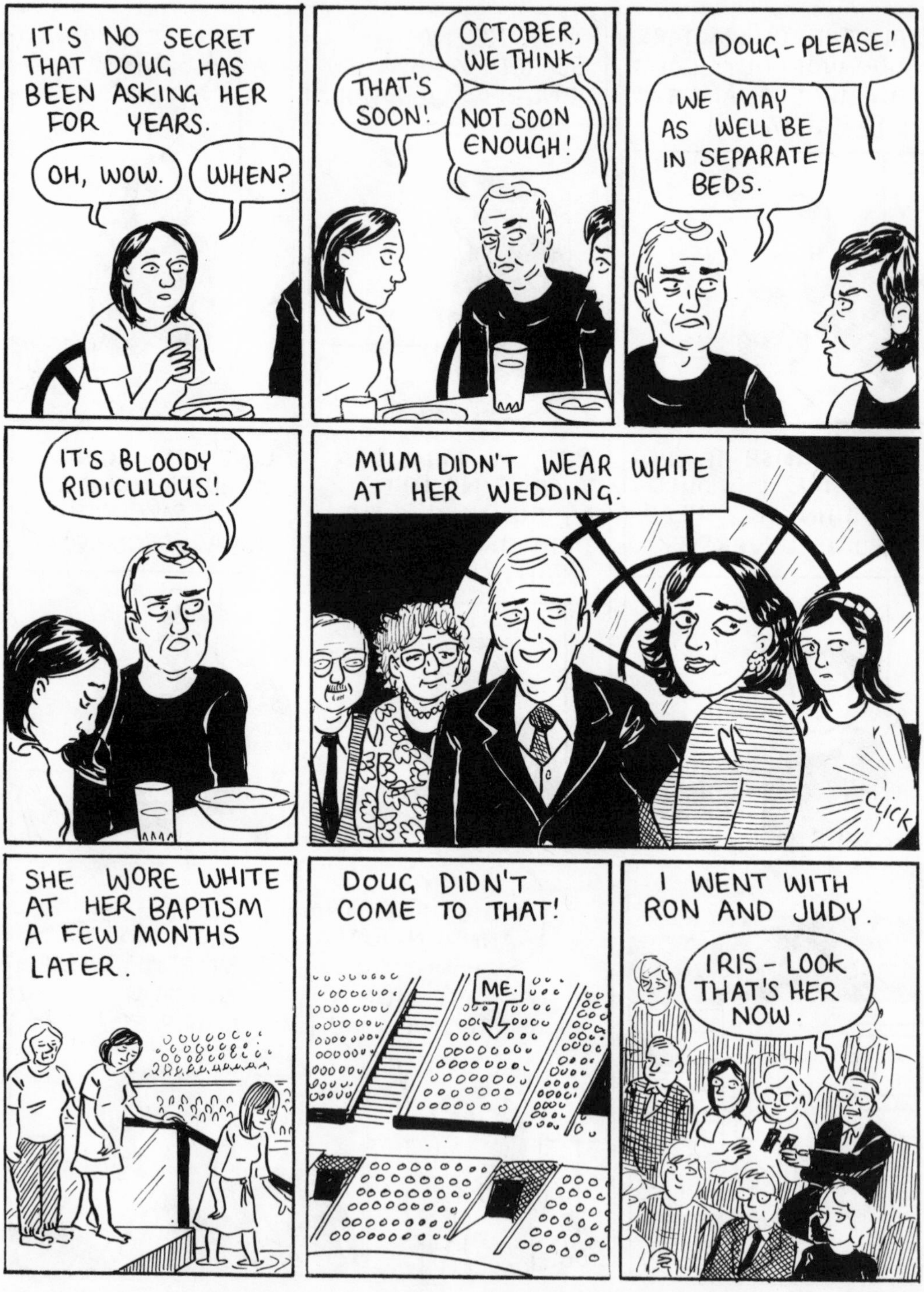
IT'S NO SECRET THAT DOUG HAS BEEN ASKING HER FOR YEARS.
OH, WOW.
WHEN?
OCTOBER, WE THINK.
THAT'S SOON!
NOT SOON ENOUGH!
DOUG - PLEASE!
WE MAY AS WELL BE IN SEPARATE BEDS.
IT'S BLOODY RIDICULOUS!
MUM DIDN'T WEAR WHITE AT HER WEDDING.
CLICK
SHE WORE WHITE AT HER BAPTISM A FEW MONTHS LATER.
DOUG DIDN'T COME TO THAT!
ME.
I WENT WITH RON AND JUDY.
IRIS - LOOK THAT'S HER NOW.

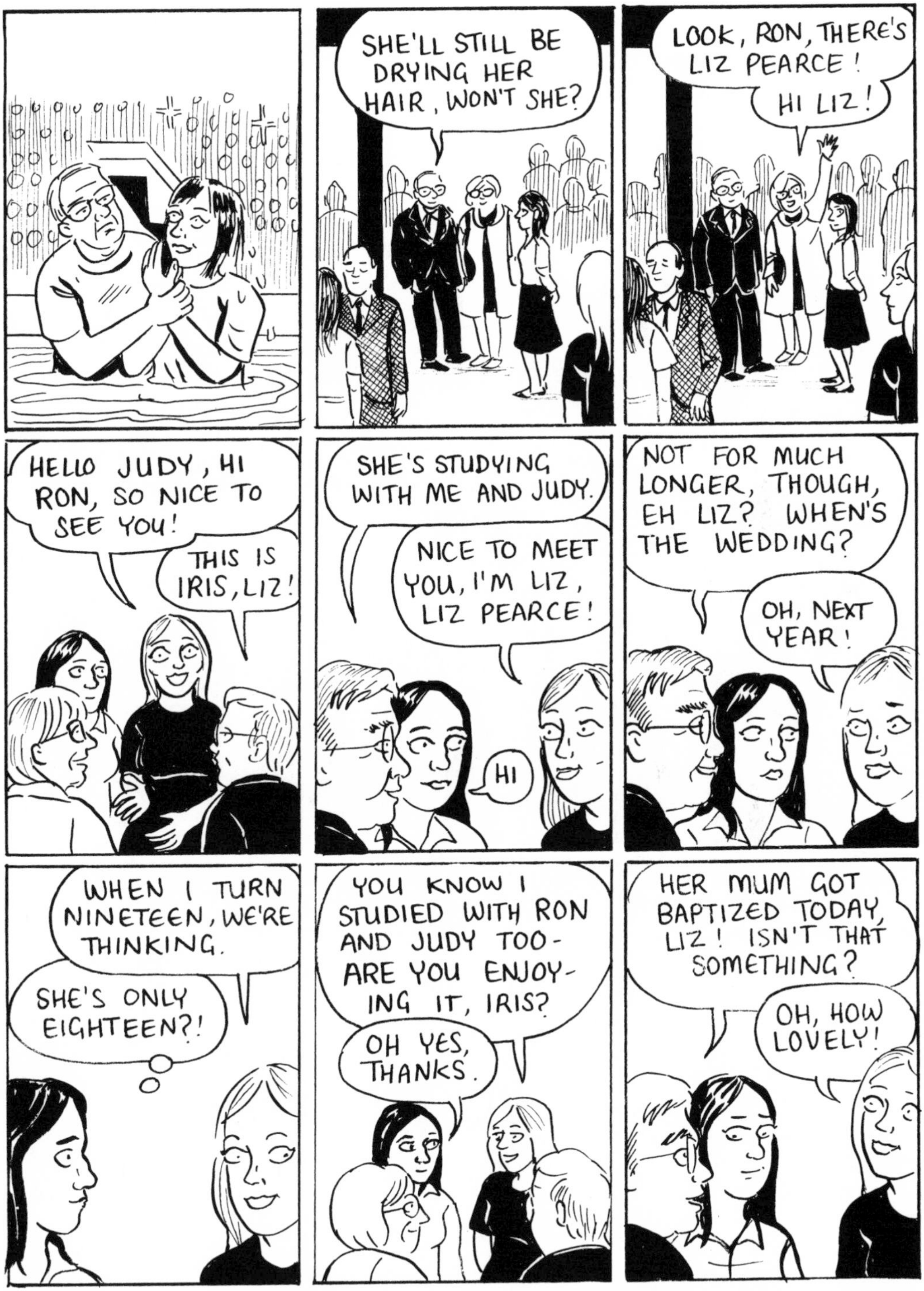
SHE'LL STILL BE DRYING HER HAIR, WON'T SHE?
LOOK, RON, THERE'S LIZ PEARCE!
HI LIZ!
HELLO JUDY, HI RON, SO NICE TO SEE YOU!
THIS IS IRIS, LIZ!
SHE'S STUDYING WITH ME AND JUDY.
NICE TO MEET YOU, I'M LIZ, LIZ PEARCE!
HI
NOT FOR MUCH LONGER, THOUGH, EH LIZ? WHEN'S THE WEDDING?
OH, NEXT YEAR!
WHEN I TURN NINETEEN, WE'RE THINKING.
SHE'S ONLY EIGHTEEN?!
YOU KNOW I STUDIED WITH RON AND JUDY TOO- ARE YOU ENJOY-ING IT, IRIS?
OH YES, THANKS.
HER MUM GOT BAPTIZED TODAY, LIZ! ISN'T THAT SOMETHING?
OH, HOW LOVELY!

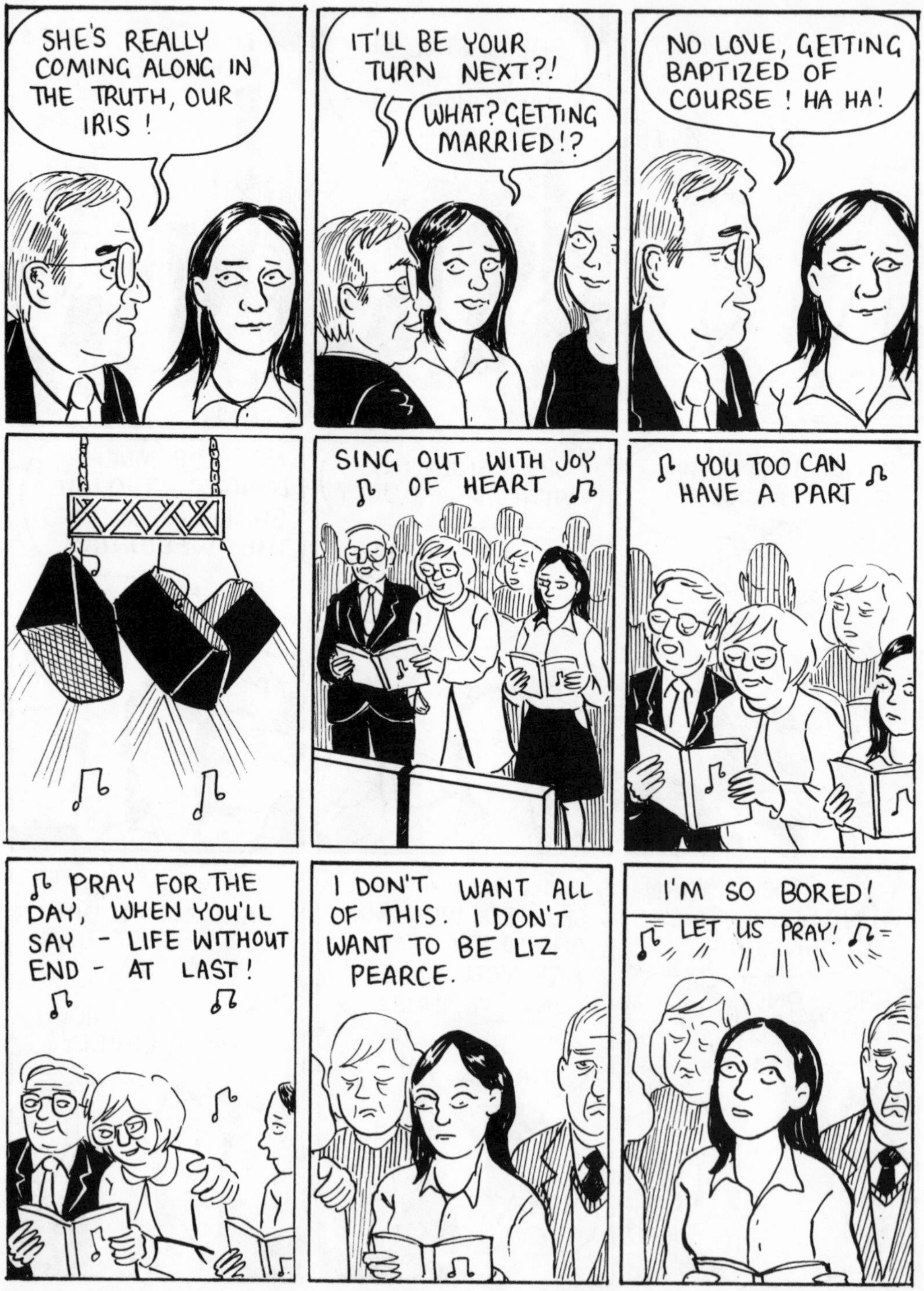
SHE'S REALLY COMING ALONG IN THE TRUTH, OUR IRIS!
IT'LL BE YOUR TURN NEXT?!
WHAT? GETTING MARRIED!?
NO LOVE, GETTING BAPTIZED OF COURSE! HA HA!
SING OUT WITH JOY OF HEART
YOU TOO CAN HAVE A PART
PRAY FOR THE DAY, WHEN YOU'LL SAY - LIFE WITHOUT END - AT LAST!
I DON'T WANT ALL OF THIS. I DON'T WANT TO BE LIZ PEARCE.
I'M SO BORED!
LET US PRAY!

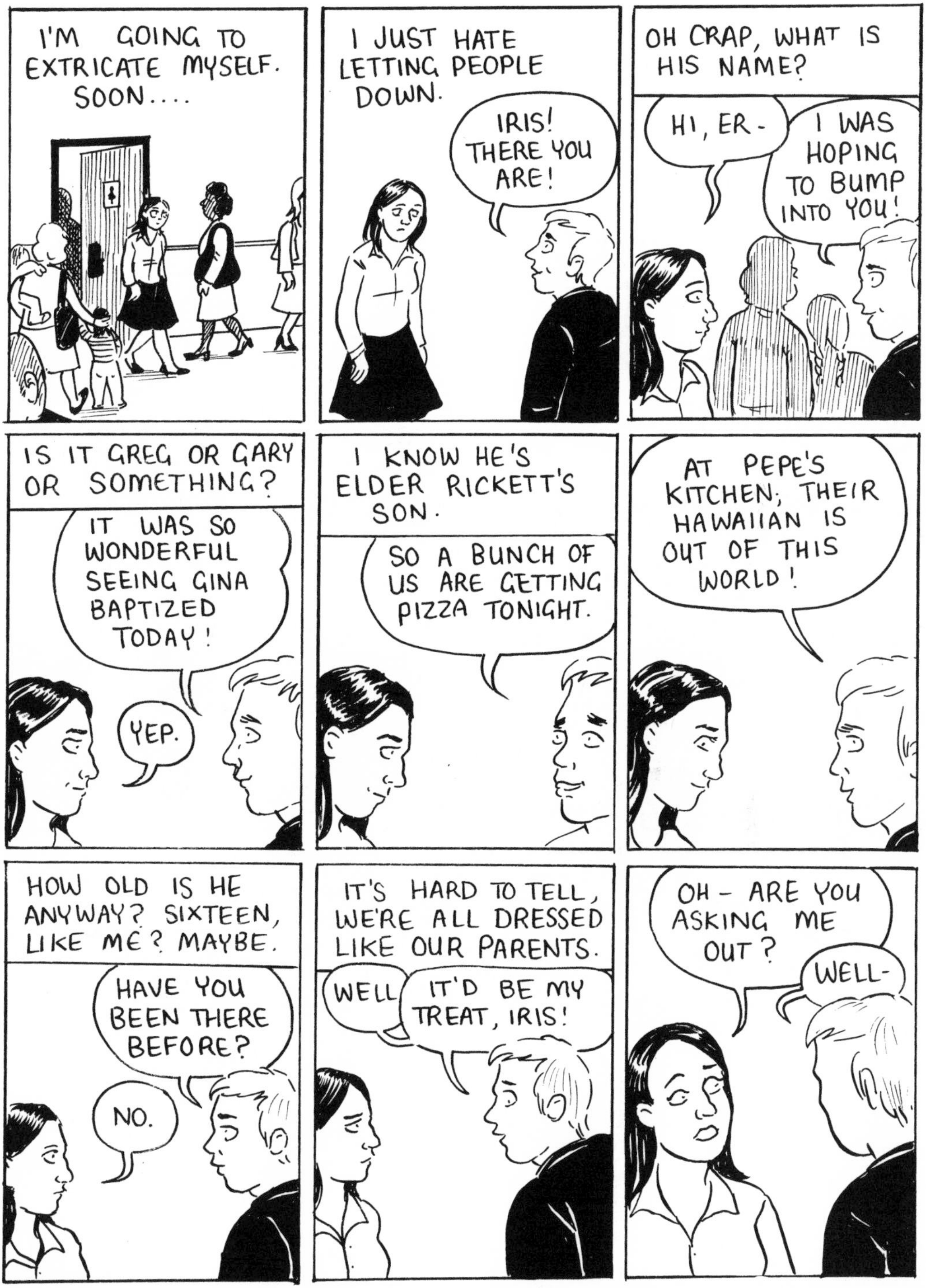
I'M GOING TO EXTRICATE MYSELF. SOON....
I JUST HATE LETTING PEOPLE DOWN.
IRIS! THERE YOU ARE!
OH CRAP, WHAT IS HIS NAME?
HI, ER-
I WAS HOPING TO BUMP INTO YOU!
IS IT GREG OR GARY OR SOMETHING?
IT WAS SO WONDERFUL SEEING GINA BAPTIZED TODAY!
YEP.
I KNOW HE'S ELDER RICKETT'S SON.
SO A BUNCH OF US ARE GETTING PIZZA TONIGHT.
AT PEPE'S KITCHEN; THEIR HAWAIIAN IS OUT OF THIS WORLD!
HOW OLD IS HE ANYWAY? SIXTEEN, LIKE ME? MAYBE.
HAVE YOU BEEN THERE BEFORE?
NO.
IT'S HARD TO TELL, WE'RE ALL DRESSED LIKE OUR PARENTS.
WELL
IT'D BE MY TREAT, IRIS!
OH - ARE YOU ASKING ME OUT?
WELL-

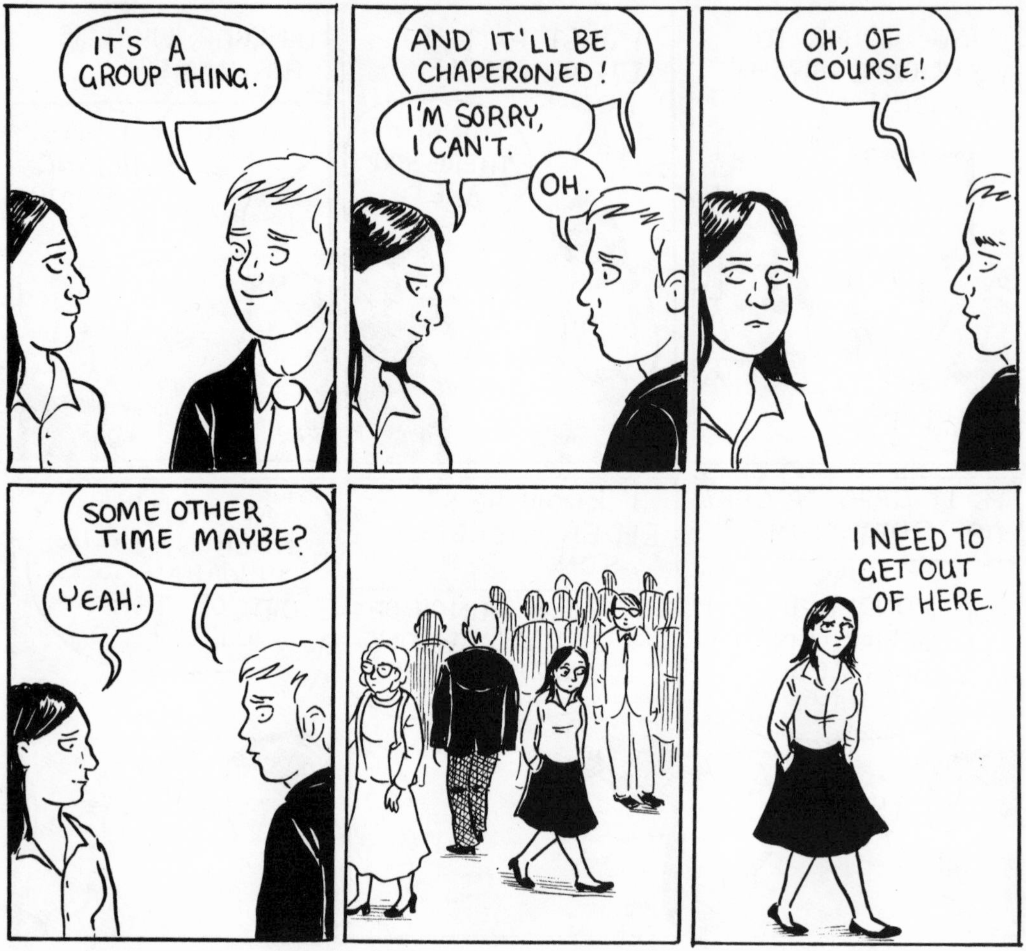
IT'S A GROUP THING.
AND IT'LL BE CHAPERONED!
I'M SORRY, I CAN'T.
OH.
OH, OF COURSE!
SOME OTHER TIME MAYBE?
YEAH.
I NEED TO GET OUT OF HERE.

THE RESPONSE

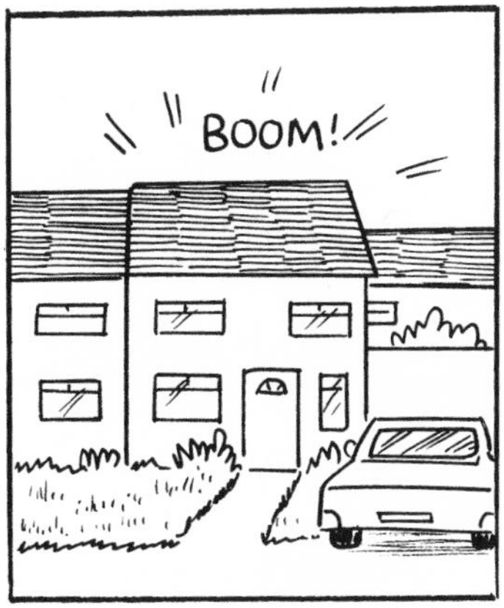
BOOM!

WAS MORE OR LESS

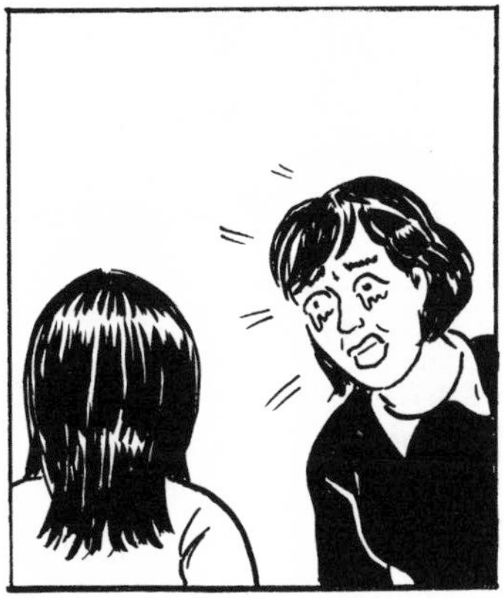

WHAT I EXPECTED.

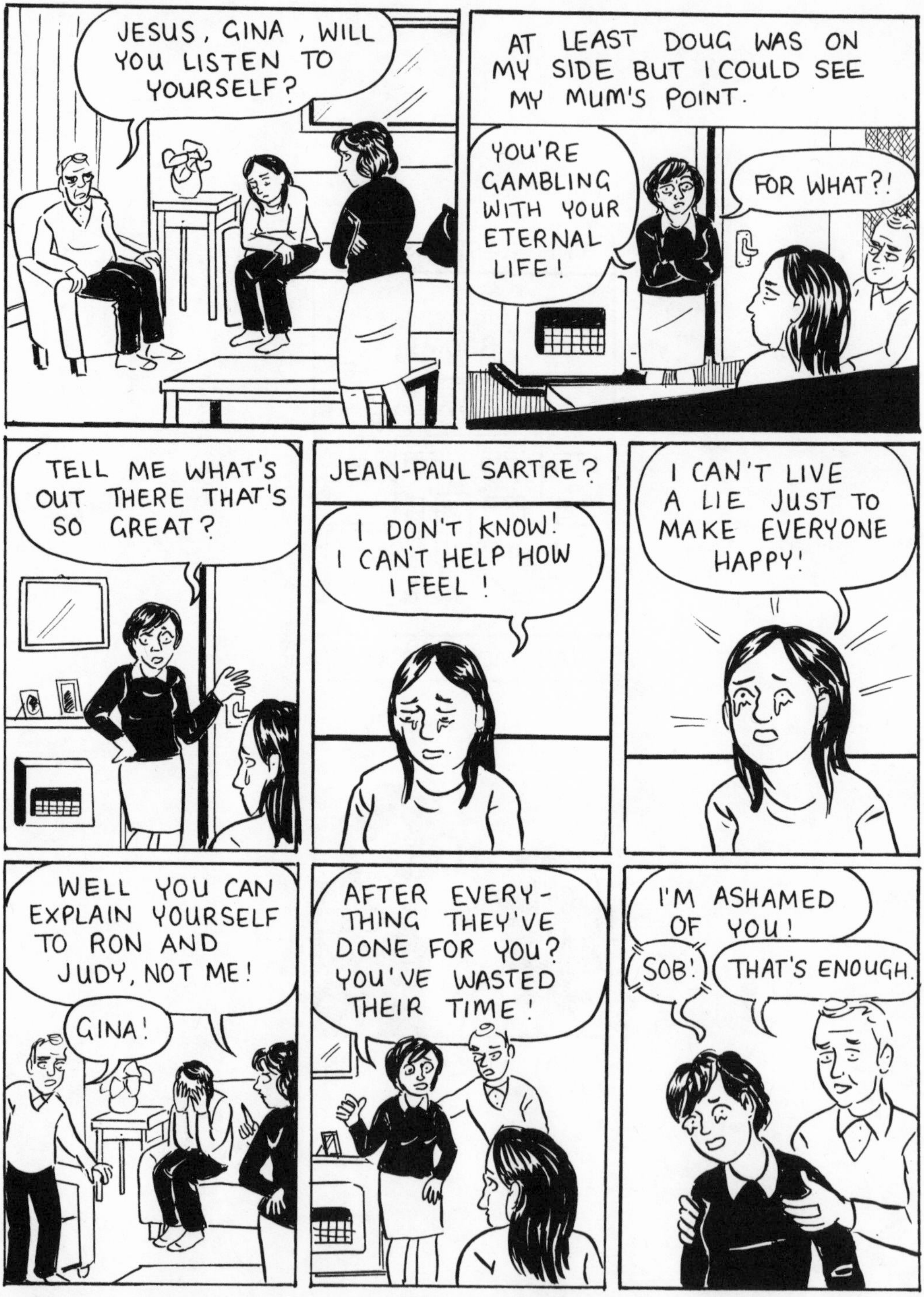
JESUS, GINA, WILL YOU LISTEN TO YOURSELF?
AT LEAST DOUG WAS ON MY SIDE BUT I COULD SEE MY MUM'S POINT.
YOU'RE GAMBLING WITH YOUR ETERNAL LIFE!
FOR WHAT?!
TELL ME WHAT'S OUT THERE THAT'S SO GREAT?
JEAN-PAUL SARTRE?
I DON'T KNOW! I CAN'T HELP HOW I FEEL!
I CAN'T LIVE A LIE JUST TO MAKE EVERYONE HAPPY!
WELL YOU CAN EXPLAIN YOURSELF TO RON AND JUDY, NOT ME!
GINA!
AFTER EVERY-THING THEY'VE DONE FOR YOU? YOU'VE WASTED THEIR TIME!
I'M ASHAMED OF YOU!
SOB!
THAT'S ENOUGH.

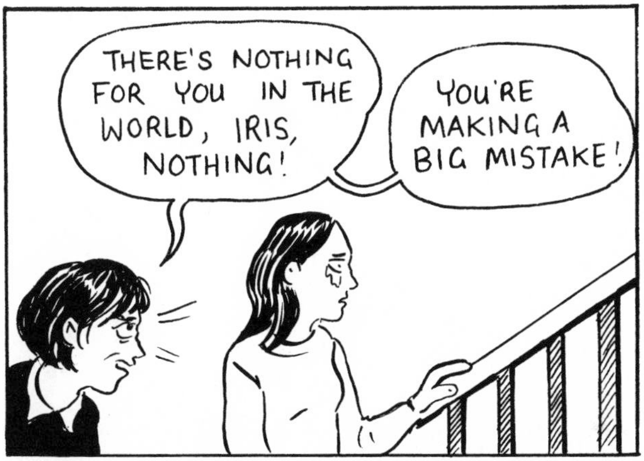
THERE'S NOTHING FOR YOU IN THE WORLD, IRIS, NOTHING!
YOU'RE MAKING A BIG MISTAKE!

sky in stereo

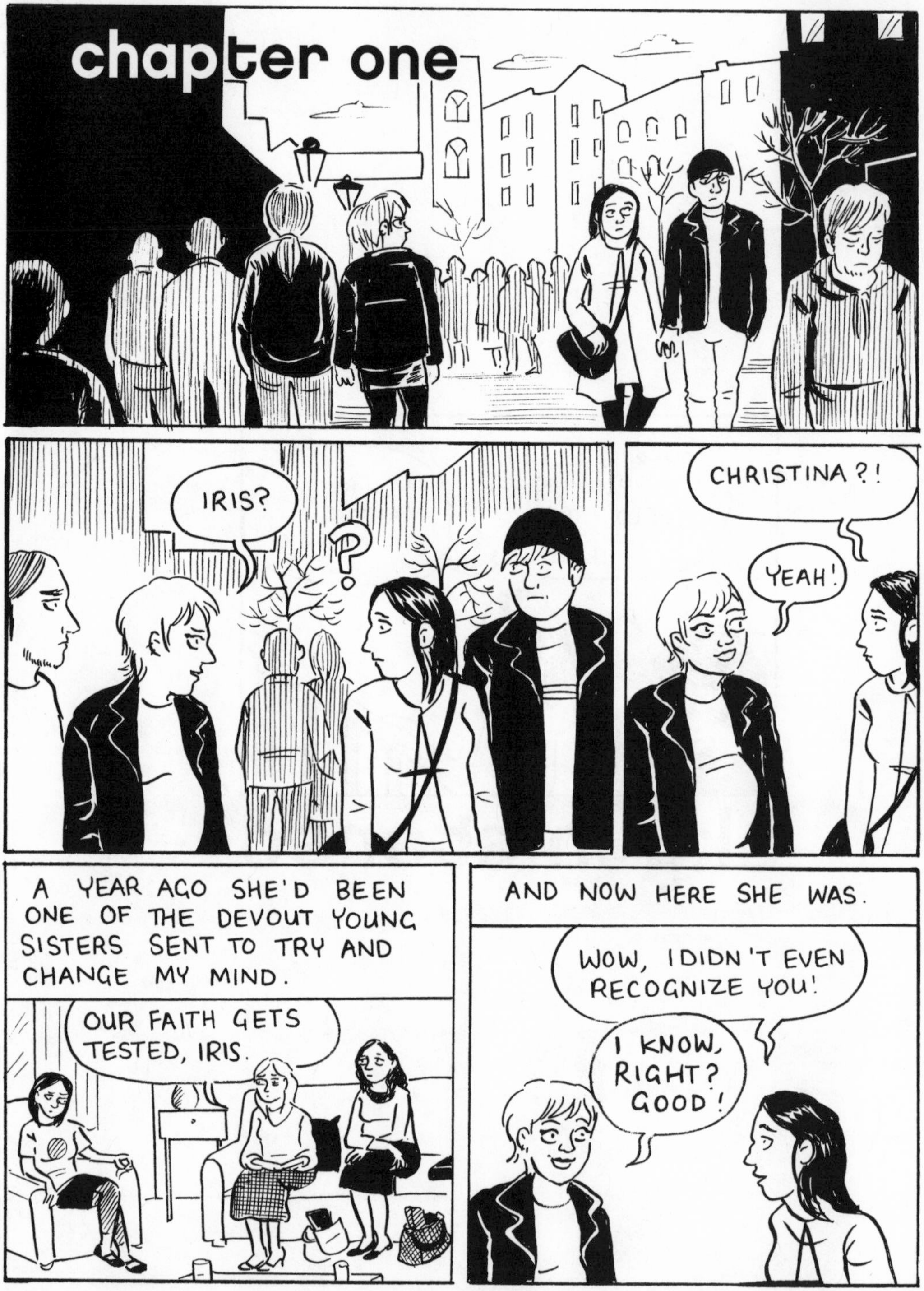
chapter one
IRIS?
?
CHRISTINA?!
YEAH!
A YEAR AGO SHE'D BEEN ONE OF THE DEVOUT YOUNG SISTERS SENT TO TRY AND CHANGE MY MIND.
OUR FAITH GETS TESTED, IRIS.
AND NOW HERE SHE WAS.
WOW, I DIDN'T EVEN RECOGNIZE YOU!
I KNOW, RIGHT? GOOD!

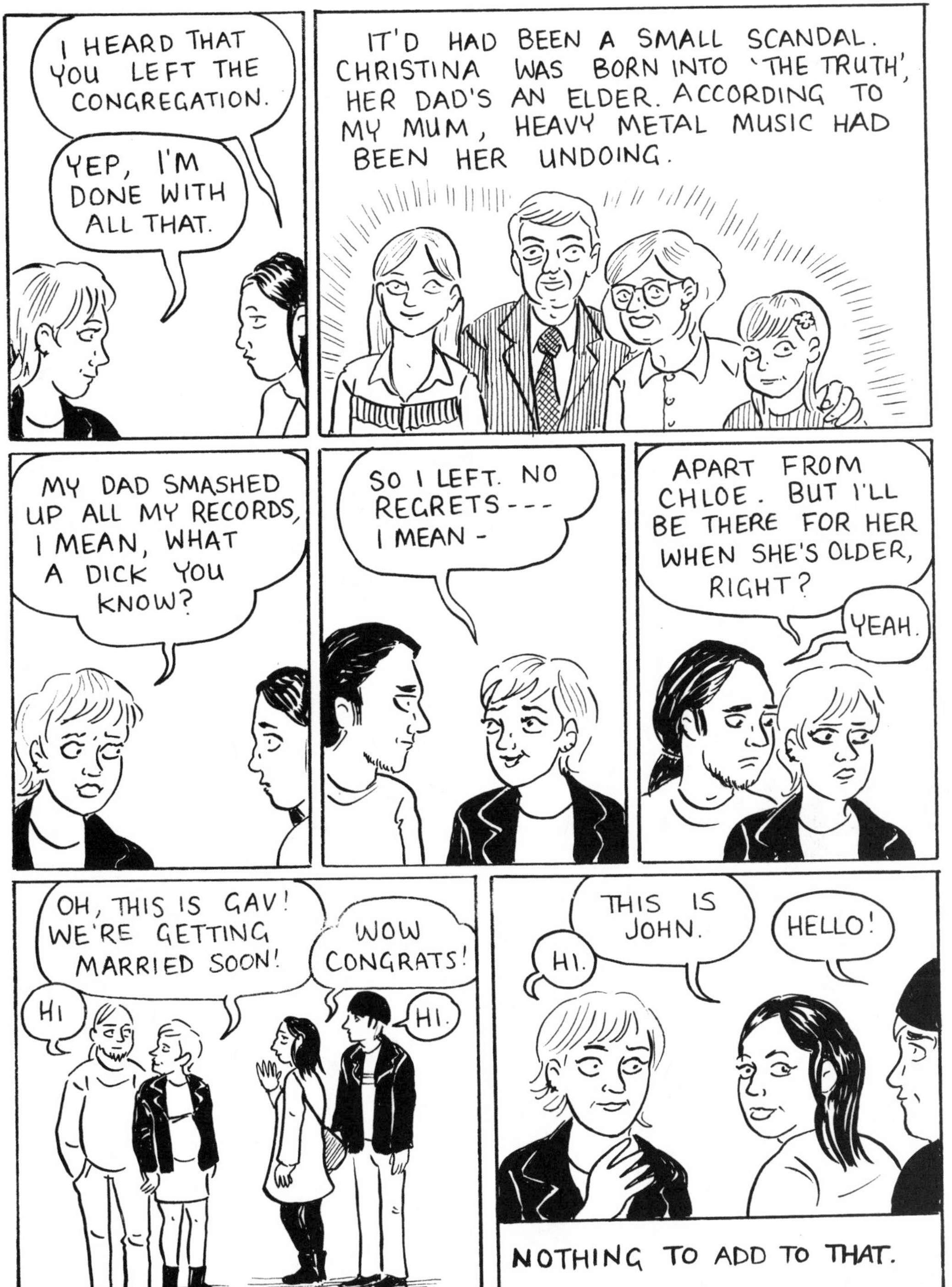
I HEARD THAT YOU LEFT THE CONGREGATION.
YEP, I'M DONE WITH ALL THAT.
IT'D HAD BEEN A SMALL SCANDAL. CHRISTINA WAS BORN INTO 'THE TRUTH', HER DAD'S AN ELDER. ACCORDING TO MY MUM, HEAVY METAL MUSIC HAD BEEN HER UNDOING.
MY DAD SMASHED UP ALL MY RECORDS, I MEAN, WHAT A DICK YOU KNOW?
SO I LEFT. NO REGRETS--- I MEAN -
APART FROM CHLOE. BUT I'LL BE THERE FOR HER WHEN SHE'S OLDER, RIGHT?
YEAH.
OH, THIS IS GAV! WE'RE GETTING MARRIED SOON!
WOW CONGRATS!
HI
HI.
THIS IS JOHN.
HELLO!
HI.
NOTHING TO ADD TO THAT.

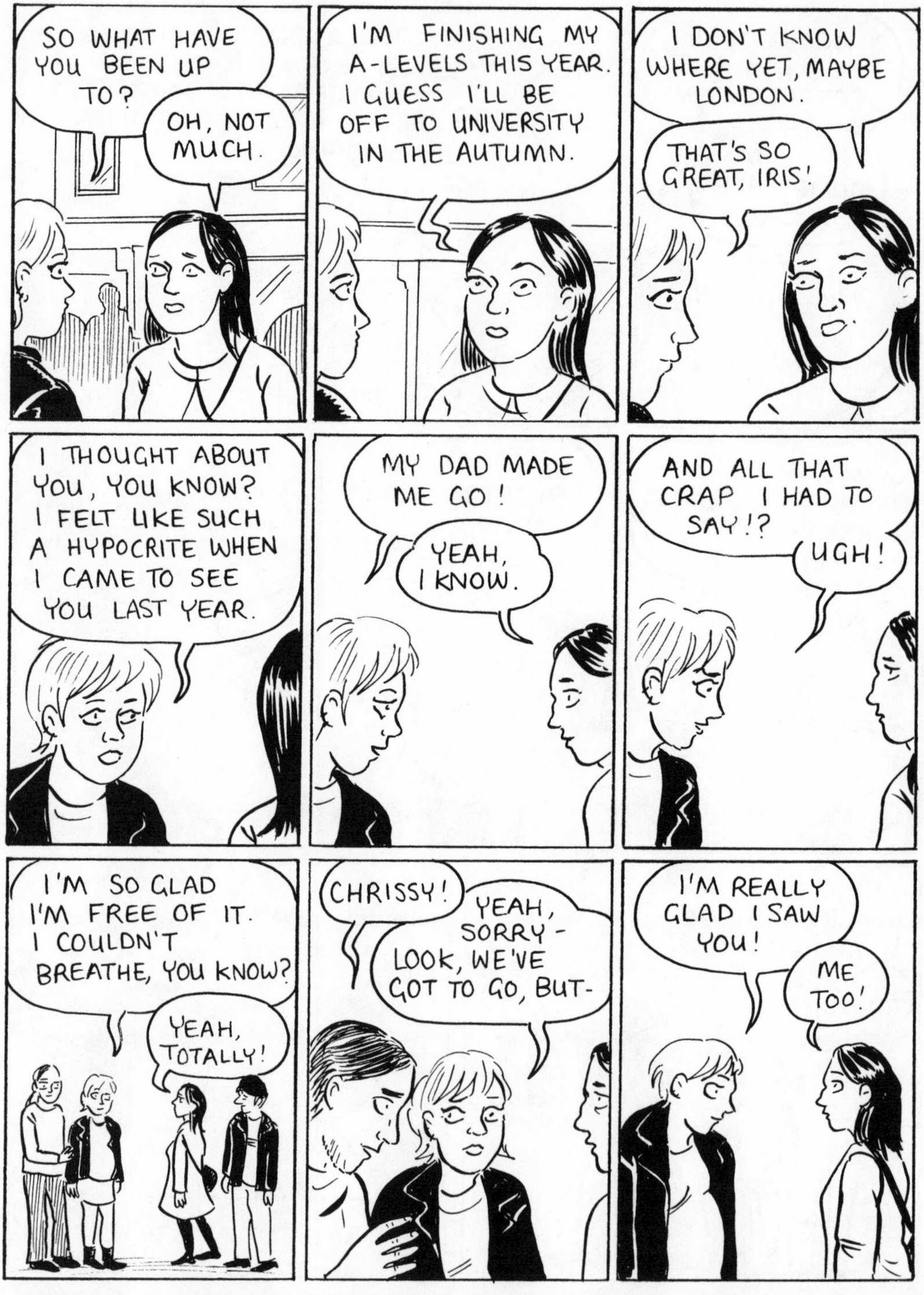
SO WHAT HAVE YOU BEEN UP TO?
OH, NOT MUCH.
I'M FINISHING MY A-LEVELS THIS YEAR. I GUESS I'LL BE OFF TO UNIVERSITY IN THE AUTUMN.
I DON'T KNOW WHERE YET, MAYBE LONDON.
THAT'S SO GREAT, IRIS!
I THOUGHT ABOUT YOU, YOU KNOW? I FELT LIKE SUCH A HYPOCRITE WHEN I CAME TO SEE YOU LAST YEAR.
MY DAD MADE ME GO!
YEAH, I KNOW.
AND ALL THAT CRAP I HAD TO SAY!?
UGH!
I'M SO GLAD I'M FREE OF IT. I COULDN'T BREATHE, YOU KNOW?
YEAH, TOTALLY!
CHRISSY!
YEAH, SORRY- LOOK, WE'VE GOT TO GO, BUT-
I'M REALLY GLAD I SAW YOU!
ME TOO!

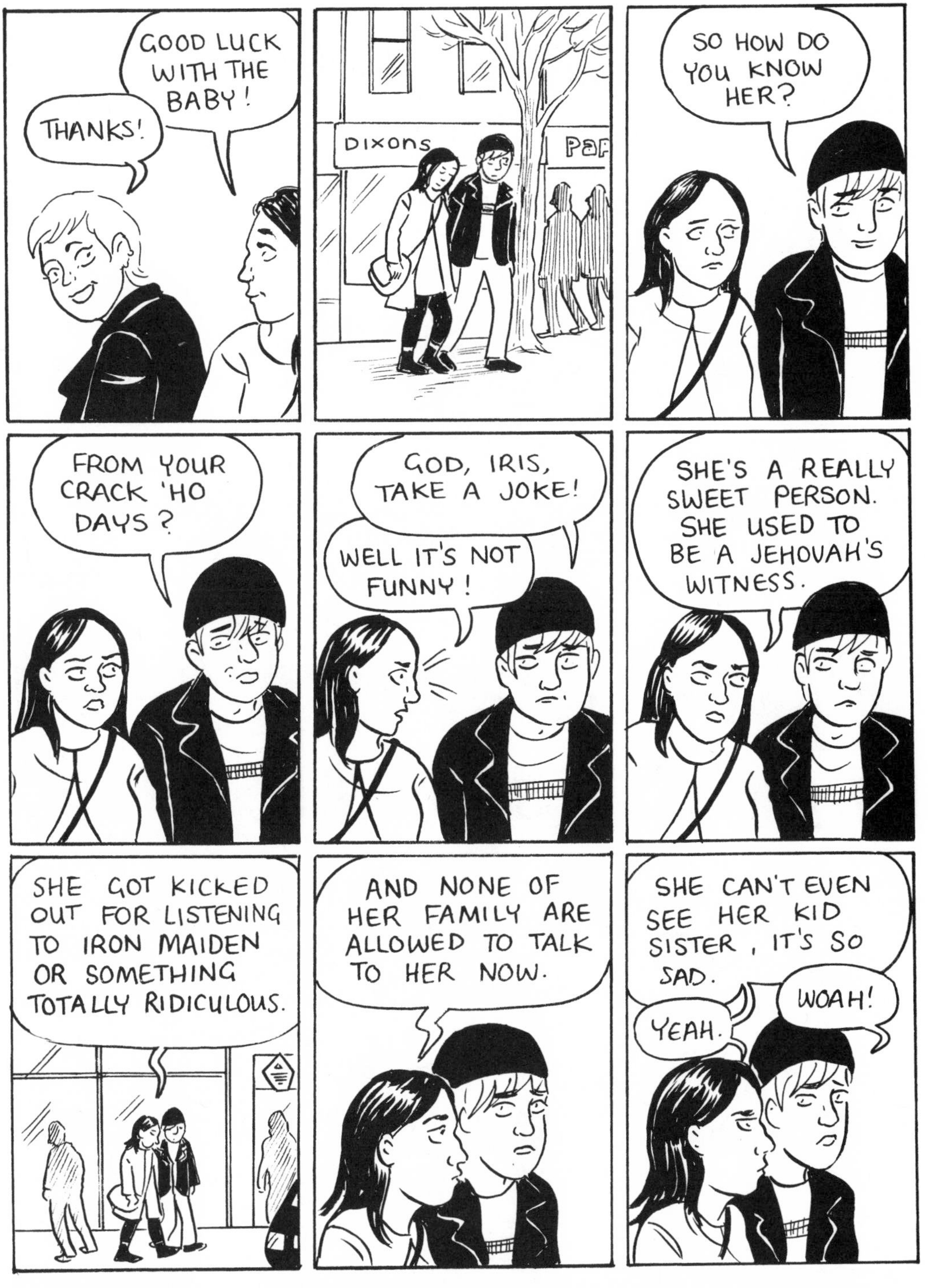
GOOD LUCK WITH THE BABY!
THANKS!
DIXONS
SO HOW DO YOU KNOW HER?
FROM YOUR CRACK 'HO DAYS?
GOD, IRIS, TAKE A JOKE!
WELL IT'S NOT FUNNY!
SHE'S A REALLY SWEET PERSON. SHE USED TO BE A JEHOVAH'S WITNESS.
SHE GOT KICKED OUT FOR LISTENING TO IRON MAIDEN OR SOMETHING TOTALLY RIDICULOUS.
AND NONE OF HER FAMILY ARE ALLOWED TO TALK TO HER NOW.
SHE CAN'T EVEN SEE HER KID SISTER, IT'S SO SAD.
YEAH.
WOAH!

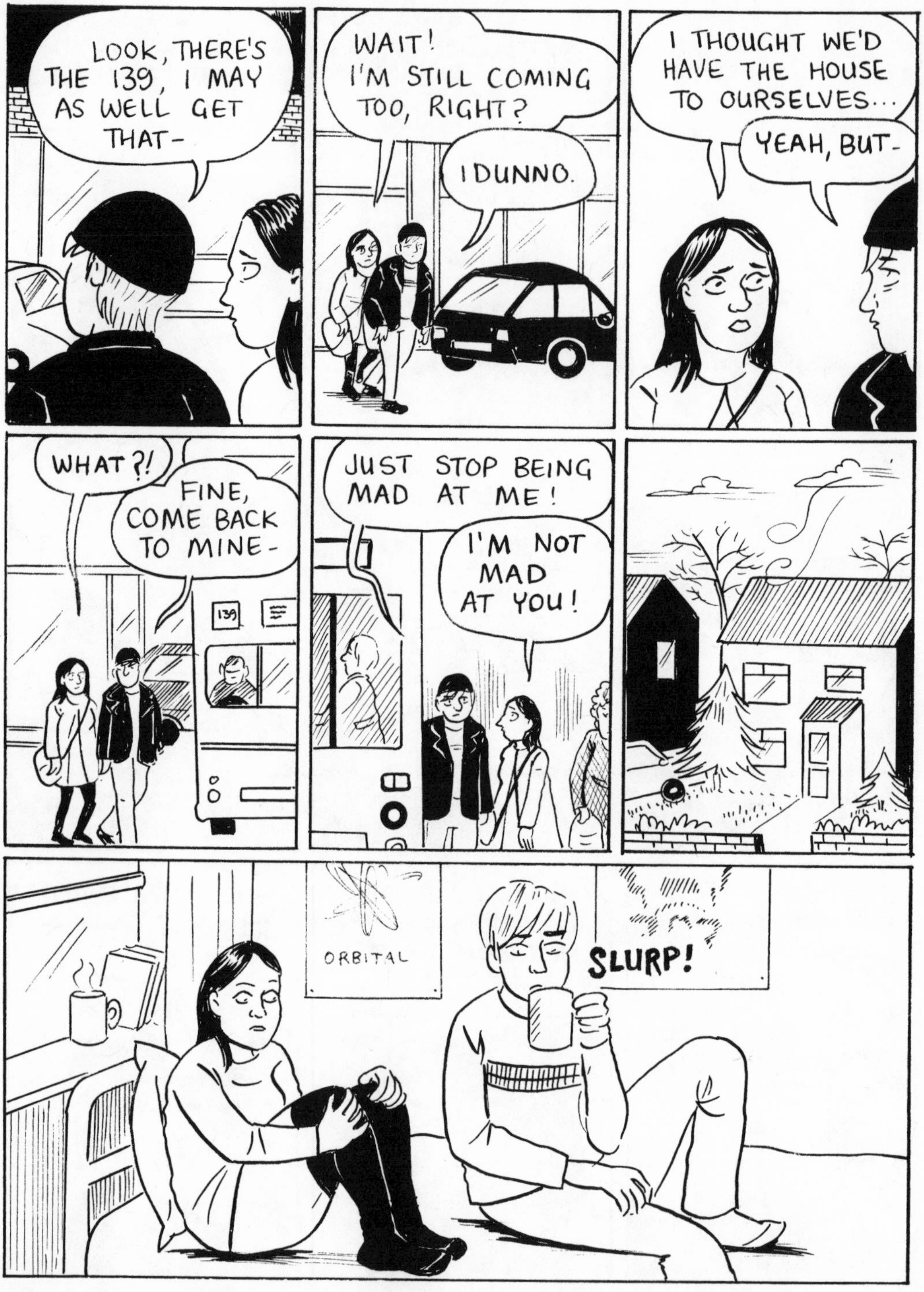
LOOK, THERE'S THE 139, I MAY AS WELL GET THAT-
WAIT! I'M STILL COMING TOO, RIGHT?
I DUNNO.
I THOUGHT WE'D HAVE THE HOUSE TO OURSELVES...
YEAH, BUT-
WHAT?!
FINE, COME BACK TO MINE-
139
JUST STOP BEING MAD AT ME!
I'M NOT MAD AT YOU!
ORBITAL
SLURP!

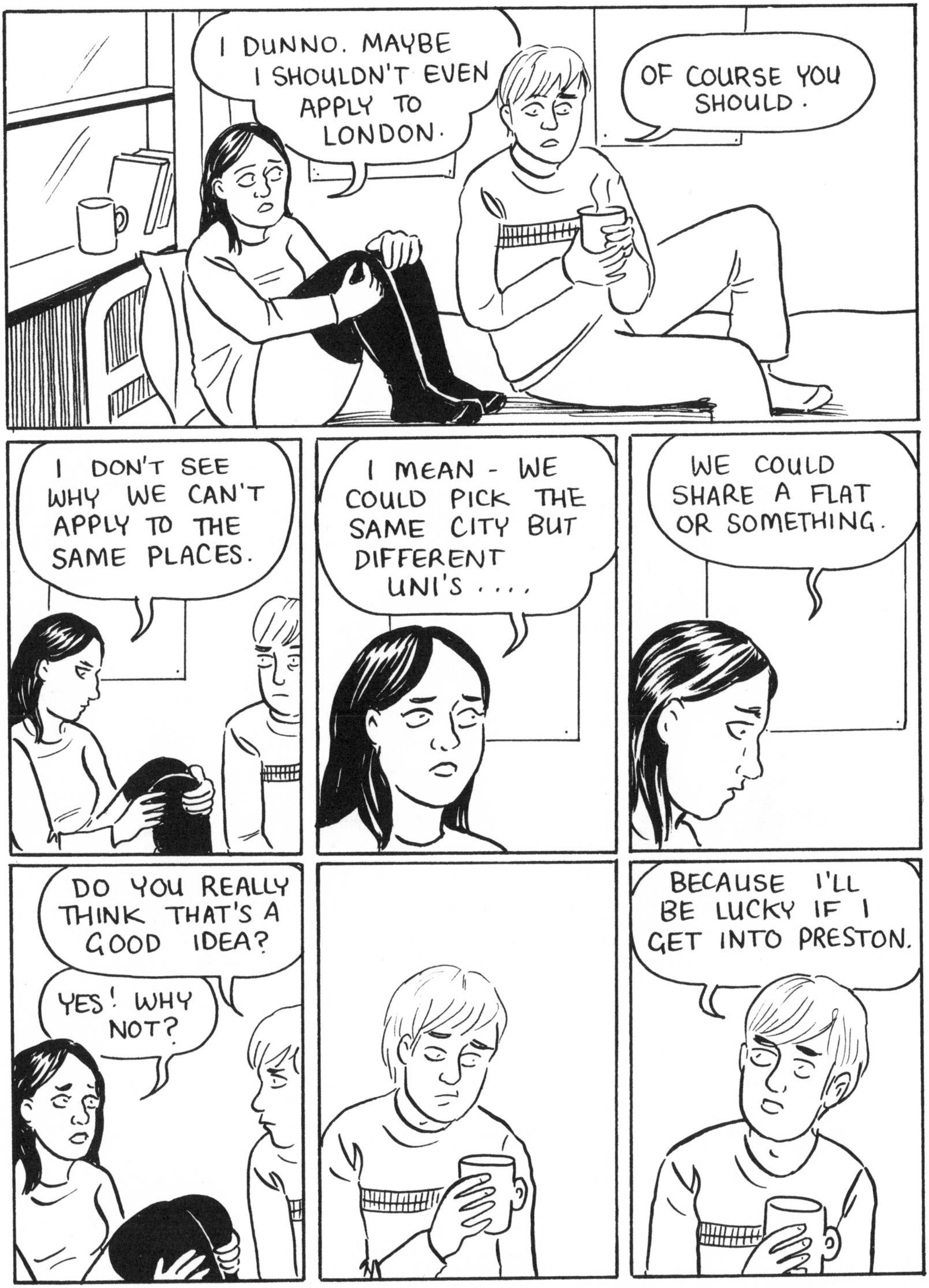
I DUNNO. MAYBE I SHOULDN'T EVEN APPLY TO LONDON.
OF COURSE YOU SHOULD.
I DON'T SEE WHY WE CAN'T APPLY TO THE SAME PLACES.
I MEAN - WE COULD PICK THE SAME CITY BUT DIFFERENT UNI'S ....
WE COULD SHARE A FLAT OR SOMETHING.
DO YOU REALLY THINK THAT'S A GOOD IDEA?
YES! WHY NOT?
BECAUSE I'LL BE LUCKY IF I GET INTO PRESTON.

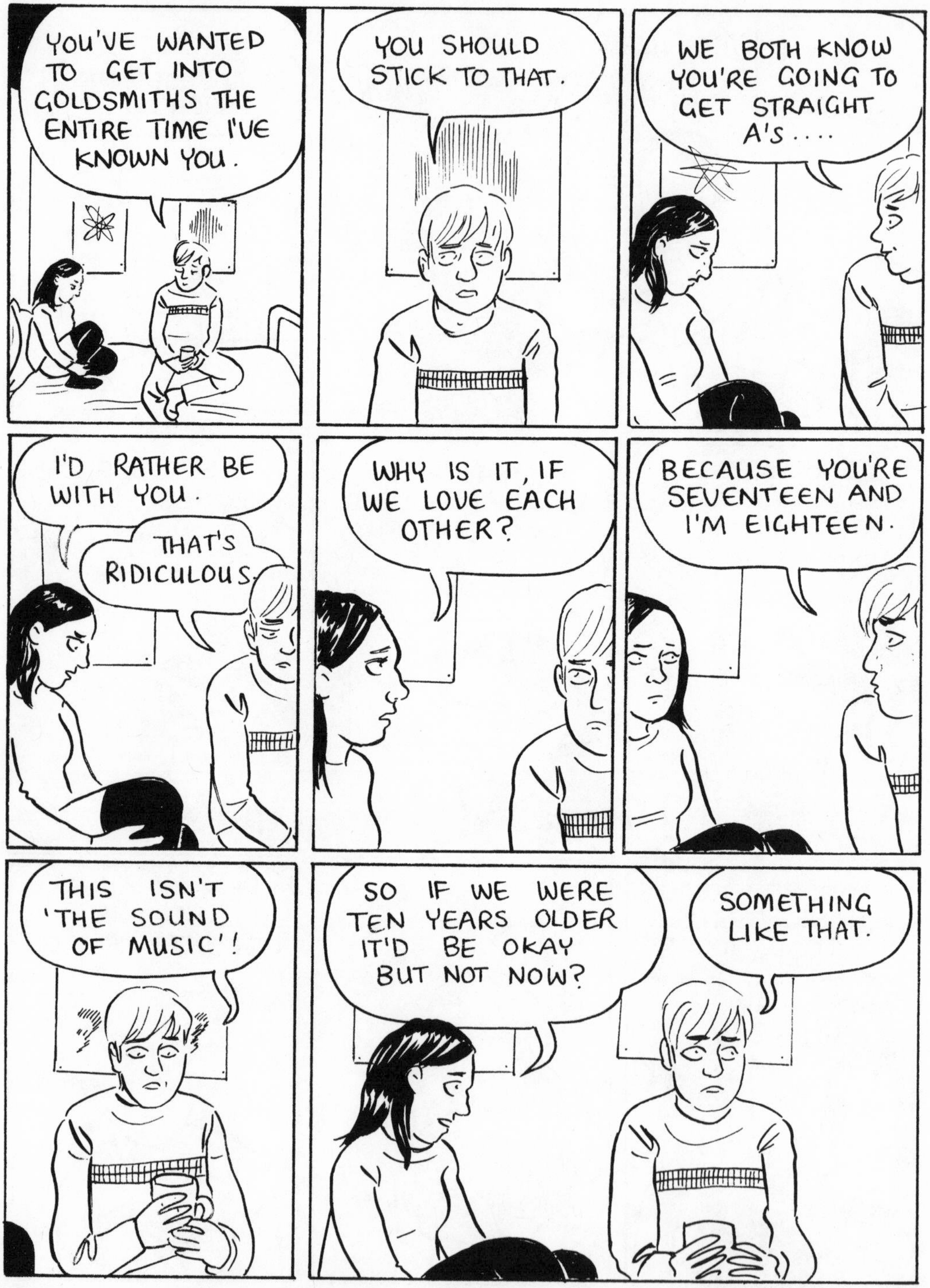
YOU'VE WANTED TO GET INTO GOLDSMITHS THE ENTIRE TIME I'VE KNOWN YOU.
YOU SHOULD STICK TO THAT.
WE BOTH KNOW YOU'RE GOING TO GET STRAIGHT A'S....
I'D RATHER BE WITH YOU.
THAT'S RIDICULOUS.
WHY IS IT, IF WE LOVE EACH OTHER?
BECAUSE YOU'RE SEVENTEEN AND I'M EIGHTEEN.
THIS ISN'T 'THE SOUND OF MUSIC'!
SO IF WE WERE TEN YEARS OLDER IT'D BE OKAY BUT NOT NOW?
SOMETHING LIKE THAT.

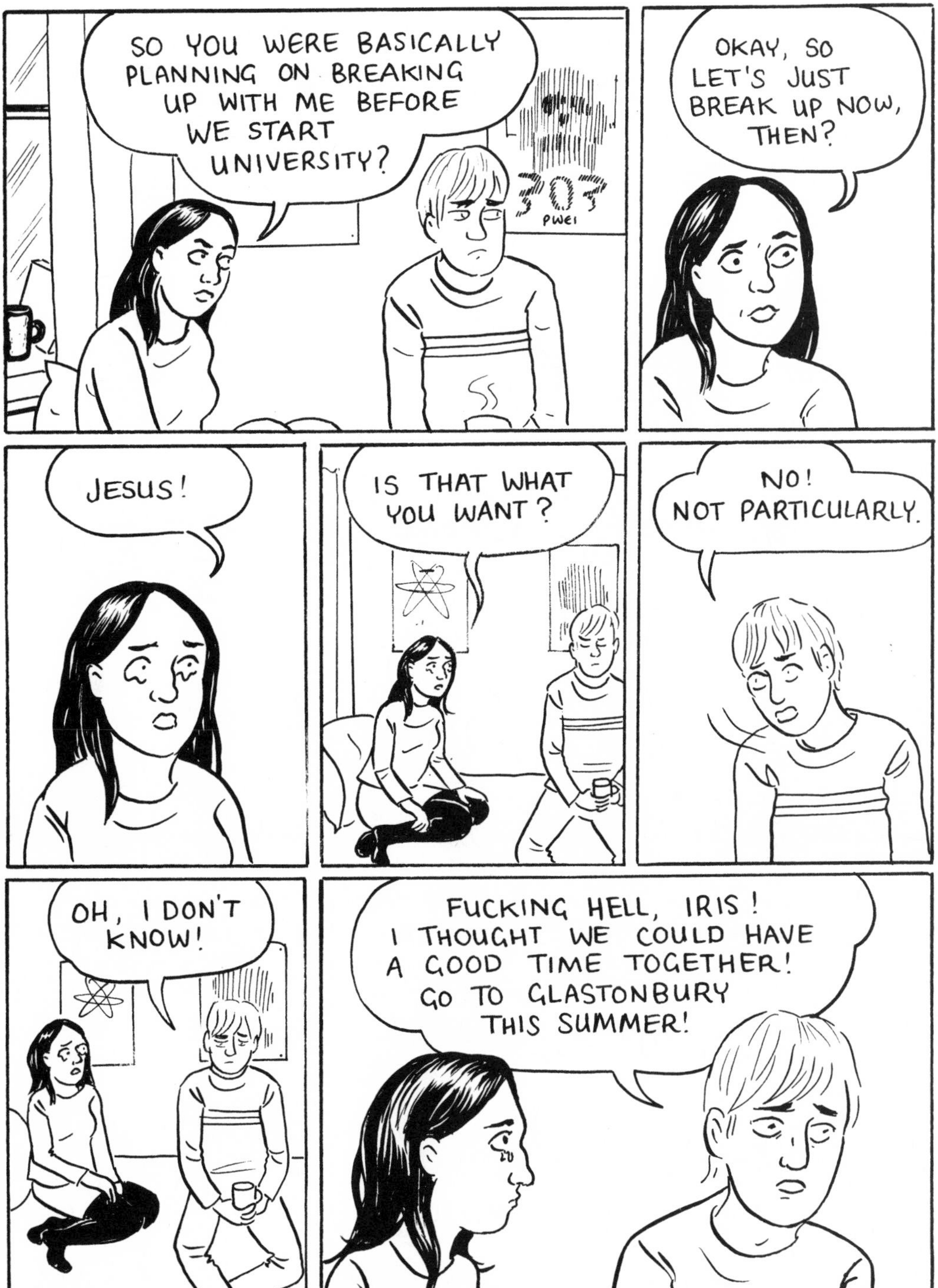
SO YOU WERE BASICALLY PLANNING ON BREAKING UP WITH ME BEFORE WE START UNIVERSITY?
303
PWEI
OKAY, SO LET'S JUST BREAK UP NOW, THEN?
JESUS!
IS THAT WHAT YOU WANT?
NO! NOT PARTICULARLY.
OH, I DON'T KNOW!
FUCKING HELL, IRIS! I THOUGHT WE COULD HAVE A GOOD TIME TOGETHER! GO TO GLASTONBURY THIS SUMMER!

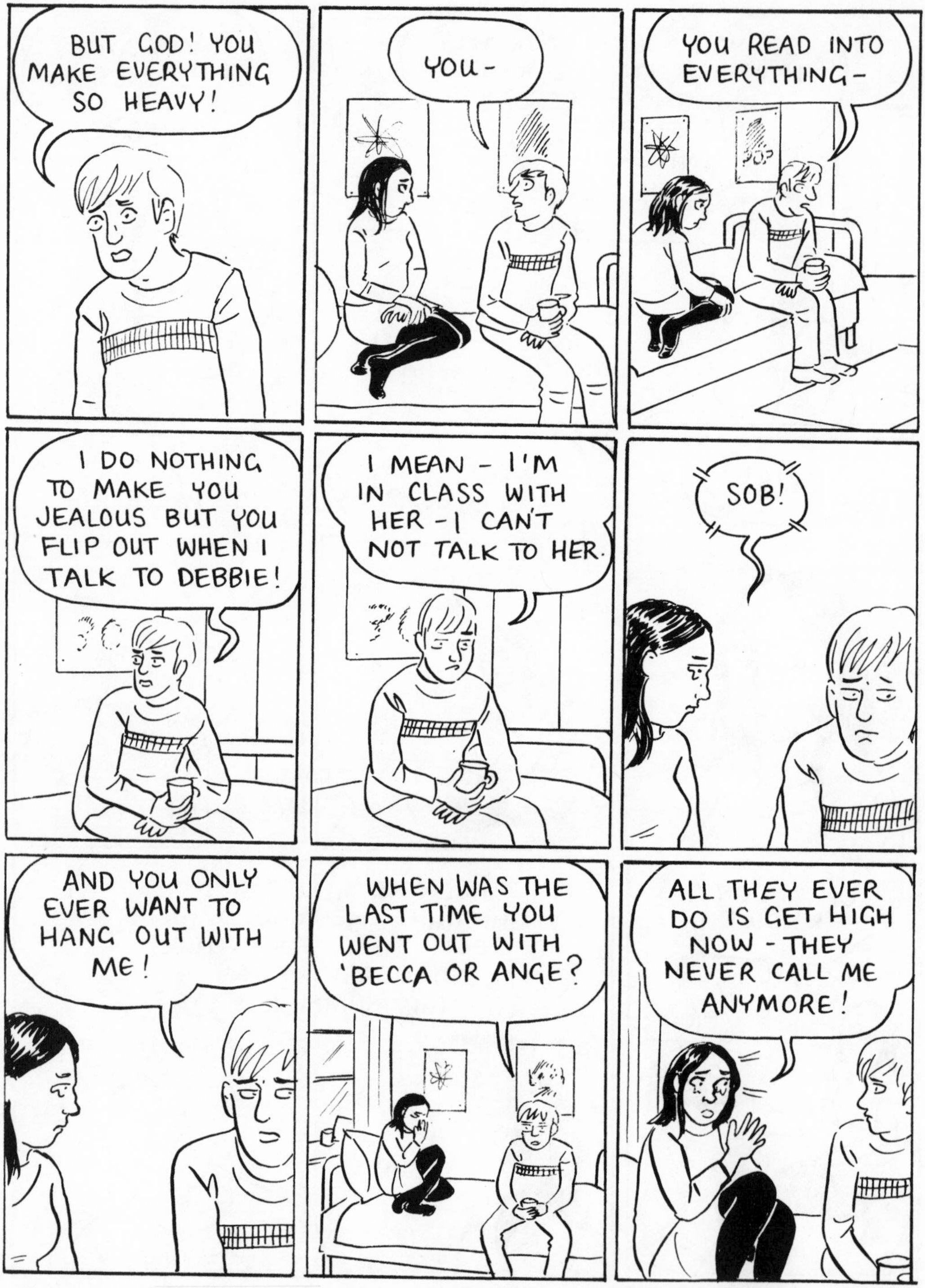
BUT GOD! YOU MAKE EVERYTHING SO HEAVY!
YOU-
YOU READ INTO EVERYTHING-
I DO NOTHING TO MAKE YOU JEALOUS BUT YOU FLIP OUT WHEN I TALK TO DEBBIE!
I MEAN - I'M IN CLASS WITH HER - I CAN'T NOT TALK TO HER.
SOB!
AND YOU ONLY EVER WANT TO HANG OUT WITH ME!
WHEN WAS THE LAST TIME YOU WENT OUT WITH 'BECCA OR ANGE?
ALL THEY EVER DO IS GET HIGH NOW - THEY NEVER CALL ME ANYMORE!

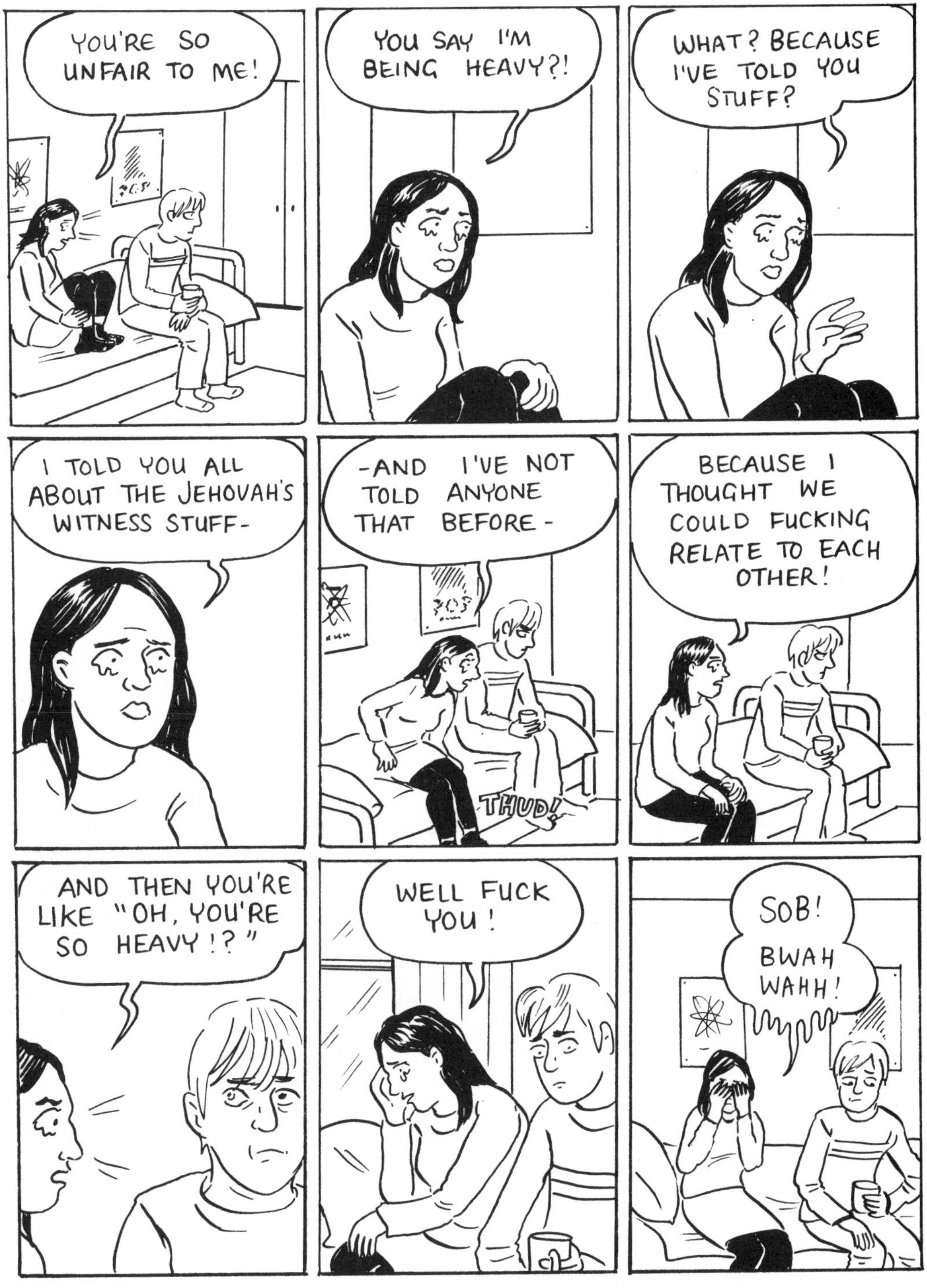
YOU'RE SO UNFAIR TO ME!
YOU SAY I'M BEING HEAVY?!
WHAT? BECAUSE I'VE TOLD YOU STUFF?
I TOLD YOU ALL ABOUT THE JEHOVAH'S WITNESS STUFF-
-AND I'VE NOT TOLD ANYONE THAT BEFORE-
THUD!
BECAUSE I THOUGHT WE COULD FUCKING RELATE TO EACH OTHER!
AND THEN YOU'RE LIKE "OH, YOU'RE SO HEAVY!?"
WELL FUCK YOU!
SOB!
BWAH WAHH!

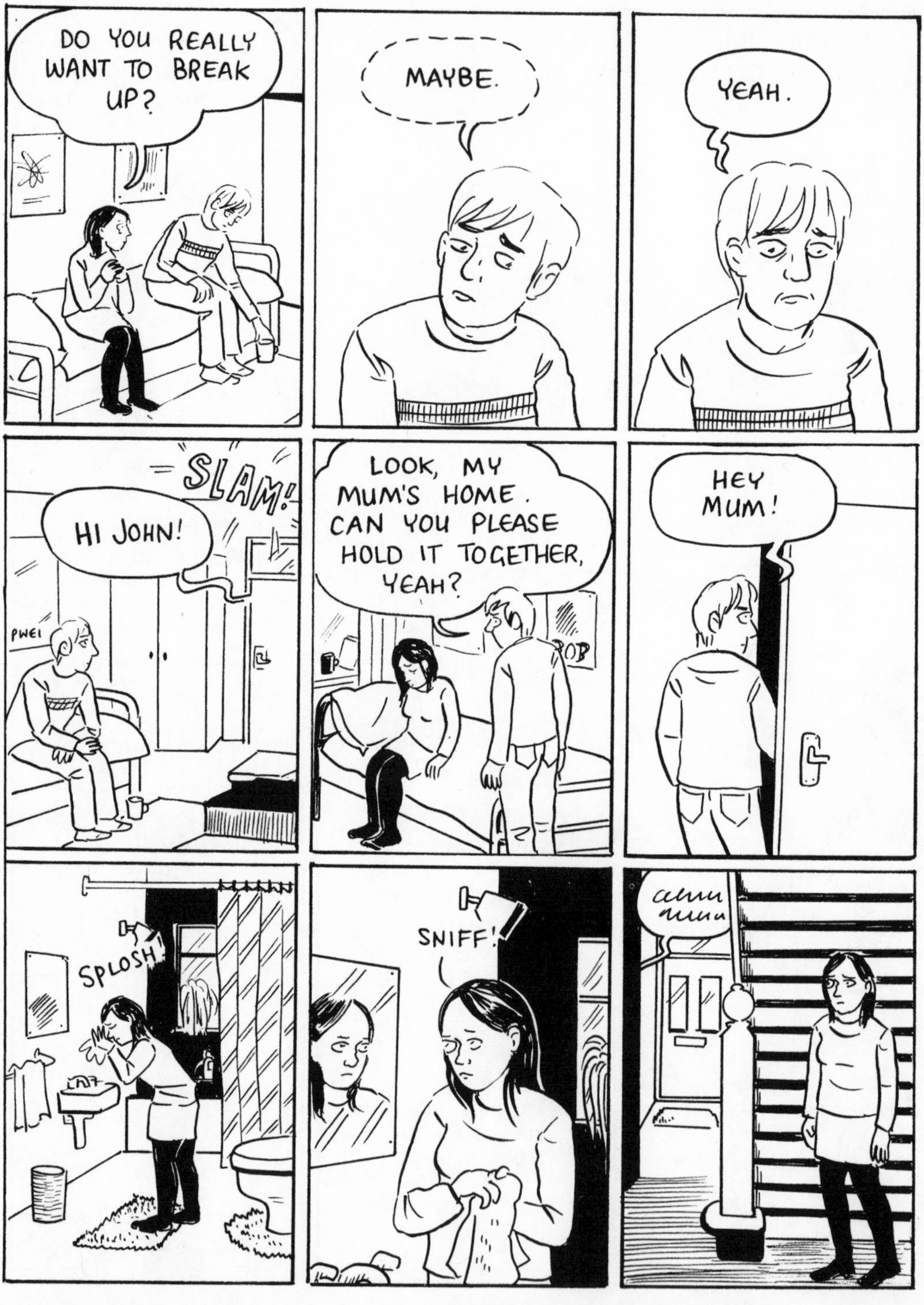
DO YOU REALLY WANT TO BREAK UP?
MAYBE.
YEAH.
SLAM!
HI JOHN!
PWEI
LOOK, MY MUM'S HOME. CAN YOU PLEASE HOLD IT TOGETHER, YEAH?
HEY MUM!
SPLOSH!
SNIFF!

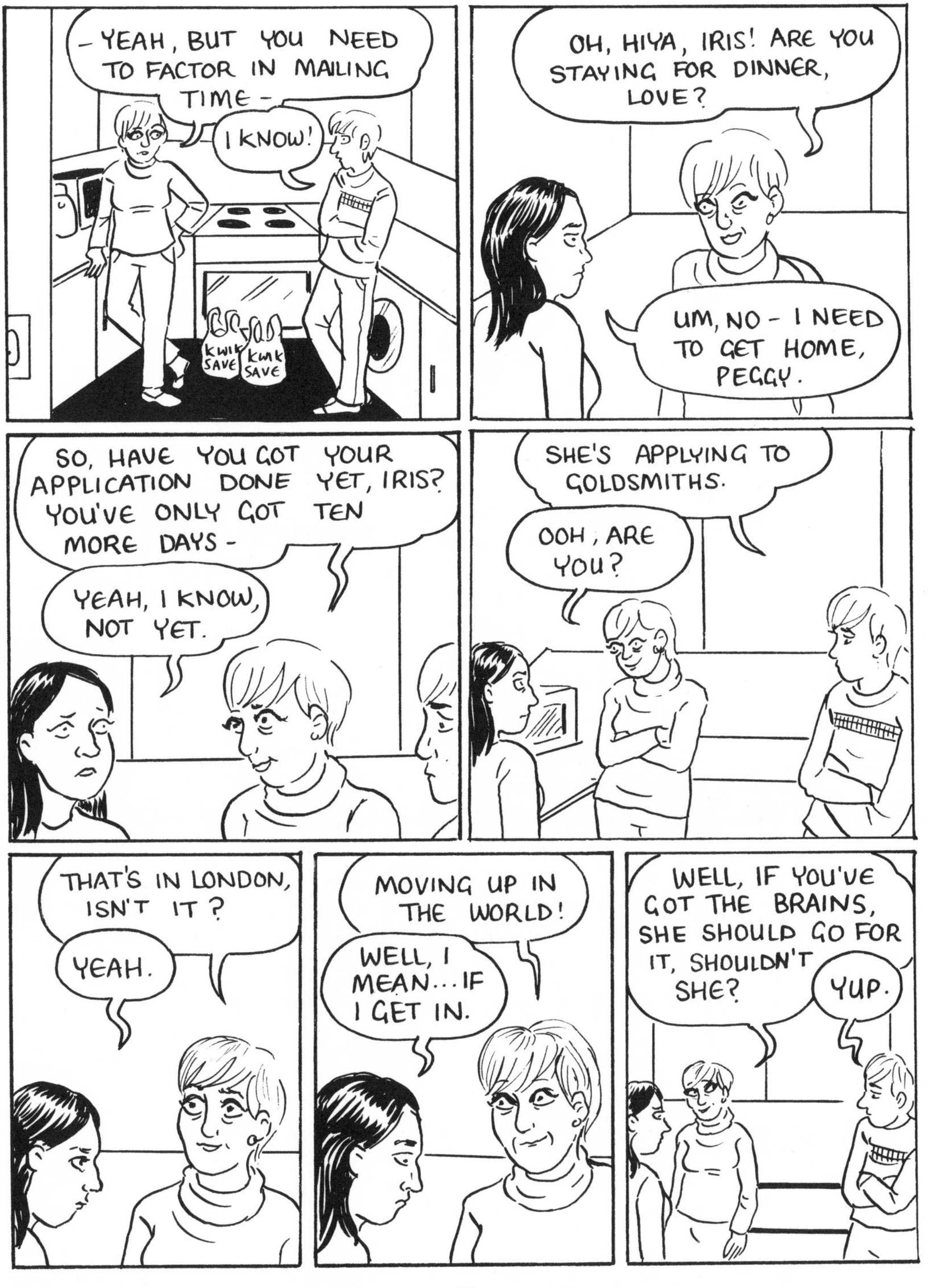
-YEAH, BUT YOU NEED TO FACTOR IN MAILING TIME-
I KNOW!
KWIK SAVE
KWIK SAVE
OH, HIYA, IRIS! ARE YOU STAYING FOR DINNER, LOVE?
UM, NO - I NEED TO GET HOME, PEGGY.
SO, HAVE YOU GOT YOUR APPLICATION DONE YET, IRIS? YOU'VE ONLY GOT TEN MORE DAYS -
YEAH, I KNOW, NOT YET.
SHE'S APPLYING TO GOLDSMITHS.
OOH, ARE YOU?
THAT'S IN LONDON, ISN'T IT?
YEAH.
MOVING UP IN THE WORLD!
WELL, I MEAN... IF I GET IN.
WELL, IF YOU'VE GOT THE BRAINS, SHE SHOULD GO FOR IT, SHOULDN'T SHE?
YUP.

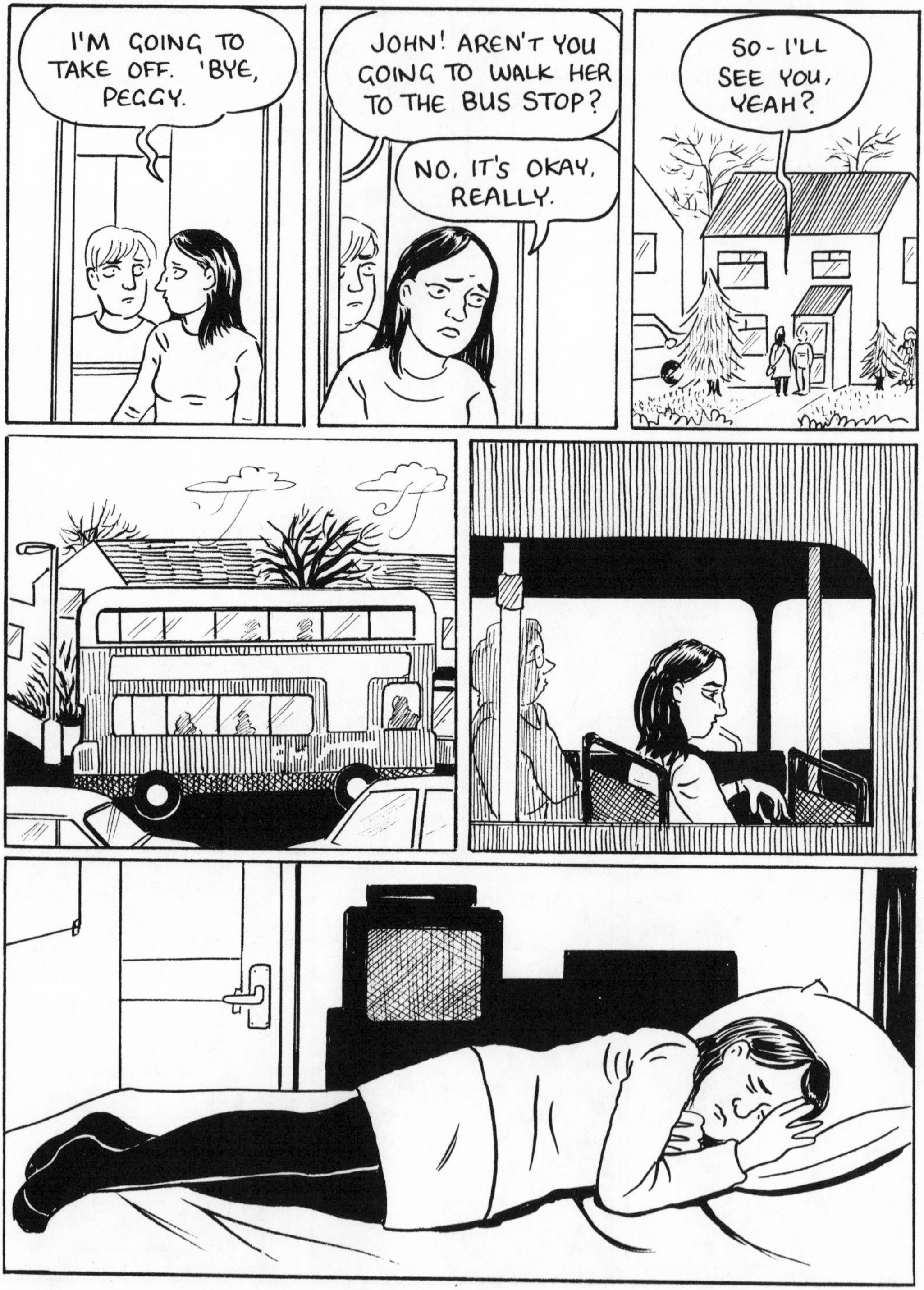
I'M GOING TO TAKE OFF. 'BYE, PEGGY.
JOHN! AREN'T YOU GOING TO WALK HER TO THE BUS STOP?
NO, IT'S OKAY, REALLY.
SO - I'LL SEE YOU, YEAH?

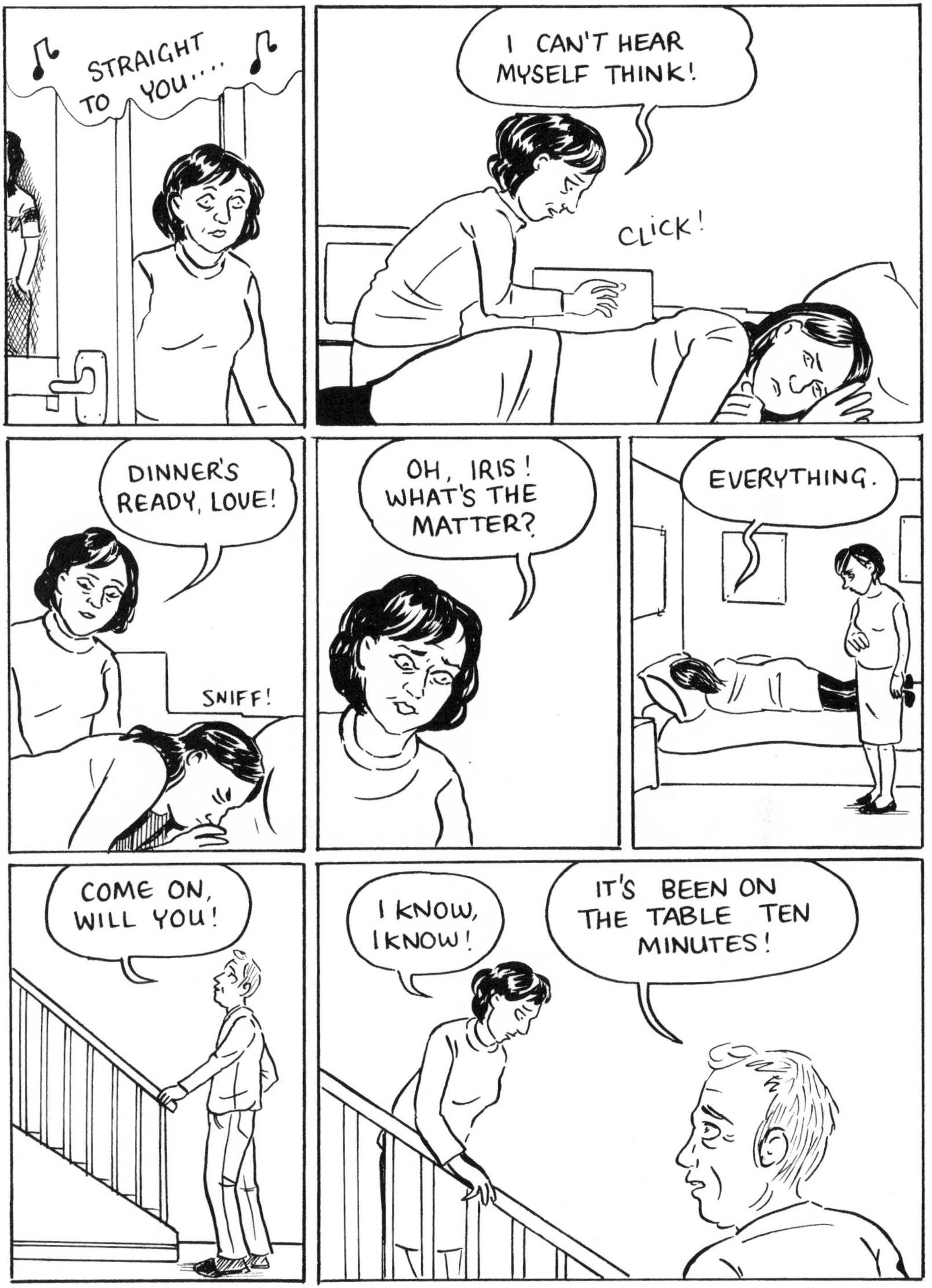
STRAIGHT TO YOU....
I CAN'T HEAR MYSELF THINK!
CLICK!
DINNER'S READY, LOVE!
SNIFF!
OH, IRIS! WHAT'S THE MATTER?
EVERYTHING.
COME ON, WILL YOU!
I KNOW, I KNOW!
IT'S BEEN ON THE TABLE TEN MINUTES!

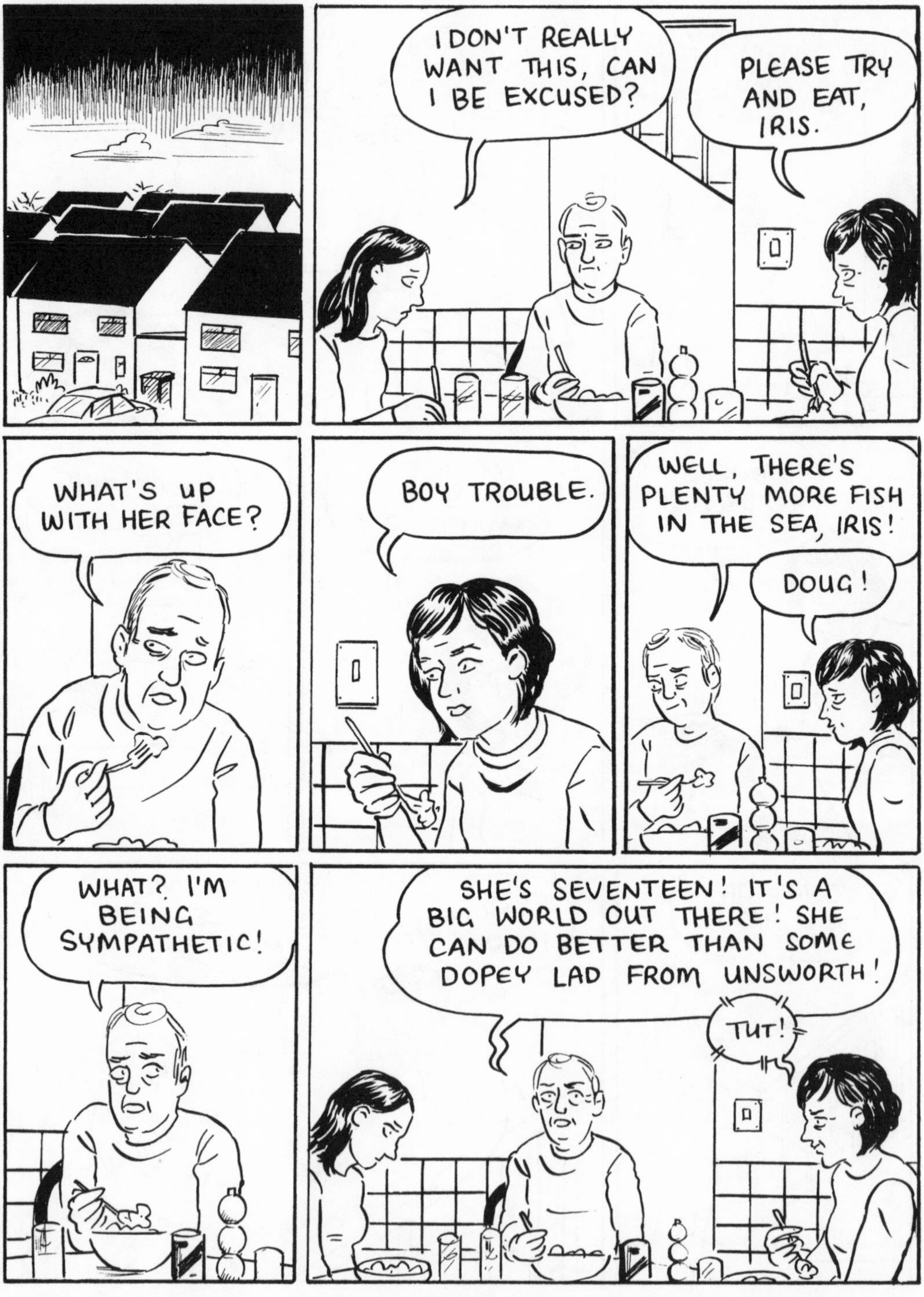

I DON'T REALLY WANT THIS, CAN I BE EXCUSED?
PLEASE TRY AND EAT, IRIS.
WHAT'S UP WITH HER FACE?
BOY TROUBLE.
WELL, THERE'S PLENTY MORE FISH IN THE SEA, IRIS!
DOUG!
WHAT? I'M BEING SYMPATHETIC!
SHE'S SEVENTEEN! IT'S A BIG WORLD OUT THERE! SHE CAN DO BETTER THAN SOME DOPEY LAD FROM UNSWORTH!
TUT!

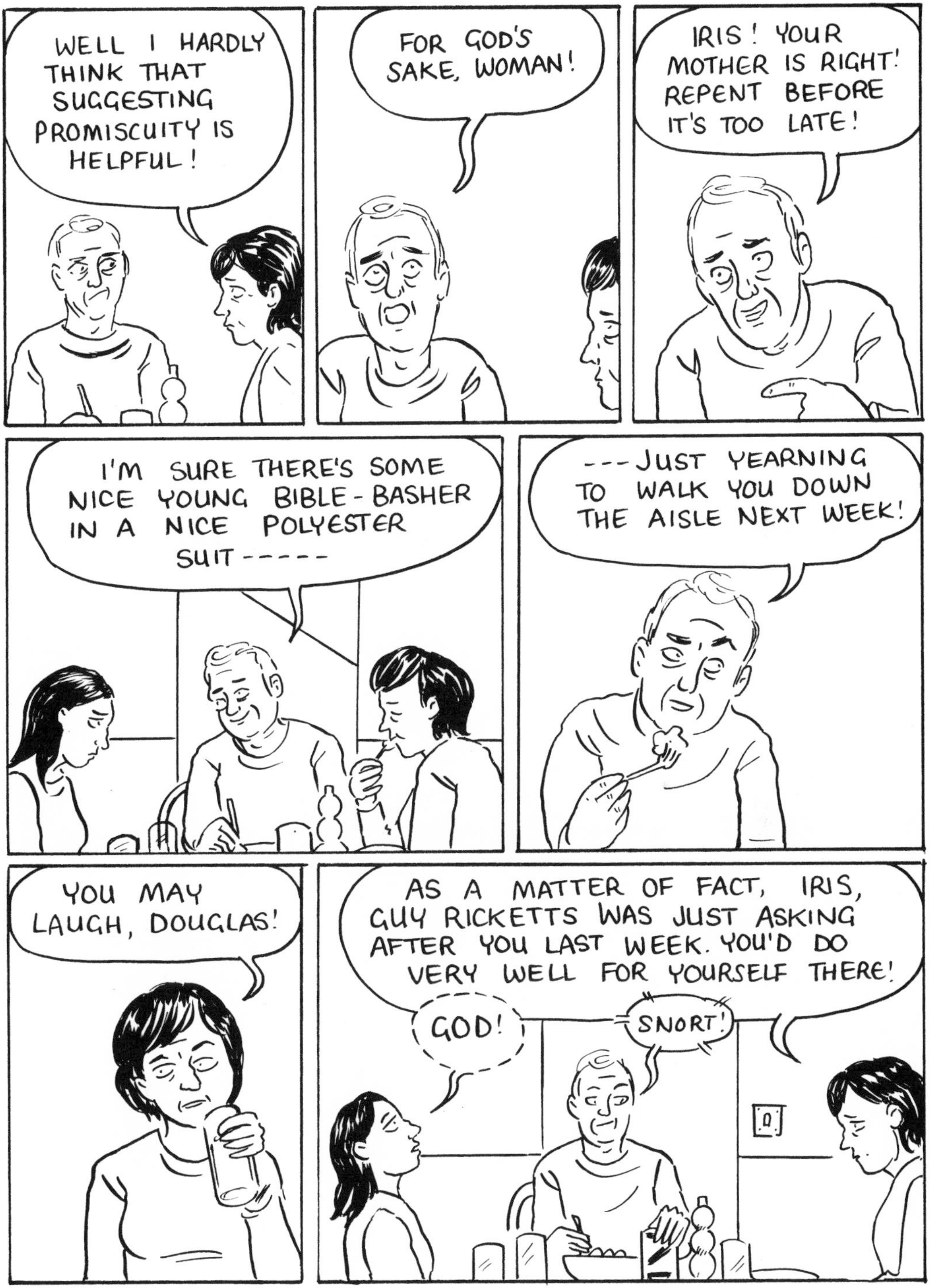
WELL I HARDLY THINK THAT SUGGESTING PROMISCUITY IS HELPFUL!
FOR GOD'S SAKE, WOMAN!
IRIS! YOUR MOTHER IS RIGHT! REPENT BEFORE IT'S TOO LATE!
I'M SURE THERE'S SOME NICE YOUNG BIBLE-BASHER IN A NICE POLYESTER SUIT-----
---JUST YEARNING TO WALK YOU DOWN THE AISLE NEXT WEEK!
YOU MAY LAUGH, DOUGLAS!
AS A MATTER OF FACT, IRIS, GUY RICKETTS WAS JUST ASKING AFTER YOU LAST WEEK. YOU'D DO VERY WELL FOR YOURSELF THERE!
GOD!
SNORT!

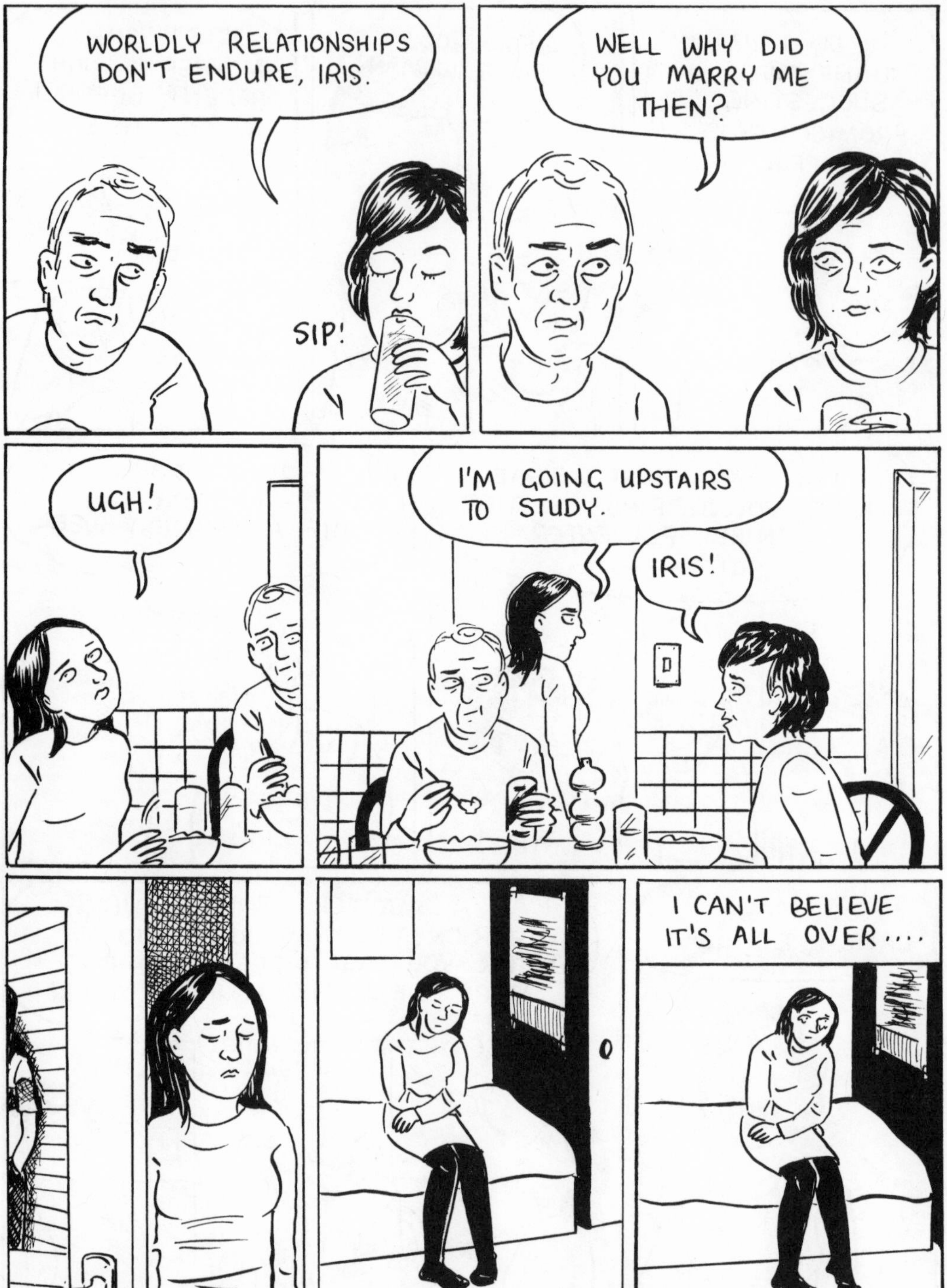
WORLDLY RELATIONSHIPS DON'T ENDURE, IRIS.
SIP!
WELL WHY DID YOU MARRY ME THEN?
UGH!
I'M GOING UPSTAIRS TO STUDY.
IRIS!
I CAN'T BELIEVE IT'S ALL OVER....

HE WAS MY FIRST---

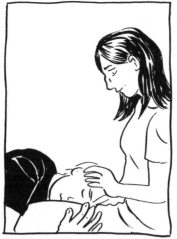

CLICK!

♪ ALL THE TOWERS OF IVORY ARE CRUMBLING... ♪

♪ ♪

SNIFF!

BEING YOUNG FEELS LIKE A CURSE.

ALL THIS TIME AHEAD OF ME....

BLANK AND GREY.

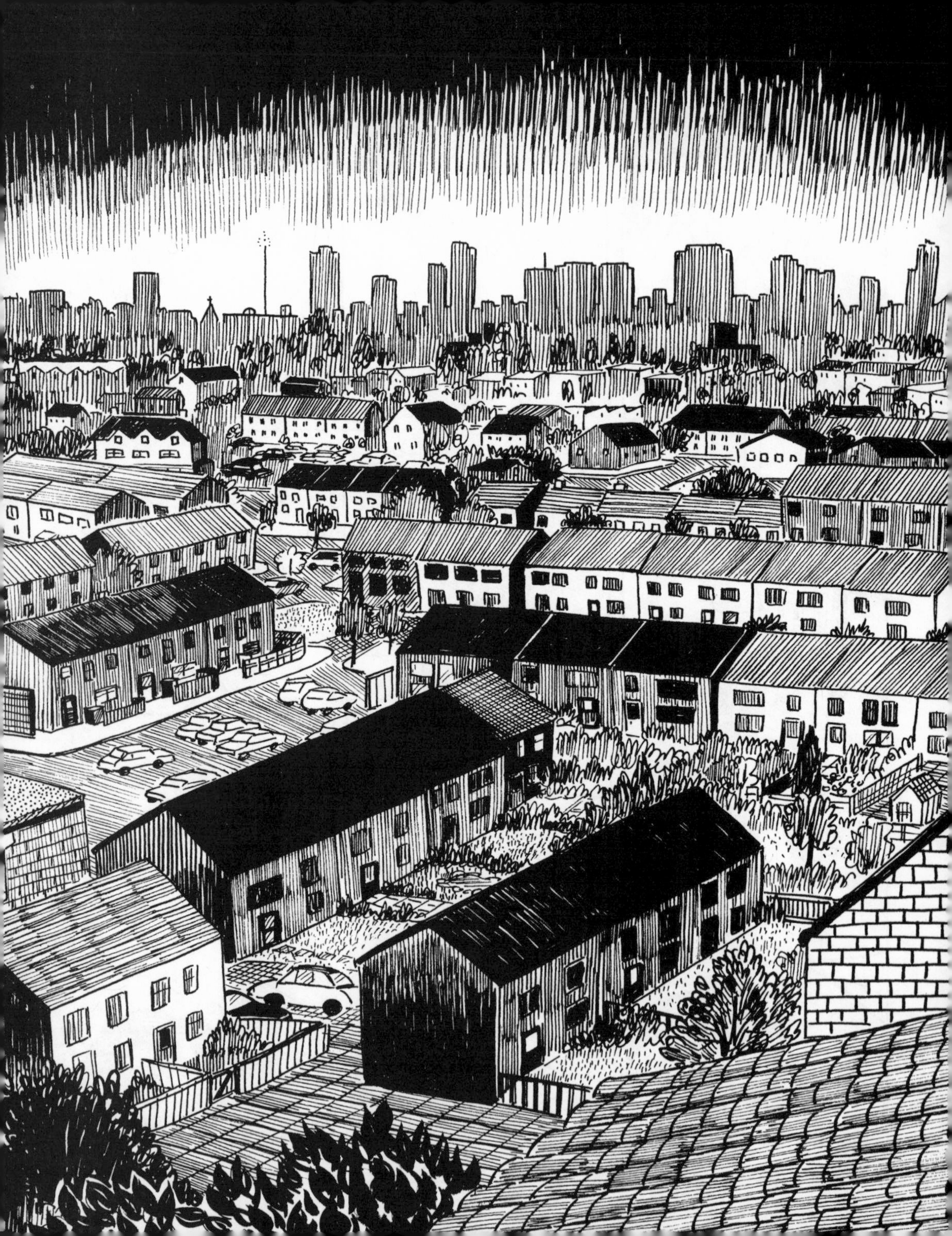

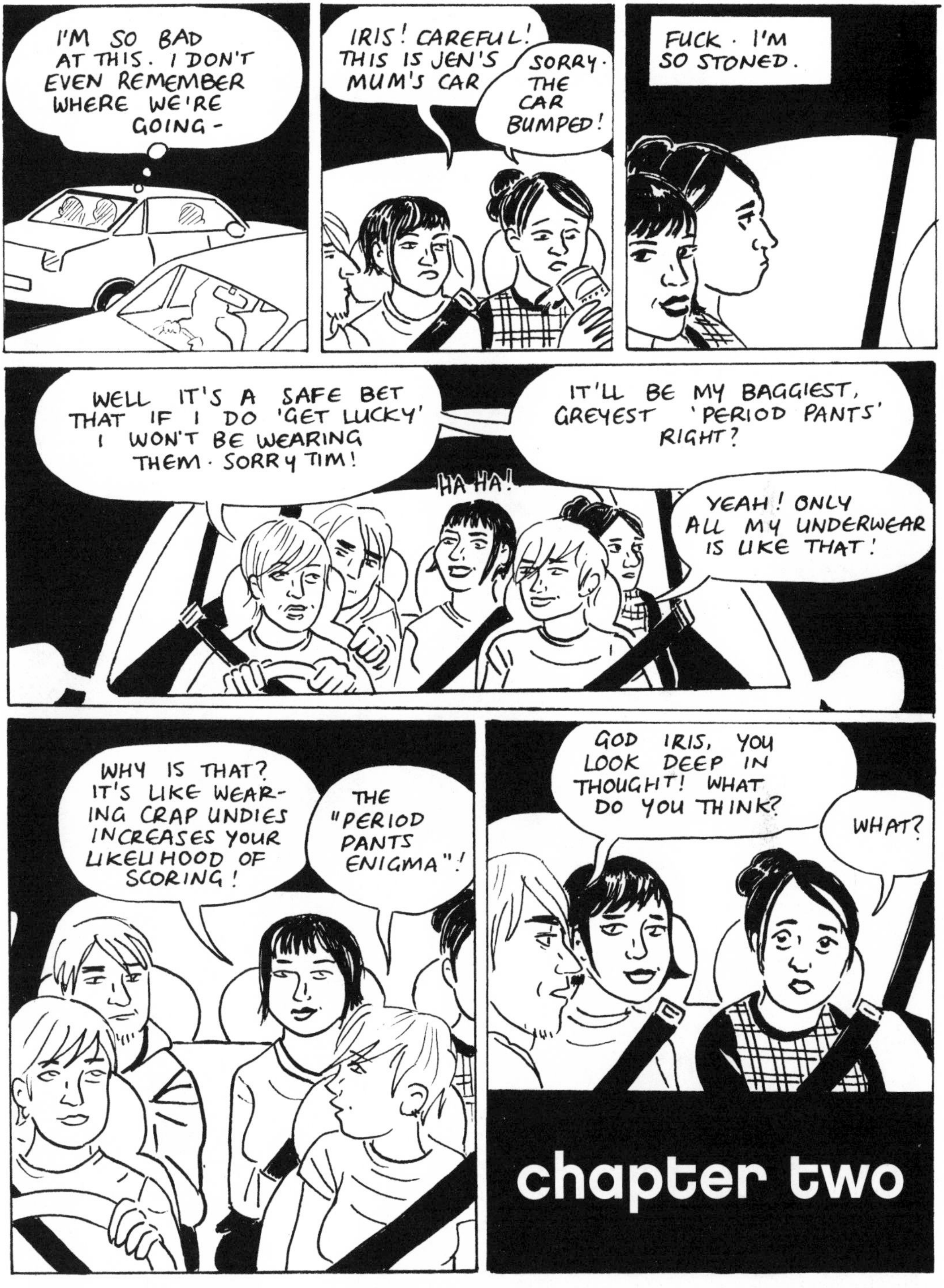
I'M SO BAD AT THIS. I DON'T EVEN REMEMBER WHERE WE'RE GOING -
IRIS! CAREFUL! THIS IS JEN'S MUM'S CAR
SORRY. THE CAR BUMPED!
FUCK. I'M SO STONED.
WELL IT'S A SAFE BET THAT IF I DO 'GET LUCKY' I WON'T BE WEARING THEM. SORRY TIM!
IT'LL BE MY BAGGIEST, GREYEST 'PERIOD PANTS' RIGHT?
HA HA!
YEAH! ONLY ALL MY UNDERWEAR IS LIKE THAT!
WHY IS THAT? IT'S LIKE WEAR-ING CRAP UNDIES INCREASES YOUR LIKELIHOOD OF SCORING!
THE "PERIOD PANTS ENIGMA"!
GOD IRIS, YOU LOOK DEEP IN THOUGHT! WHAT DO YOU THINK?
WHAT?
chapter two

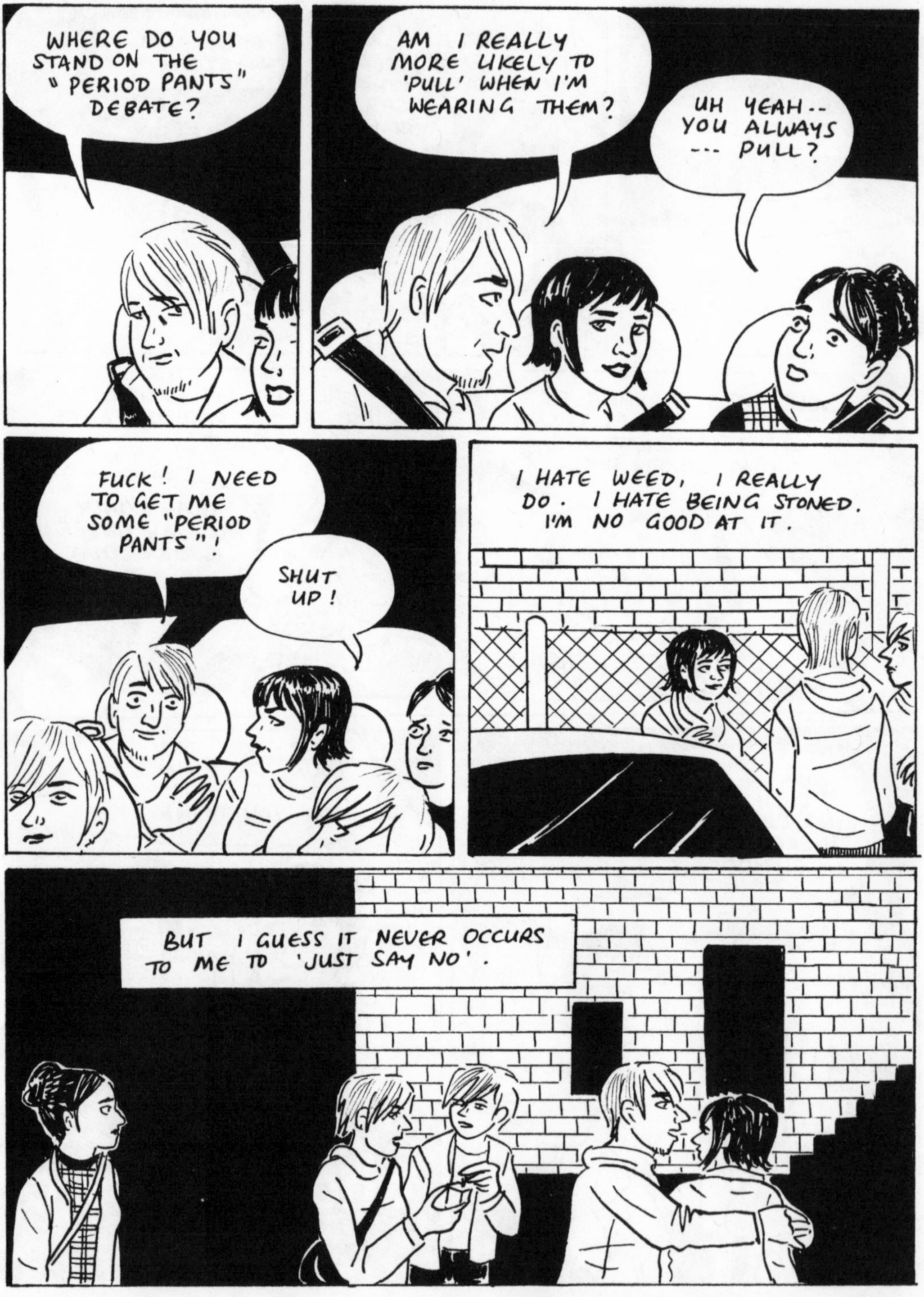
WHERE DO YOU STAND ON THE "PERIOD PANTS" DEBATE?
AM I REALLY MORE LIKELY TO 'PULL' WHEN I'M WEARING THEM?
UH YEAH -- YOU ALWAYS --- PULL?
FUCK! I NEED TO GET ME SOME "PERIOD PANTS"!
SHUT UP!
I HATE WEED, I REALLY DO. I HATE BEING STONED. I'M NO GOOD AT IT.
BUT I GUESS IT NEVER OCCURS TO ME TO 'JUST SAY NO'.

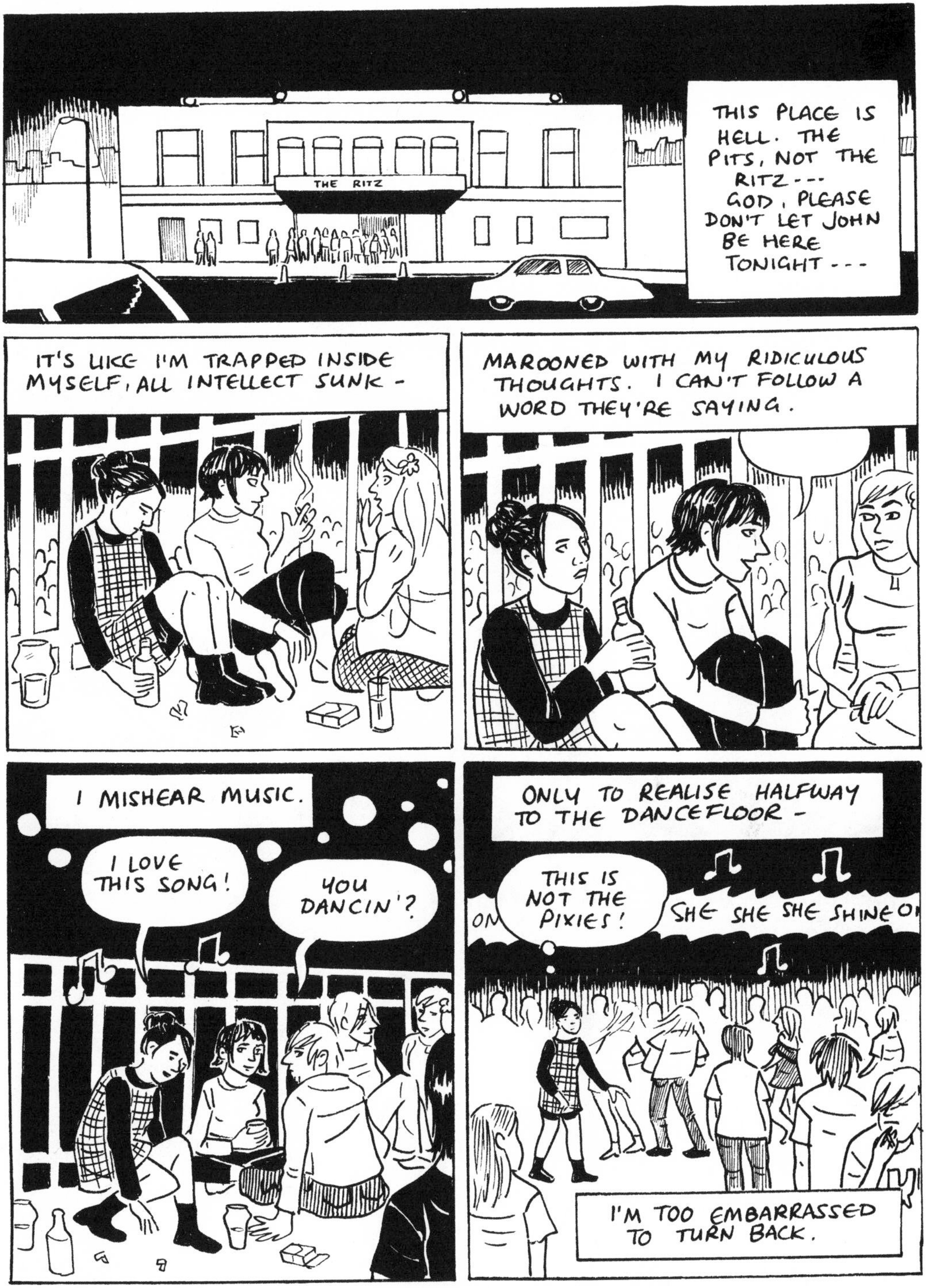
THE RITZ
THIS PLACE IS HELL. THE PITS, NOT THE RITZ--- GOD, PLEASE DON'T LET JOHN BE HERE TONIGHT---
IT'S LIKE I'M TRAPPED INSIDE MYSELF, ALL INTELLECT SUNK -
MAROONED WITH MY RIDICULOUS THOUGHTS. I CAN'T FOLLOW A WORD THEY'RE SAYING.
I MISHEAR MUSIC.
I LOVE THIS SONG!
YOU DANCIN'?
ONLY TO REALISE HALFWAY TO THE DANCEFLOOR -
THIS IS NOT THE PIXIES!
ON SHE SHE SHE SHINE ON
I'M TOO EMBARRASSED TO TURN BACK.

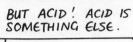

BUT ACID! ACID IS SOMETHING ELSE.

PETE SAYS HE'S ONLY GOT THREE.

I WAS READY FOR IT. I'D READ THE 'DOORS OF PERCEPTION'!

ALRIGHT, LET'S JUST GET THEM ANYWAY —

IT'S IRIS'S FIRST TIME, WE CAN SPLIT ONE.

OKAY.

NOTHING HAPPENED THE FIRST TIME I TRIED IT.

YOU NEITHER HUH?

STUPID HIPPY PETE.

I WASN'T SCARED TO TRY IT AGAIN.

THE WORLD WAS SO ABSURDLY WARPED AND FUNNY ON ACID.

OH GOD!

HA HA HA!

NOT WHAT I WAS EXPECTING. I COULD HARDLY IMAGINE ALDOUS HUXLEY FAILING AT BUYING FAST FOOD —

WE CAN DO IT! I BELIEVE IN US!

— ON A DAMP SPRING EVENING IN MANCHESTER!

BECCA, I REALLY, REALLY WANT CHIPS!

ME TOO! ME TOO!

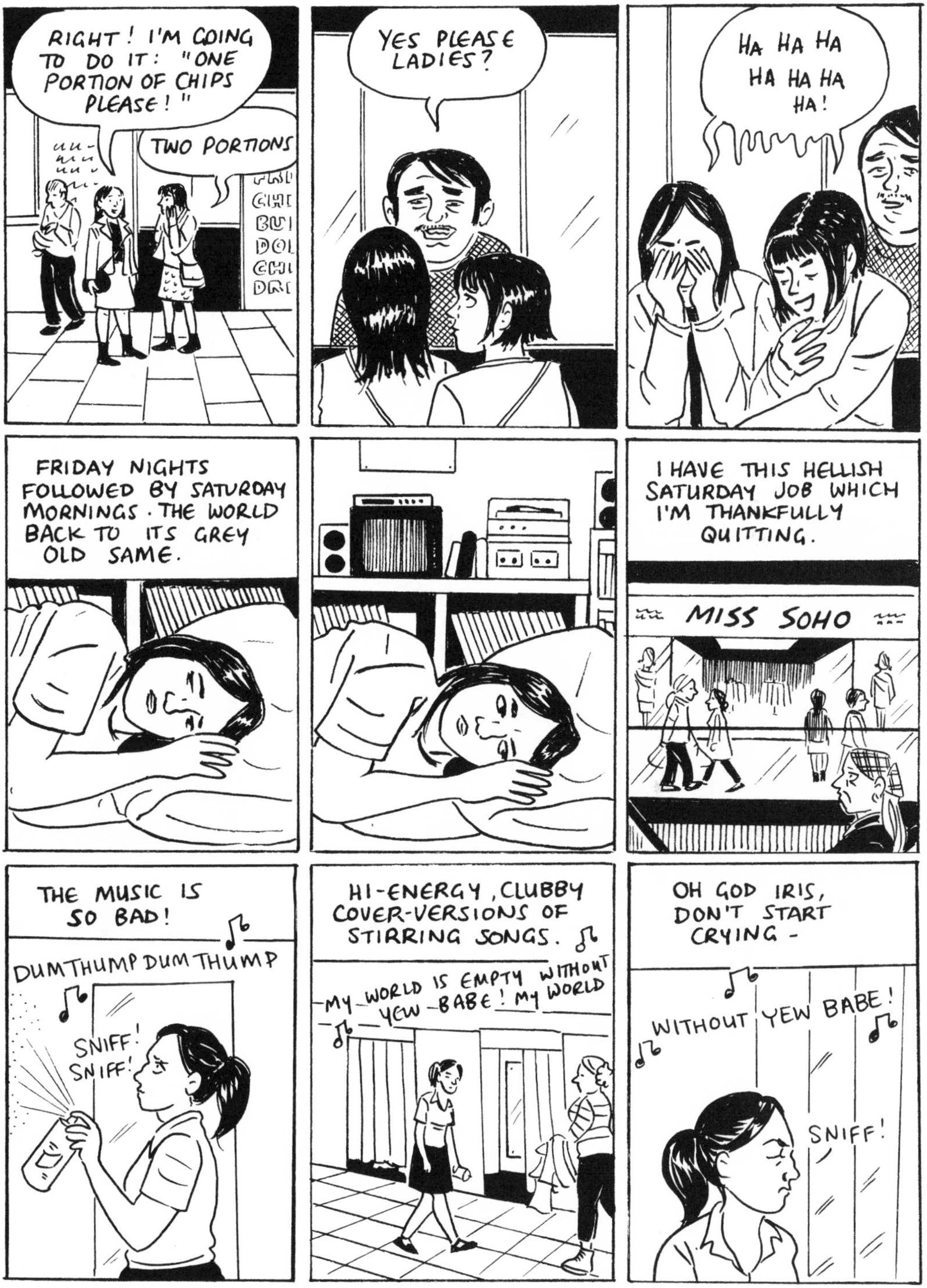
RIGHT! I'M GOING TO DO IT: "ONE PORTION OF CHIPS PLEASE!"
TWO PORTIONS
YES PLEASE LADIES?
HA HA HA HA HA HA HA!
FRIDAY NIGHTS FOLLOWED BY SATURDAY MORNINGS. THE WORLD BACK TO ITS GREY OLD SAME.
I HAVE THIS HELLISH SATURDAY JOB WHICH I'M THANKFULLY QUITTING.
MISS SOHO
THE MUSIC IS SO BAD!
DUMTHUMP DUM THUMP
SNIFF! SNIFF!
HI-ENERGY, CLUBBY COVER-VERSIONS OF STIRRING SONGS.
MY WORLD IS EMPTY WITHOUT YEW BABE! MY WORLD
OH GOD IRIS, DON'T START CRYING -
WITHOUT YEW BABE!
SNIFF!

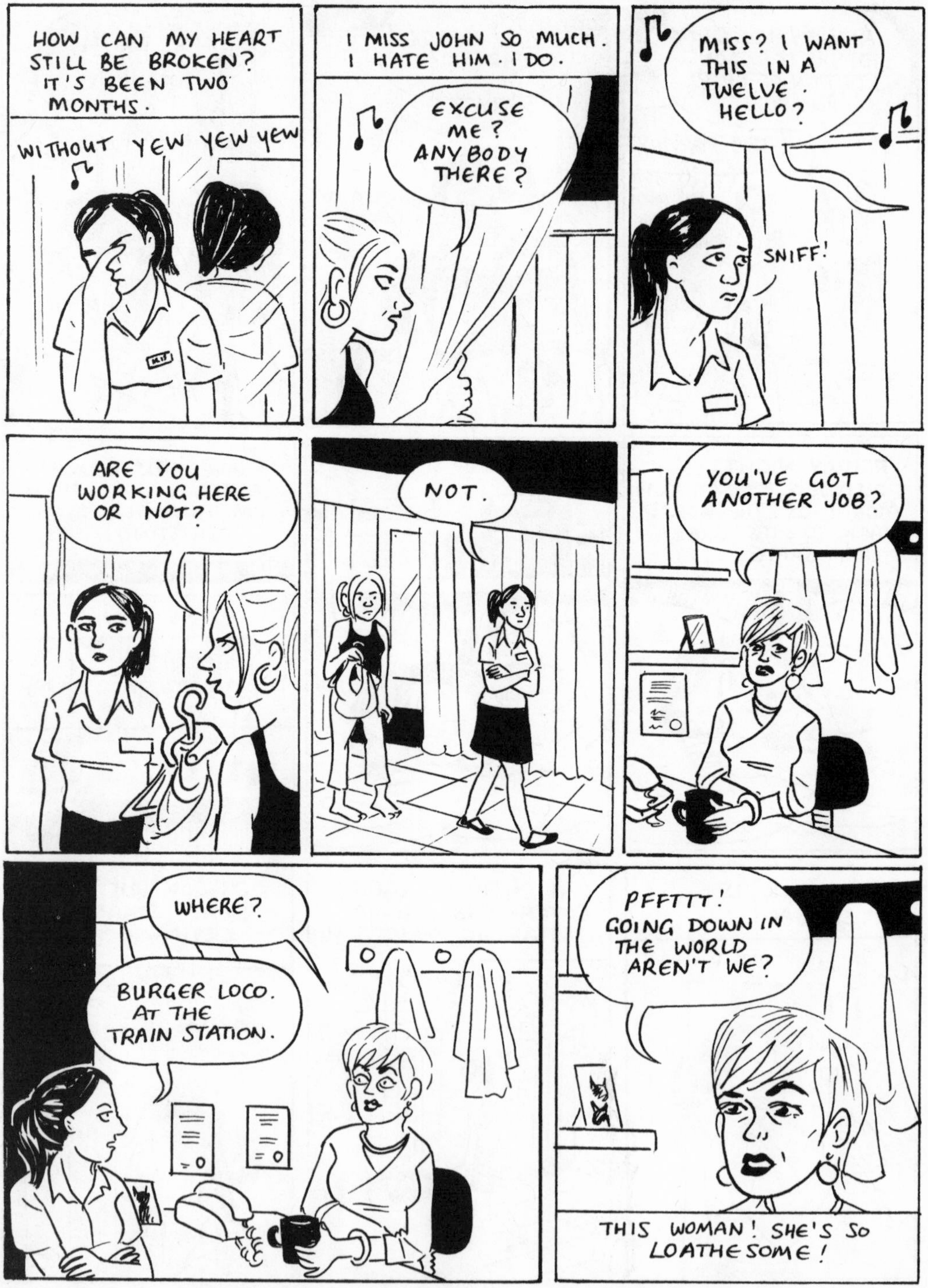
HOW CAN MY HEART STILL BE BROKEN? IT'S BEEN TWO MONTHS.
WITHOUT YEW YEW YEW
I MISS JOHN SO MUCH. I HATE HIM. I DO.
EXCUSE ME? ANYBODY THERE?
MISS? I WANT THIS IN A TWELVE. HELLO?
SNIFF!
ARE YOU WORKING HERE OR NOT?
NOT.
YOU'VE GOT ANOTHER JOB?
WHERE?
BURGER LOCO. AT THE TRAIN STATION.
PFFTTT! GOING DOWN IN THE WORLD AREN'T WE?
THIS WOMAN! SHE'S SO LOATHESOME!

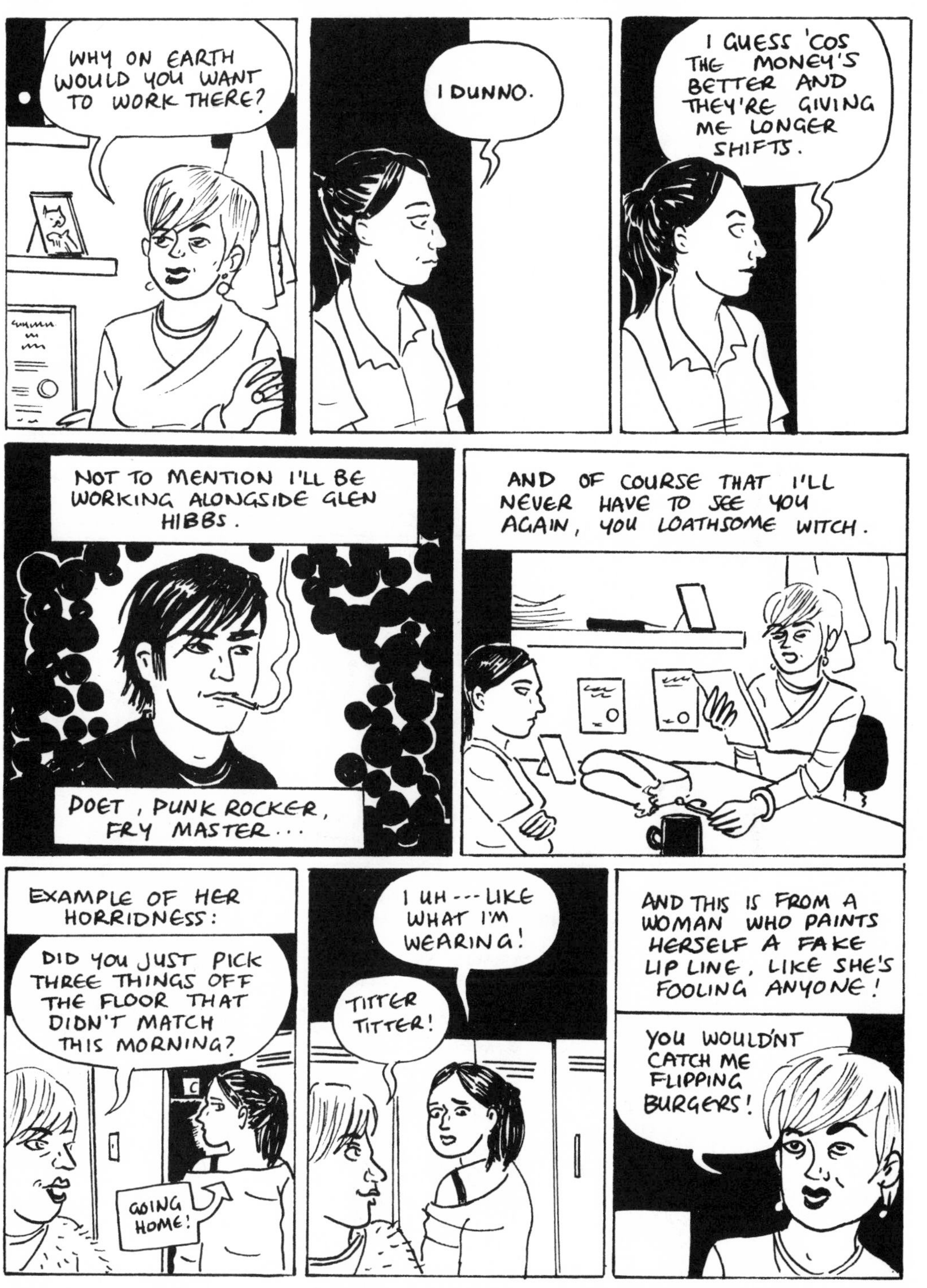
WHY ON EARTH WOULD YOU WANT TO WORK THERE?
I DUNNO.
I GUESS 'COS THE MONEY'S BETTER AND THEY'RE GIVING ME LONGER SHIFTS.
NOT TO MENTION I'LL BE WORKING ALONGSIDE GLEN HIBBS.
POET, PUNK ROCKER, FRY MASTER...
AND OF COURSE THAT I'LL NEVER HAVE TO SEE YOU AGAIN, YOU LOATHSOME WITCH.
EXAMPLE OF HER HORRIDNESS:
DID YOU JUST PICK THREE THINGS OFF THE FLOOR THAT DIDN'T MATCH THIS MORNING?
GOING HOME!
I UH---LIKE WHAT I'M WEARING!
TITTER TITTER!
AND THIS IS FROM A WOMAN WHO PAINTS HERSELF A FAKE LIP LINE, LIKE SHE'S FOOLING ANYONE!
YOU WOULDN'T CATCH ME FLIPPING BURGERS!

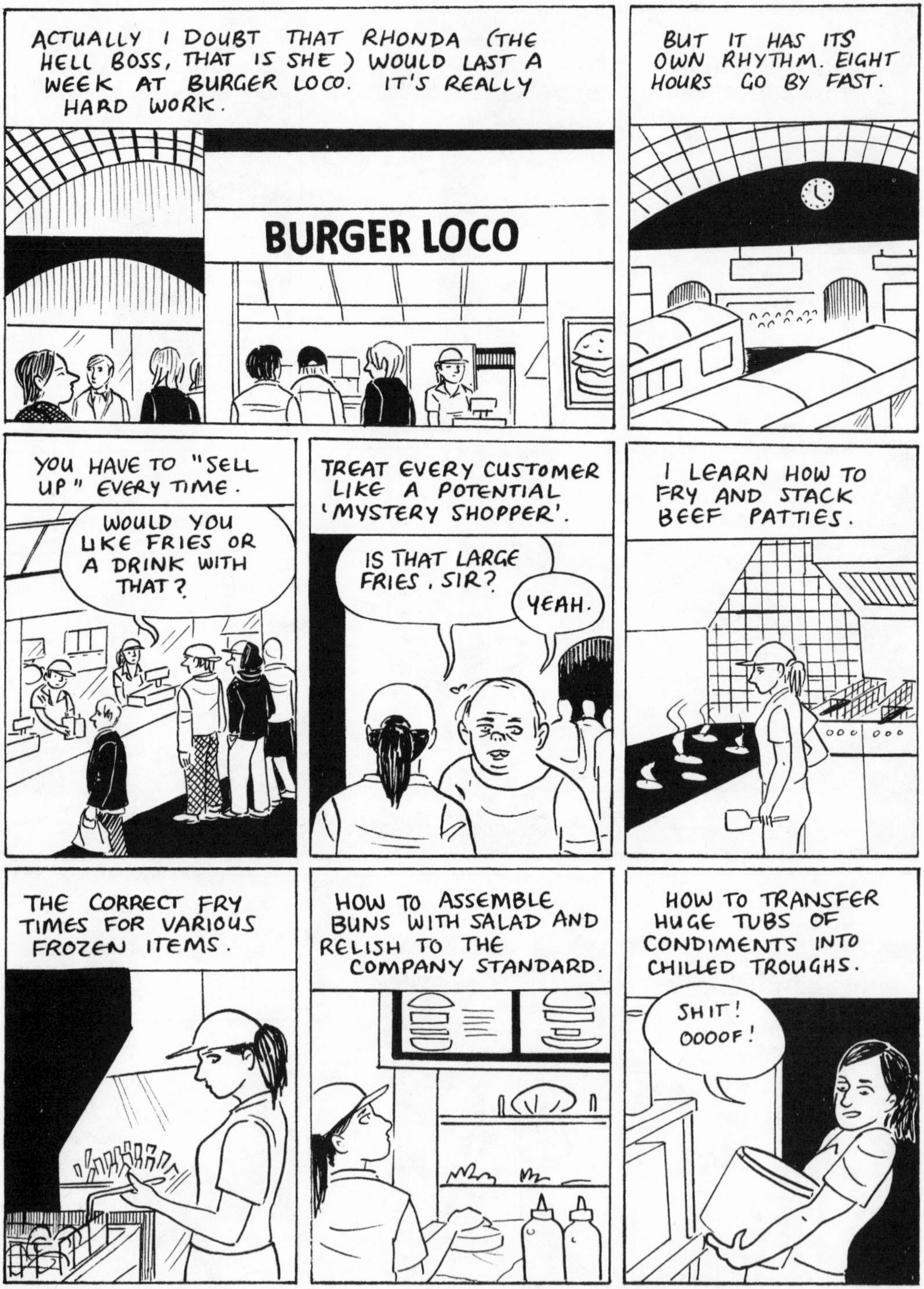
ACTUALLY I DOUBT THAT RHONDA (THE HELL BOSS, THAT IS SHE) WOULD LAST A WEEK AT BURGER LOCO. IT'S REALLY HARD WORK.
BURGER LOCO
BUT IT HAS ITS OWN RHYTHM. EIGHT HOURS GO BY FAST.
YOU HAVE TO "SELL UP" EVERY TIME.
WOULD YOU LIKE FRIES OR A DRINK WITH THAT?
TREAT EVERY CUSTOMER LIKE A POTENTIAL 'MYSTERY SHOPPER'.
IS THAT LARGE FRIES, SIR?
YEAH.
I LEARN HOW TO FRY AND STACK BEEF PATTIES.
THE CORRECT FRY TIMES FOR VARIOUS FROZEN ITEMS.
HOW TO ASSEMBLE BUNS WITH SALAD AND RELISH TO THE COMPANY STANDARD.
HOW TO TRANSFER HUGE TUBS OF CONDIMENTS INTO CHILLED TROUGHS.
SHIT! OOOOF!

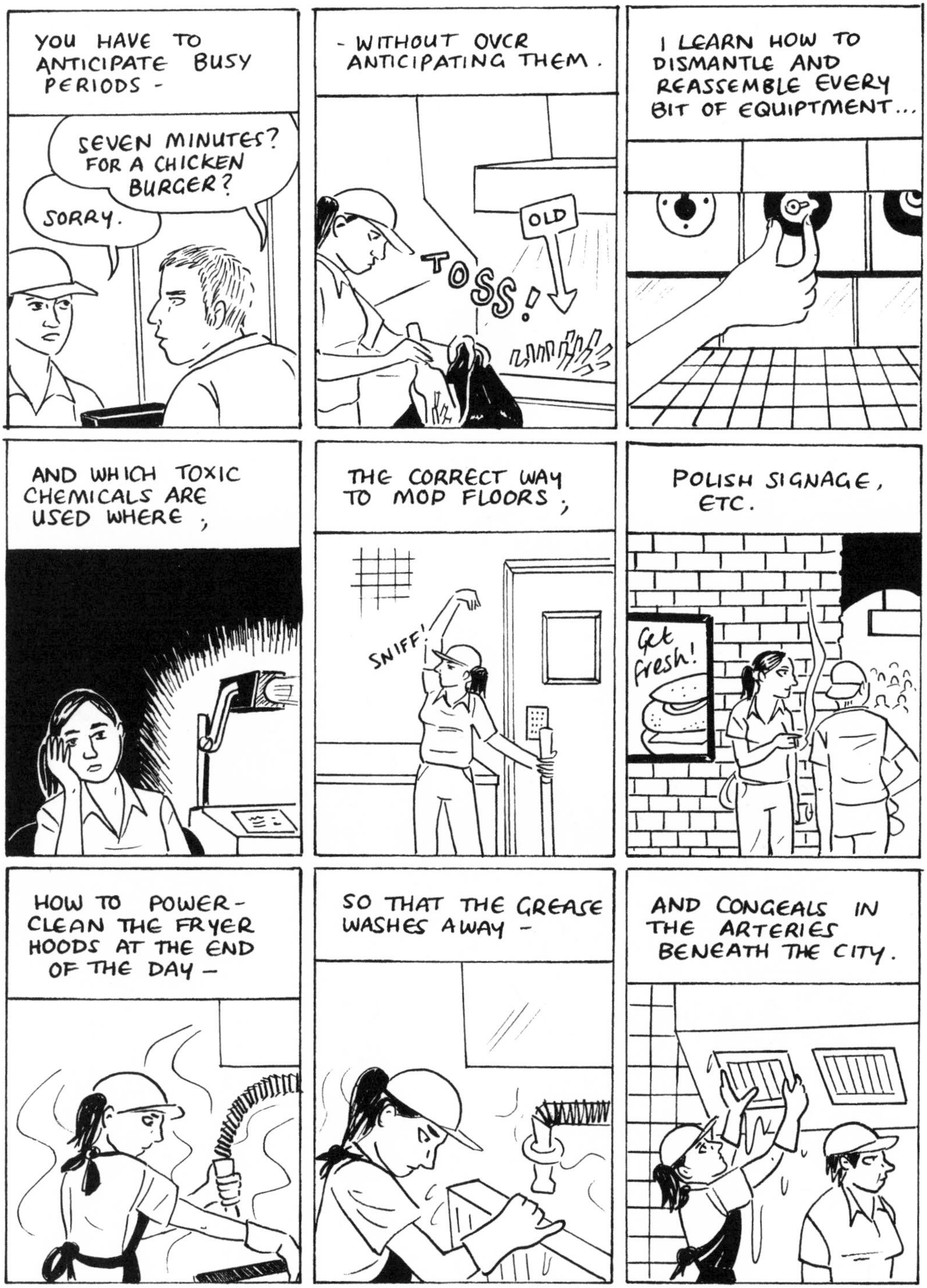
YOU HAVE TO ANTICIPATE BUSY PERIODS -
SEVEN MINUTES? FOR A CHICKEN BURGER?
SORRY.
- WITHOUT OVER ANTICIPATING THEM.
OLD
TOSS!
I LEARN HOW TO DISMANTLE AND REASSEMBLE EVERY BIT OF EQUIPTMENT...
AND WHICH TOXIC CHEMICALS ARE USED WHERE;
THE CORRECT WAY TO MOP FLOORS;
SNIFF!
POLISH SIGNAGE, ETC.
Get fresh!
HOW TO POWER-CLEAN THE FRYER HOODS AT THE END OF THE DAY -
SO THAT THE GREASE WASHES AWAY -
AND CONGEALS IN THE ARTERIES BENEATH THE CITY.

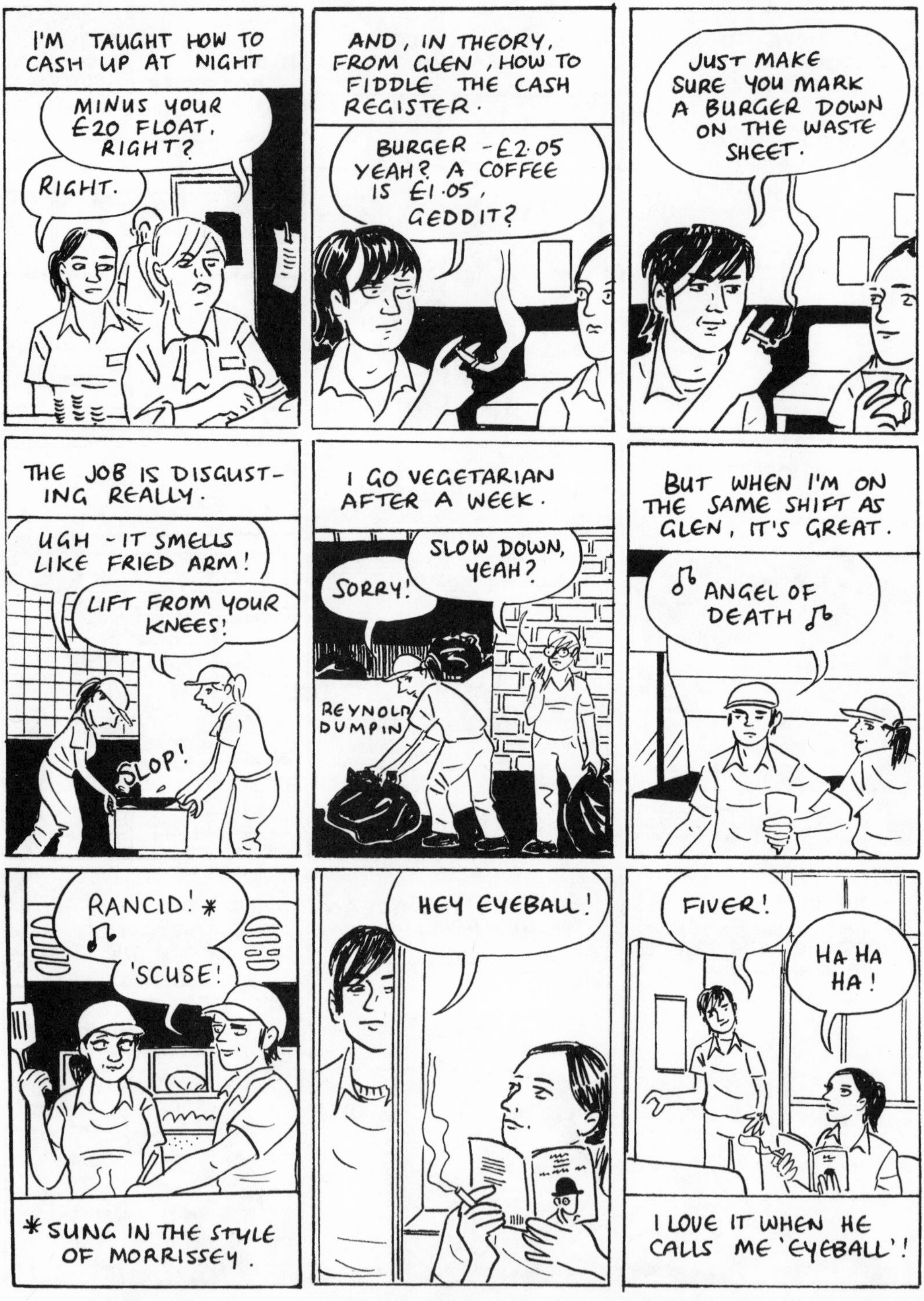
I'M TAUGHT HOW TO CASH UP AT NIGHT
MINUS YOUR £20 FLOAT, RIGHT?
RIGHT.
AND, IN THEORY, FROM GLEN, HOW TO FIDDLE THE CASH REGISTER.
BURGER - £2.05 YEAH? A COFFEE IS £1.05, GEDDIT?
JUST MAKE SURE YOU MARK A BURGER DOWN ON THE WASTE SHEET.
THE JOB IS DISGUSTING REALLY.
UGH - IT SMELLS LIKE FRIED ARM!
LIFT FROM YOUR KNEES!
SLOP!
I GO VEGETARIAN AFTER A WEEK.
SLOW DOWN, YEAH?
SORRY!
BUT WHEN I'M ON THE SAME SHIFT AS GLEN, IT'S GREAT.
ANGEL OF DEATH
RANCID! *
'SCUSE!
* SUNG IN THE STYLE OF MORRISSEY.
HEY EYEBALL!
FIVER!
HA HA HA!
I LOVE IT WHEN HE CALLS ME 'EYEBALL'!

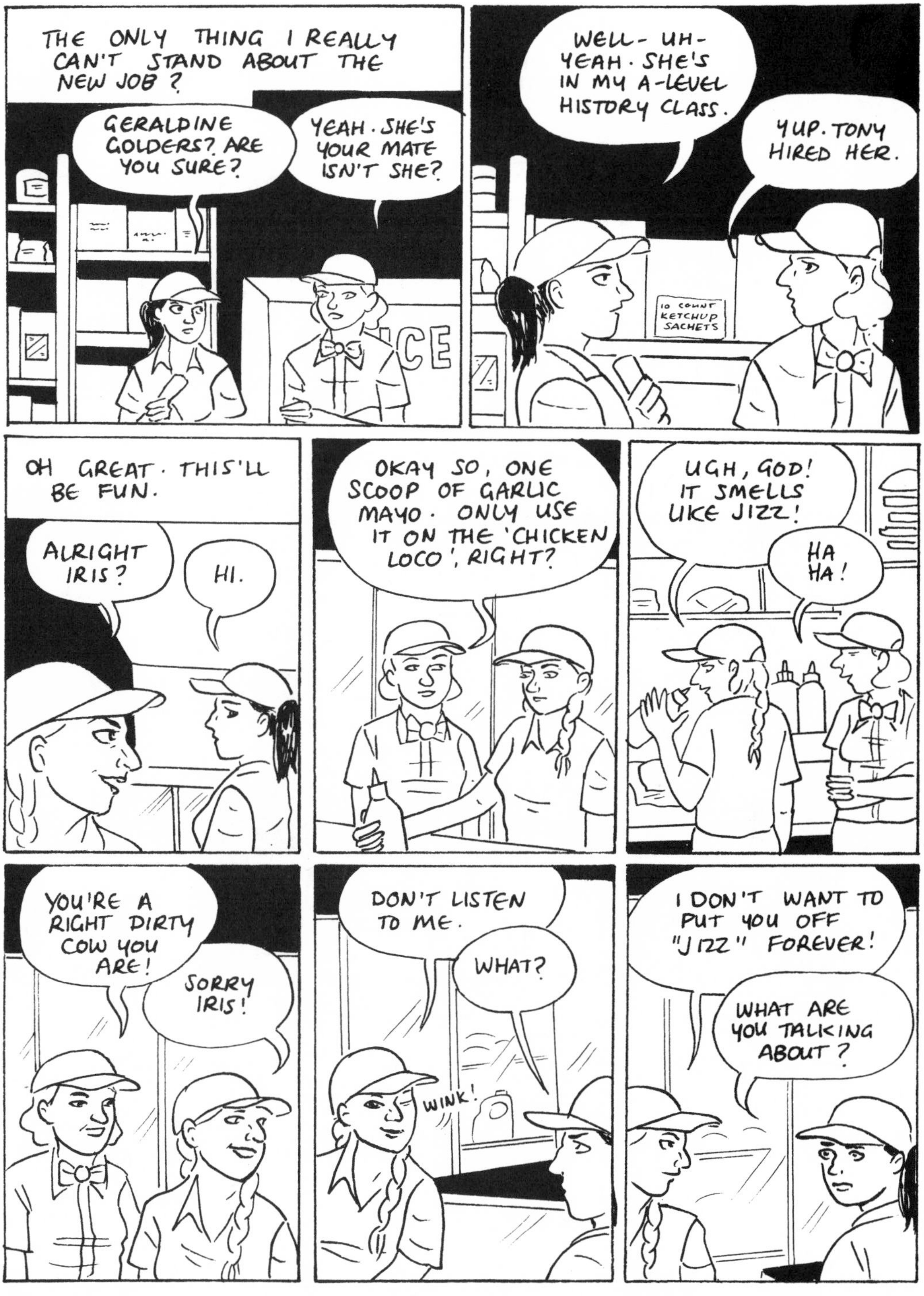
THE ONLY THING I REALLY CAN'T STAND ABOUT THE NEW JOB?
GERALDINE GOLDERS? ARE YOU SURE?
YEAH. SHE'S YOUR MATE ISN'T SHE?
ICE
WELL- UH- YEAH. SHE'S IN MY A-LEVEL HISTORY CLASS.
YUP. TONY HIRED HER.
10 COUNT KETCHUP SACHETS
OH GREAT. THIS'LL BE FUN.
ALRIGHT IRIS?
HI.
OKAY SO, ONE SCOOP OF GARLIC MAYO. ONLY USE IT ON THE 'CHICKEN LOCO', RIGHT?
UGH, GOD! IT SMELLS LIKE JIZZ!
HA HA!
YOU'RE A RIGHT DIRTY COW YOU ARE!
SORRY IRIS!
DON'T LISTEN TO ME.
WHAT?
WINK!
I DON'T WANT TO PUT YOU OFF "JIZZ" FOREVER!
WHAT ARE YOU TALKING ABOUT?

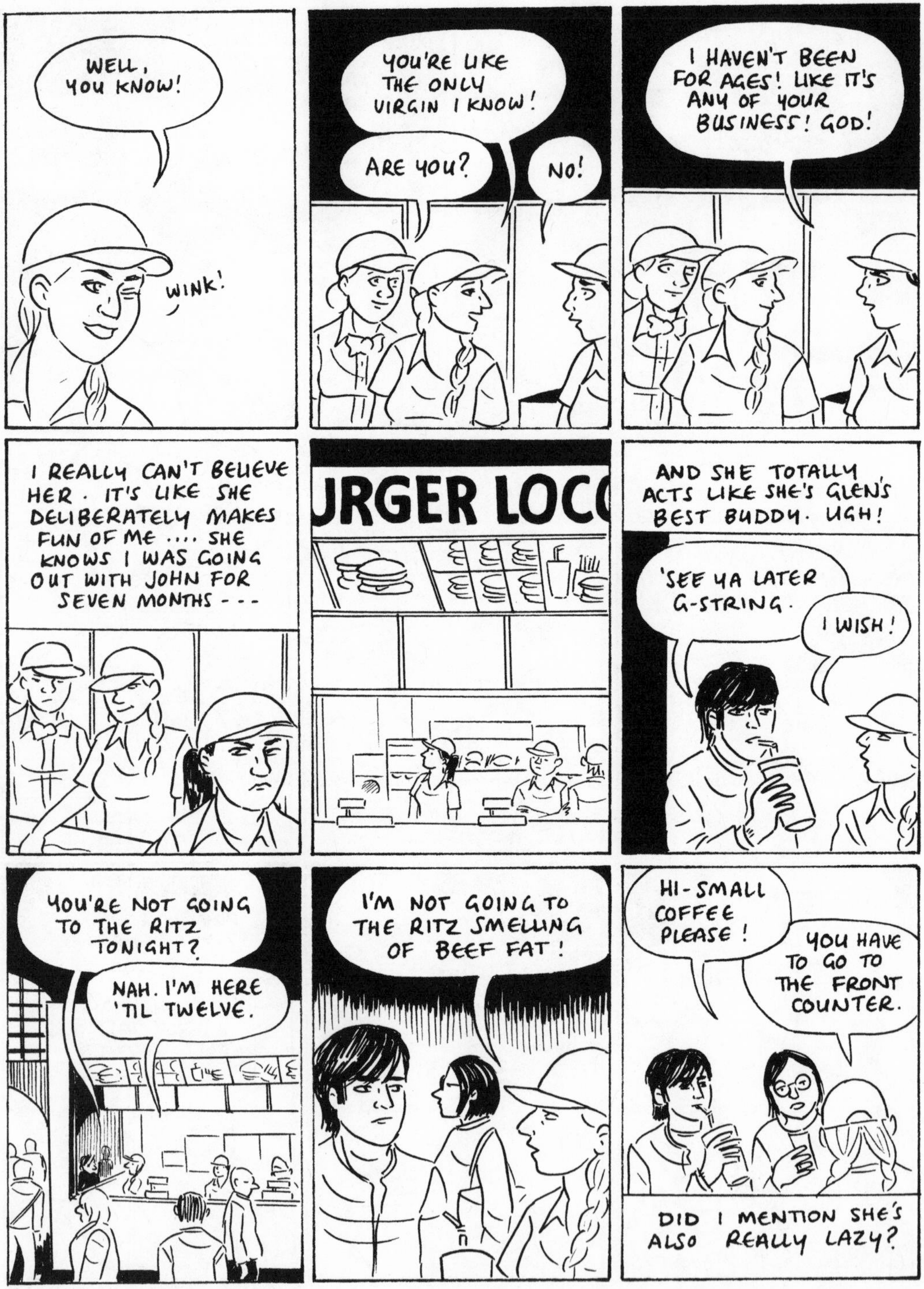
WELL, YOU KNOW!
WINK!
YOU'RE LIKE THE ONLY VIRGIN I KNOW!
ARE YOU?
NO!
I HAVEN'T BEEN FOR AGES! LIKE IT'S ANY OF YOUR BUSINESS! GOD!
I REALLY CAN'T BELIEVE HER. IT'S LIKE SHE DELIBERATELY MAKES FUN OF ME .... SHE KNOWS I WAS GOING OUT WITH JOHN FOR SEVEN MONTHS ---
URGER LOC
AND SHE TOTALLY ACTS LIKE SHE'S GLEN'S BEST BUDDY. UGH!
'SEE YA LATER G-STRING.
I WISH!
YOU'RE NOT GOING TO THE RITZ TONIGHT?
NAH. I'M HERE 'TIL TWELVE.
I'M NOT GOING TO THE RITZ SMELLING OF BEEF FAT!
HI-SMALL COFFEE PLEASE!
YOU HAVE TO GO TO THE FRONT COUNTER.
DID I MENTION SHE'S ALSO REALLY LAZY?

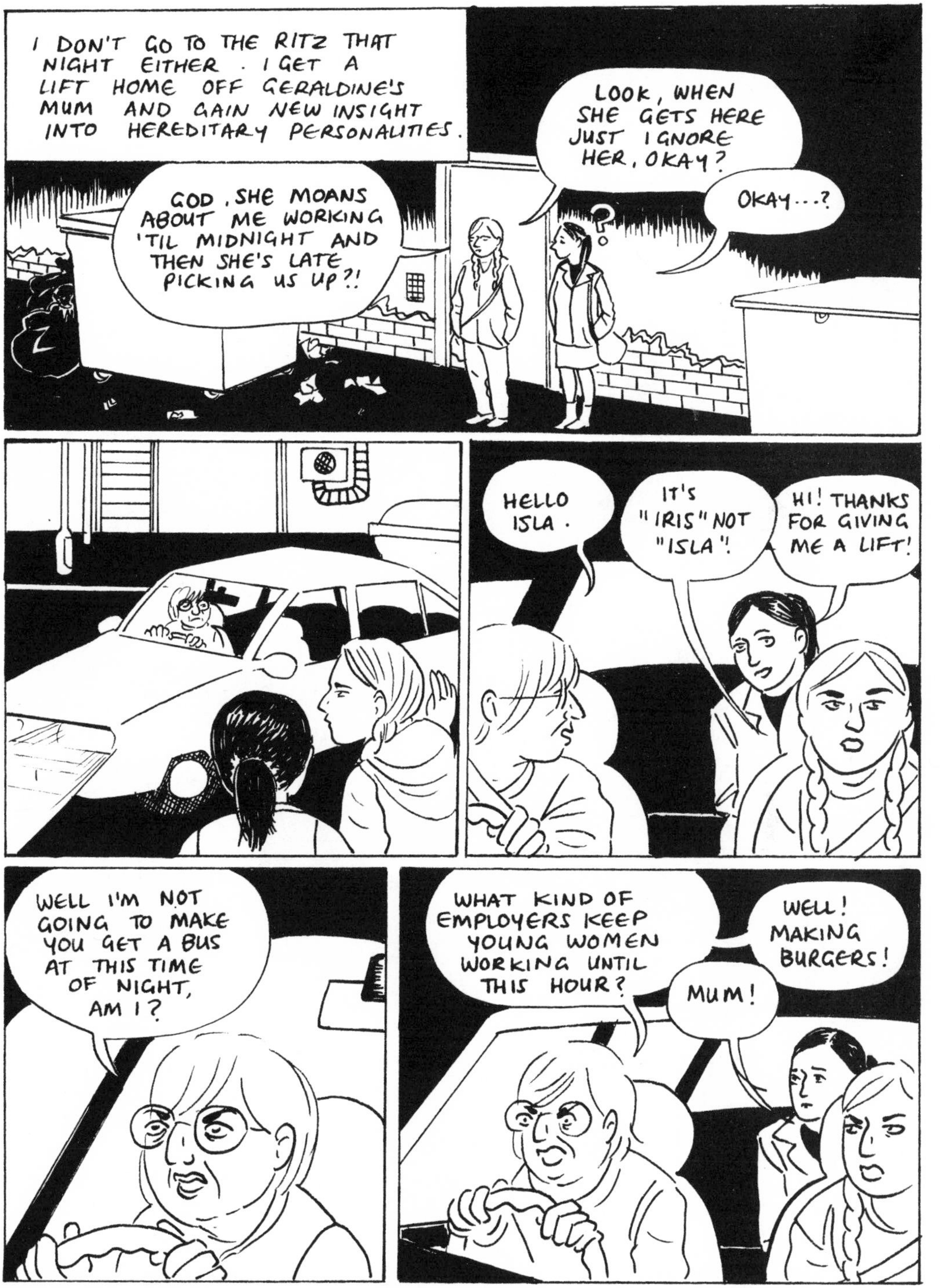
I DON'T GO TO THE RITZ THAT NIGHT EITHER. I GET A LIFT HOME OFF GERALDINE'S MUM AND GAIN NEW INSIGHT INTO HEREDITARY PERSONALITIES.
GOD, SHE MOANS ABOUT ME WORKING 'TIL MIDNIGHT AND THEN SHE'S LATE PICKING US UP?!
LOOK, WHEN SHE GETS HERE JUST IGNORE HER, OKAY?
?
OKAY...?
HELLO ISLA.
IT'S "IRIS" NOT "ISLA"!
HI! THANKS FOR GIVING ME A LIFT!
WELL I'M NOT GOING TO MAKE YOU GET A BUS AT THIS TIME OF NIGHT, AM I?
WHAT KIND OF EMPLOYERS KEEP YOUNG WOMEN WORKING UNTIL THIS HOUR?
WELL! MAKING BURGERS!
MUM!

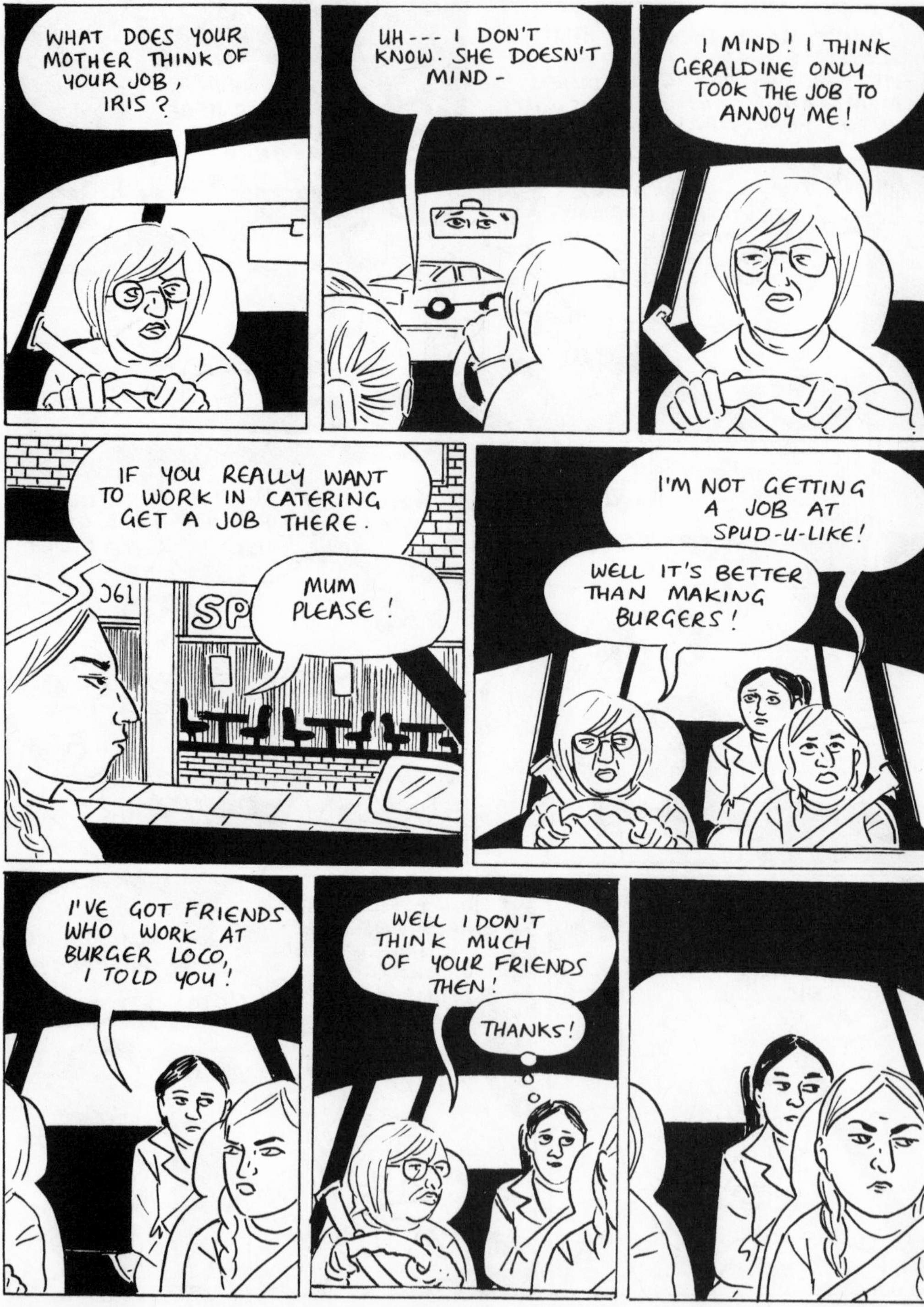
WHAT DOES YOUR MOTHER THINK OF YOUR JOB, IRIS?
UH--- I DON'T KNOW. SHE DOESN'T MIND -
I MIND! I THINK GERALDINE ONLY TOOK THE JOB TO ANNOY ME!
IF YOU REALLY WANT TO WORK IN CATERING GET A JOB THERE.
J61
SP
MUM PLEASE!
I'M NOT GETTING A JOB AT SPUD-U-LIKE!
WELL IT'S BETTER THAN MAKING BURGERS!
I'VE GOT FRIENDS WHO WORK AT BURGER LOCO, I TOLD YOU!
WELL I DON'T THINK MUCH OF YOUR FRIENDS THEN!
THANKS!

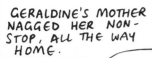

GERALDINE'S MOTHER NAGGED HER NON-STOP, ALL THE WAY HOME.

YOU CO
ASKED
ANNABE
HER M

CAN'T YOU JUST BE HAPPY THAT I'LL HAVE A JOB THIS SUMMER? JESUS!

UH-THIS IS ME!

THANKS FOR THE LIFT!

SEE YA.

YEAH

GOOD GRIEF!

VRRRMMM

SPLOSH!

TICK TOCK TICK

TOCK TICK TO

?

♡ IRIS

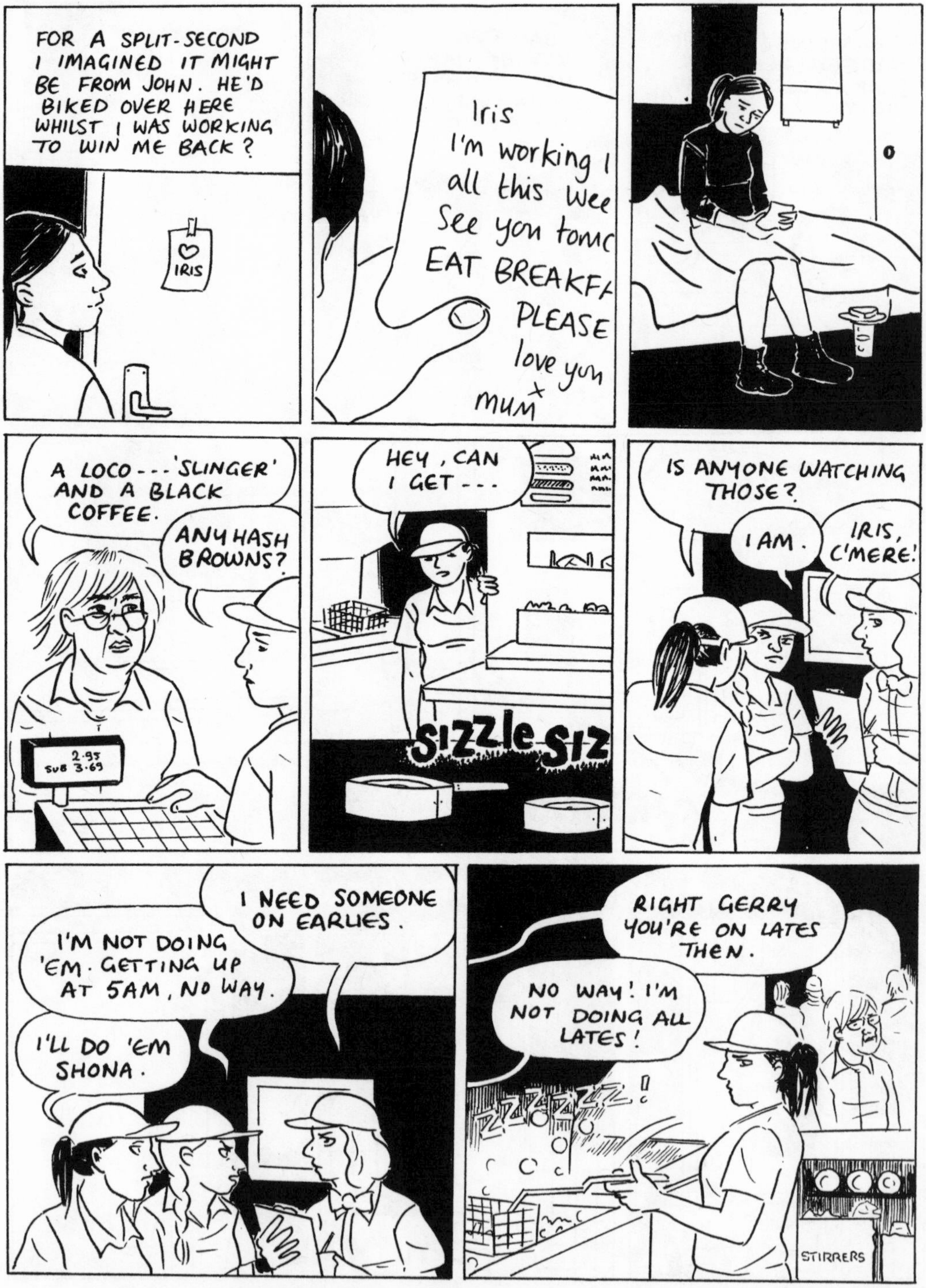
FOR A SPLIT-SECOND I IMAGINED IT MIGHT BE FROM JOHN. HE'D BIKED OVER HERE WHILST I WAS WORKING TO WIN ME BACK?
IRIS
Iris
I'm working l
all this wee
See you tomo
EAT BREAKFA
PLEASE
love you
mum
A LOCO---'SLINGER' AND A BLACK COFFEE.
ANY HASH BROWNS?
2.95
SUB 3.69
HEY, CAN I GET---
SIZZLE SIZ
IS ANYONE WATCHING THOSE?
I AM.
IRIS, C'MERE!
I NEED SOMEONE ON EARLIES.
I'M NOT DOING 'EM. GETTING UP AT 5AM, NO WAY.
I'LL DO 'EM SHONA.
RIGHT GERRY YOU'RE ON LATES THEN.
NO WAY! I'M NOT DOING ALL LATES!
ZZZZZZZ!
STIRRERS

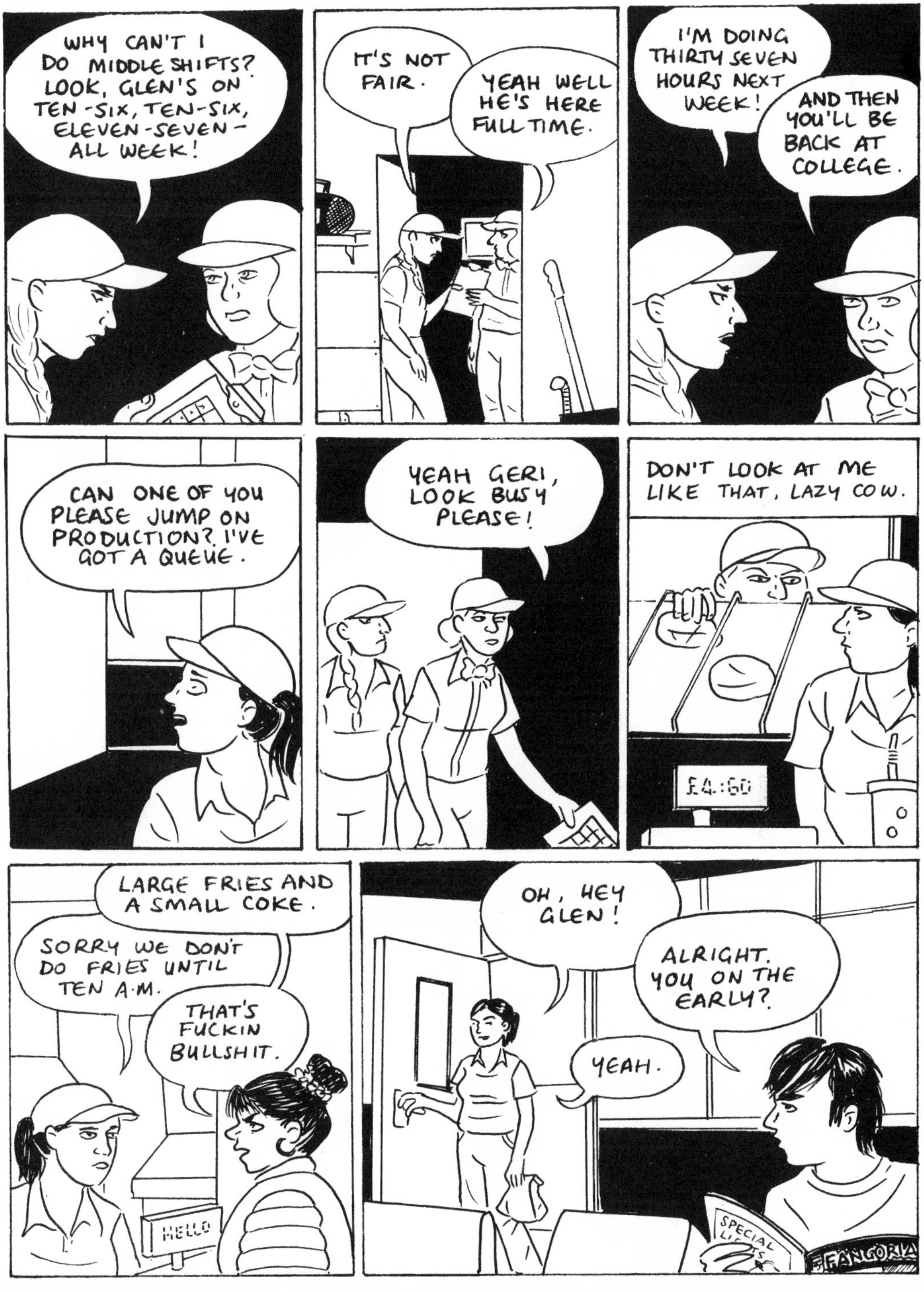
WHY CAN'T I DO MIDDLE SHIFTS? LOOK, GLEN'S ON TEN-SIX, TEN-SIX, ELEVEN-SEVEN - ALL WEEK!
IT'S NOT FAIR.
YEAH WELL HE'S HERE FULL TIME.
I'M DOING THIRTY SEVEN HOURS NEXT WEEK!
AND THEN YOU'LL BE BACK AT COLLEGE.
CAN ONE OF YOU PLEASE JUMP ON PRODUCTION? I'VE GOT A QUEUE.
YEAH GERI, LOOK BUSY PLEASE!
DON'T LOOK AT ME LIKE THAT, LAZY COW.
£4.60
LARGE FRIES AND A SMALL COKE.
SORRY WE DON'T DO FRIES UNTIL TEN A.M.
THAT'S FUCKIN BULLSHIT.
HELLO
OH, HEY GLEN!
ALRIGHT. YOU ON THE EARLY?
YEAH.
FANGORIA

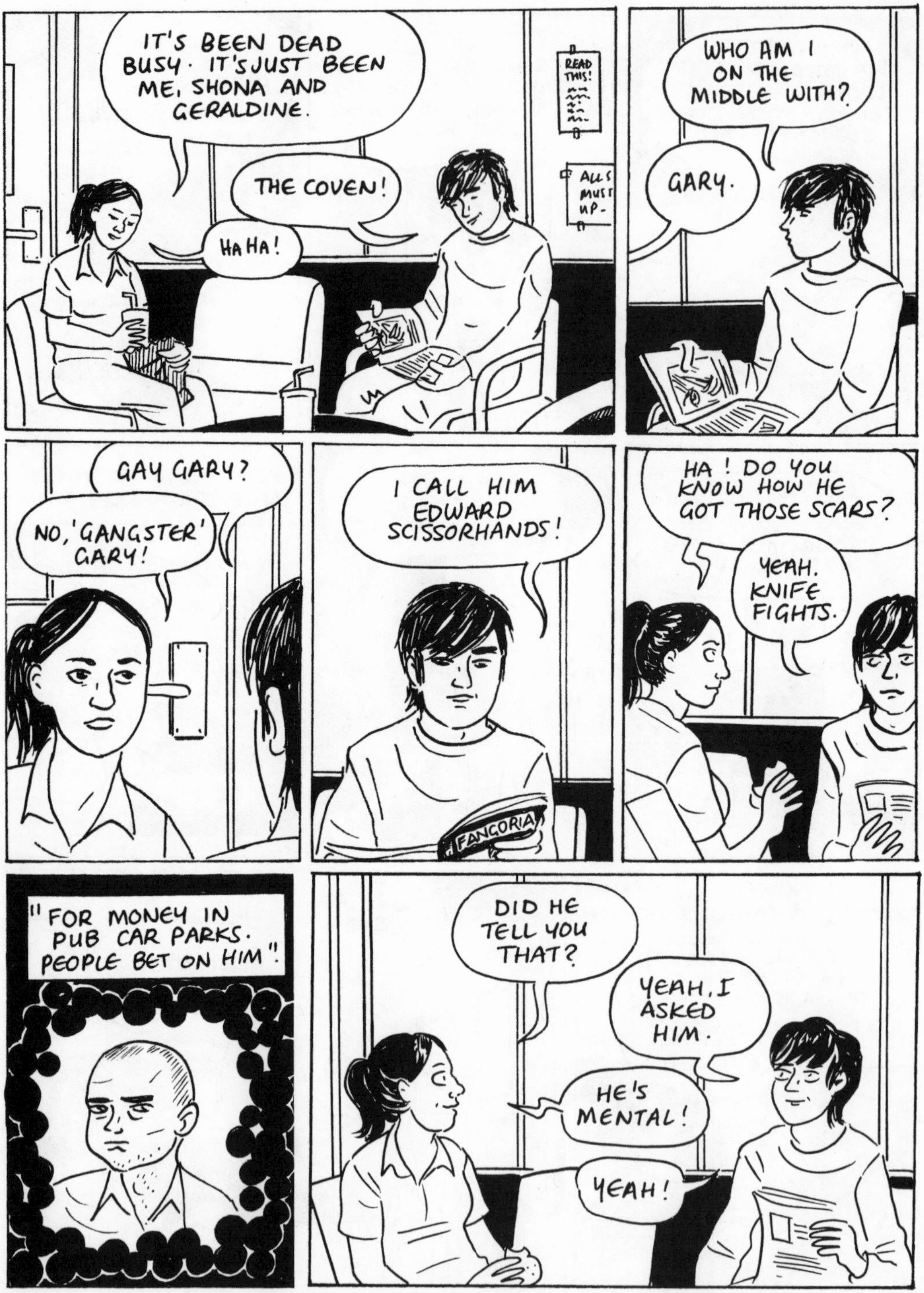
IT'S BEEN DEAD BUSY. IT'S JUST BEEN ME, SHONA AND GERALDINE.
THE COVEN!
HA HA!
READ THIS!
WHO AM I ON THE MIDDLE WITH?
GARY.
GAY GARY?
NO, 'GANGSTER' GARY!
I CALL HIM EDWARD SCISSORHANDS!
FANGORIA
HA! DO YOU KNOW HOW HE GOT THOSE SCARS?
YEAH. KNIFE FIGHTS.
"FOR MONEY IN PUB CAR PARKS. PEOPLE BET ON HIM".
DID HE TELL YOU THAT?
YEAH, I ASKED HIM.
HE'S MENTAL!
YEAH!

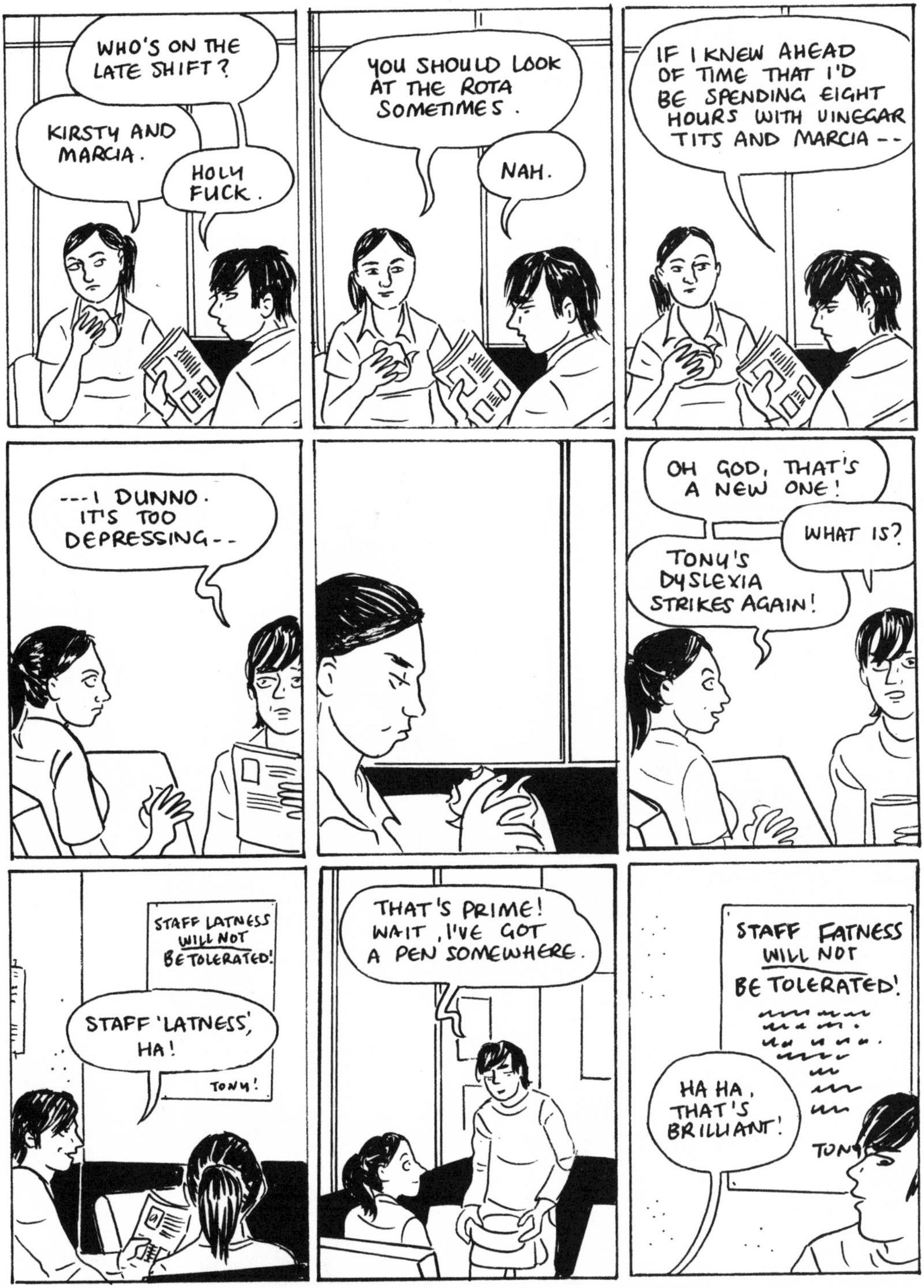
WHO'S ON THE LATE SHIFT?
KIRSTY AND MARCIA.
HOLY FUCK.
YOU SHOULD LOOK AT THE ROTA SOMETIMES.
NAH.
IF I KNEW AHEAD OF TIME THAT I'D BE SPENDING EIGHT HOURS WITH VINEGAR TITS AND MARCIA --
---I DUNNO. IT'S TOO DEPRESSING--
OH GOD, THAT'S A NEW ONE!
WHAT IS?
TONY'S DYSLEXIA STRIKES AGAIN!
STAFF LATNESS WILL NOT BE TOLERATED!
TONY!
STAFF 'LATNESS', HA!
THAT'S PRIME! WAIT, I'VE GOT A PEN SOMEWHERE.
STAFF FATNESS WILL NOT BE TOLERATED!
TONY
HA HA, THAT'S BRILLIANT!

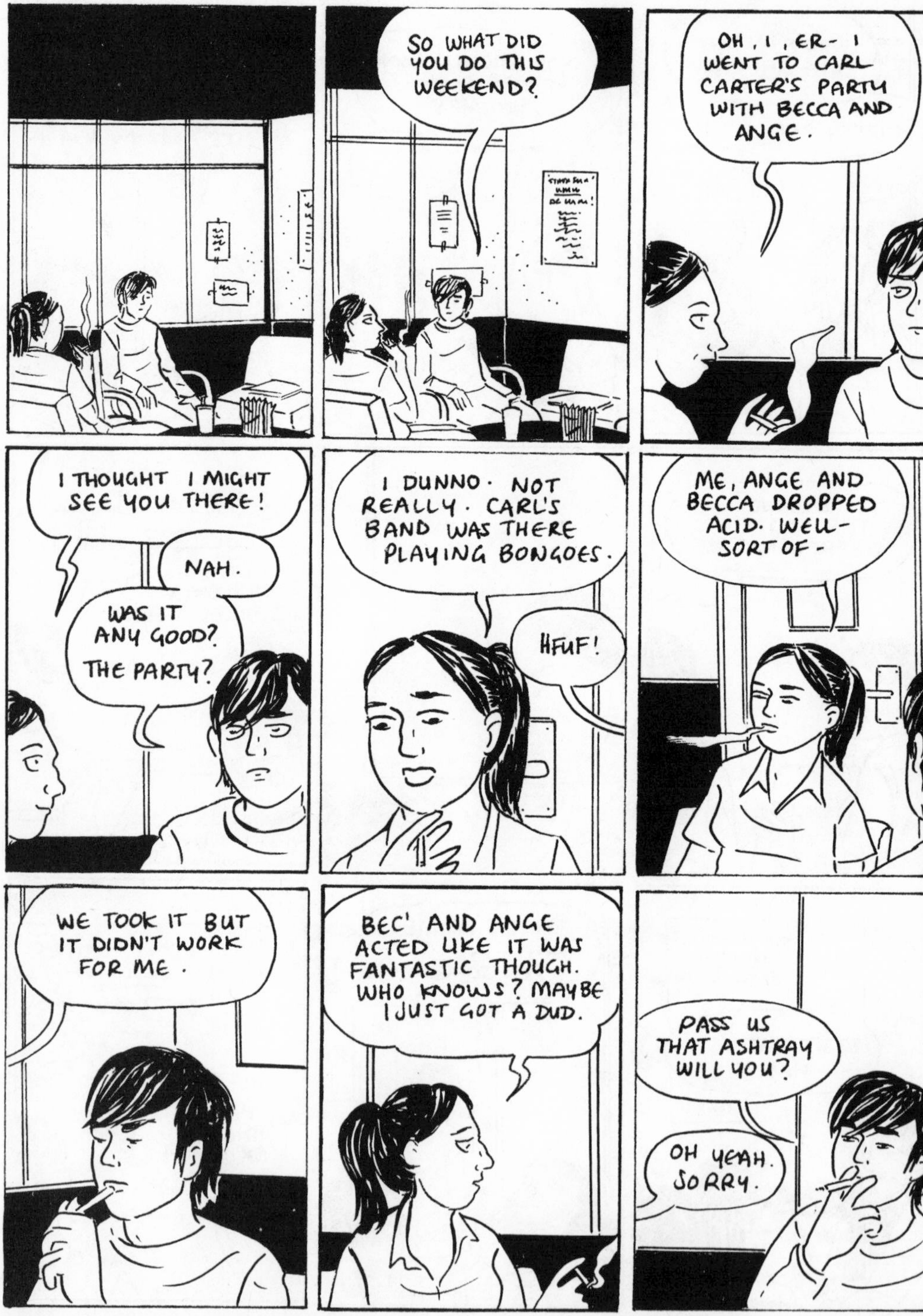
SO WHAT DID YOU DO THIS WEEKEND?
OH, I, ER- I WENT TO CARL CARTER'S PARTY WITH BECCA AND ANGE.
I THOUGHT I MIGHT SEE YOU THERE!
NAH.
WAS IT ANY GOOD? THE PARTY?
I DUNNO. NOT REALLY. CARL'S BAND WAS THERE PLAYING BONGOES.
HFUF!
ME, ANGE AND BECCA DROPPED ACID. WELL- SORT OF-
WE TOOK IT BUT IT DIDN'T WORK FOR ME.
BEC' AND ANGE ACTED LIKE IT WAS FANTASTIC THOUGH. WHO KNOWS? MAYBE I JUST GOT A DUD.
PASS US THAT ASHTRAY WILL YOU?
OH YEAH. SORRY.

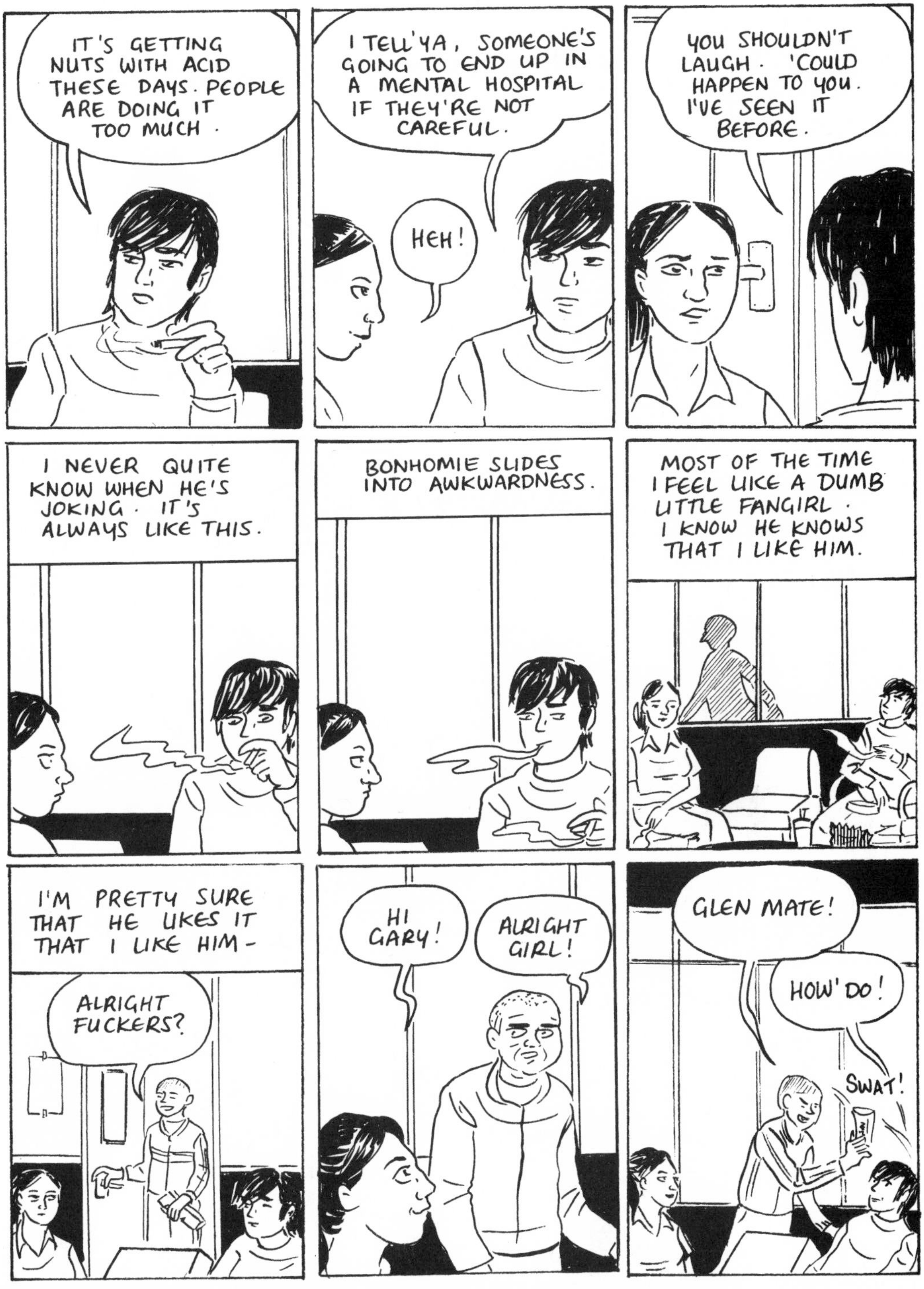
IT'S GETTING NUTS WITH ACID THESE DAYS. PEOPLE ARE DOING IT TOO MUCH.
I TELL'YA, SOMEONE'S GOING TO END UP IN A MENTAL HOSPITAL IF THEY'RE NOT CAREFUL.
HEH!
YOU SHOULDN'T LAUGH. 'COULD HAPPEN TO YOU. I'VE SEEN IT BEFORE.
I NEVER QUITE KNOW WHEN HE'S JOKING. IT'S ALWAYS LIKE THIS.
BONHOMIE SLIDES INTO AWKWARDNESS.
MOST OF THE TIME I FEEL LIKE A DUMB LITTLE FANGIRL. I KNOW HE KNOWS THAT I LIKE HIM.
I'M PRETTY SURE THAT HE LIKES IT THAT I LIKE HIM-
ALRIGHT FUCKERS?
HI GARY!
ALRIGHT GIRL!
GLEN MATE!
HOW'DO!
SWAT!

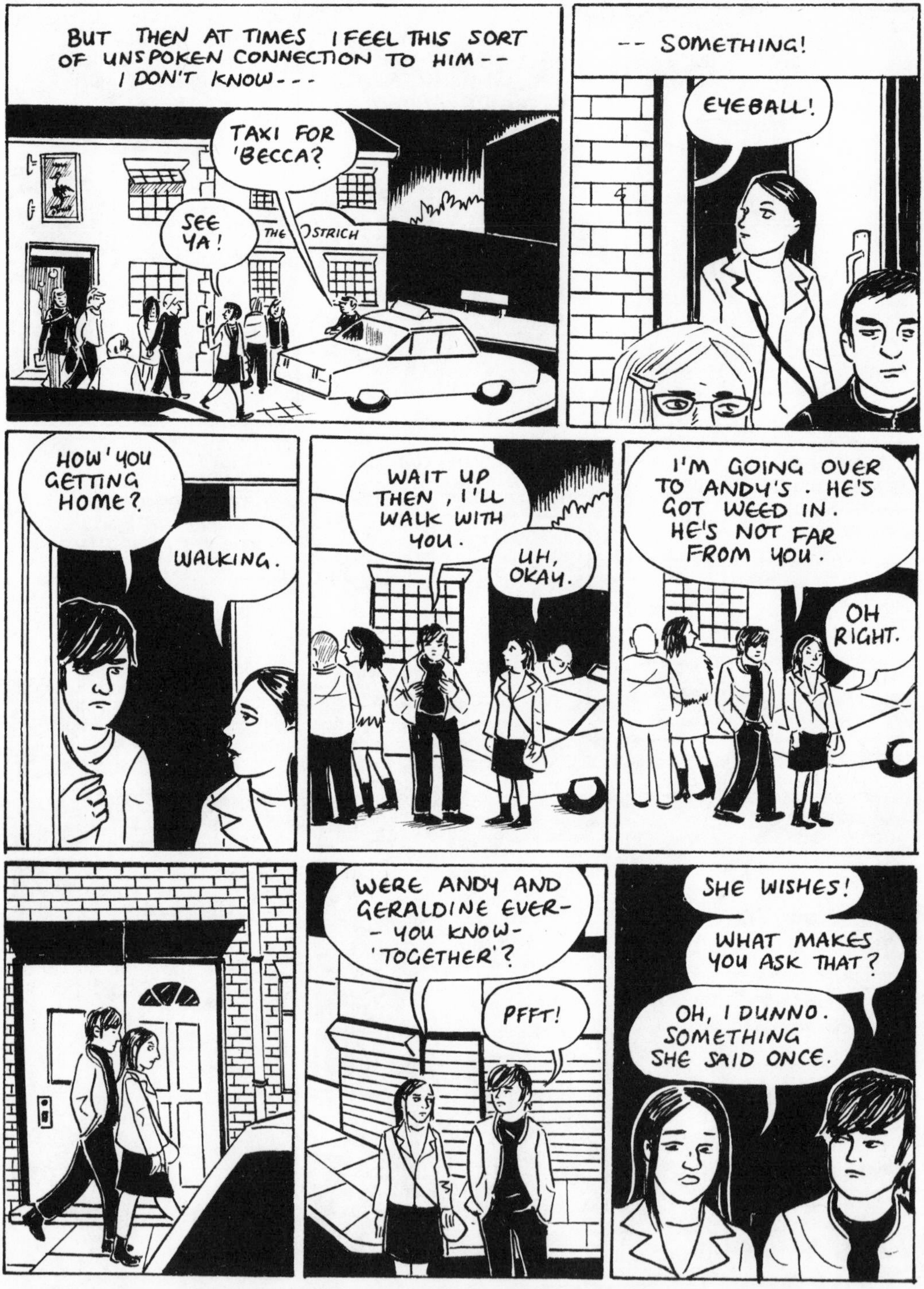
BUT THEN AT TIMES I FEEL THIS SORT OF UNSPOKEN CONNECTION TO HIM -- I DON'T KNOW---
TAXI FOR 'BECCA?
SEE YA!
THE OSTRICH
-- SOMETHING!
EYEBALL!
HOW' YOU GETTING HOME?
WALKING.
WAIT UP THEN, I'LL WALK WITH YOU.
UH, OKAY.
I'M GOING OVER TO ANDY'S. HE'S GOT WEED IN. HE'S NOT FAR FROM YOU.
OH RIGHT.
WERE ANDY AND GERALDINE EVER- - YOU KNOW- 'TOGETHER'?
PFFT!
SHE WISHES!
WHAT MAKES YOU ASK THAT?
OH, I DUNNO. SOMETHING SHE SAID ONCE.

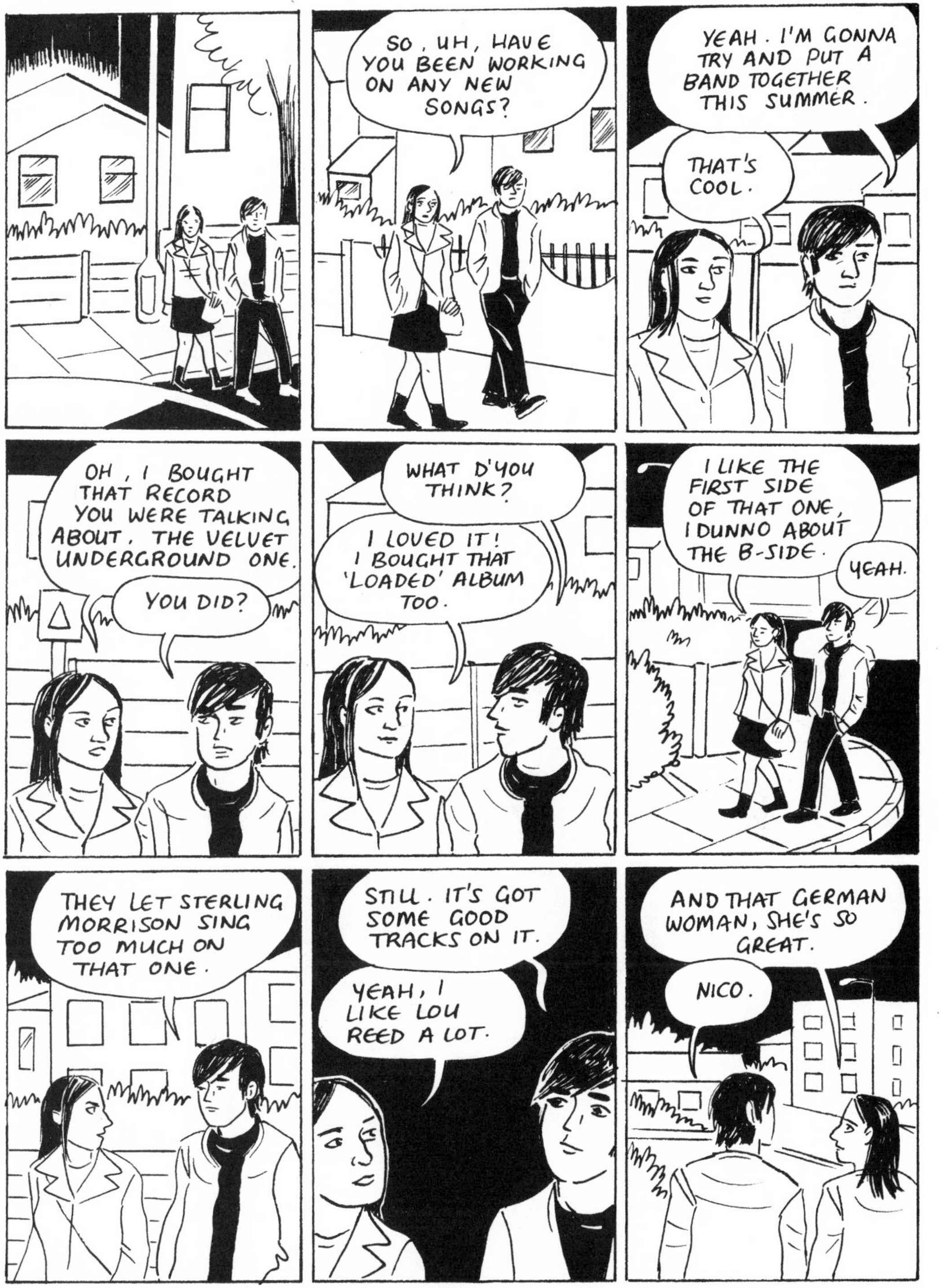
SO, UH, HAVE YOU BEEN WORKING ON ANY NEW SONGS?
YEAH. I'M GONNA TRY AND PUT A BAND TOGETHER THIS SUMMER.
THAT'S COOL.
OH, I BOUGHT THAT RECORD YOU WERE TALKING ABOUT. THE VELVET UNDERGROUND ONE.
YOU DID?
WHAT D'YOU THINK?
I LOVED IT! I BOUGHT THAT 'LOADED' ALBUM TOO.
I LIKE THE FIRST SIDE OF THAT ONE, I DUNNO ABOUT THE B-SIDE.
YEAH.
THEY LET STERLING MORRISON SING TOO MUCH ON THAT ONE.
STILL. IT'S GOT SOME GOOD TRACKS ON IT.
YEAH, I LIKE LOU REED A LOT.
AND THAT GERMAN WOMAN, SHE'S SO GREAT.
NICO.

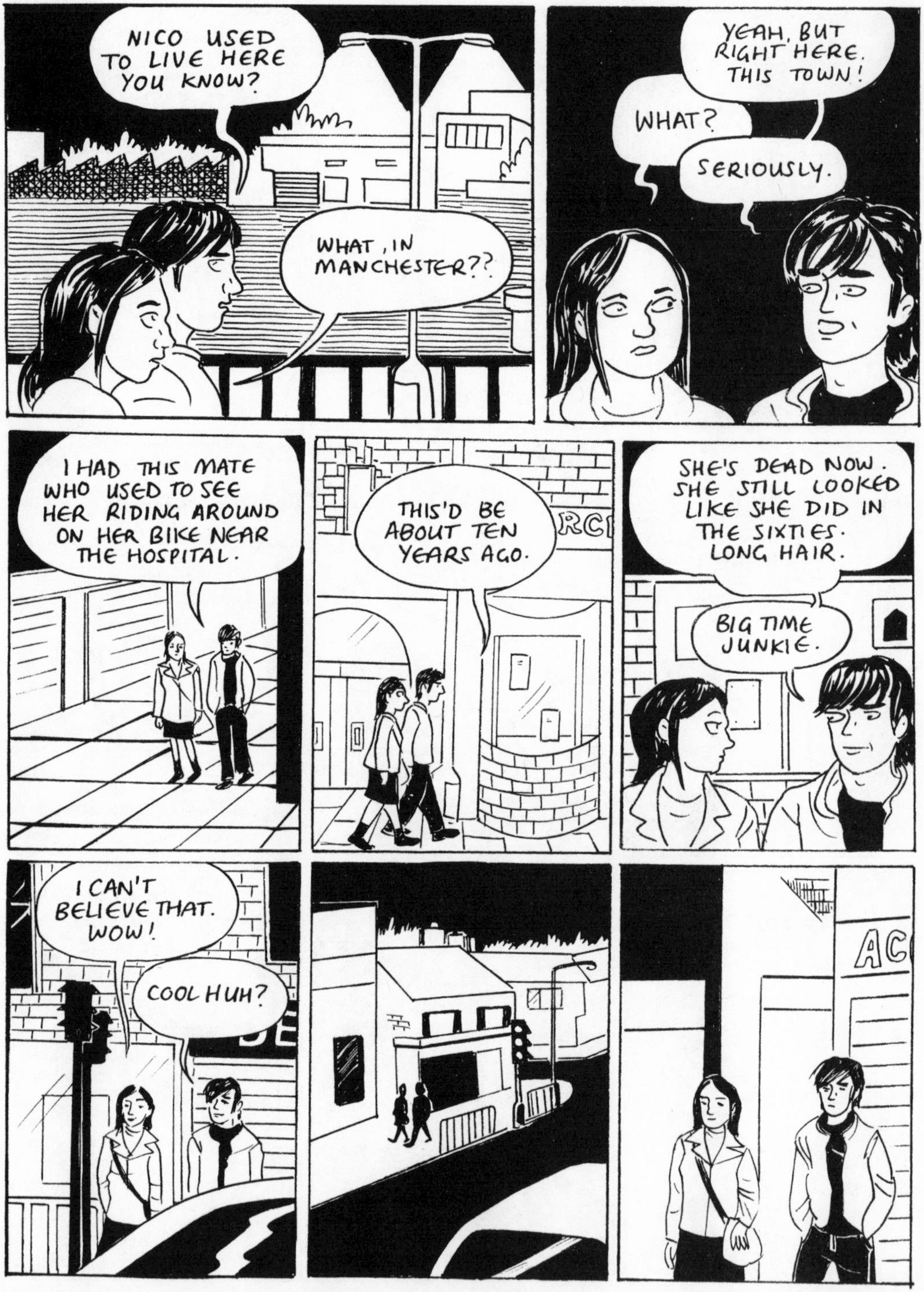
NICO USED TO LIVE HERE YOU KNOW?
WHAT, IN MANCHESTER??
YEAH, BUT RIGHT HERE. THIS TOWN!
WHAT?
SERIOUSLY.
I HAD THIS MATE WHO USED TO SEE HER RIDING AROUND ON HER BIKE NEAR THE HOSPITAL.
THIS'D BE ABOUT TEN YEARS AGO.
RCI
SHE'S DEAD NOW. SHE STILL LOOKED LIKE SHE DID IN THE SIXTIES. LONG HAIR.
BIG TIME JUNKIE.
I CAN'T BELIEVE THAT. WOW!
COOL HUH?
AC

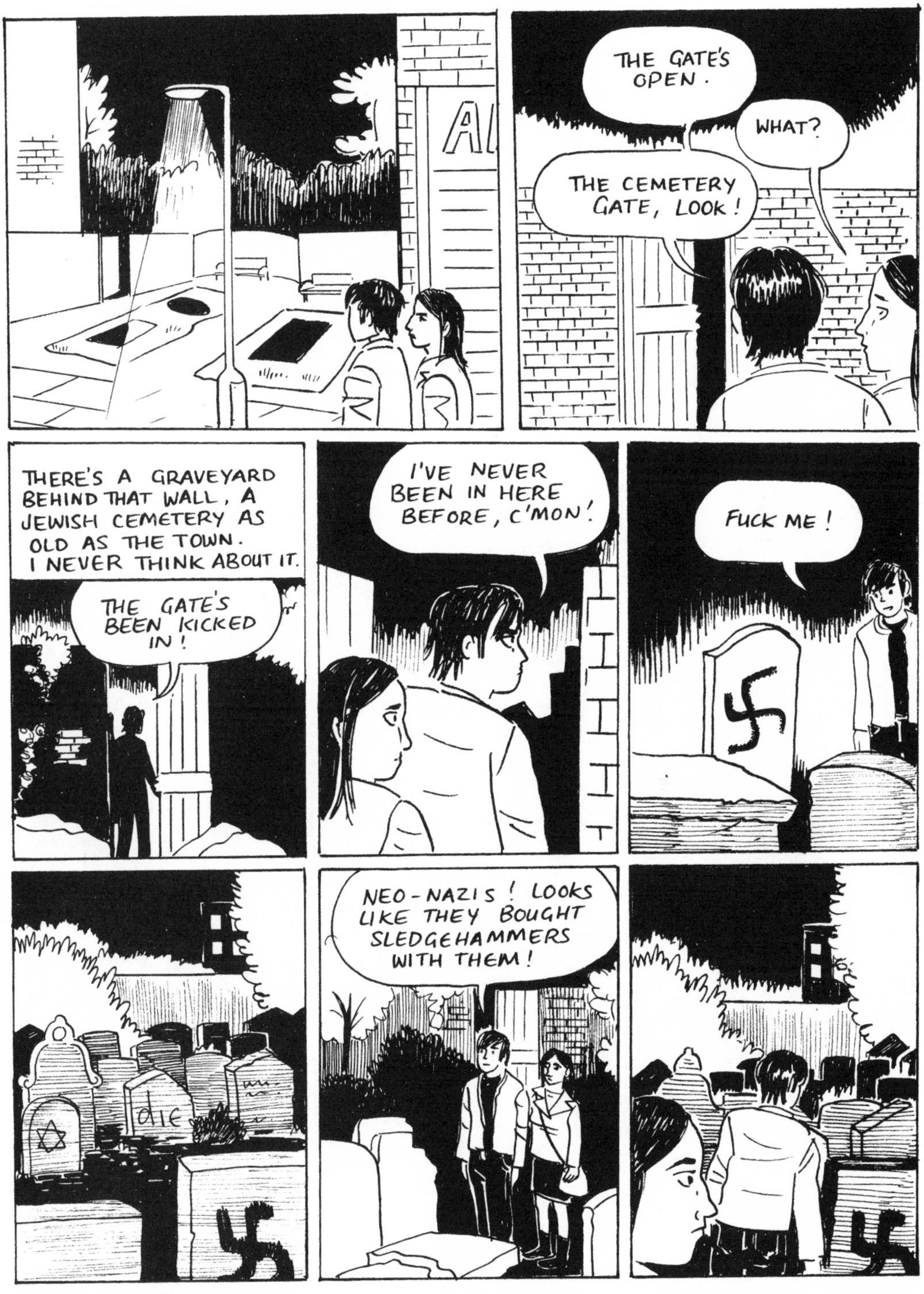
THE GATE'S OPEN.
THE CEMETERY GATE, LOOK!
WHAT?
THERE'S A GRAVEYARD BEHIND THAT WALL, A JEWISH CEMETERY AS OLD AS THE TOWN. I NEVER THINK ABOUT IT.
THE GATE'S BEEN KICKED IN!
I'VE NEVER BEEN IN HERE BEFORE, C'MON!
FUCK ME!
die
NEO-NAZIS! LOOKS LIKE THEY BOUGHT SLEDGEHAMMERS WITH THEM!

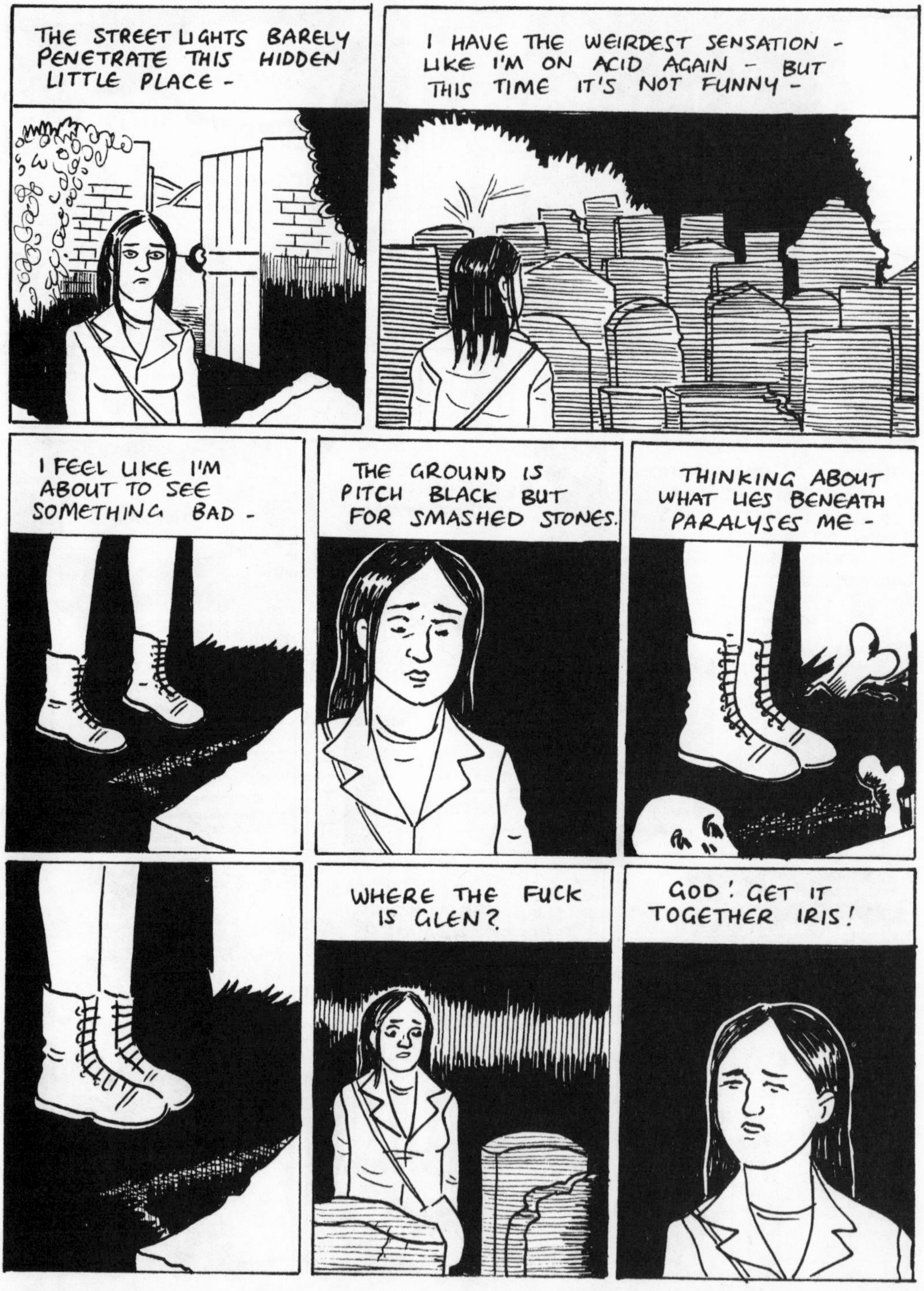
THE STREET LIGHTS BARELY PENETRATE THIS HIDDEN LITTLE PLACE -
I HAVE THE WEIRDEST SENSATION - LIKE I'M ON ACID AGAIN - BUT THIS TIME IT'S NOT FUNNY -
I FEEL LIKE I'M ABOUT TO SEE SOMETHING BAD -
THE GROUND IS PITCH BLACK BUT FOR SMASHED STONES.
THINKING ABOUT WHAT LIES BENEATH PARALYSES ME -
WHERE THE FUCK IS GLEN?
GOD! GET IT TOGETHER IRIS!

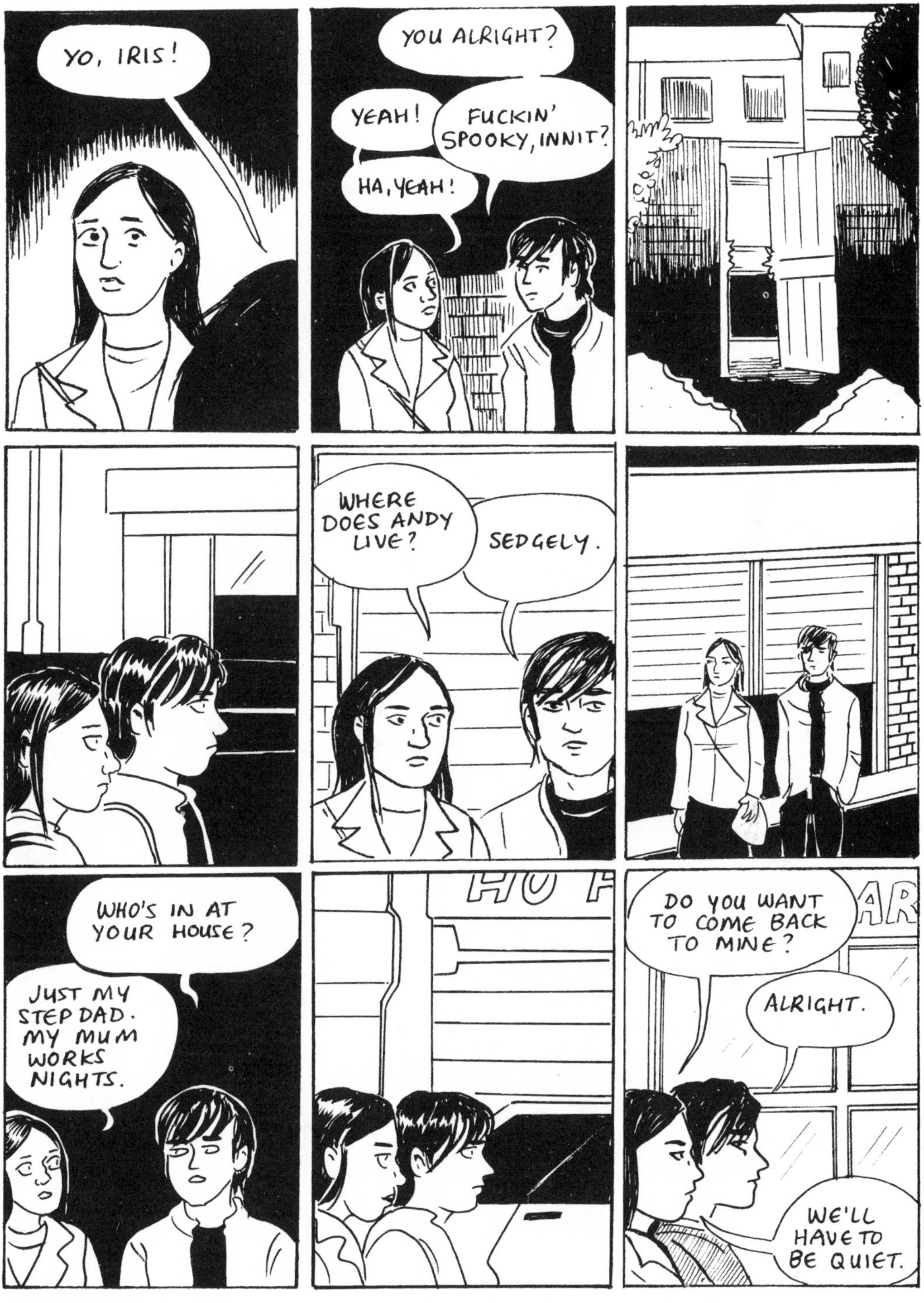
YO, IRIS!
YOU ALRIGHT?
YEAH!
FUCKIN' SPOOKY, INNIT?
HA, YEAH!
WHERE DOES ANDY LIVE?
SEDGELY.
WHO'S IN AT YOUR HOUSE?
JUST MY STEP DAD. MY MUM WORKS NIGHTS.
HO
DO YOU WANT TO COME BACK TO MINE?
ALRIGHT.
WE'LL HAVE TO BE QUIET.

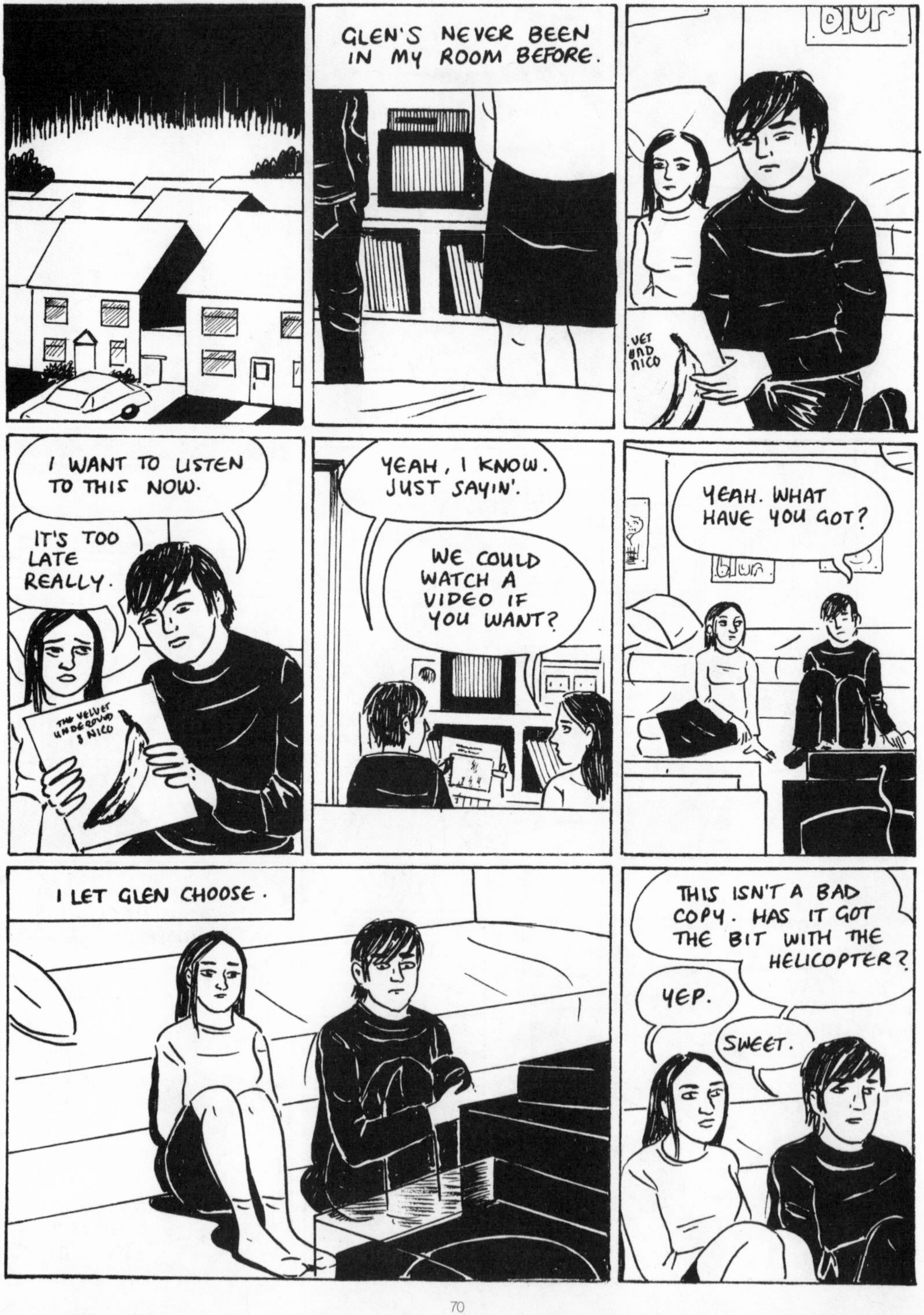
GLEN'S NEVER BEEN IN MY ROOM BEFORE.
blur
VET UND NICO
I WANT TO LISTEN TO THIS NOW.
IT'S TOO LATE REALLY.
THE VELVET UNDERGROUND & NICO
YEAH, I KNOW. JUST SAYIN'.
WE COULD WATCH A VIDEO IF YOU WANT?
YEAH. WHAT HAVE YOU GOT?
blur
I LET GLEN CHOOSE.
THIS ISN'T A BAD COPY. HAS IT GOT THE BIT WITH THE HELICOPTER?
YEP.
SWEET.

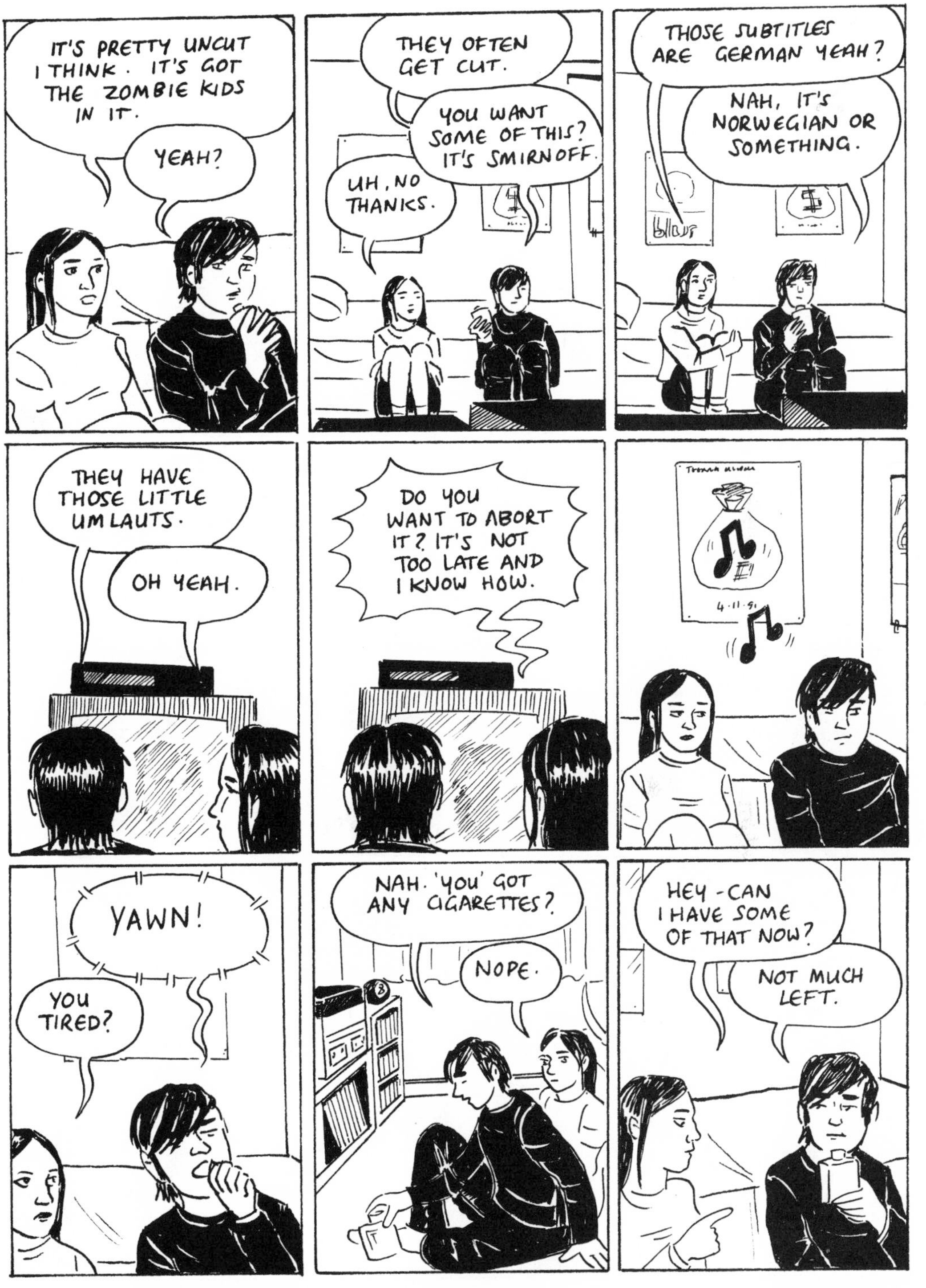
IT'S PRETTY UNCUT I THINK. IT'S GOT THE ZOMBIE KIDS IN IT.
YEAH?
THEY OFTEN GET CUT.
YOU WANT SOME OF THIS? IT'S SMIRNOFF.
UH, NO THANKS.
THOSE SUBTITLES ARE GERMAN YEAH?
NAH, IT'S NORWEGIAN OR SOMETHING.
THEY HAVE THOSE LITTLE UMLAUTS.
OH YEAH.
DO YOU WANT TO ABORT IT? IT'S NOT TOO LATE AND I KNOW HOW.
YAWN!
YOU TIRED?
NAH. 'YOU' GOT ANY CIGARETTES?
NOPE.
HEY - CAN I HAVE SOME OF THAT NOW?
NOT MUCH LEFT.

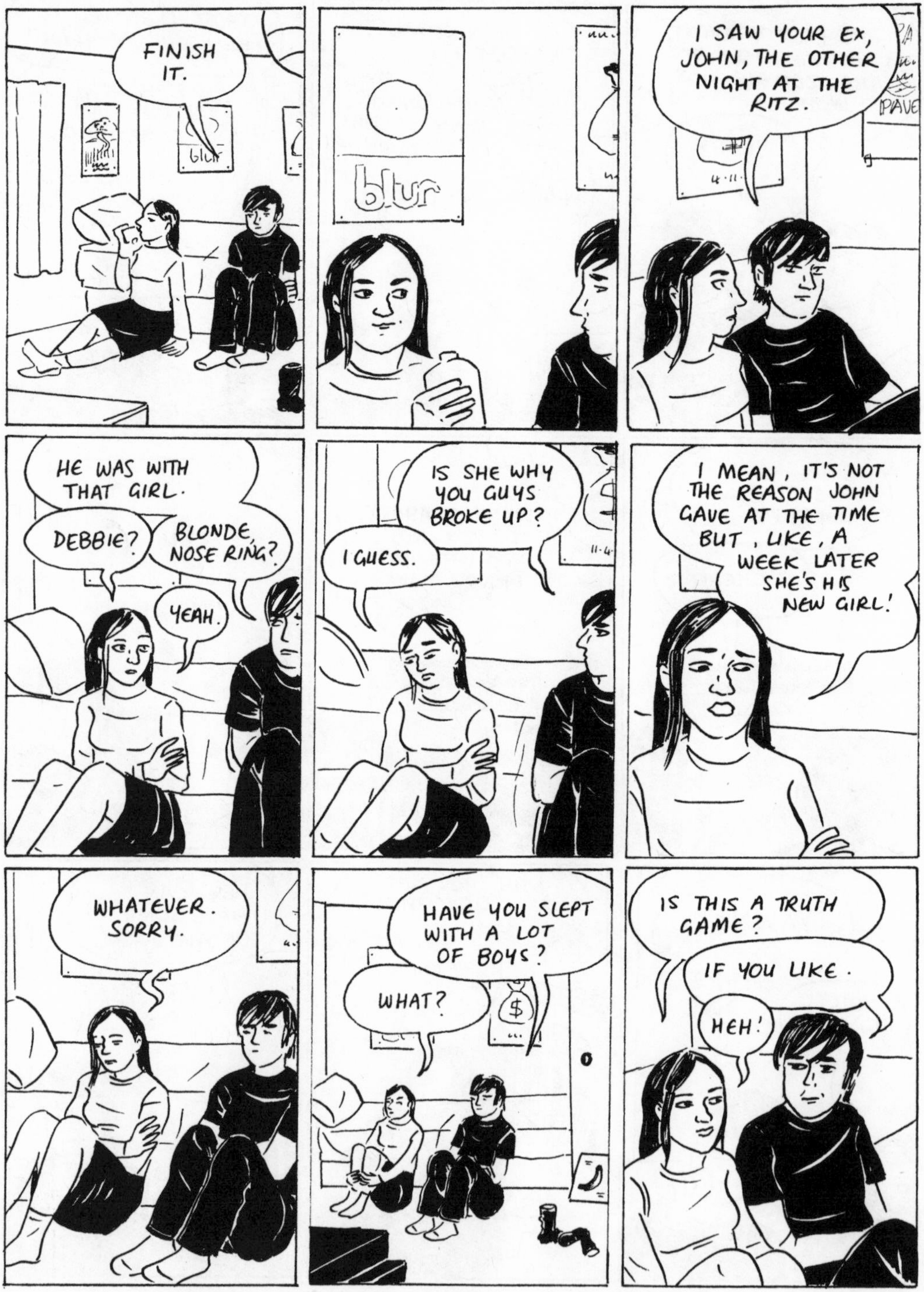
FINISH IT.
blur
I SAW YOUR EX, JOHN, THE OTHER NIGHT AT THE RITZ.
HE WAS WITH THAT GIRL.
DEBBIE?
BLONDE, NOSE RING?
YEAH.
IS SHE WHY YOU GUYS BROKE UP?
I GUESS.
I MEAN, IT'S NOT THE REASON JOHN GAVE AT THE TIME BUT, LIKE, A WEEK LATER SHE'S HIS NEW GIRL!
WHATEVER. SORRY.
HAVE YOU SLEPT WITH A LOT OF BOYS?
WHAT?
IS THIS A TRUTH GAME?
IF YOU LIKE.
HEH!

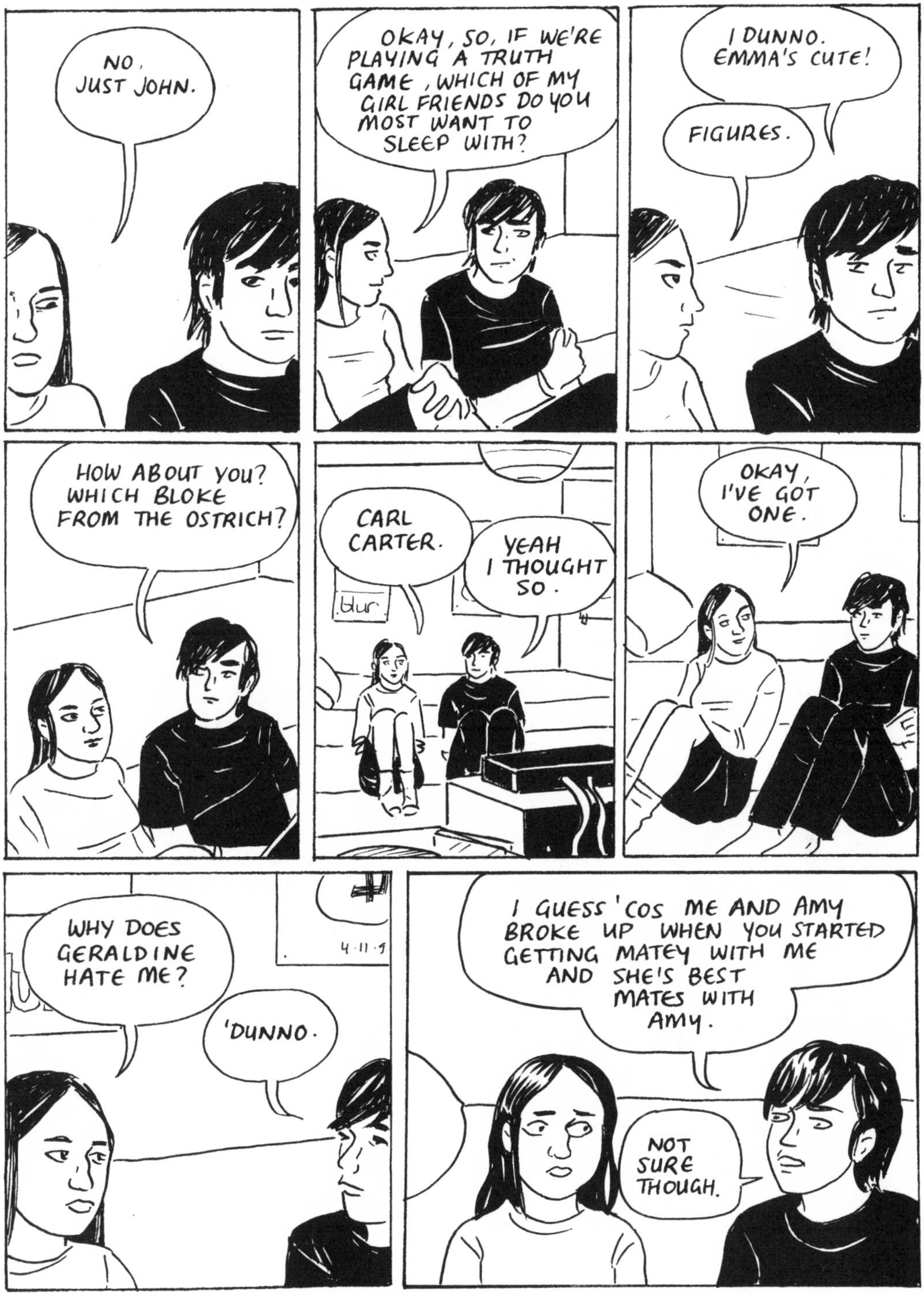
NO. JUST JOHN.
OKAY, SO, IF WE'RE PLAYING A TRUTH GAME, WHICH OF MY GIRL FRIENDS DO YOU MOST WANT TO SLEEP WITH?
I DUNNO. EMMA'S CUTE!
FIGURES.
HOW ABOUT YOU? WHICH BLOKE FROM THE OSTRICH?
CARL CARTER.
YEAH I THOUGHT SO.
blur
OKAY, I'VE GOT ONE.
WHY DOES GERALDINE HATE ME?
'DUNNO.
4·11·9
I GUESS 'COS ME AND AMY BROKE UP WHEN YOU STARTED GETTING MATEY WITH ME AND SHE'S BEST MATES WITH AMY.
NOT SURE THOUGH.

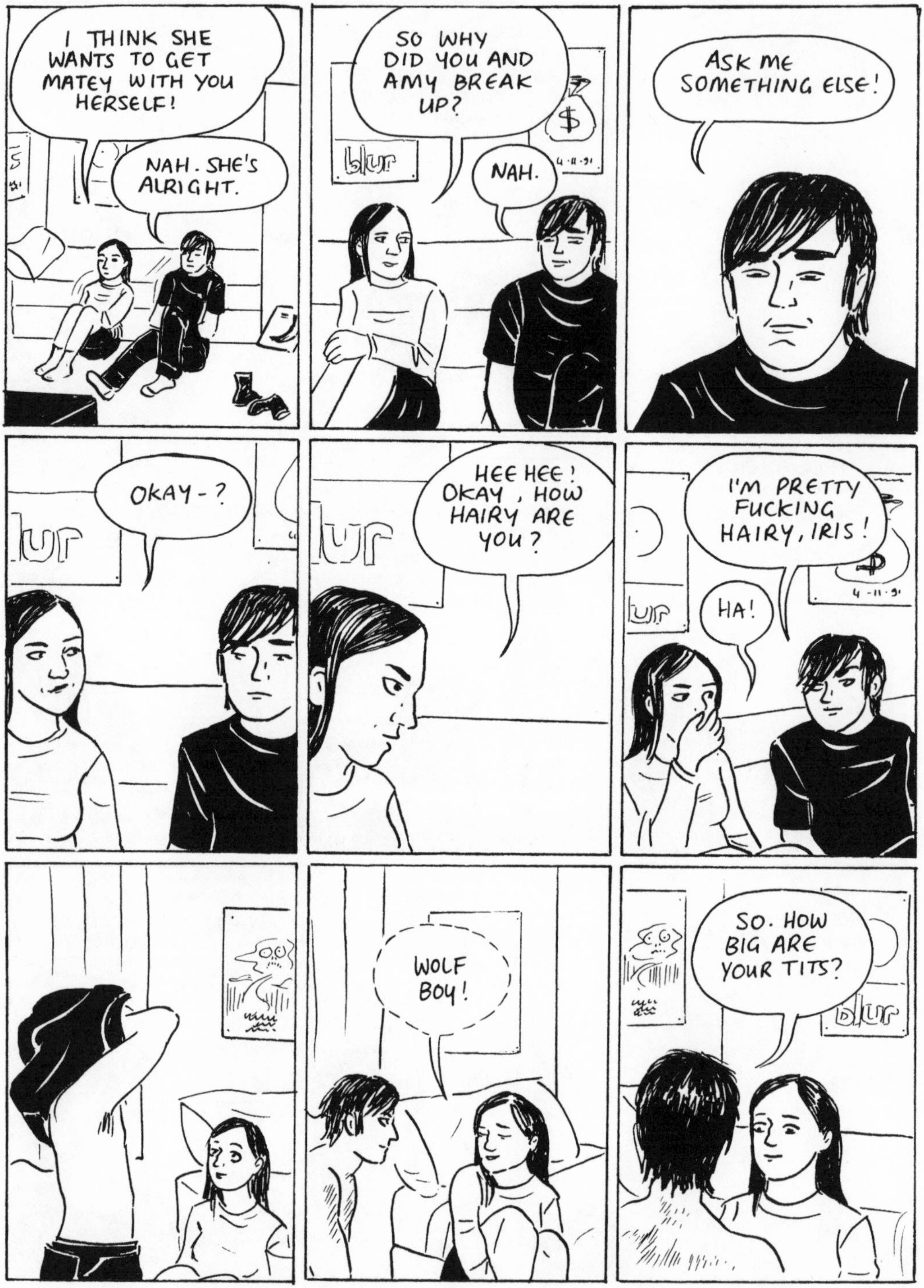
I THINK SHE WANTS TO GET MATEY WITH YOU HERSELF!
NAH. SHE'S ALRIGHT.
SO WHY DID YOU AND AMY BREAK UP?
NAH.
4-11-91
ASK ME SOMETHING ELSE!
OKAY-?
HEE HEE! OKAY, HOW HAIRY ARE YOU?
I'M PRETTY FUCKING HAIRY, IRIS!
HA!
4-11-91
WOLF BOY!
SO. HOW BIG ARE YOUR TITS?

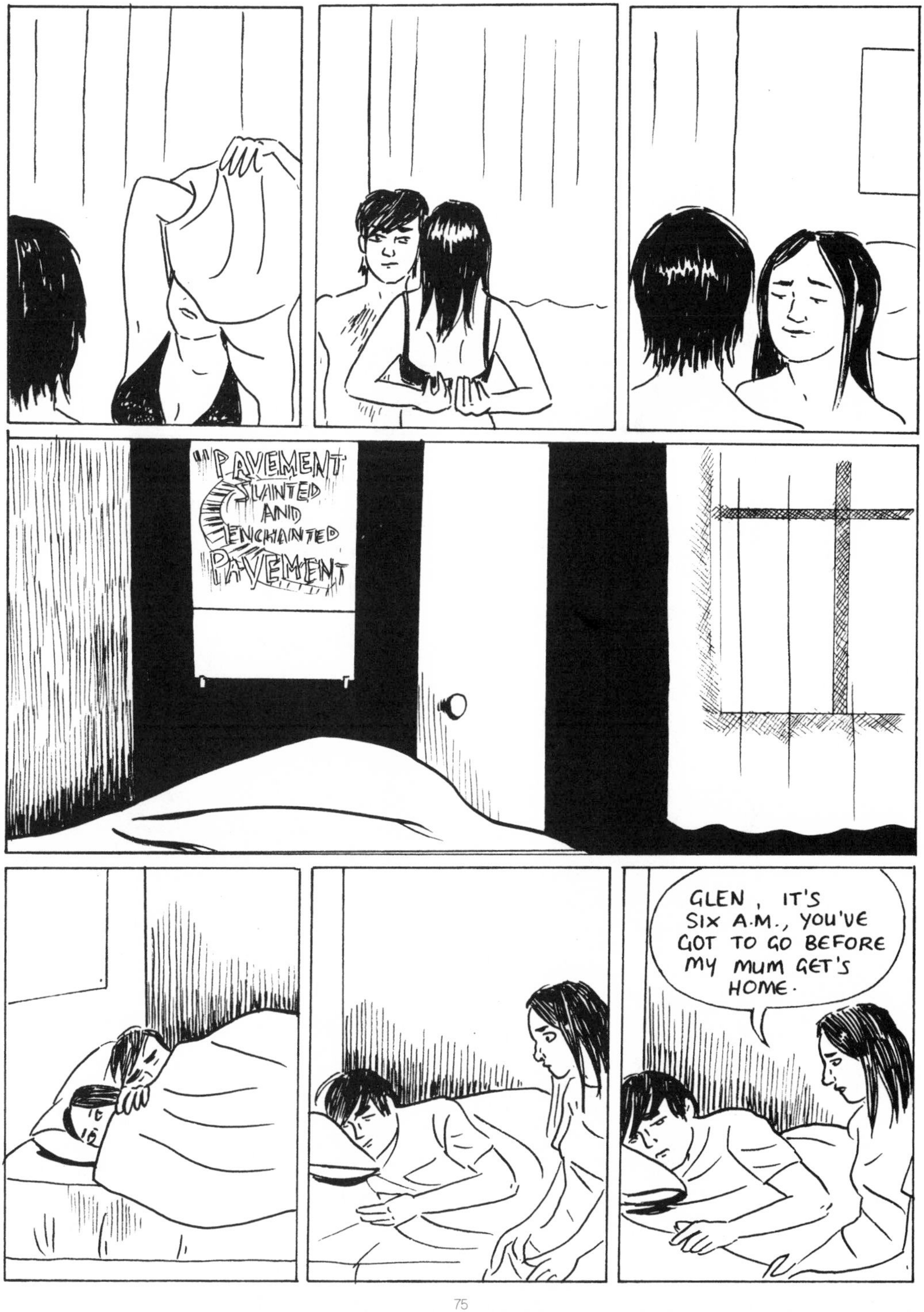
"PAVEMENT
SLANTED AND ENCHANTED
PAVEMENT
GLEN, IT'S SIX A.M., YOU'VE GOT TO GO BEFORE MY MUM GET'S HOME.

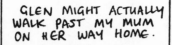

GLEN MIGHT ACTUALLY WALK PAST MY MUM ON HER WAY HOME.

SHE SAYS 'HELLO' TO PEOPLE ON THE STREET.

MAYBE EVEN TO ODD BOYS LIKE GLEN.

IT WAS AWKWARD THIS MORNING, WATCHING GLEN GET DRESSED.

SNIFF!

I KNOW THINGS WILL BE NO DIFFERENT NEXT TIME I SEE HIM.

WE BUILD UP TO THESE LITTLE OCCASIONS. I FORGET MY SHYNESS, HE ACTS LIKE HE LIKES ME —

AND THEN, HE SLIPS AWAY.

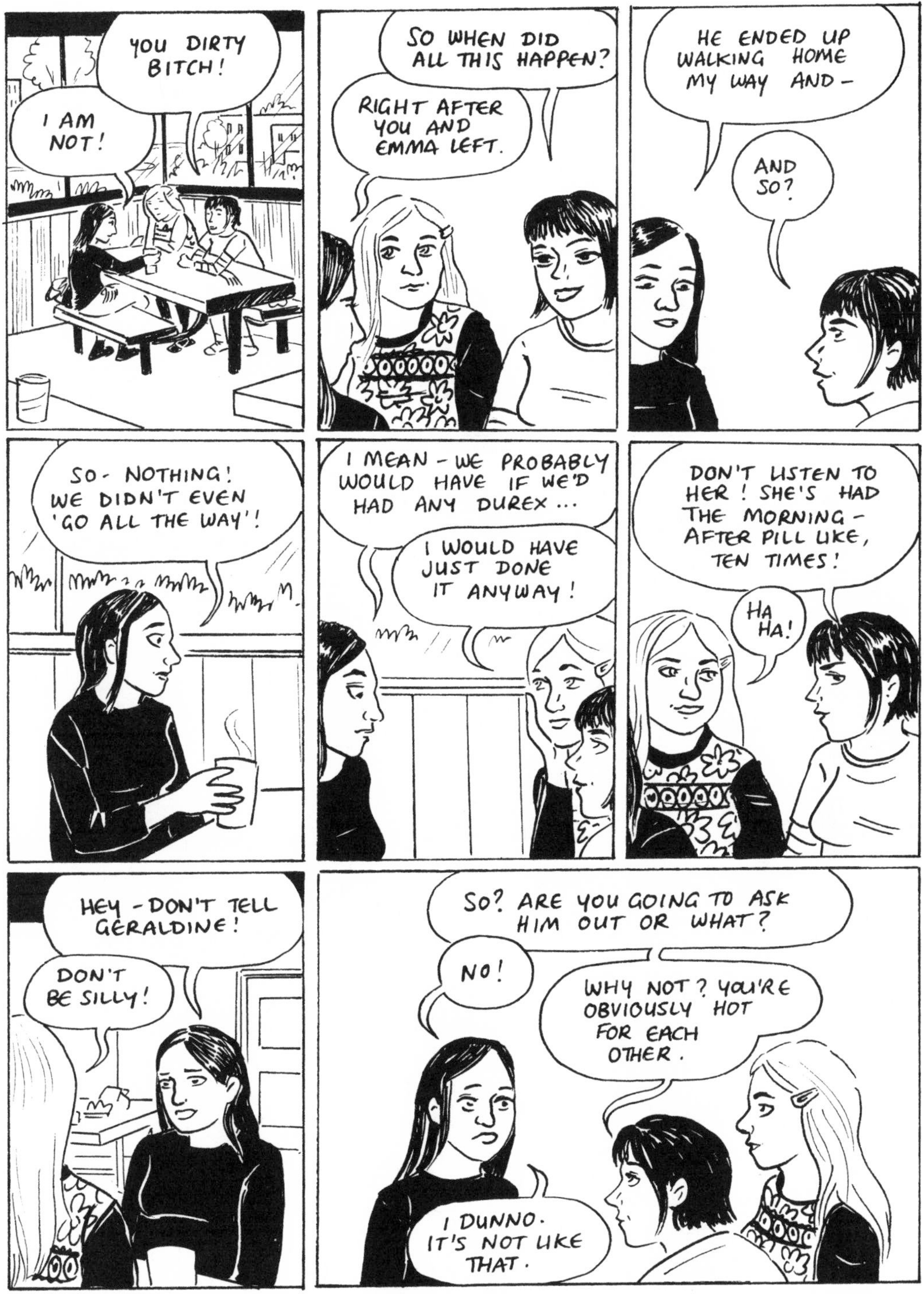
YOU DIRTY BITCH!
I AM NOT!
SO WHEN DID ALL THIS HAPPEN?
RIGHT AFTER YOU AND EMMA LEFT.
HE ENDED UP WALKING HOME MY WAY AND -
AND SO?
SO- NOTHING! WE DIDN'T EVEN 'GO ALL THE WAY'!
I MEAN - WE PROBABLY WOULD HAVE IF WE'D HAD ANY DUREX ...
I WOULD HAVE JUST DONE IT ANYWAY!
DON'T LISTEN TO HER! SHE'S HAD THE MORNING-AFTER PILL LIKE, TEN TIMES!
HA HA!
HEY - DON'T TELL GERALDINE!
DON'T BE SILLY!
SO? ARE YOU GOING TO ASK HIM OUT OR WHAT?
NO!
WHY NOT? YOU'RE OBVIOUSLY HOT FOR EACH OTHER.
I DUNNO. IT'S NOT LIKE THAT.

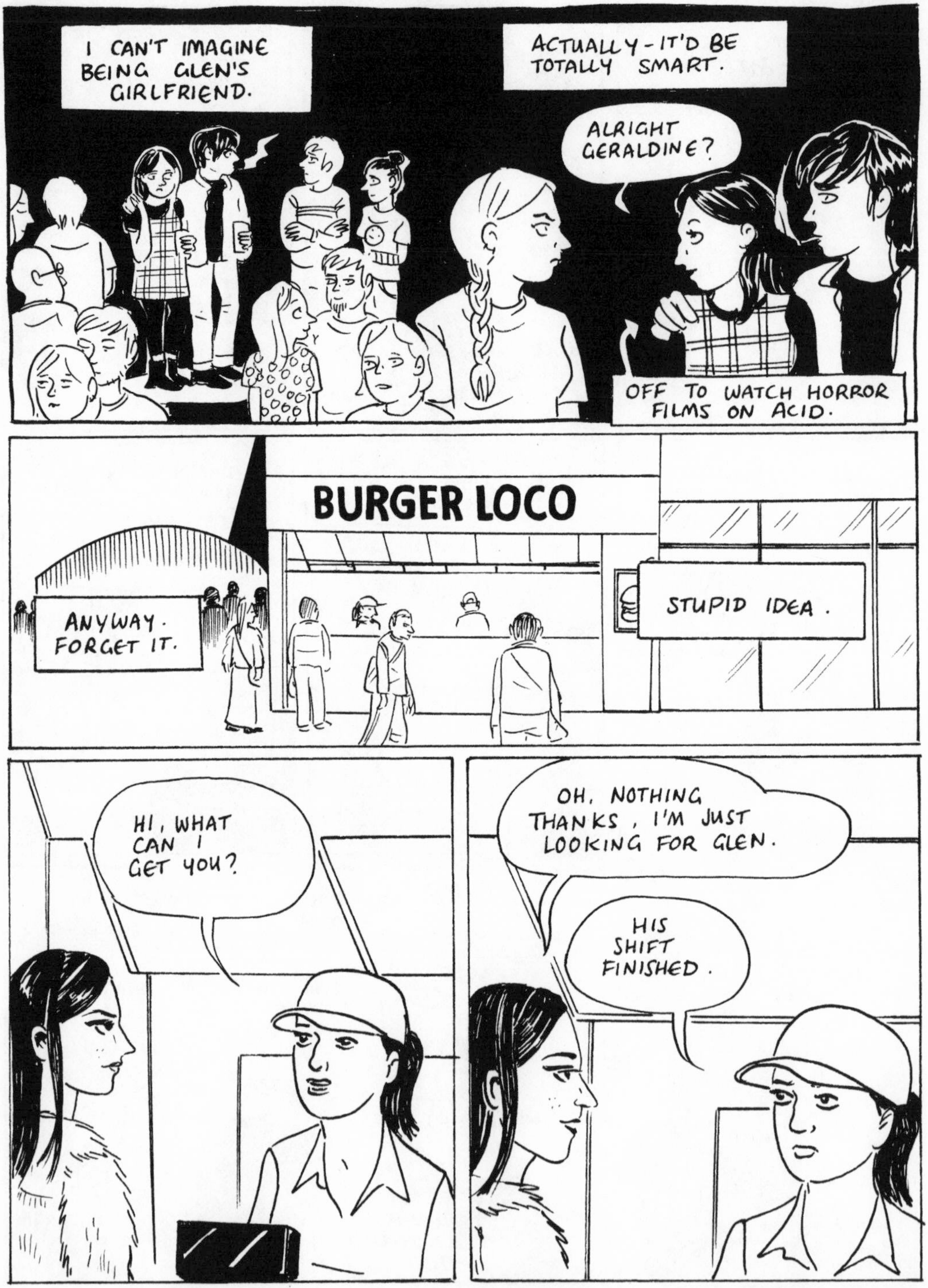
I CAN'T IMAGINE BEING GLEN'S GIRLFRIEND.
ACTUALLY - IT'D BE TOTALLY SMART.
ALRIGHT GERALDINE?
OFF TO WATCH HORROR FILMS ON ACID.
BURGER LOCO
ANYWAY. FORGET IT.
STUPID IDEA.
HI, WHAT CAN I GET YOU?
OH, NOTHING THANKS, I'M JUST LOOKING FOR GLEN.
HIS SHIFT FINISHED.

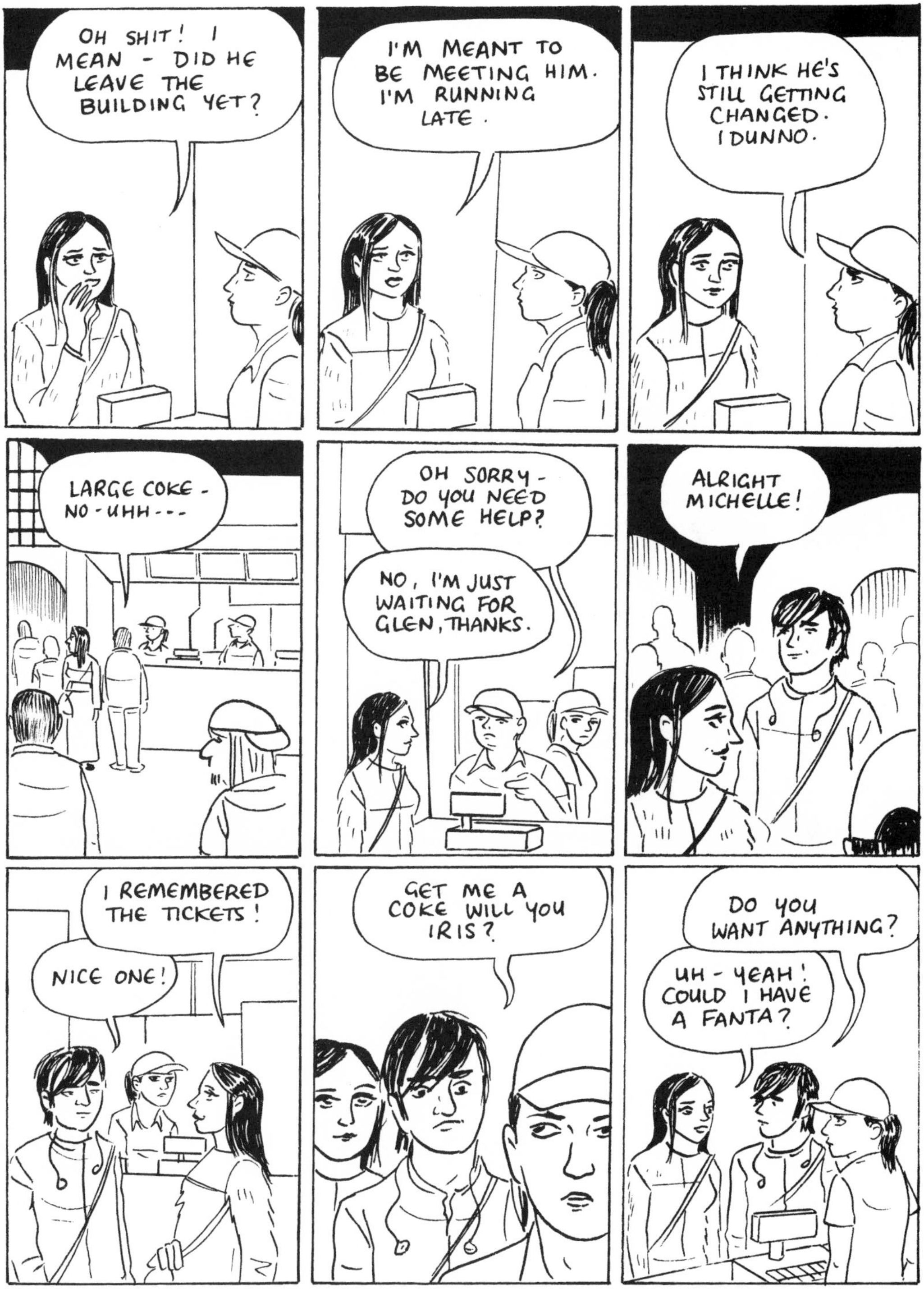
OH SHIT! I MEAN - DID HE LEAVE THE BUILDING YET?
I'M MEANT TO BE MEETING HIM. I'M RUNNING LATE.
I THINK HE'S STILL GETTING CHANGED. I DUNNO.
LARGE COKE - NO - UHH - - -
OH SORRY - DO YOU NEED SOME HELP?
NO, I'M JUST WAITING FOR GLEN, THANKS.
ALRIGHT MICHELLE!
I REMEMBERED THE TICKETS!
NICE ONE!
GET ME A COKE WILL YOU IRIS?
DO YOU WANT ANYTHING?
UH - YEAH! COULD I HAVE A FANTA?

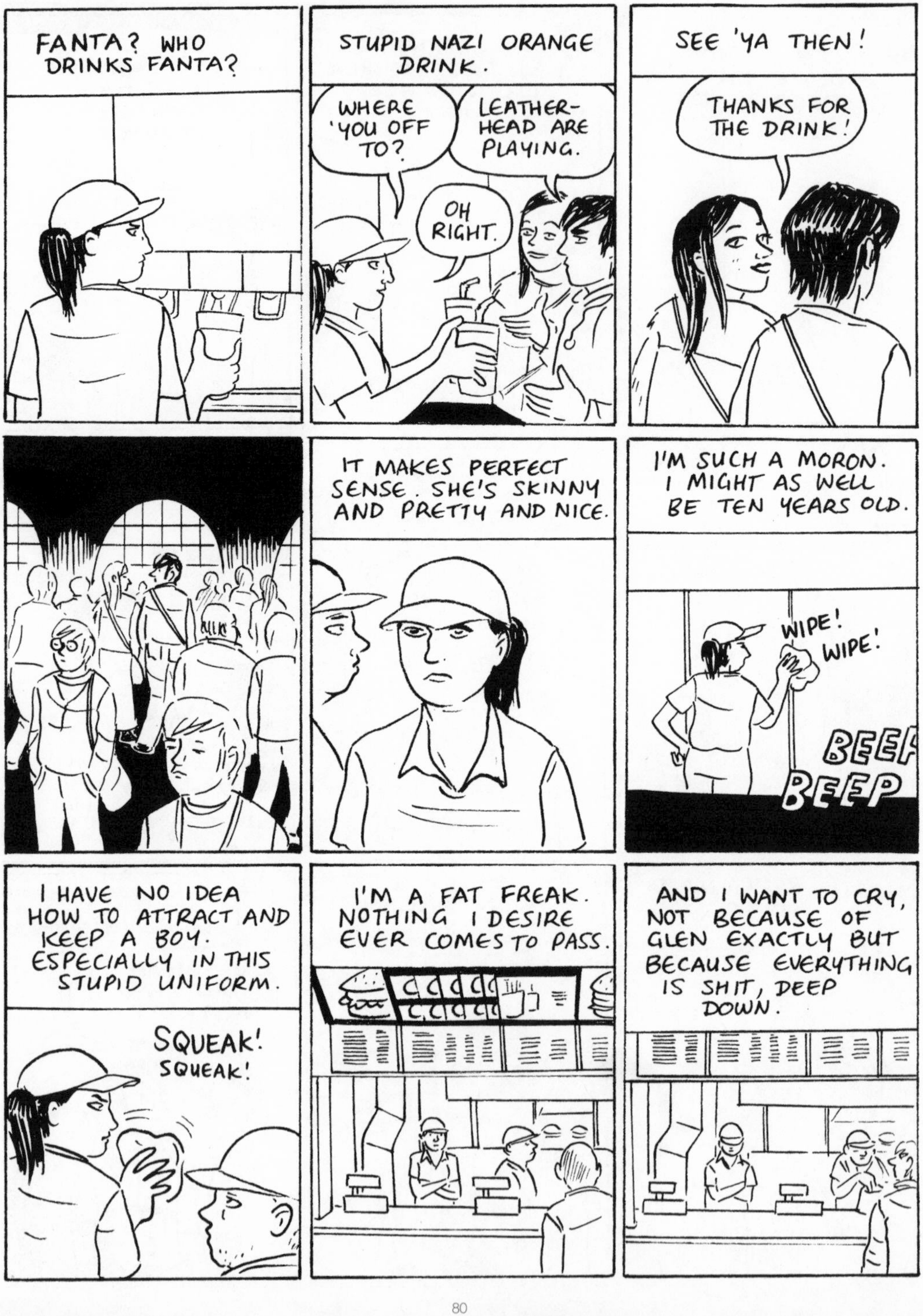
FANTA? WHO DRINKS FANTA?
STUPID NAZI ORANGE DRINK.
WHERE 'YOU OFF TO?
LEATHER-HEAD ARE PLAYING.
OH RIGHT.
SEE 'YA THEN!
THANKS FOR THE DRINK!
IT MAKES PERFECT SENSE. SHE'S SKINNY AND PRETTY AND NICE.
I'M SUCH A MORON. I MIGHT AS WELL BE TEN YEARS OLD.
WIPE!
WIPE!
BEEP
BEEP
I HAVE NO IDEA HOW TO ATTRACT AND KEEP A BOY. ESPECIALLY IN THIS STUPID UNIFORM.
SQUEAK!
SQUEAK!
I'M A FAT FREAK. NOTHING I DESIRE EVER COMES TO PASS.
AND I WANT TO CRY, NOT BECAUSE OF GLEN EXACTLY BUT BECAUSE EVERYTHING IS SHIT, DEEP DOWN.

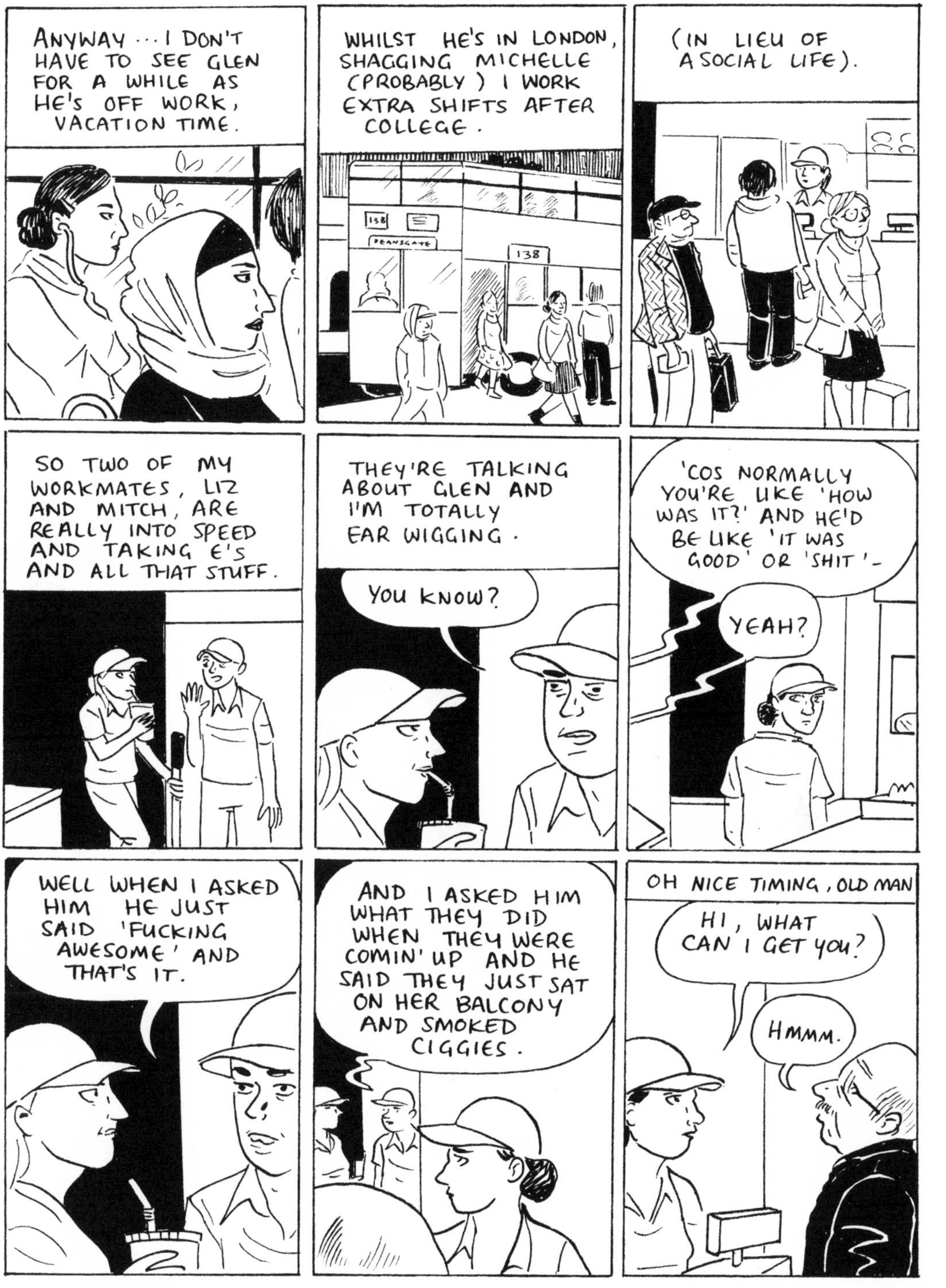
ANYWAY ... I DON'T HAVE TO SEE GLEN FOR A WHILE AS HE'S OFF WORK, VACATION TIME.
WHILST HE'S IN LONDON, SHAGGING MICHELLE (PROBABLY) I WORK EXTRA SHIFTS AFTER COLLEGE.
(IN LIEU OF A SOCIAL LIFE).
SO TWO OF MY WORKMATES, LIZ AND MITCH, ARE REALLY INTO SPEED AND TAKING E'S AND ALL THAT STUFF.
THEY'RE TALKING ABOUT GLEN AND I'M TOTALLY EAR WIGGING.
YOU KNOW?
'COS NORMALLY YOU'RE LIKE 'HOW WAS IT?' AND HE'D BE LIKE 'IT WAS GOOD' OR 'SHIT'–
YEAH?
WELL WHEN I ASKED HIM HE JUST SAID 'FUCKING AWESOME' AND THAT'S IT.
AND I ASKED HIM WHAT THEY DID WHEN THEY WERE COMIN' UP AND HE SAID THEY JUST SAT ON HER BALCONY AND SMOKED CIGGIES.
OH NICE TIMING, OLD MAN
HI, WHAT CAN I GET YOU?
HMMM.

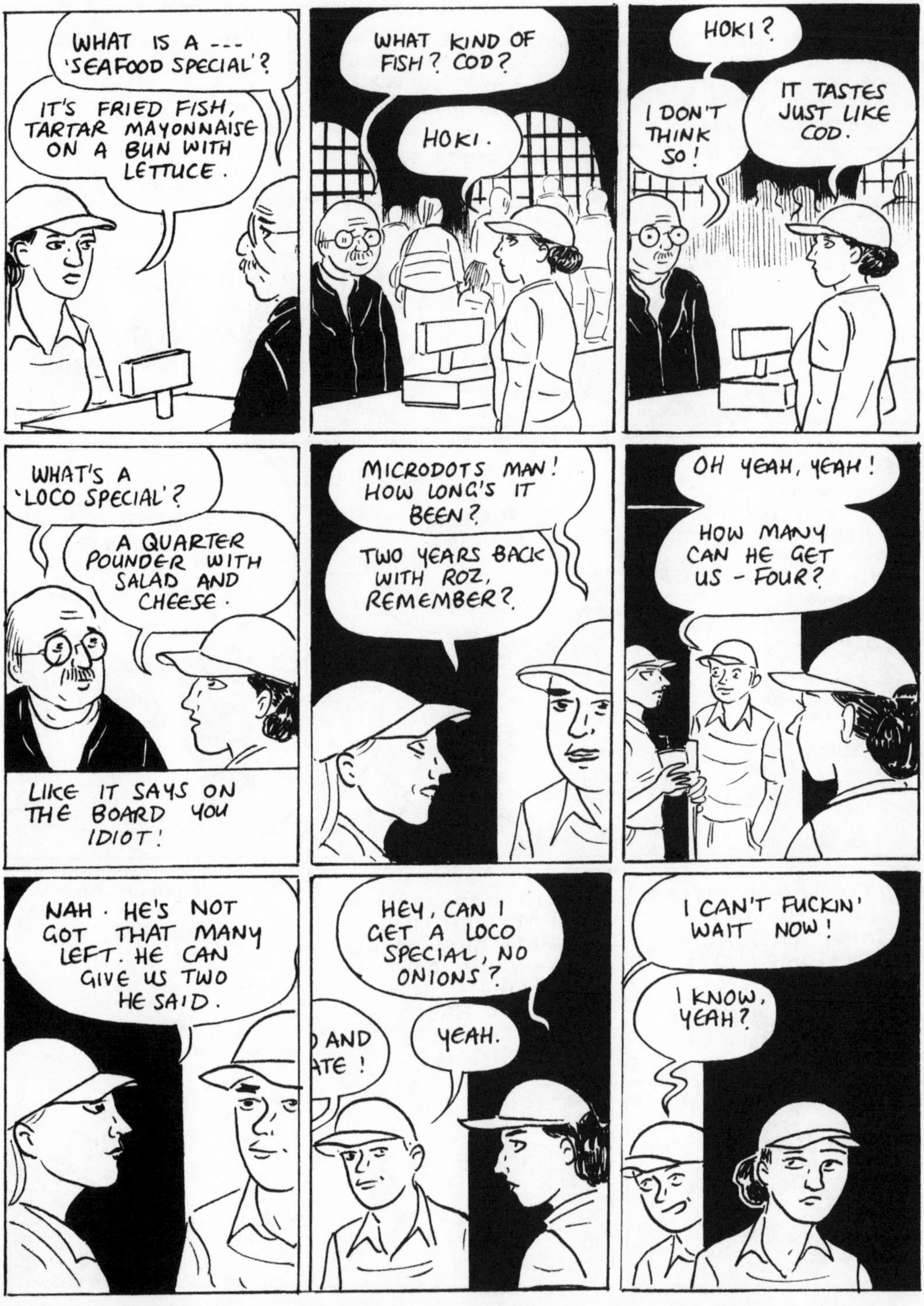
WHAT IS A --- 'SEAFOOD SPECIAL'?
IT'S FRIED FISH, TARTAR MAYONNAISE ON A BUN WITH LETTUCE.
WHAT KIND OF FISH? COD?
HOKI.
HOKI?
I DON'T THINK SO!
IT TASTES JUST LIKE COD.
WHAT'S A 'LOCO SPECIAL'?
A QUARTER POUNDER WITH SALAD AND CHEESE.
LIKE IT SAYS ON THE BOARD YOU IDIOT!
MICRODOTS MAN! HOW LONG'S IT BEEN?
TWO YEARS BACK WITH ROZ, REMEMBER?
OH YEAH, YEAH!
HOW MANY CAN HE GET US - FOUR?
NAH. HE'S NOT GOT THAT MANY LEFT. HE CAN GIVE US TWO HE SAID.
HEY, CAN I GET A LOCO SPECIAL, NO ONIONS?
AND ATE!
YEAH.
I CAN'T FUCKIN' WAIT NOW!
I KNOW, YEAH?

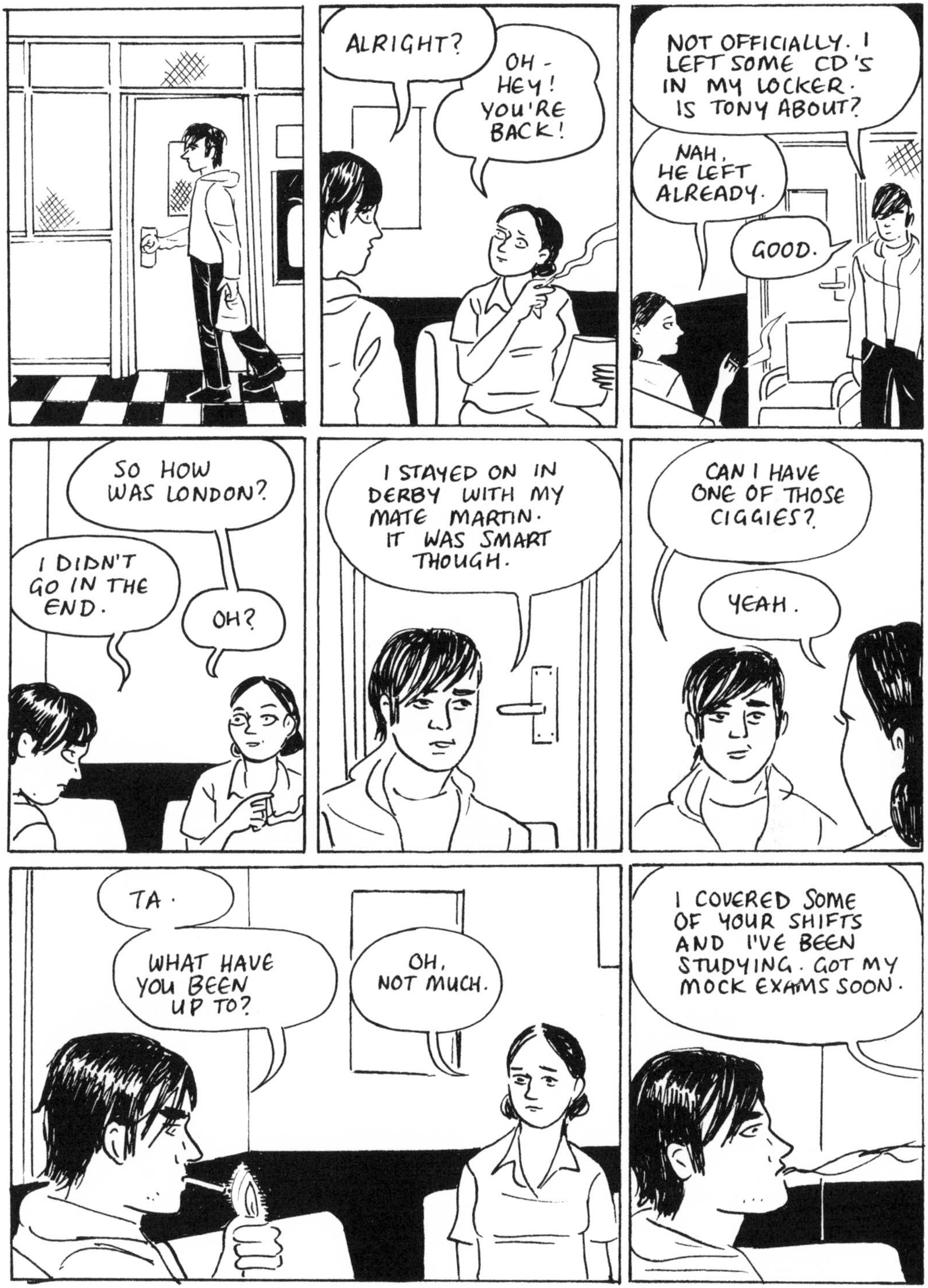
ALRIGHT?
OH - HEY! YOU'RE BACK!
NOT OFFICIALLY. I LEFT SOME CD'S IN MY LOCKER. IS TONY ABOUT?
NAH, HE LEFT ALREADY.
GOOD.
SO HOW WAS LONDON?
I DIDN'T GO IN THE END.
OH?
I STAYED ON IN DERBY WITH MY MATE MARTIN. IT WAS SMART THOUGH.
CAN I HAVE ONE OF THOSE CIGGIES?
YEAH.
TA.
WHAT HAVE YOU BEEN UP TO?
OH, NOT MUCH.
I COVERED SOME OF YOUR SHIFTS AND I'VE BEEN STUDYING. GOT MY MOCK EXAMS SOON.

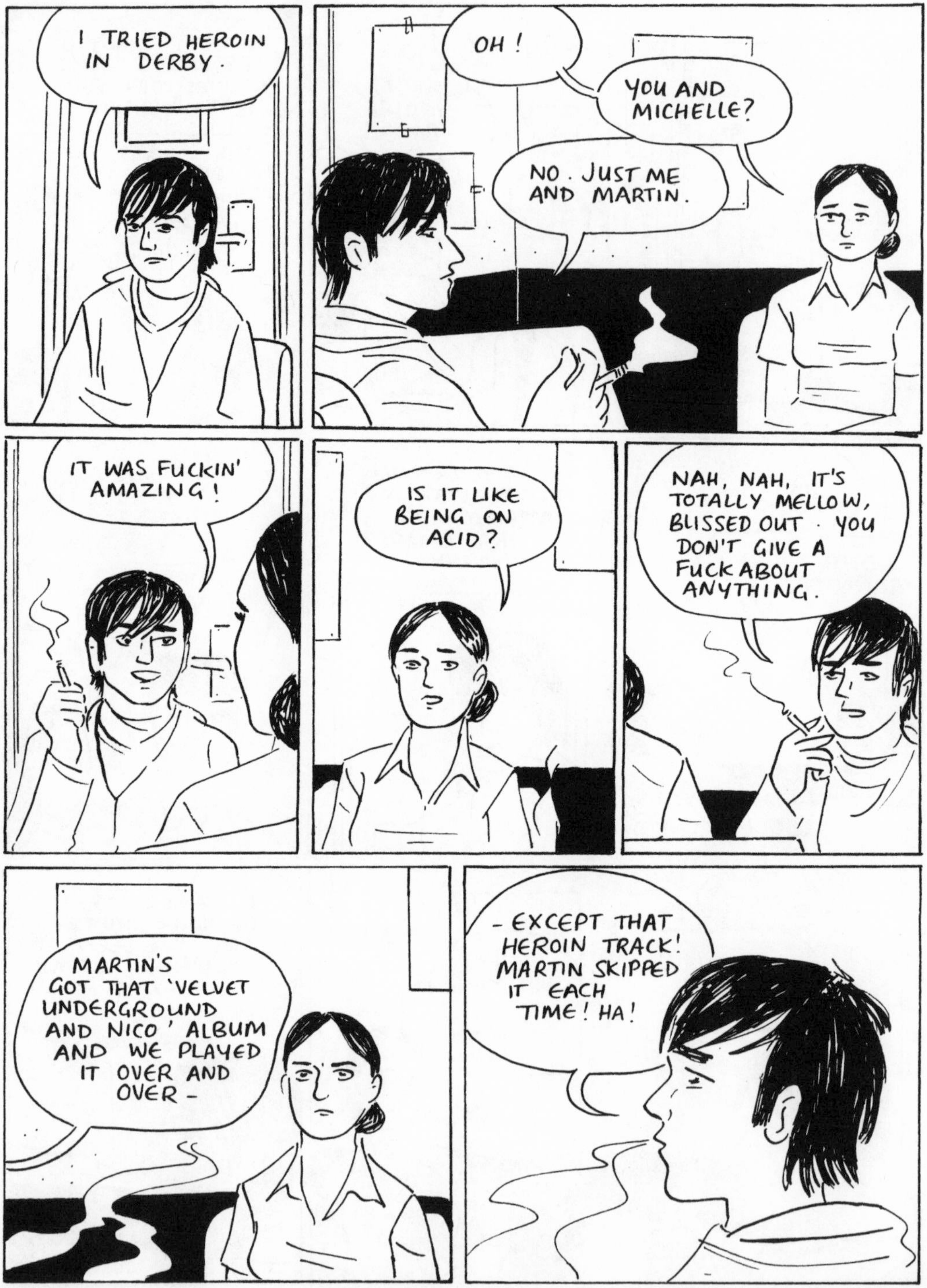

I TRIED HEROIN IN DERBY.
OH!
YOU AND MICHELLE?
NO. JUST ME AND MARTIN.
IT WAS FUCKIN' AMAZING!
IS IT LIKE BEING ON ACID?
NAH, NAH, IT'S TOTALLY MELLOW, BLISSED OUT. YOU DON'T GIVE A FUCK ABOUT ANYTHING.
MARTIN'S GOT THAT 'VELVET UNDERGROUND AND NICO' ALBUM AND WE PLAYED IT OVER AND OVER -
- EXCEPT THAT HEROIN TRACK! MARTIN SKIPPED IT EACH TIME! HA!

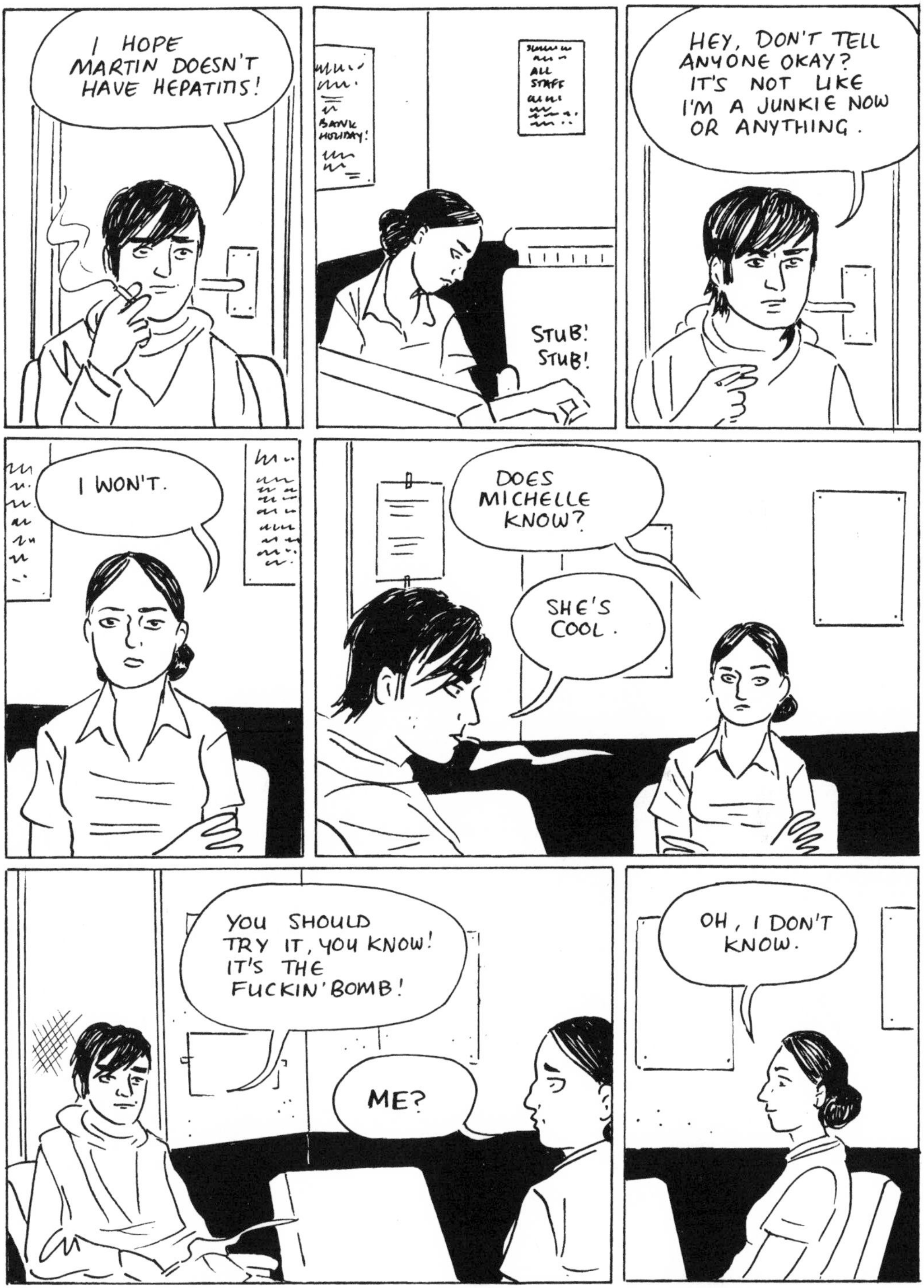
I HOPE MARTIN DOESN'T HAVE HEPATITIS!
ALL STAFF
BANK HOLIDAY!
STUB! STUB!
HEY, DON'T TELL ANYONE OKAY? IT'S NOT LIKE I'M A JUNKIE NOW OR ANYTHING.
I WON'T.
DOES MICHELLE KNOW?
SHE'S COOL.
YOU SHOULD TRY IT, YOU KNOW! IT'S THE FUCKIN' BOMB!
ME?
OH, I DON'T KNOW.

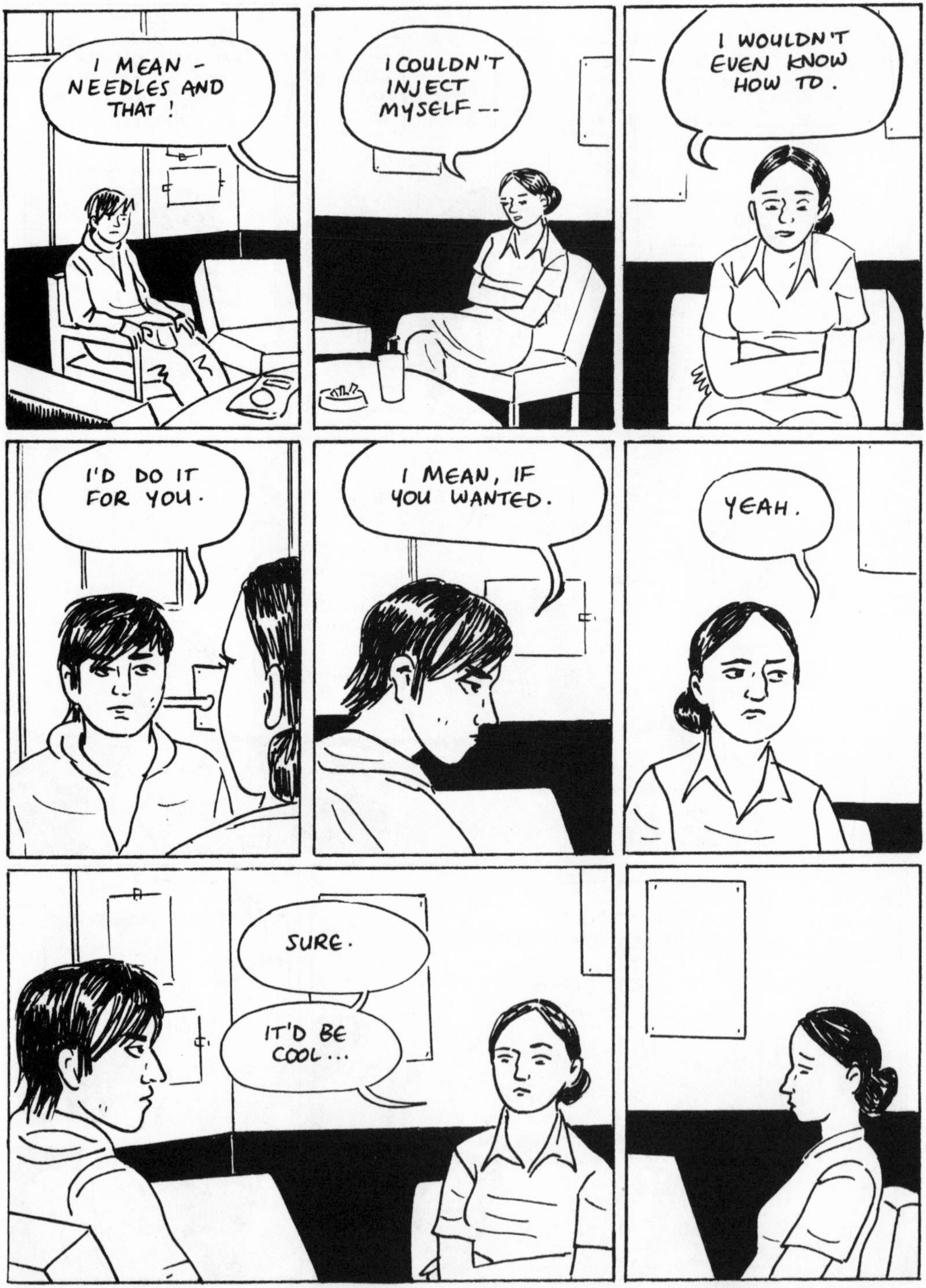
I MEAN - NEEDLES AND THAT!
I COULDN'T INJECT MYSELF --
I WOULDN'T EVEN KNOW HOW TO.
I'D DO IT FOR YOU.
I MEAN, IF YOU WANTED.
YEAH.
SURE.
IT'D BE COOL...

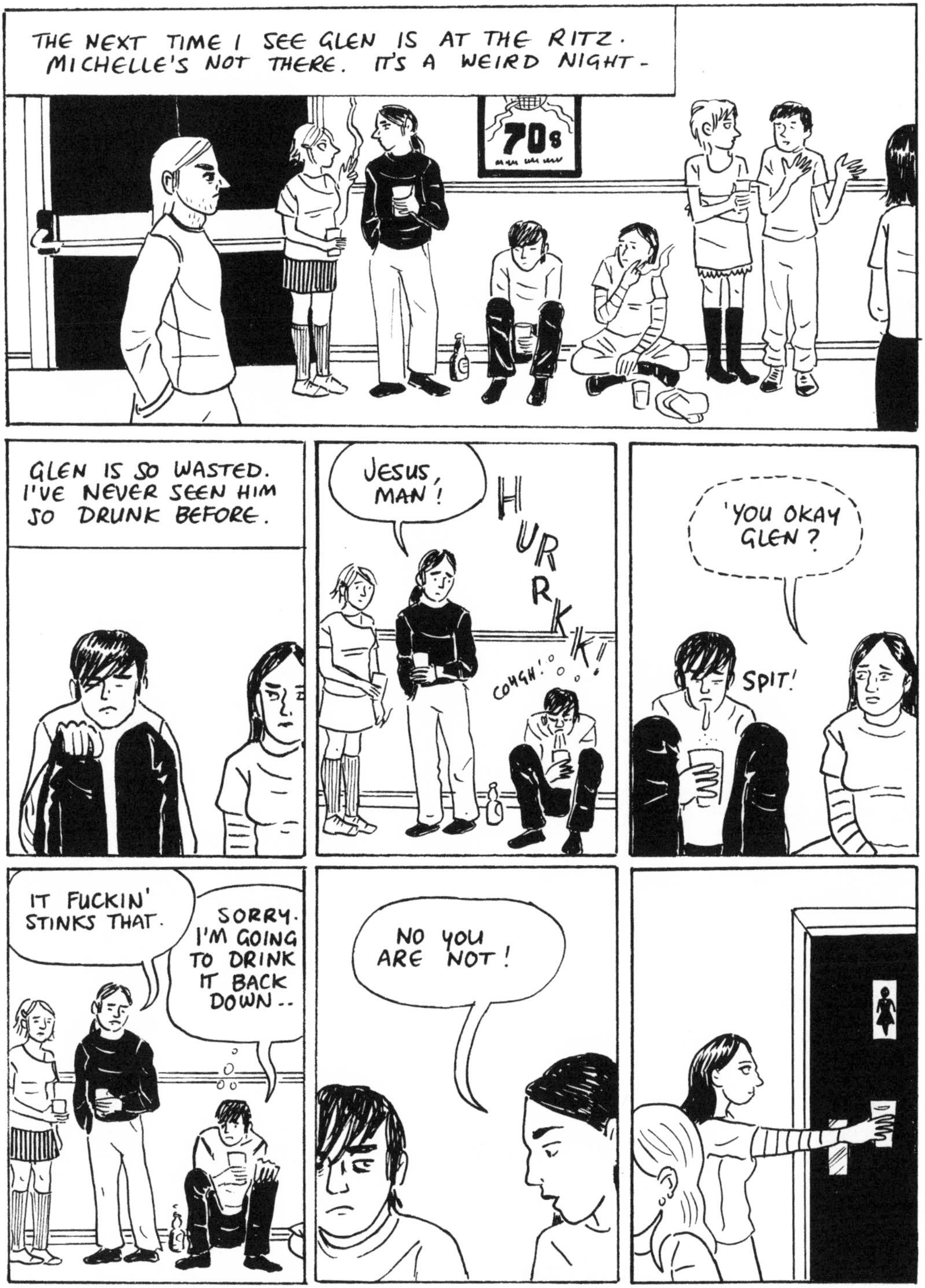
THE NEXT TIME I SEE GLEN IS AT THE RITZ. MICHELLE'S NOT THERE. IT'S A WEIRD NIGHT -
70s
GLEN IS SO WASTED. I'VE NEVER SEEN HIM SO DRUNK BEFORE.
JESUS, MAN!
HURRKK!
COUGH!
'YOU OKAY GLEN?
SPIT!
IT FUCKIN' STINKS THAT.
SORRY. I'M GOING TO DRINK IT BACK DOWN..
NO YOU ARE NOT!

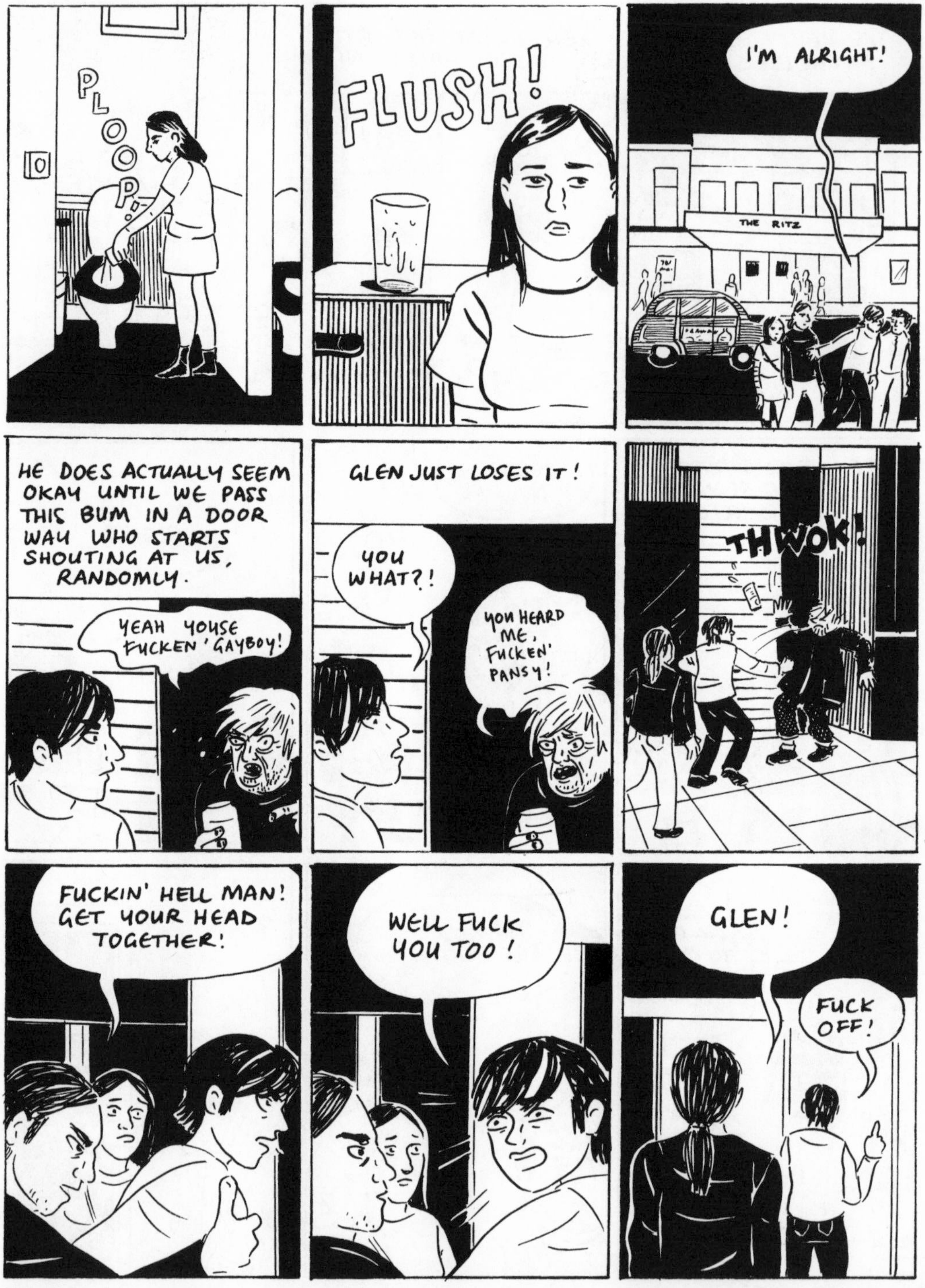
PLOOP!
FLUSH!
I'M ALRIGHT!
THE RITZ
HE DOES ACTUALLY SEEM OKAY UNTIL WE PASS THIS BUM IN A DOOR WAY WHO STARTS SHOUTING AT US, RANDOMLY.
YEAH YOUSE FUCKEN 'GAYBOY!
GLEN JUST LOSES IT!
YOU WHAT?!
YOU HEARD ME, FUCKEN' PANSY!
THWOK!
FUCKIN' HELL MAN! GET YOUR HEAD TOGETHER!
WELL FUCK YOU TOO!
GLEN!
FUCK OFF!

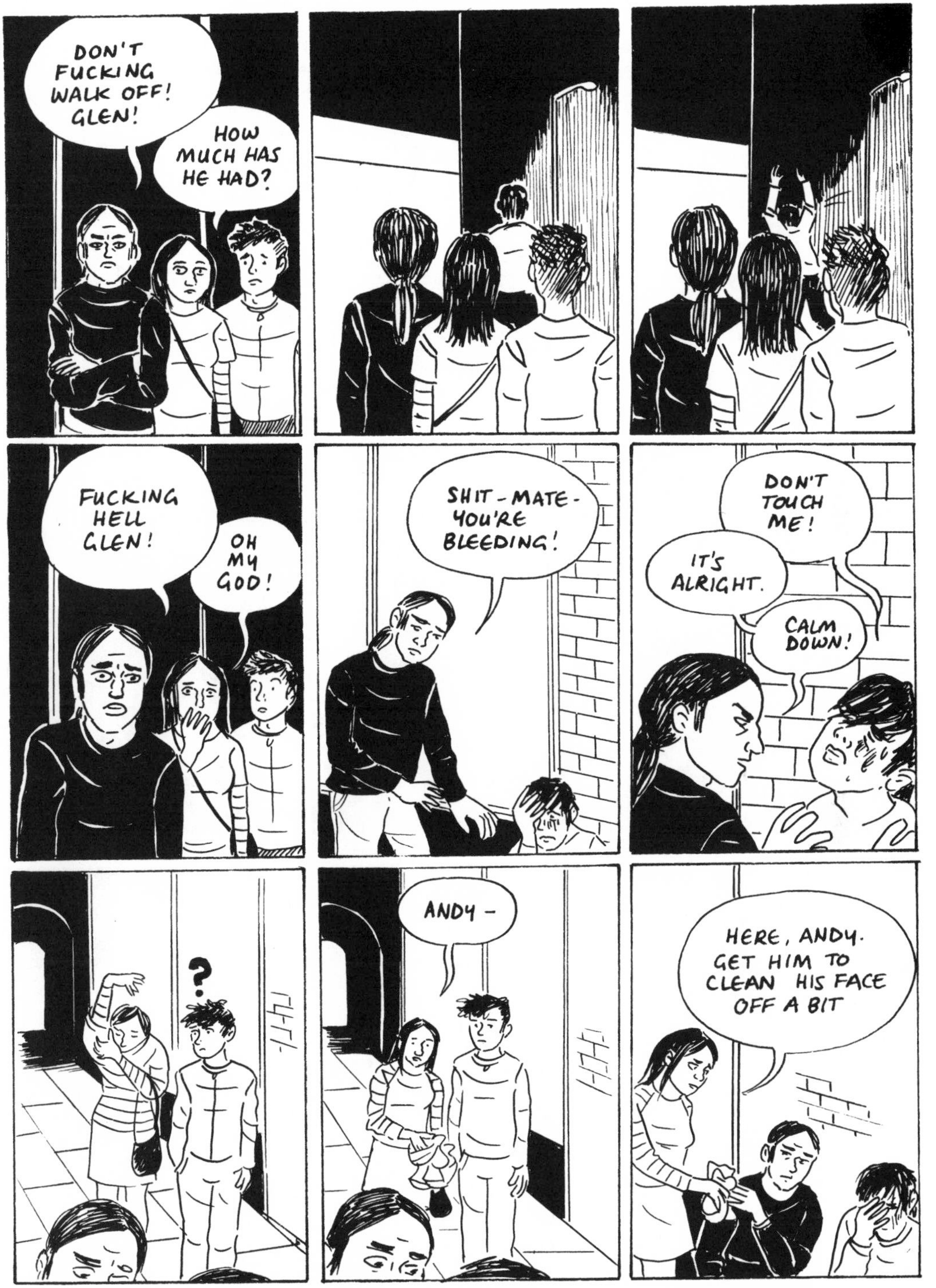
DON'T FUCKING WALK OFF! GLEN!
HOW MUCH HAS HE HAD?
FUCKING HELL GLEN!
OH MY GOD!
SHIT - MATE - YOU'RE BLEEDING!
DON'T TOUCH ME!
IT'S ALRIGHT.
CALM DOWN!
?
ANDY -
HERE, ANDY. GET HIM TO CLEAN HIS FACE OFF A BIT

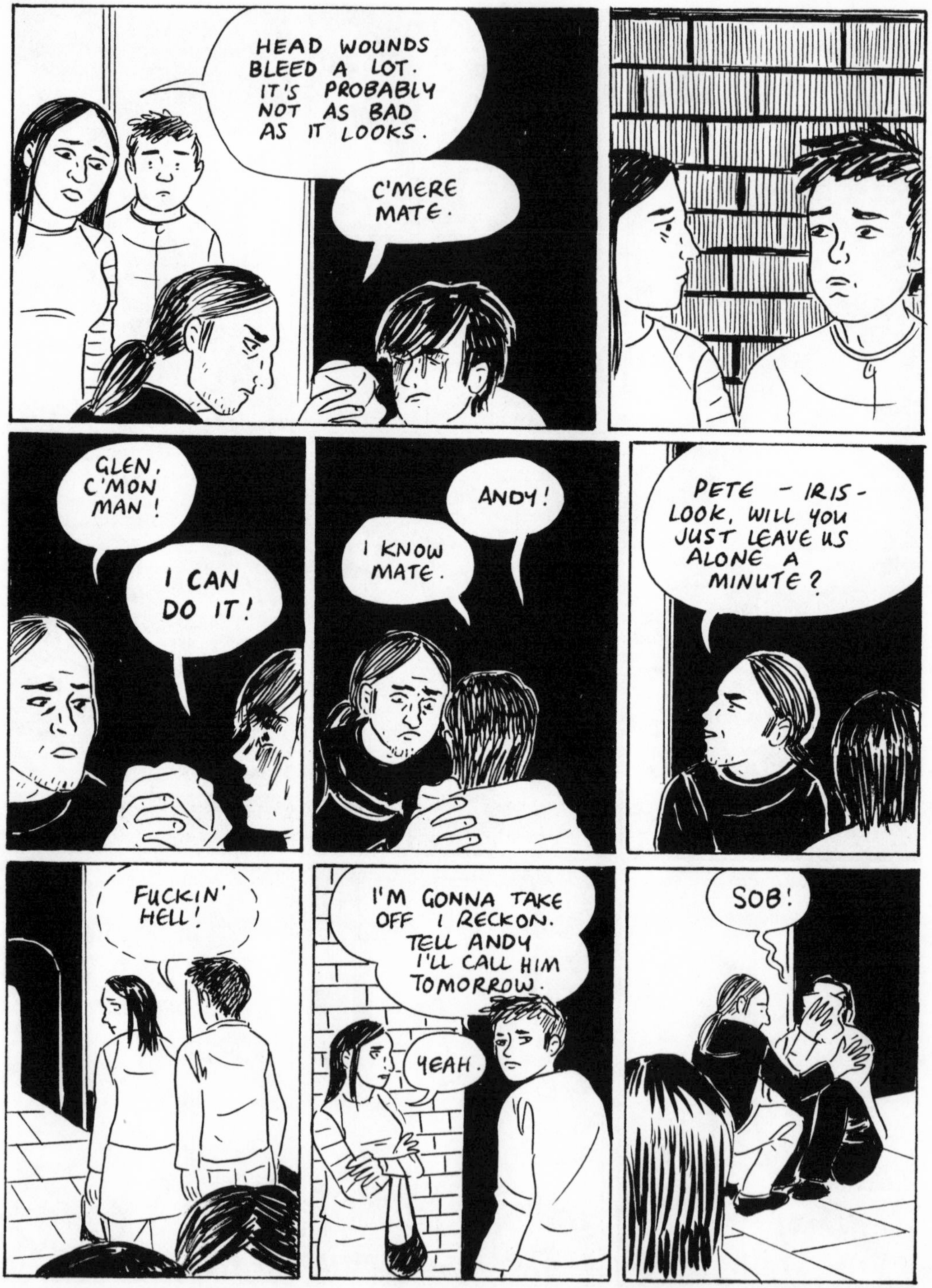
HEAD WOUNDS BLEED A LOT. IT'S PROBABLY NOT AS BAD AS IT LOOKS.
C'MERE MATE.
GLEN, C'MON MAN!
I CAN DO IT!
ANDY!
I KNOW MATE.
PETE - IRIS - LOOK, WILL YOU JUST LEAVE US ALONE A MINUTE?
FUCKIN' HELL!
I'M GONNA TAKE OFF I RECKON. TELL ANDY I'LL CALL HIM TOMORROW.
YEAH.
SOB!

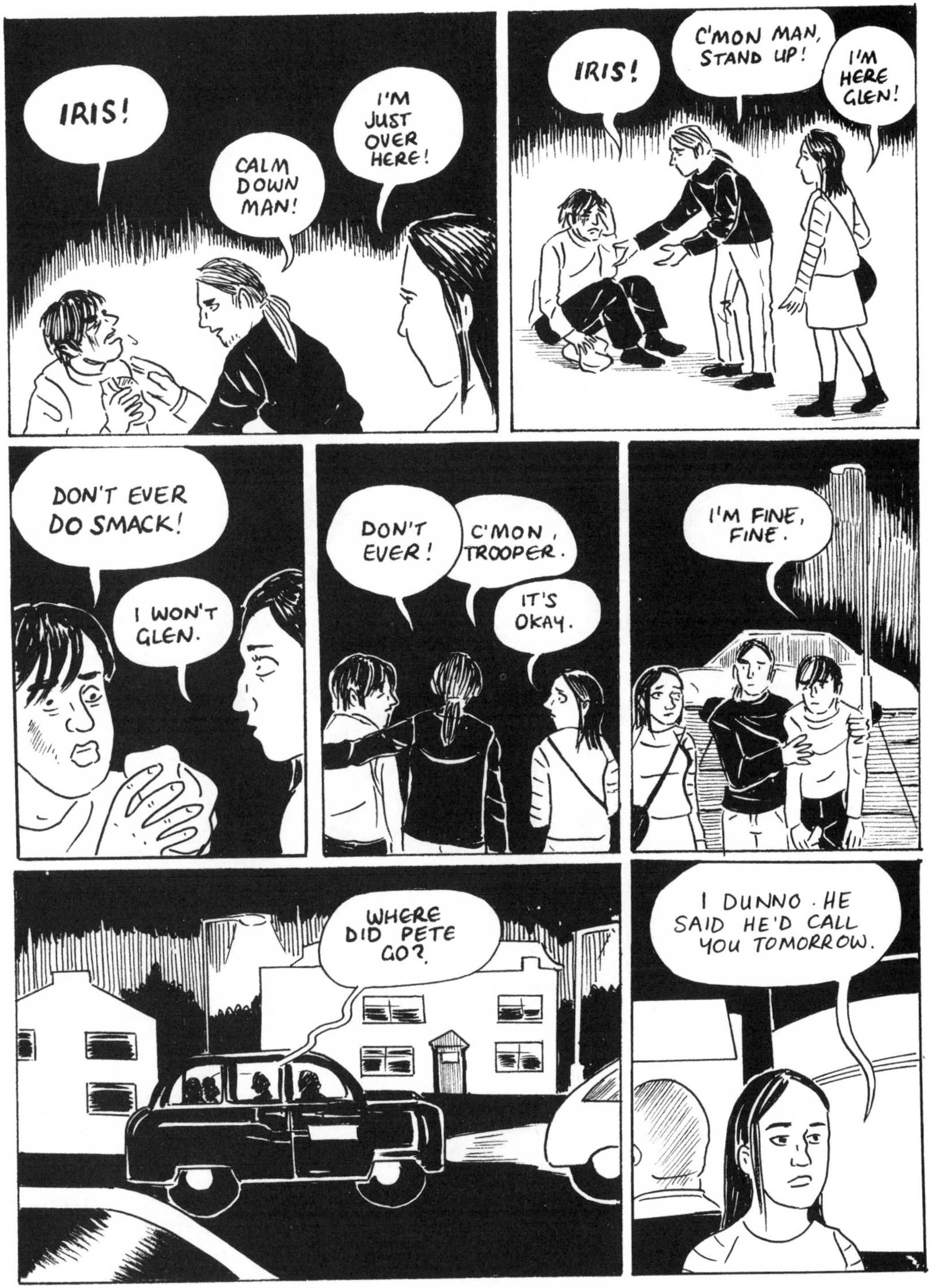
IRIS!
CALM DOWN MAN!
I'M JUST OVER HERE!
IRIS!
C'MON MAN, STAND UP!
I'M HERE GLEN!
DON'T EVER DO SMACK!
I WON'T GLEN.
DON'T EVER!
C'MON, TROOPER.
IT'S OKAY.
I'M FINE, FINE.
WHERE DID PETE GO?
I DUNNO. HE SAID HE'D CALL YOU TOMORROW.

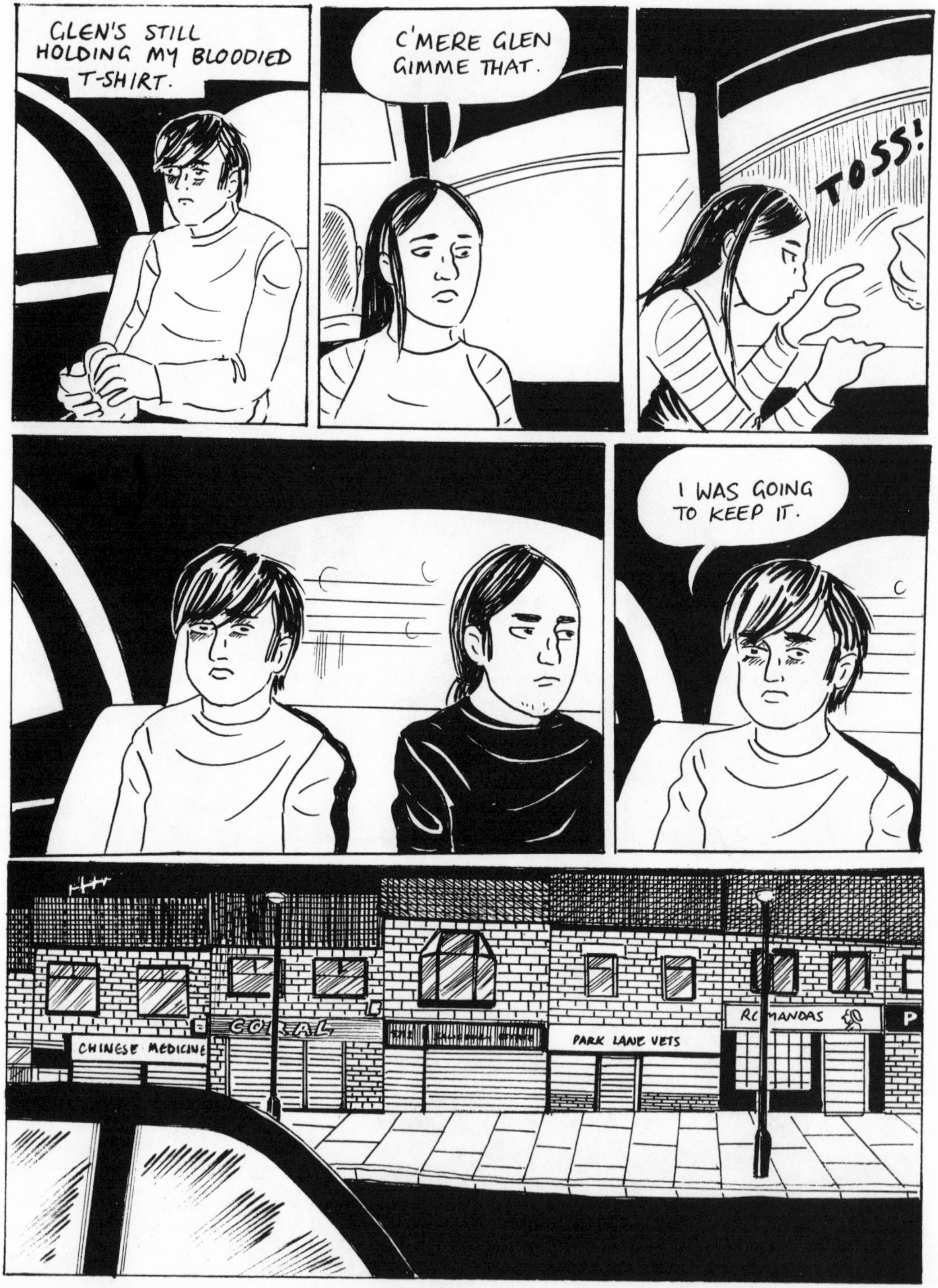
GLEN'S STILL HOLDING MY BLOODIED T-SHIRT.
C'MERE GLEN GIMME THAT.
TOSS!
I WAS GOING TO KEEP IT.
CHINESE MEDICINE
CORAL
PARK LANE VETS

chapter three

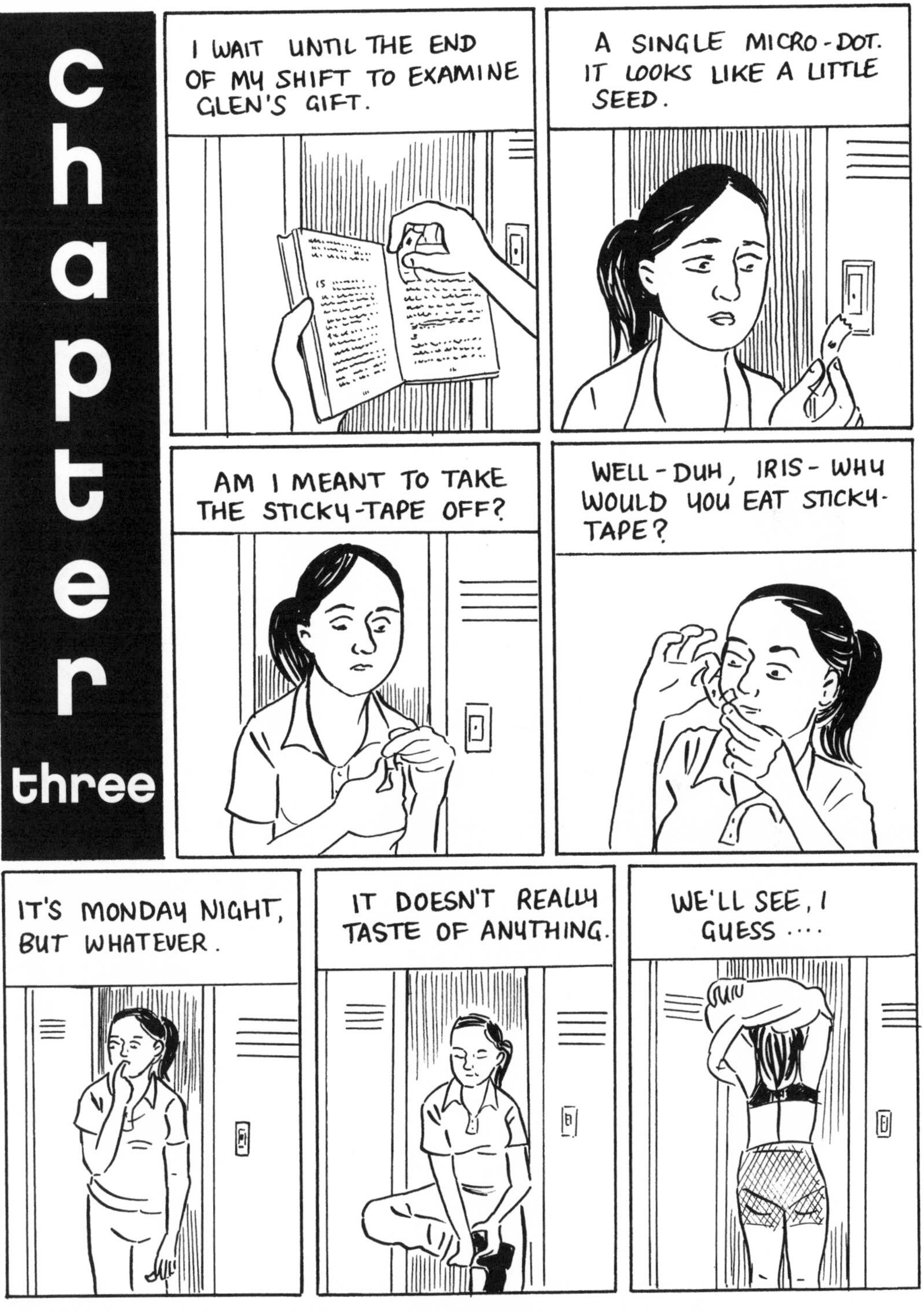

I WAIT UNTIL THE END OF MY SHIFT TO EXAMINE GLEN'S GIFT.
A SINGLE MICRO-DOT. IT LOOKS LIKE A LITTLE SEED.
AM I MEANT TO TAKE THE STICKY-TAPE OFF?
WELL-DUH, IRIS- WHY WOULD YOU EAT STICKY-TAPE?
IT'S MONDAY NIGHT, BUT WHATEVER.
IT DOESN'T REALLY TASTE OF ANYTHING.
WE'LL SEE, I GUESS ....

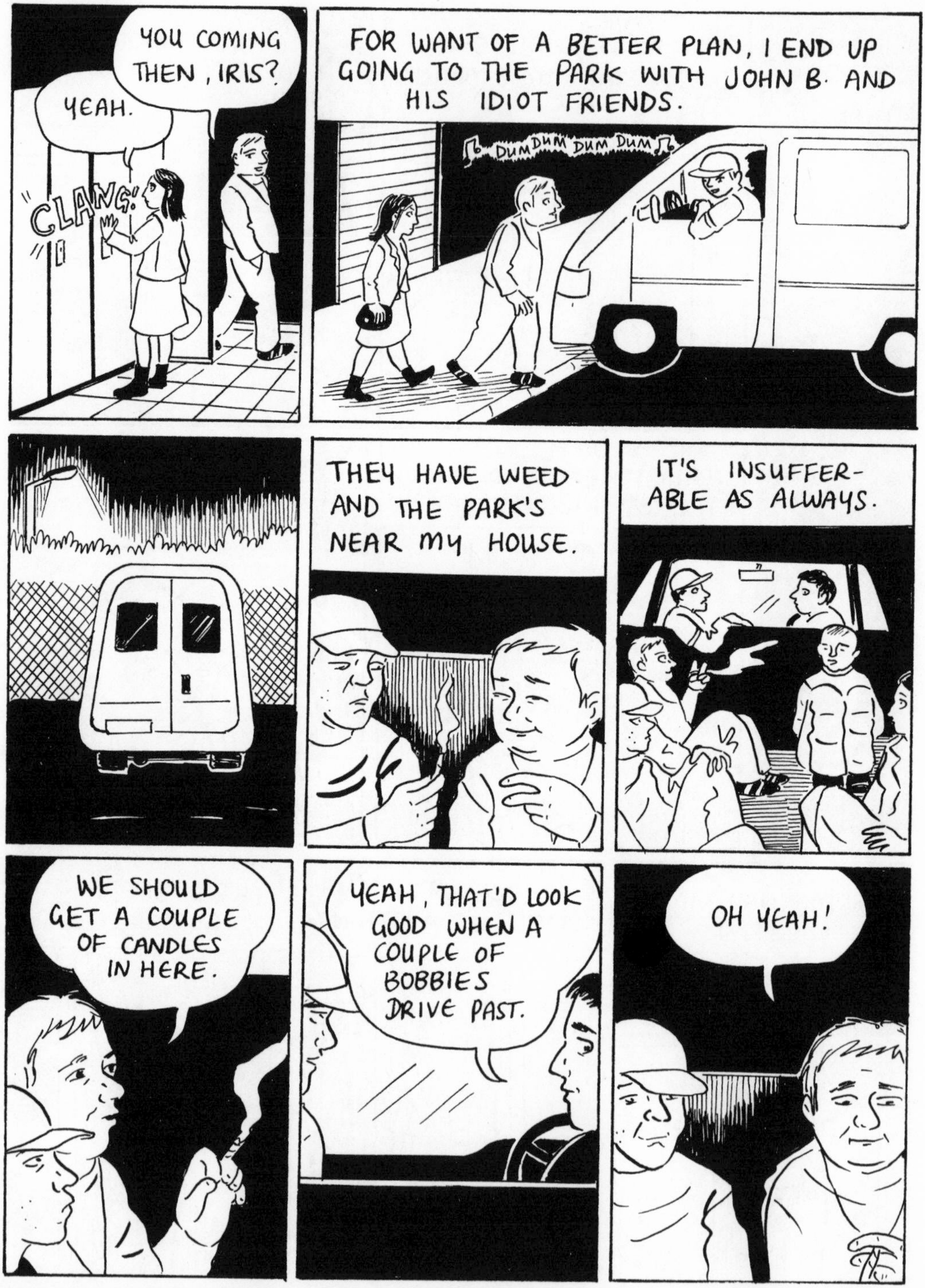
YOU COMING THEN, IRIS?
YEAH.
CLANG!
FOR WANT OF A BETTER PLAN, I END UP GOING TO THE PARK WITH JOHN B. AND HIS IDIOT FRIENDS.
DUM DUM DUM DUM
THEY HAVE WEED AND THE PARK'S NEAR MY HOUSE.
IT'S INSUFFERABLE AS ALWAYS.
WE SHOULD GET A COUPLE OF CANDLES IN HERE.
YEAH, THAT'D LOOK GOOD WHEN A COUPLE OF BOBBIES DRIVE PAST.
OH YEAH!

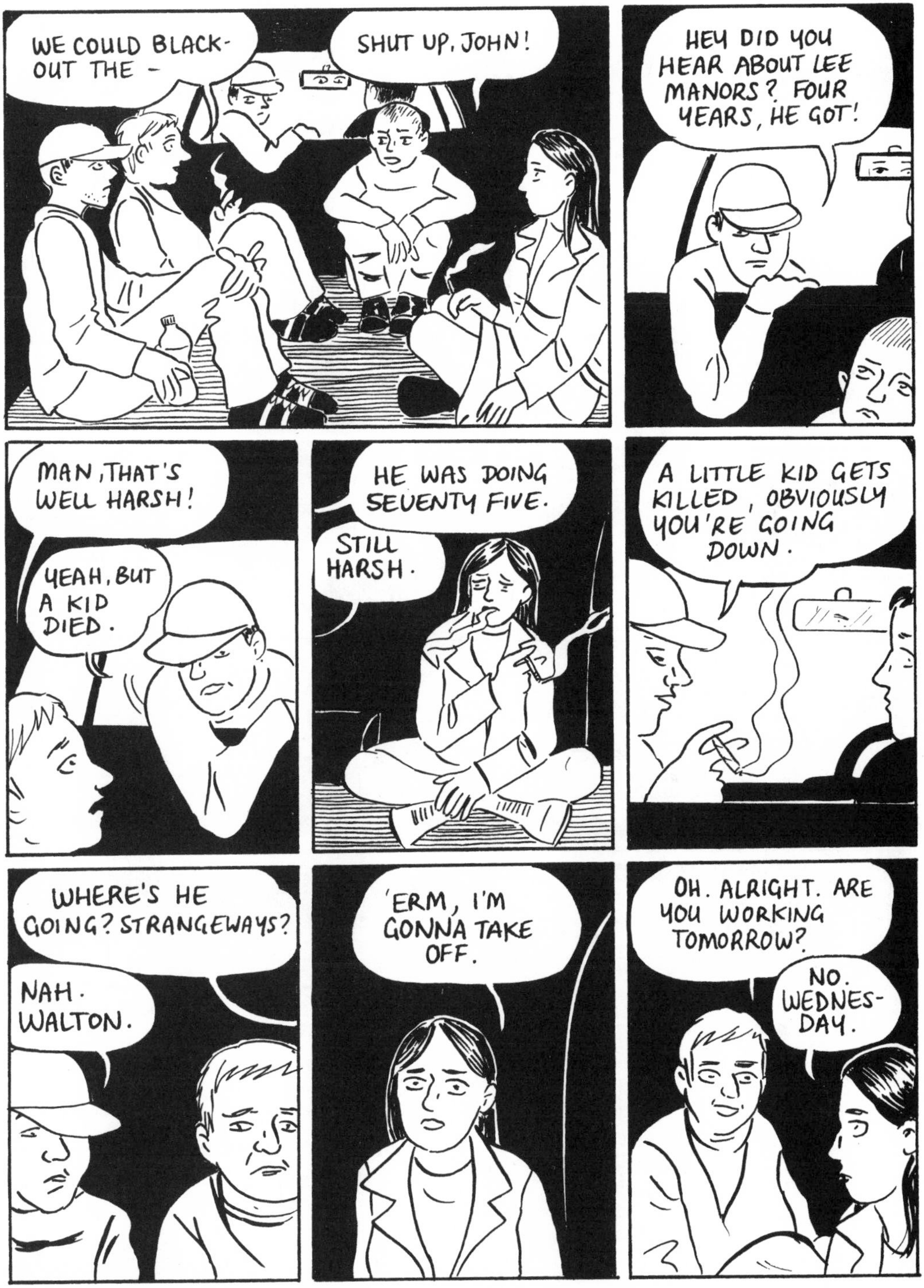
WE COULD BLACK-OUT THE -
SHUT UP, JOHN!
HEY DID YOU HEAR ABOUT LEE MANORS? FOUR YEARS, HE GOT!
MAN, THAT'S WELL HARSH!
YEAH, BUT A KID DIED.
HE WAS DOING SEVENTY FIVE.
STILL HARSH.
A LITTLE KID GETS KILLED, OBVIOUSLY YOU'RE GOING DOWN.
WHERE'S HE GOING? STRANGEWAYS?
NAH. WALTON.
'ERM, I'M GONNA TAKE OFF.
OH. ALRIGHT. ARE YOU WORKING TOMORROW?
NO. WEDNES-DAY.

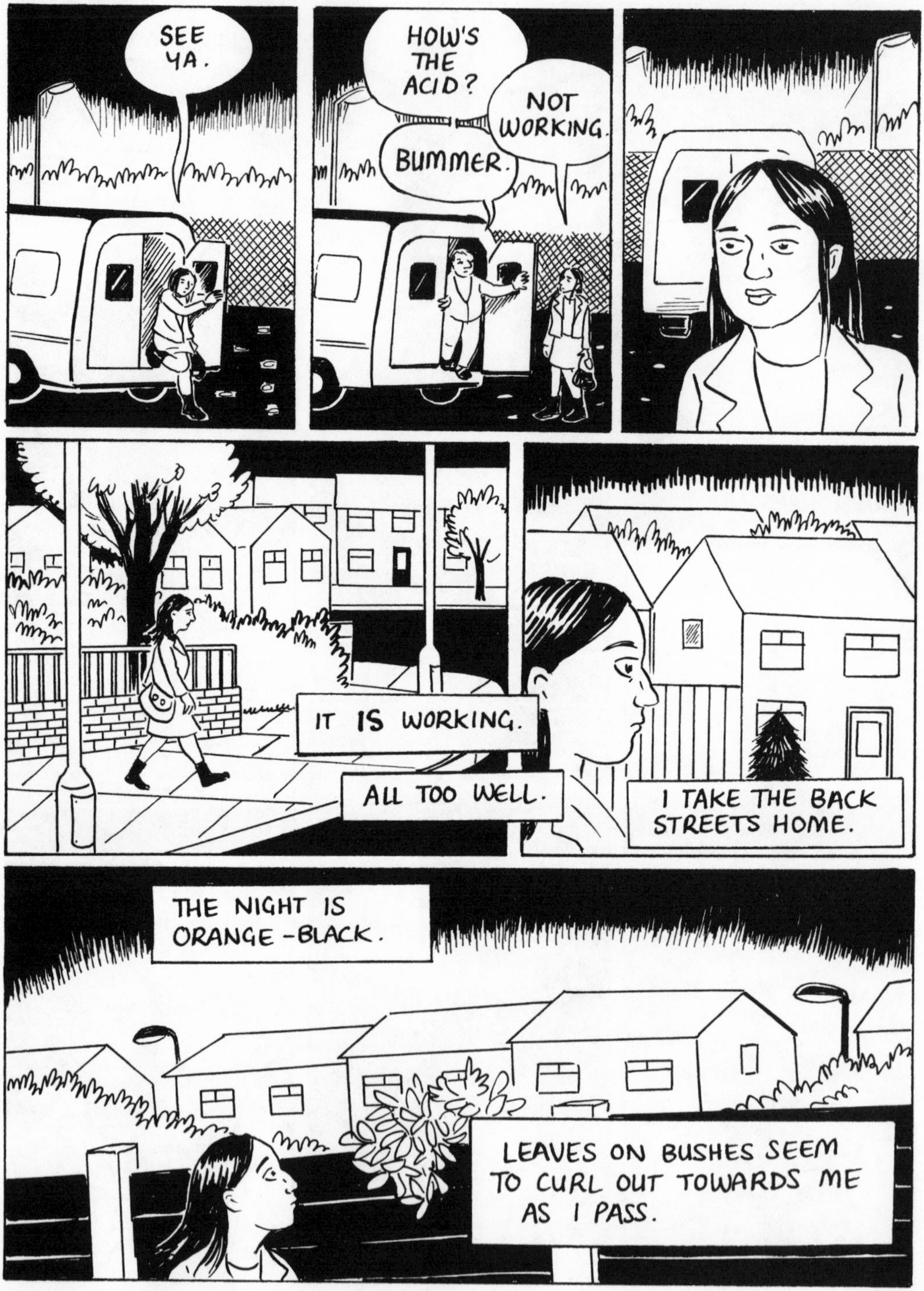
SEE YA.
HOW'S THE ACID?
NOT WORKING.
BUMMER.
IT IS WORKING.
ALL TOO WELL.
I TAKE THE BACK STREETS HOME.
THE NIGHT IS ORANGE-BLACK.
LEAVES ON BUSHES SEEM TO CURL OUT TOWARDS ME AS I PASS.

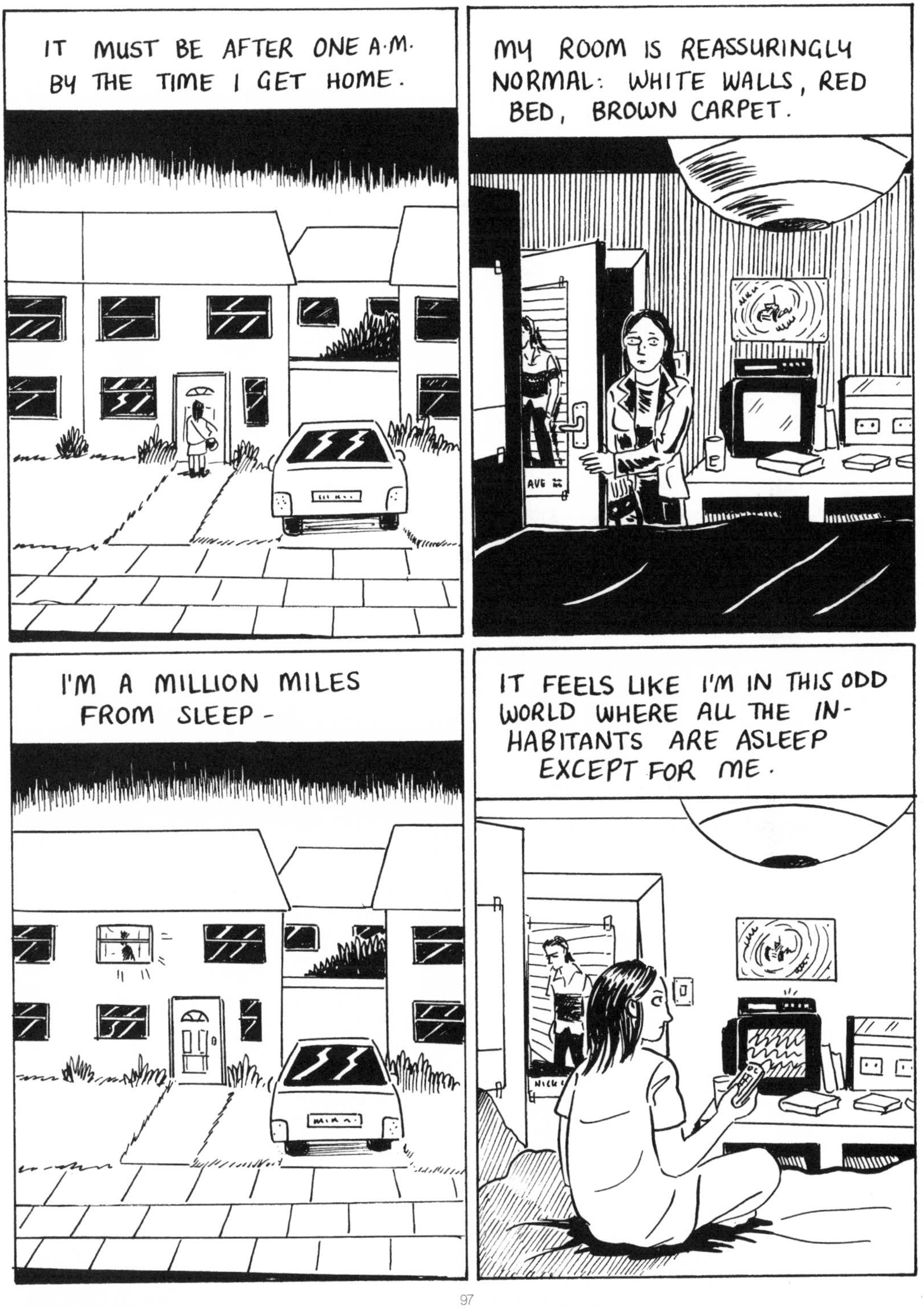
IT MUST BE AFTER ONE A.M. BY THE TIME I GET HOME.
MY ROOM IS REASSURINGLY NORMAL: WHITE WALLS, RED BED, BROWN CARPET.
I'M A MILLION MILES FROM SLEEP -
IT FEELS LIKE I'M IN THIS ODD WORLD WHERE ALL THE IN-HABITANTS ARE ASLEEP EXCEPT FOR ME.

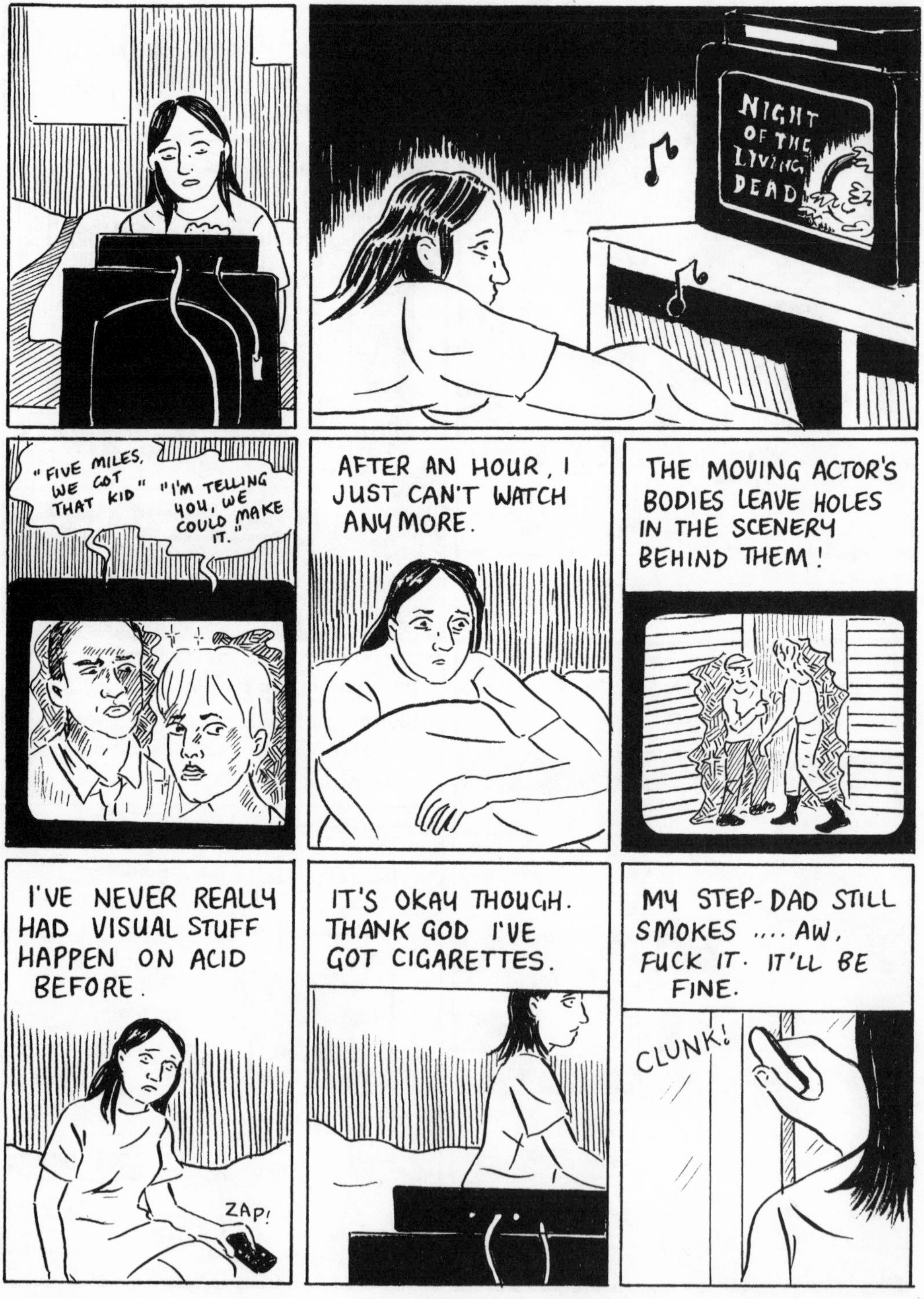
NIGHT OF THE LIVING DEAD
"FIVE MILES, WE GOT THAT KID"
"I'M TELLING YOU, WE COULD MAKE IT."
AFTER AN HOUR, I JUST CAN'T WATCH ANYMORE.
THE MOVING ACTOR'S BODIES LEAVE HOLES IN THE SCENERY BEHIND THEM!
I'VE NEVER REALLY HAD VISUAL STUFF HAPPEN ON ACID BEFORE.
ZAP!
IT'S OKAY THOUGH. THANK GOD I'VE GOT CIGARETTES.
MY STEP-DAD STILL SMOKES .... AW, FUCK IT. IT'LL BE FINE.
CLUNK!

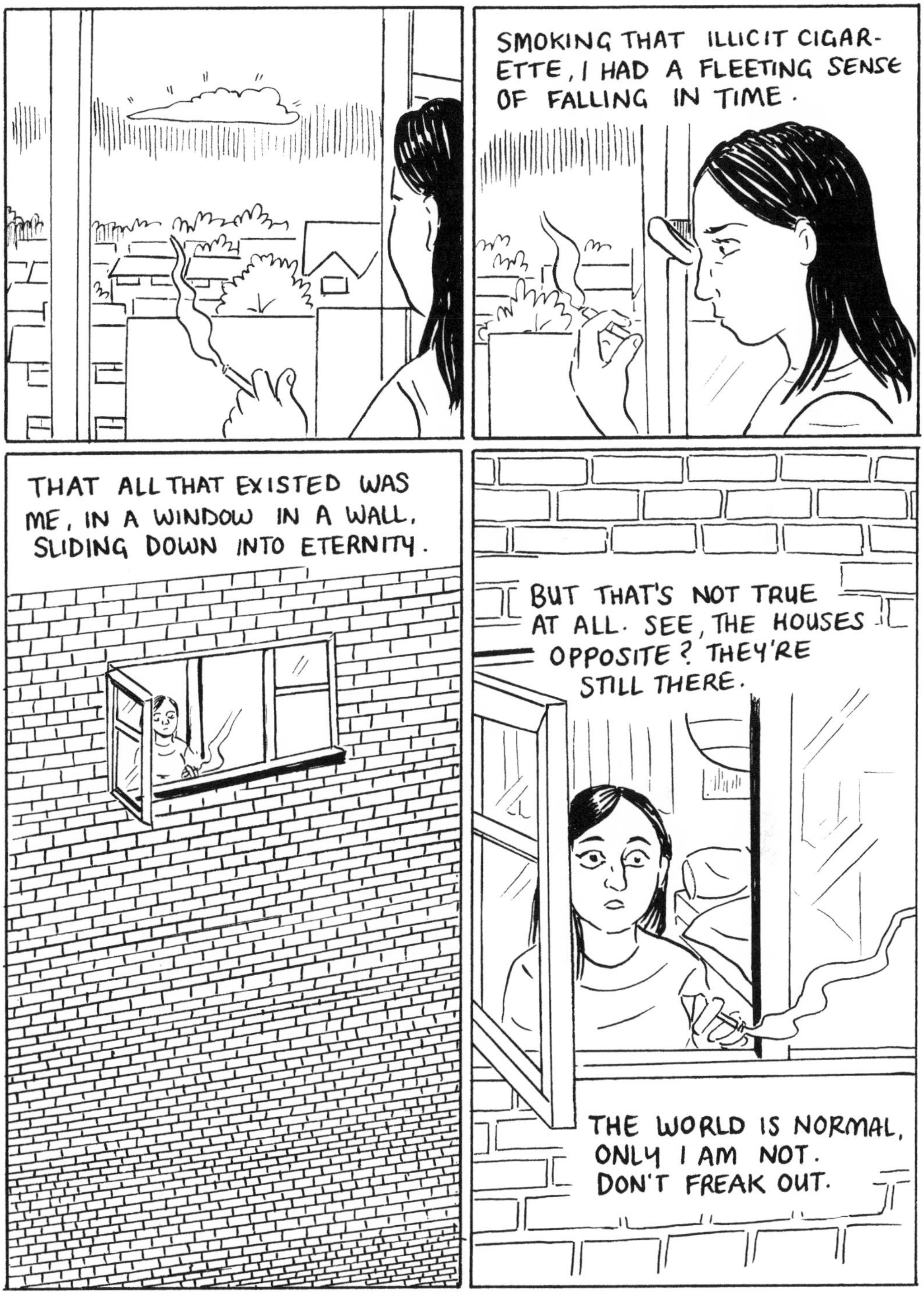
SMOKING THAT ILLICIT CIGAR-ETTE, I HAD A FLEETING SENSE OF FALLING IN TIME.
THAT ALL THAT EXISTED WAS ME, IN A WINDOW IN A WALL, SLIDING DOWN INTO ETERNITY.
BUT THAT'S NOT TRUE AT ALL. SEE, THE HOUSES OPPOSITE? THEY'RE STILL THERE.
THE WORLD IS NORMAL, ONLY I AM NOT. DON'T FREAK OUT.

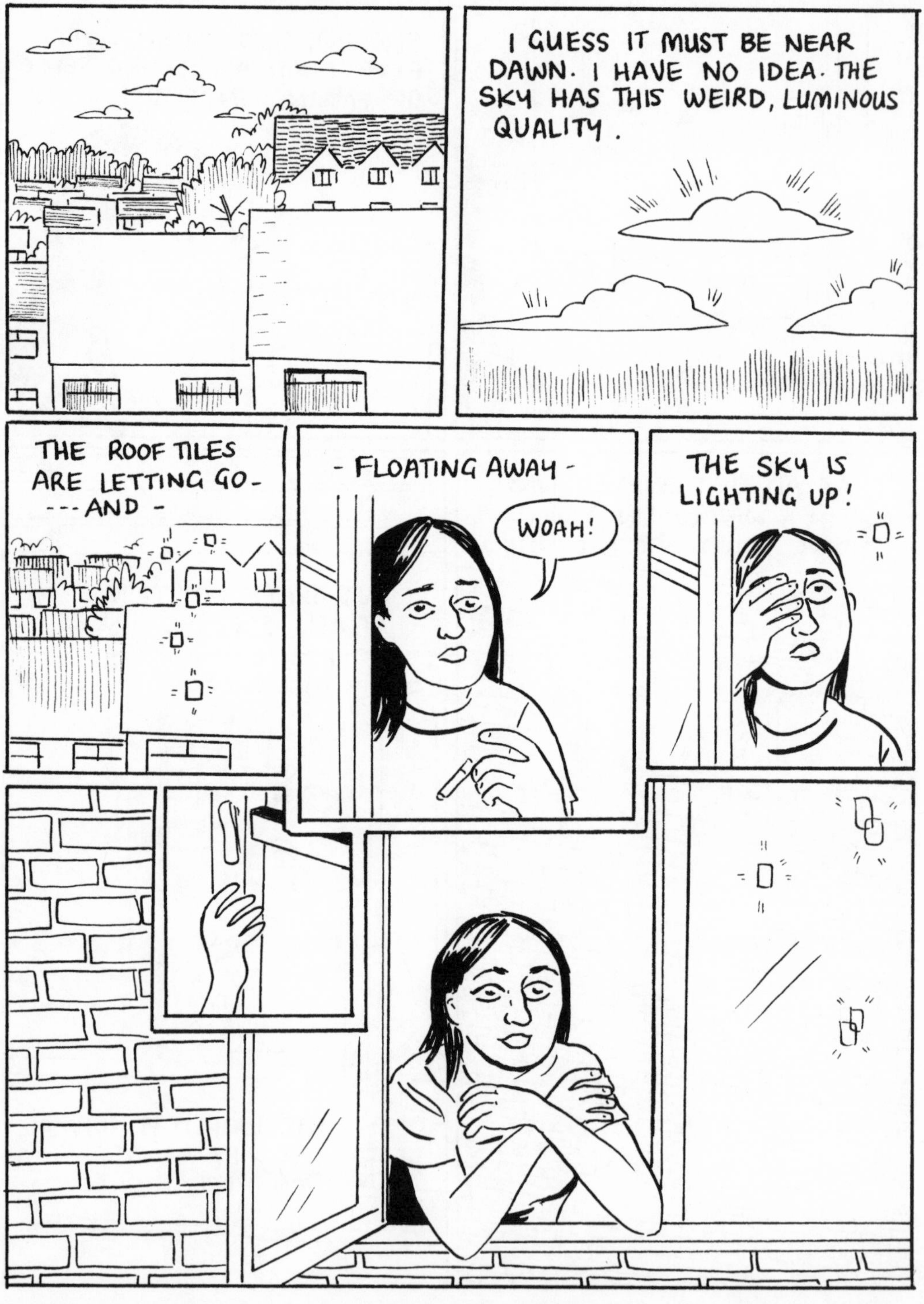
I GUESS IT MUST BE NEAR DAWN. I HAVE NO IDEA. THE SKY HAS THIS WEIRD, LUMINOUS QUALITY.
THE ROOF TILES ARE LETTING GO- ---AND -
- FLOATING AWAY -
WOAH!
THE SKY IS LIGHTING UP!

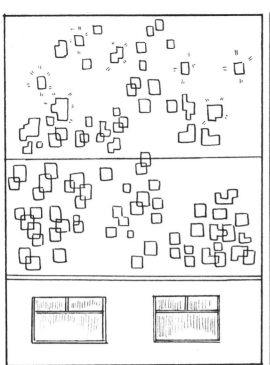

- IT JUST MELTS INTO ITSELF!

I CAN'T HELP LAUGHING AT ALL THIS CHAOTIC BEAUTY - I KNOW THAT PATTERN! IT WAS STACY'S EMBOSSED BEDROOM WALLPAPER!

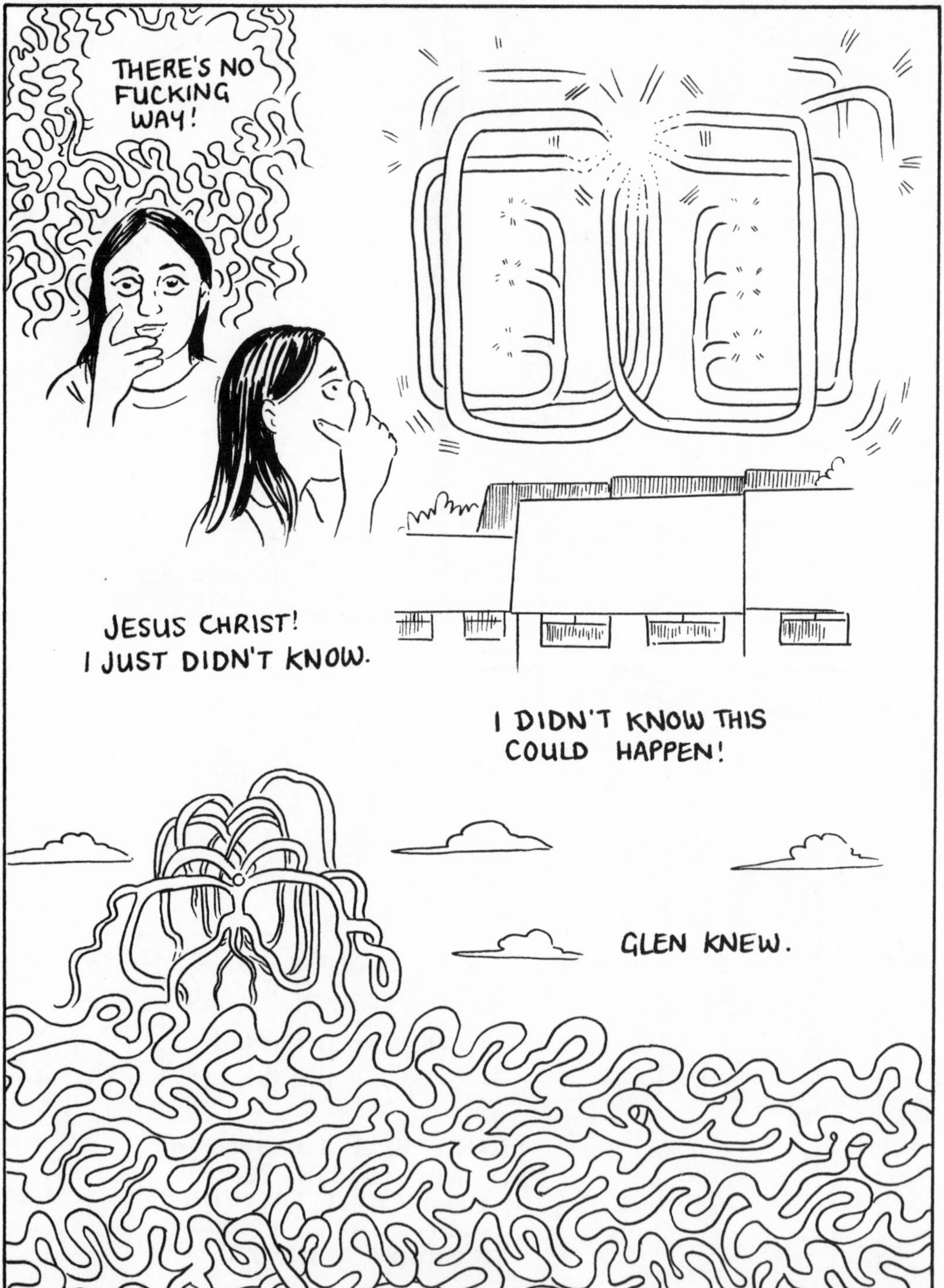
THERE'S NO FUCKING WAY!
JESUS CHRIST! I JUST DIDN'T KNOW.
I DIDN'T KNOW THIS COULD HAPPEN!
GLEN KNEW.

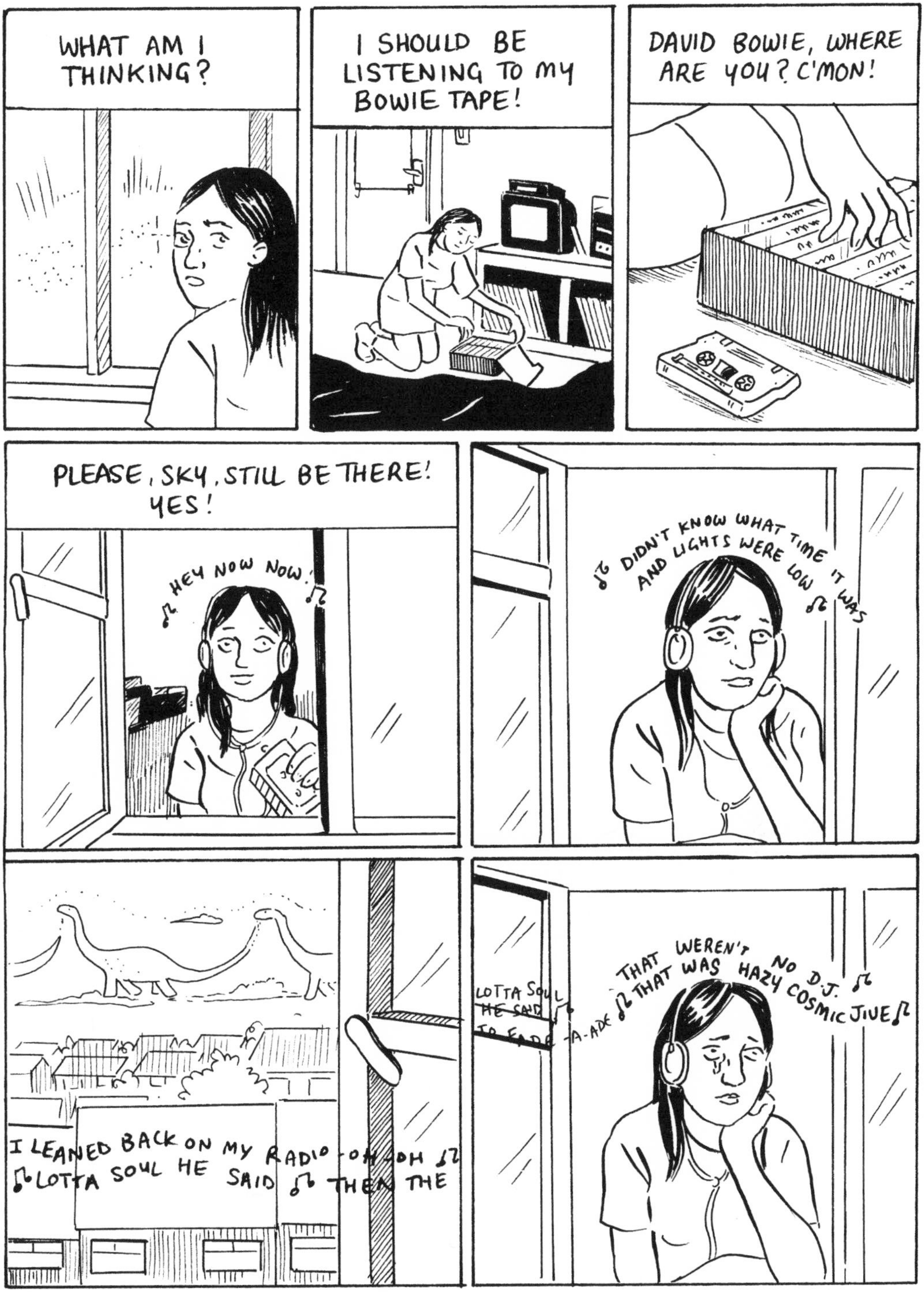
WHAT AM I THINKING?
I SHOULD BE LISTENING TO MY BOWIE TAPE!
DAVID BOWIE, WHERE ARE YOU? C'MON!
PLEASE, SKY, STILL BE THERE! YES!
HEY NOW NOW!
DIDN'T KNOW WHAT TIME IT WAS AND LIGHTS WERE LOW
I LEANED BACK ON MY RADIO-OH-OH
LOTTA SOUL HE SAID THEN THE
LOTTA SOUL HE SAID TO FADE-A-ADE
THAT WEREN'T NO D.J. THAT WAS HAZY COSMIC JIVE

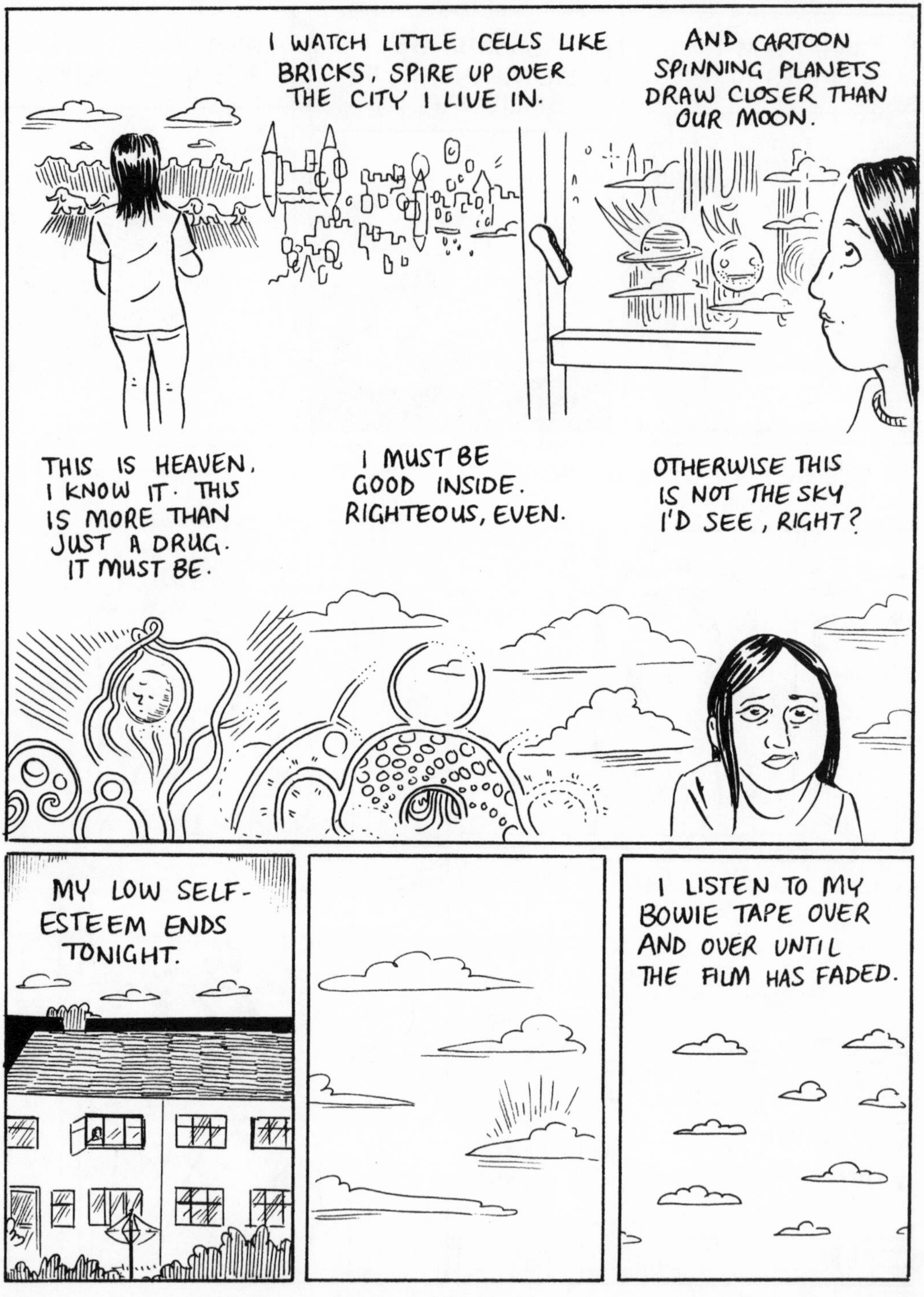
I WATCH LITTLE CELLS LIKE BRICKS, SPIRE UP OVER THE CITY I LIVE IN.
AND CARTOON SPINNING PLANETS DRAW CLOSER THAN OUR MOON.
THIS IS HEAVEN. I KNOW IT. THIS IS MORE THAN JUST A DRUG. IT MUST BE.
I MUST BE GOOD INSIDE. RIGHTEOUS, EVEN.
OTHERWISE THIS IS NOT THE SKY I'D SEE, RIGHT?
MY LOW SELF-ESTEEM ENDS TONIGHT.
I LISTEN TO MY BOWIE TAPE OVER AND OVER UNTIL THE FILM HAS FADED.

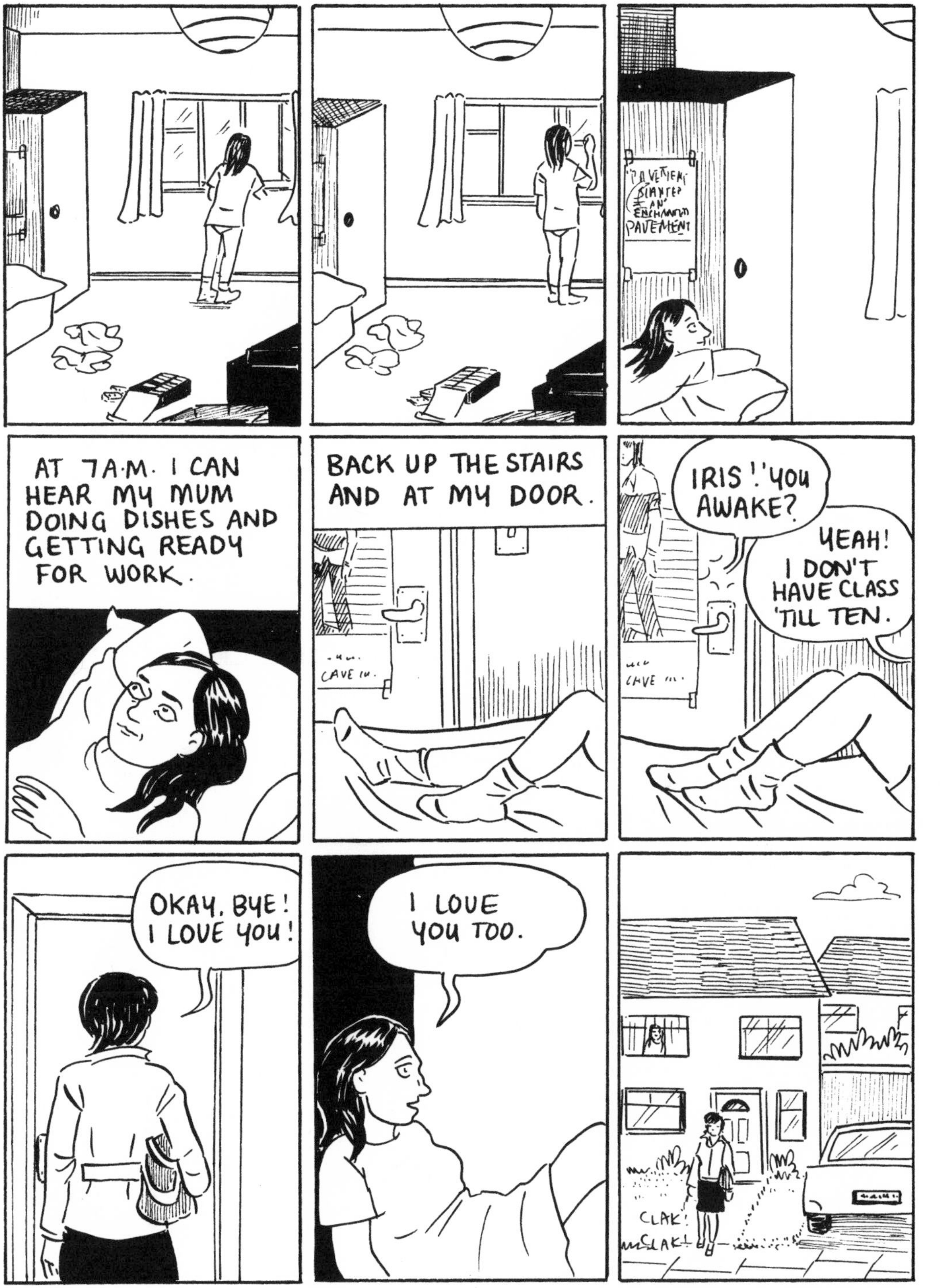
AT 7A.M. I CAN HEAR MY MUM DOING DISHES AND GETTING READY FOR WORK.
BACK UP THE STAIRS AND AT MY DOOR.
IRIS! YOU AWAKE?
YEAH! I DON'T HAVE CLASS 'TILL TEN.
OKAY. BYE! I LOVE YOU!
I LOVE YOU TOO.
CLAK!
CLAK!

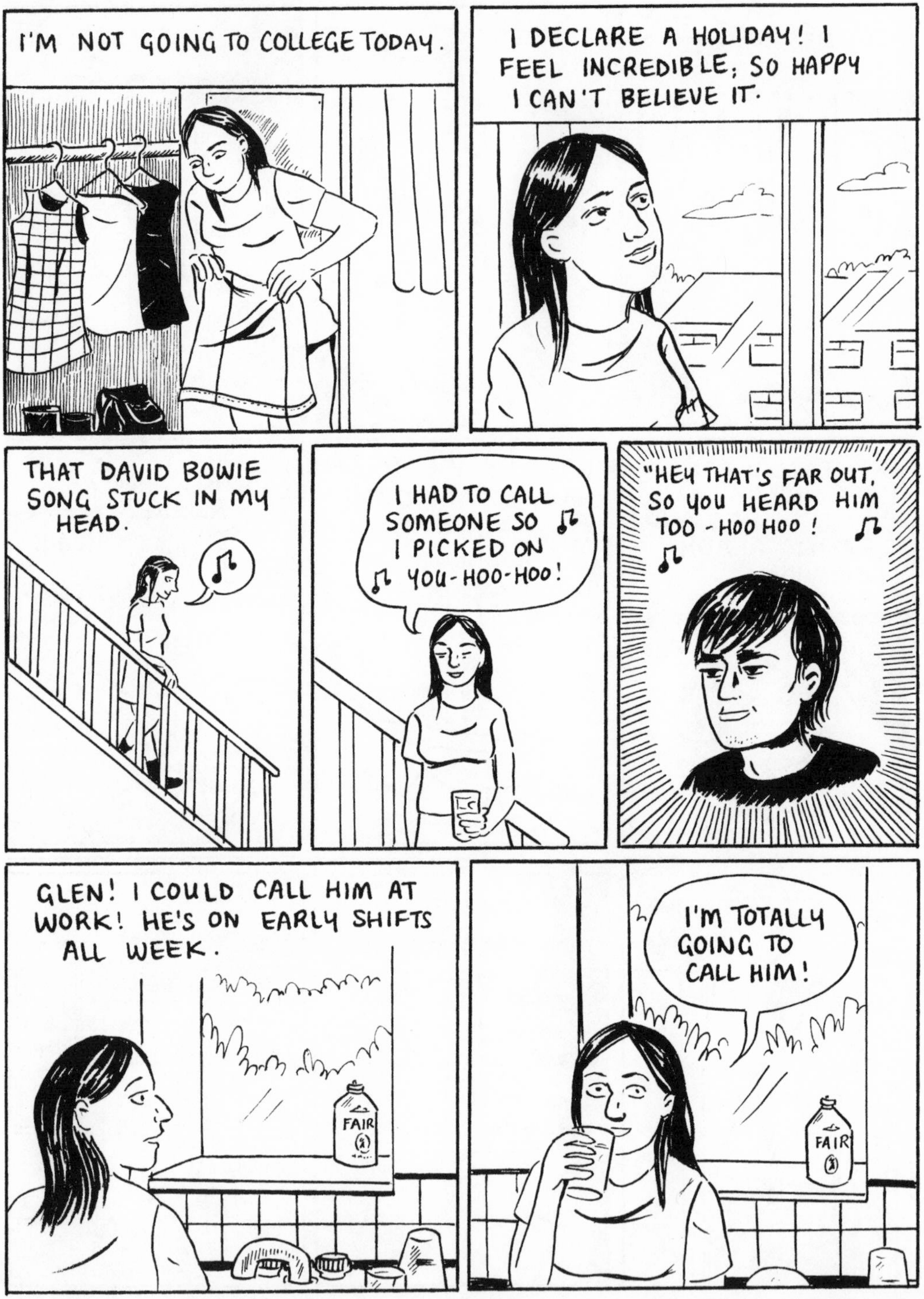
I'M NOT GOING TO COLLEGE TODAY.
I DECLARE A HOLIDAY! I FEEL INCREDIBLE; SO HAPPY I CAN'T BELIEVE IT.
THAT DAVID BOWIE SONG STUCK IN MY HEAD.
I HAD TO CALL SOMEONE SO I PICKED ON YOU-HOO-HOO!
"HEY THAT'S FAR OUT, SO YOU HEARD HIM TOO-HOO HOO!
GLEN! I COULD CALL HIM AT WORK! HE'S ON EARLY SHIFTS ALL WEEK.
FAIR
I'M TOTALLY GOING TO CALL HIM!
FAIR

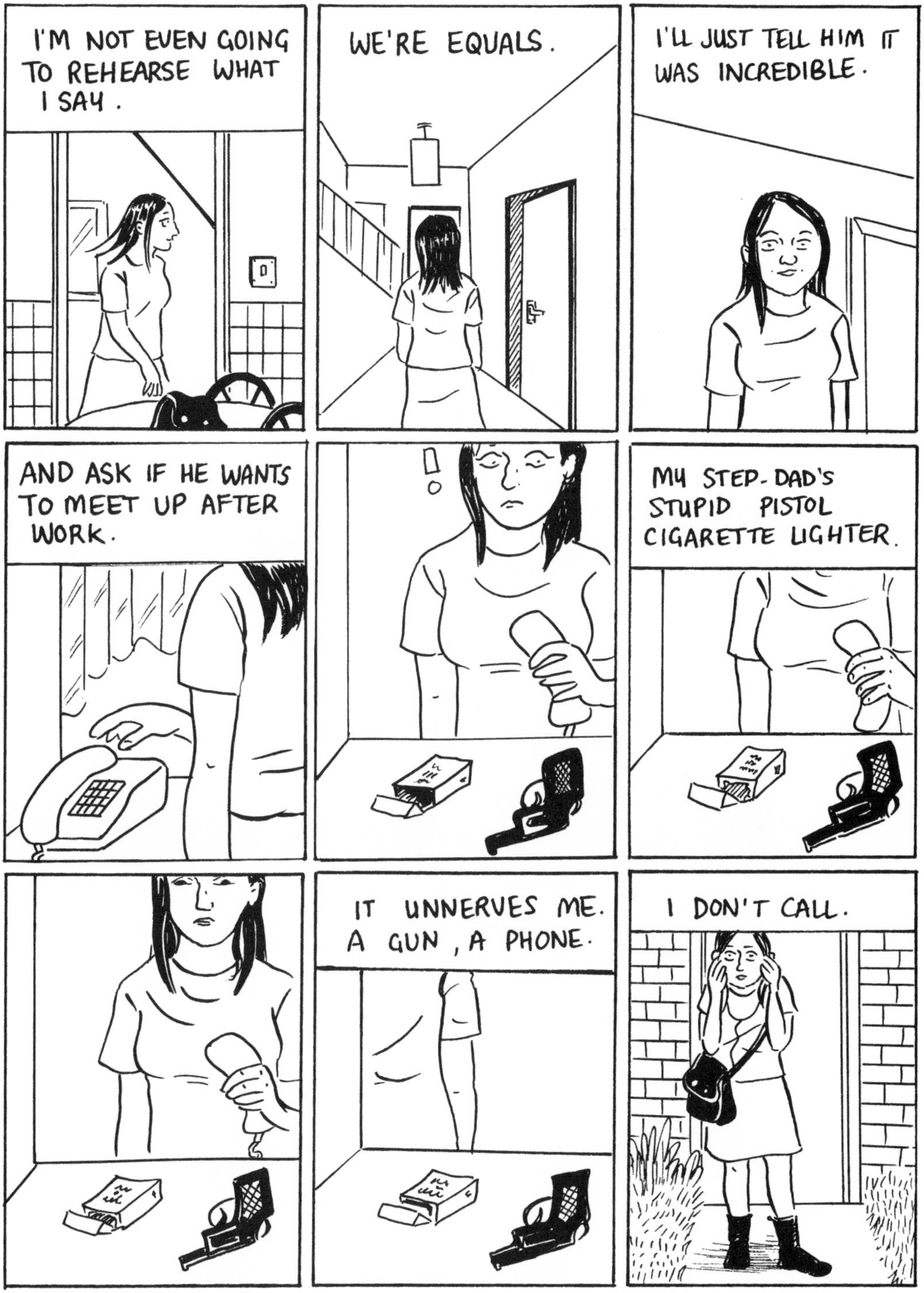
I'M NOT EVEN GOING TO REHEARSE WHAT I SAY.
WE'RE EQUALS.
I'LL JUST TELL HIM IT WAS INCREDIBLE.
AND ASK IF HE WANTS TO MEET UP AFTER WORK.
!
MY STEP-DAD'S STUPID PISTOL CIGARETTE LIGHTER.
IT UNNERVES ME. A GUN, A PHONE.
I DON'T CALL.

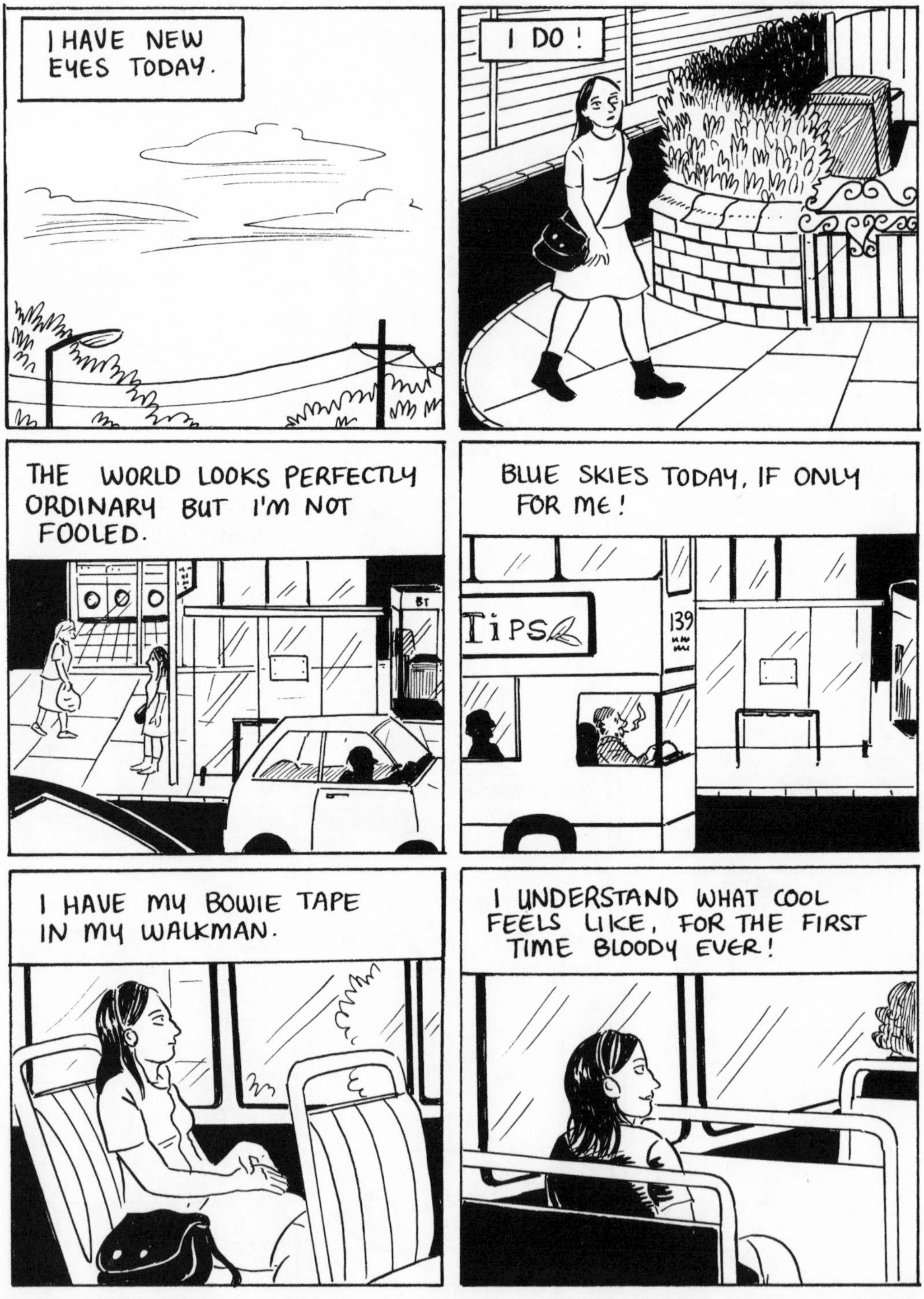
I HAVE NEW EYES TODAY.
I DO!
THE WORLD LOOKS PERFECTLY ORDINARY BUT I'M NOT FOOLED.
BT
BLUE SKIES TODAY, IF ONLY FOR ME!
TIPS
139
I HAVE MY BOWIE TAPE IN MY WALKMAN.
I UNDERSTAND WHAT COOL FEELS LIKE, FOR THE FIRST TIME BLOODY EVER!

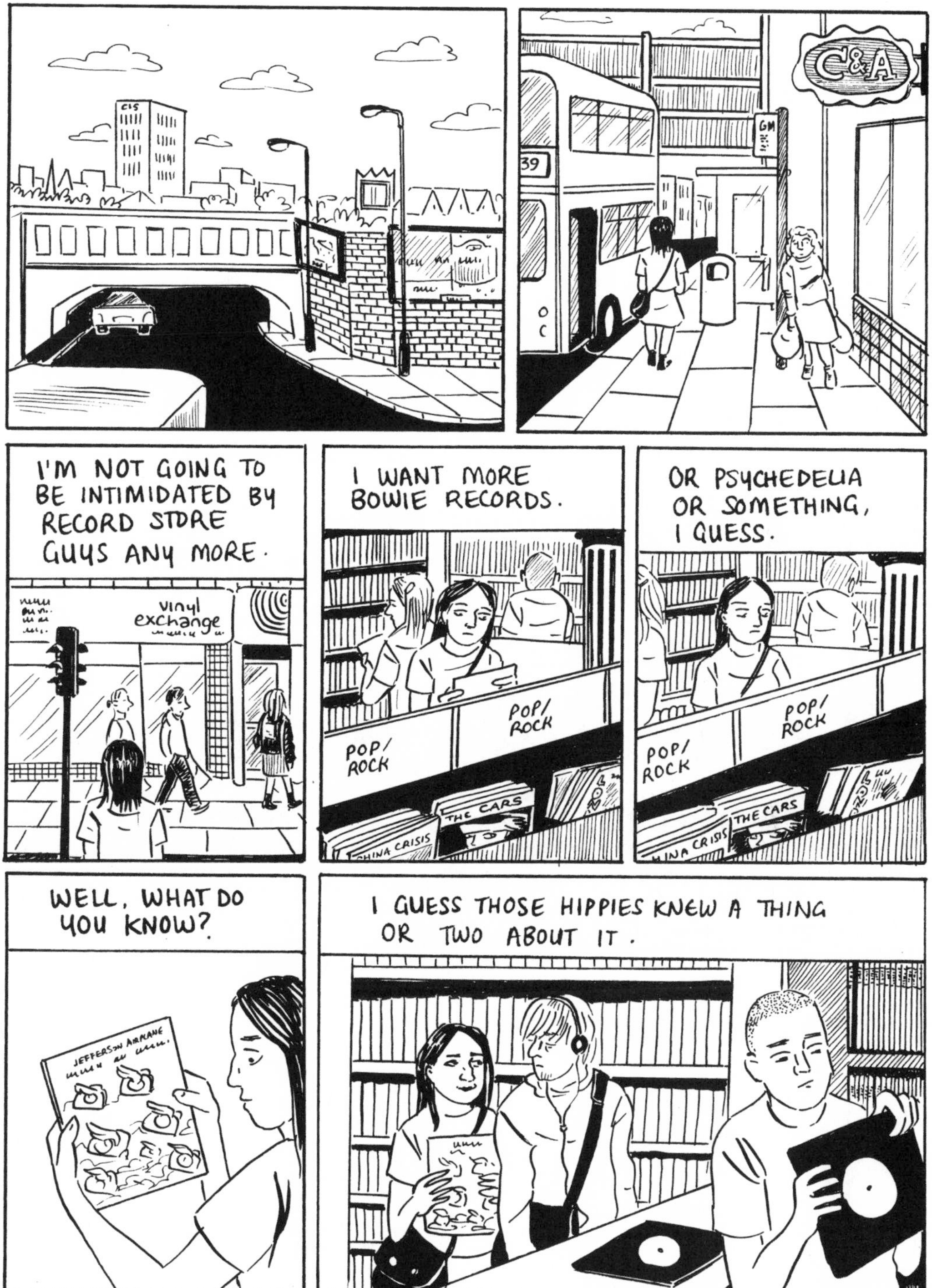
C&A
vinyl exchange
I'M NOT GOING TO BE INTIMIDATED BY RECORD STORE GUYS ANY MORE.
I WANT MORE BOWIE RECORDS.
POP/ROCK
POP/ROCK
THE CARS
CHINA CRISIS
OR PSYCHEDELIA OR SOMETHING, I GUESS.
POP/ROCK
POP/ROCK
THE CARS
WELL, WHAT DO YOU KNOW?
JEFFERSON AIRPLANE
I GUESS THOSE HIPPIES KNEW A THING OR TWO ABOUT IT.

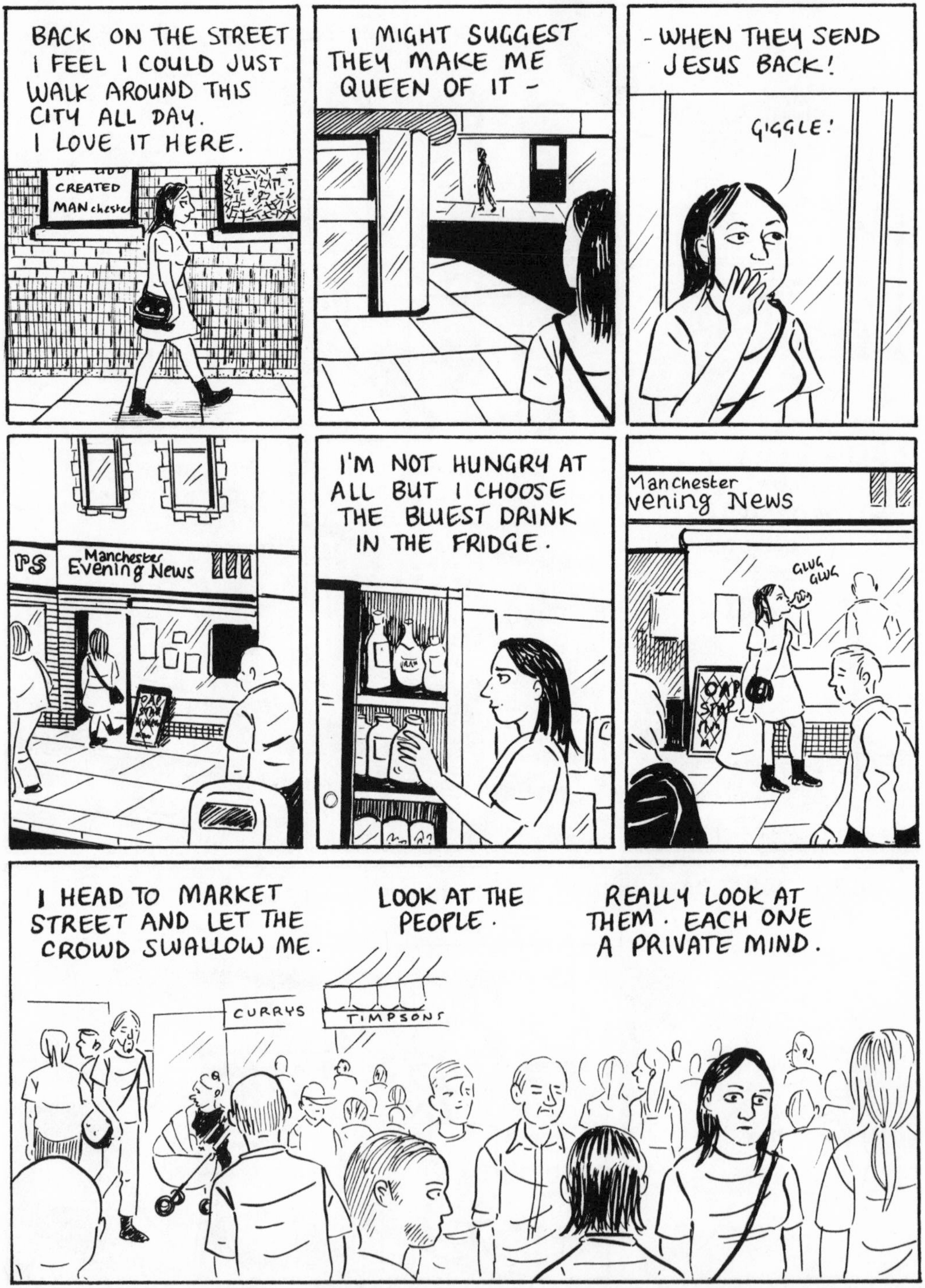
BACK ON THE STREET I FEEL I COULD JUST WALK AROUND THIS CITY ALL DAY. I LOVE IT HERE.
CREATED
MANchester
I MIGHT SUGGEST THEY MAKE ME QUEEN OF IT -
- WHEN THEY SEND JESUS BACK!
GIGGLE!
Manchester Evening News
I'M NOT HUNGRY AT ALL BUT I CHOOSE THE BLUEST DRINK IN THE FRIDGE.
Manchester
vening News
GLUG GLUG
I HEAD TO MARKET STREET AND LET THE CROWD SWALLOW ME.
LOOK AT THE PEOPLE.
REALLY LOOK AT THEM. EACH ONE A PRIVATE MIND.
CURRYS
TIMPSONS

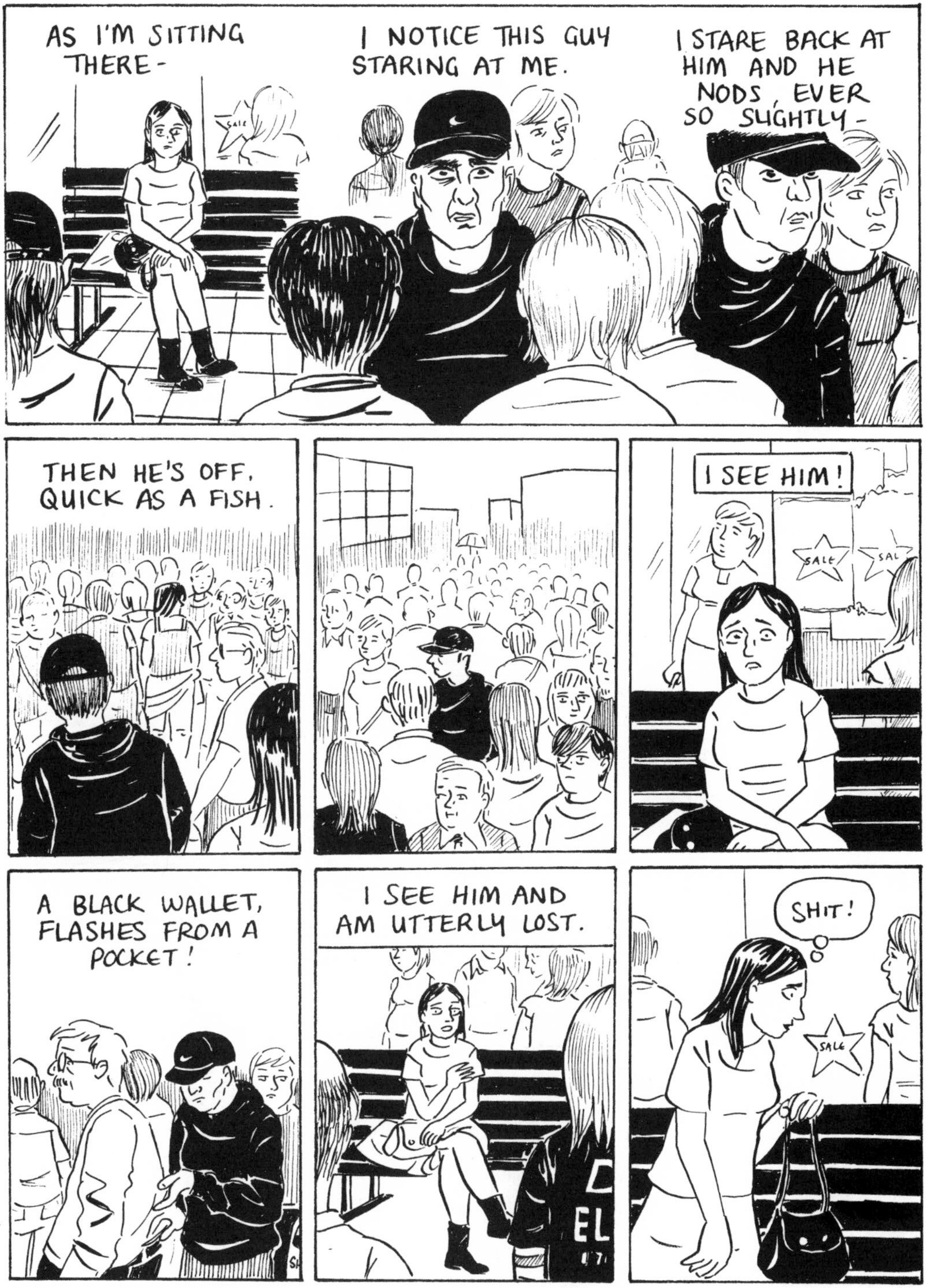
AS I'M SITTING THERE-
I NOTICE THIS GUY STARING AT ME.
I STARE BACK AT HIM AND HE NODS, EVER SO SLIGHTLY-
THEN HE'S OFF, QUICK AS A FISH.
I SEE HIM!
A BLACK WALLET, FLASHES FROM A POCKET!
I SEE HIM AND AM UTTERLY LOST.
SHIT!

HAVE YOU SEEN THE SAUCERS?

blur

I'M SUFFOCATING. I CAN'T BE INSIDE.

I TAKE MY STASH AND WALKMAN AND TAKE A WALK DOWN TO THE RESERVOIR, PAST THE SCRUBLAND, PAST THE OLD WORLD WAR TWO BUNKERS. I SIT ACROSS FROM THE OLD POWERSTATION.

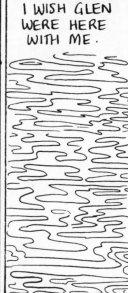

I WISH GLEN WERE HERE WITH ME.

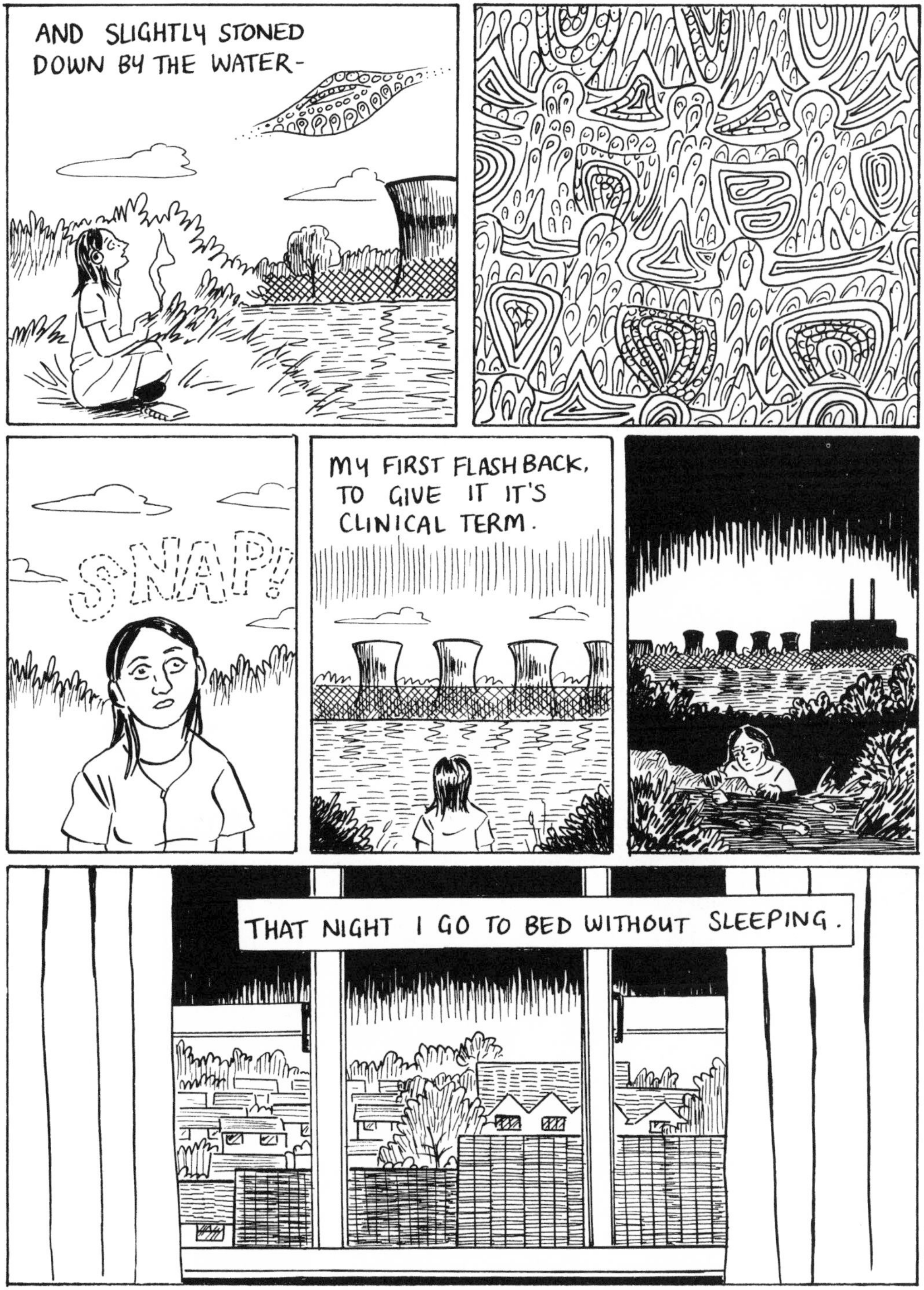
AND SLIGHTLY STONED DOWN BY THE WATER-
SNAP!
MY FIRST FLASHBACK, TO GIVE IT IT'S CLINICAL TERM.
THAT NIGHT I GO TO BED WITHOUT SLEEPING.

THE NEXT MORNING I AVOID MY PARENTS AND GO TO COLLEGE.

BUT INSTEAD OF GOING TO CLASS, I SMOKE WEED WITH THIS GUY SAMIR.

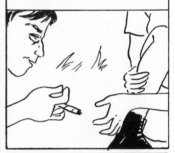

THERE'S THIS FIELD AT THE BACK OF THE CAMPUS WITH THESE ABANDONED CABINS. I GUESS THEY USED TO BE CLASSROOMS. ANYWAY, IT'S A GOOD PLACE FOR A SMOKE...

WELL, HE'S A NICE PERSON, REALLY FUNNY, BUT I FEEL SO TONGUE-TIED, IT'S AWFUL.

AND I HAVE NO IDEA WHAT HE JUST SAID TO ME.

RIGHT?

FAR OUT!

WHY THE HELL DID I SAY THAT? I'M SUCH A SPAZ.

HA HA, FUCKIN' YEAH, HA HA!

?

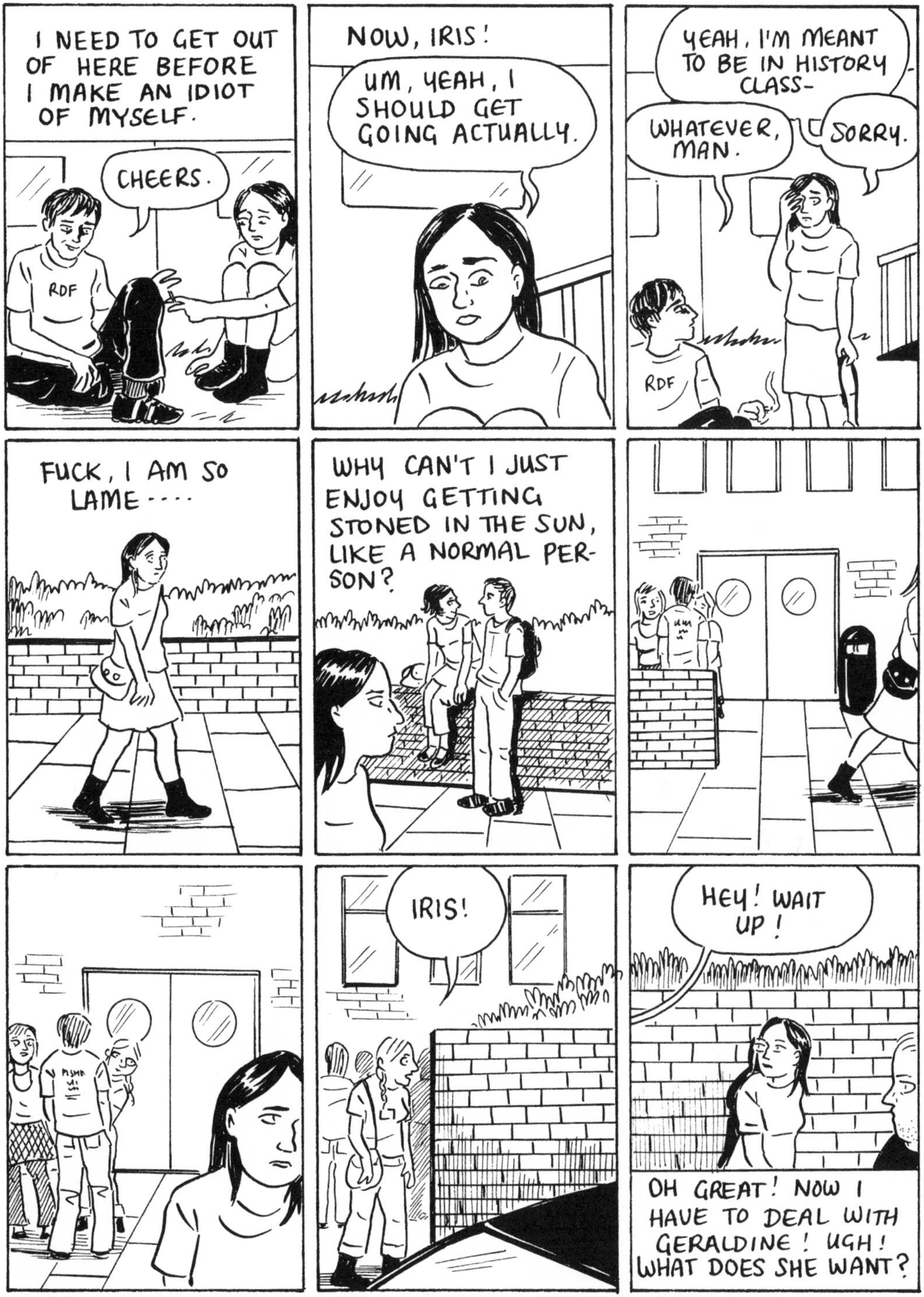
I NEED TO GET OUT OF HERE BEFORE I MAKE AN IDIOT OF MYSELF.
CHEERS.
RDF
NOW, IRIS!
UM, YEAH, I SHOULD GET GOING ACTUALLY.
YEAH, I'M MEANT TO BE IN HISTORY CLASS-
WHATEVER, MAN.
SORRY.
RDF
FUCK, I AM SO LAME....
WHY CAN'T I JUST ENJOY GETTING STONED IN THE SUN, LIKE A NORMAL PER-SON?
IRIS!
HEY! WAIT UP!
OH GREAT! NOW I HAVE TO DEAL WITH GERALDINE! UGH! WHAT DOES SHE WANT?

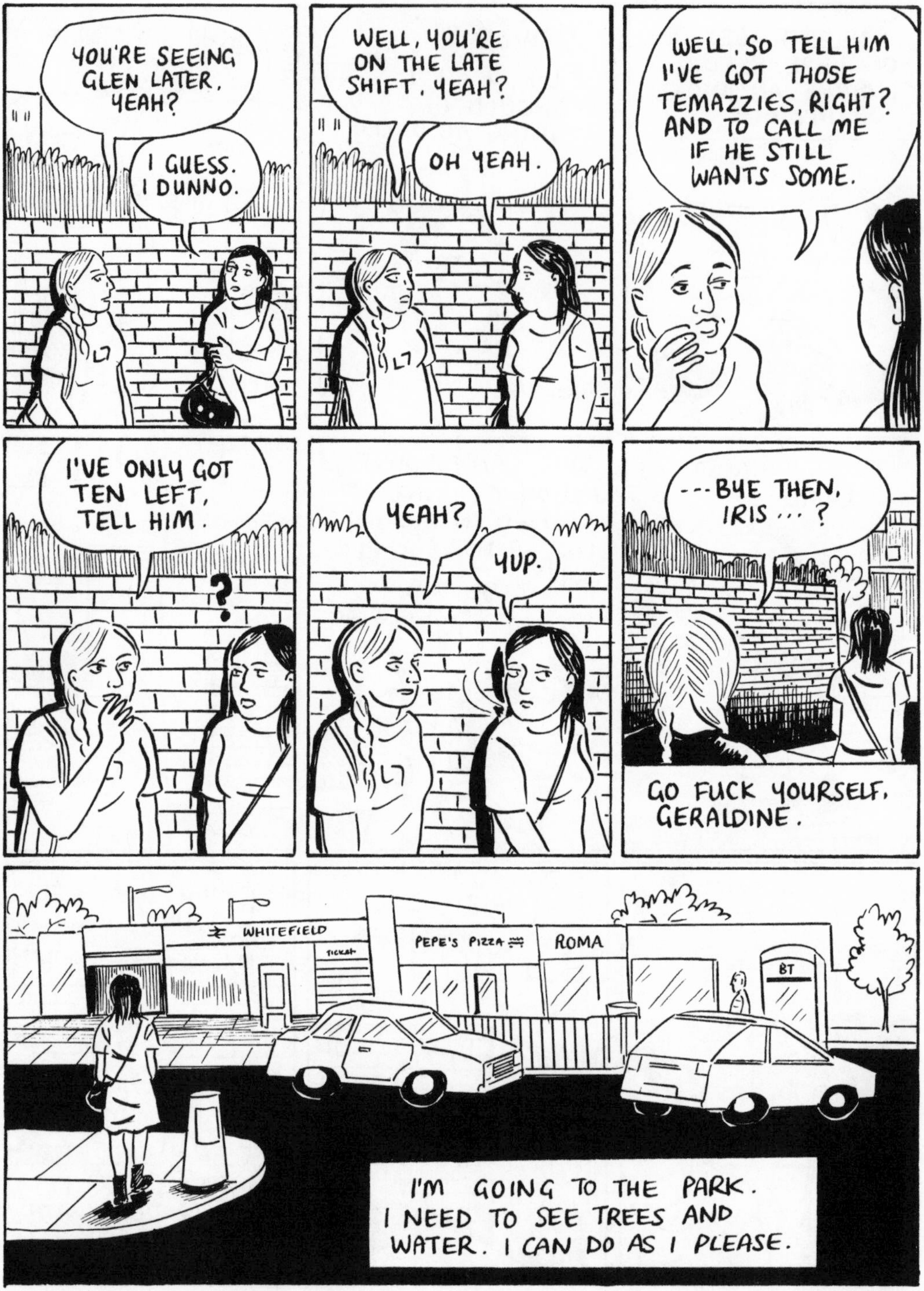
YOU'RE SEEING GLEN LATER, YEAH?
I GUESS. I DUNNO.
WELL, YOU'RE ON THE LATE SHIFT, YEAH?
OH YEAH.
WELL, SO TELL HIM I'VE GOT THOSE TEMAZZIES, RIGHT? AND TO CALL ME IF HE STILL WANTS SOME.
I'VE ONLY GOT TEN LEFT, TELL HIM.
?
YEAH?
YUP.
---BYE THEN, IRIS ... ?
GO FUCK YOURSELF, GERALDINE.
WHITEFIELD
PEPE'S PIZZA
ROMA
BT
I'M GOING TO THE PARK. I NEED TO SEE TREES AND WATER. I CAN DO AS I PLEASE.

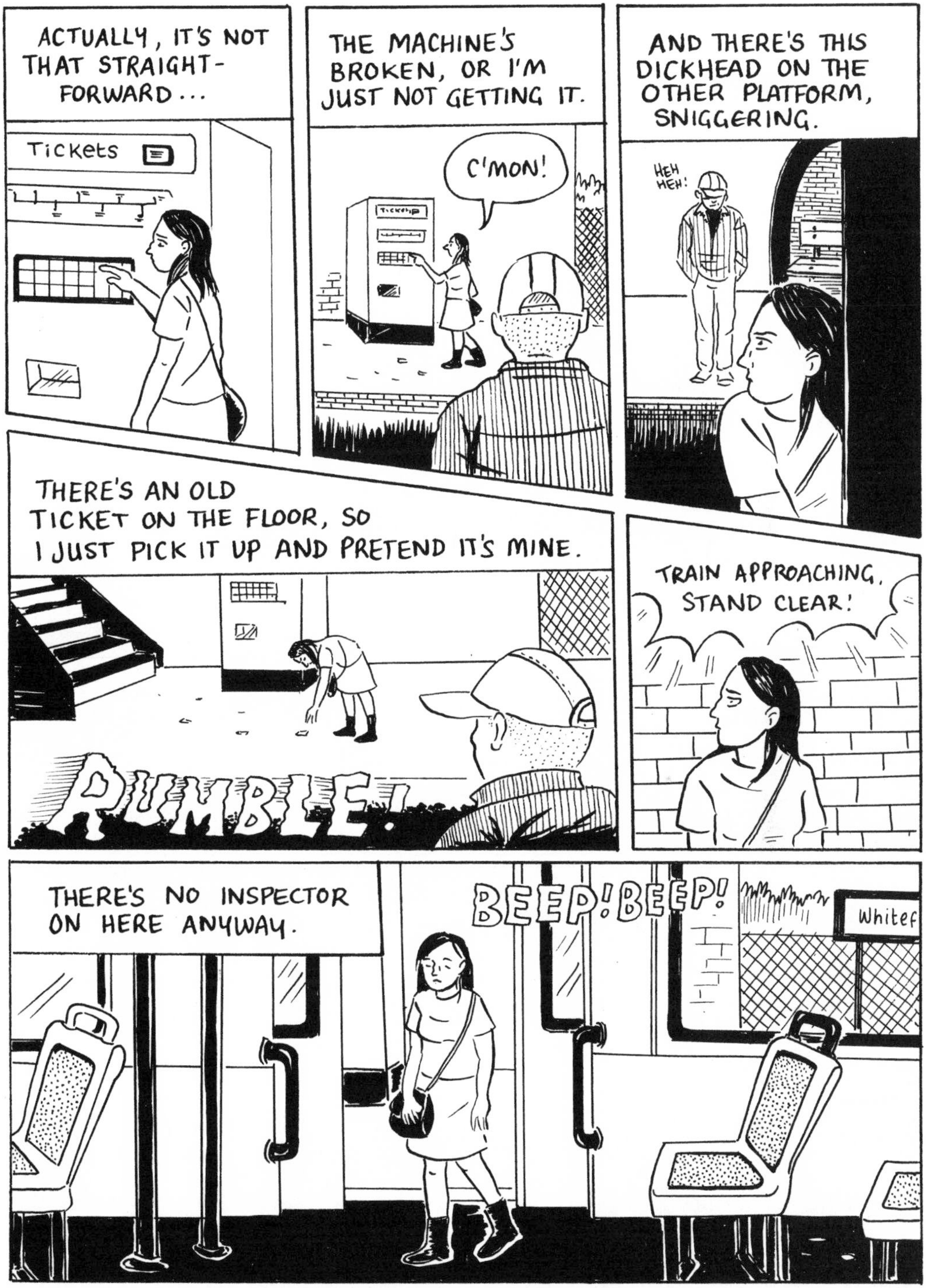

ACTUALLY, IT'S NOT THAT STRAIGHT-FORWARD...
Tickets
THE MACHINE'S BROKEN, OR I'M JUST NOT GETTING IT.
C'MON!
AND THERE'S THIS DICKHEAD ON THE OTHER PLATFORM, SNIGGERING.
HEH HEH!
THERE'S AN OLD TICKET ON THE FLOOR, SO I JUST PICK IT UP AND PRETEND IT'S MINE.
RUMBLE!
TRAIN APPROACHING. STAND CLEAR!
THERE'S NO INSPECTOR ON HERE ANYWAY.
BEEP! BEEP!
Whitef

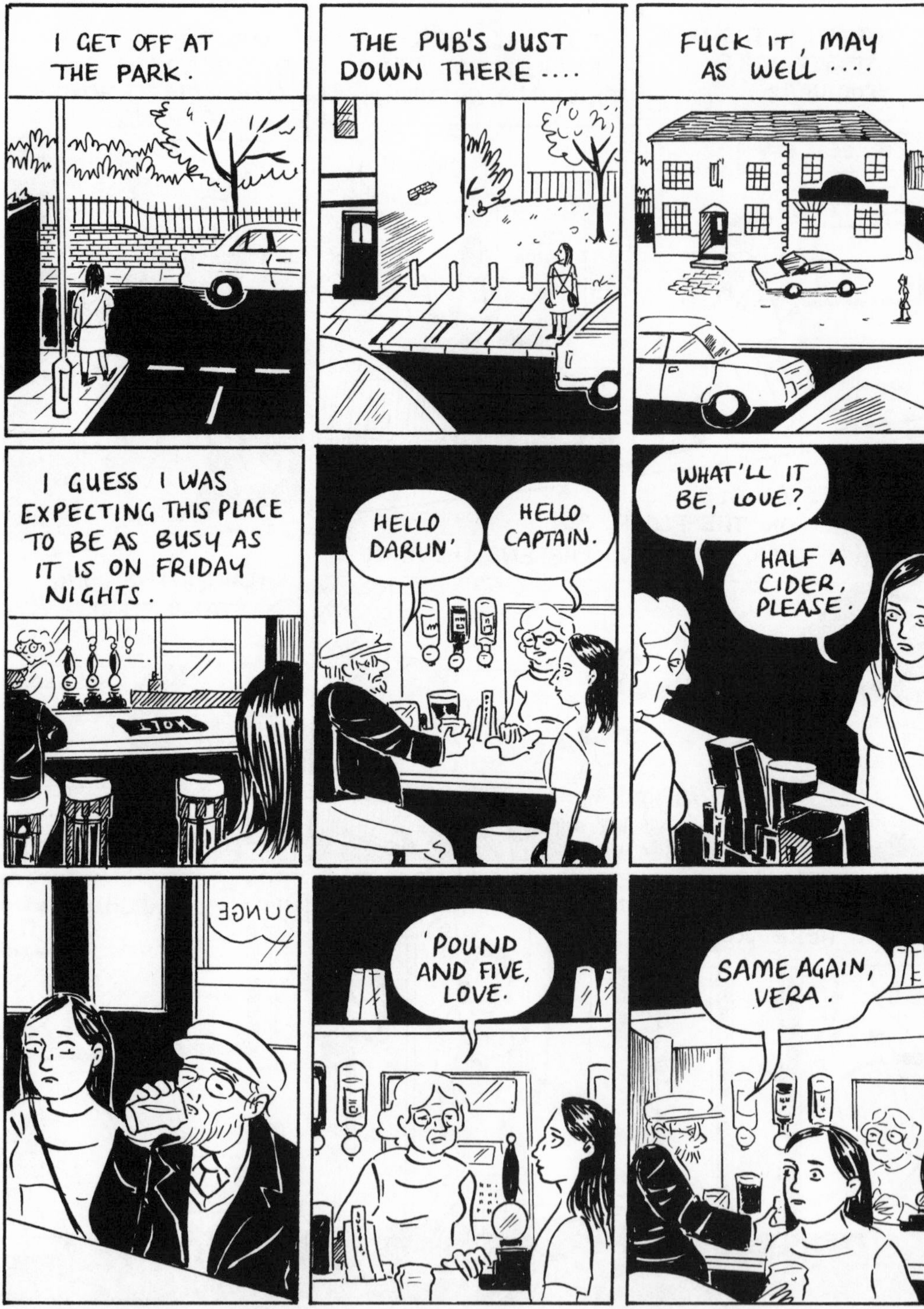
I GET OFF AT THE PARK.
THE PUB'S JUST DOWN THERE....
FUCK IT, MAY AS WELL....
I GUESS I WAS EXPECTING THIS PLACE TO BE AS BUSY AS IT IS ON FRIDAY NIGHTS.
HELLO DARLIN'
HELLO CAPTAIN.
WHAT'LL IT BE, LOVE?
HALF A CIDER, PLEASE.
'POUND AND FIVE, LOVE.
SAME AGAIN, VERA.

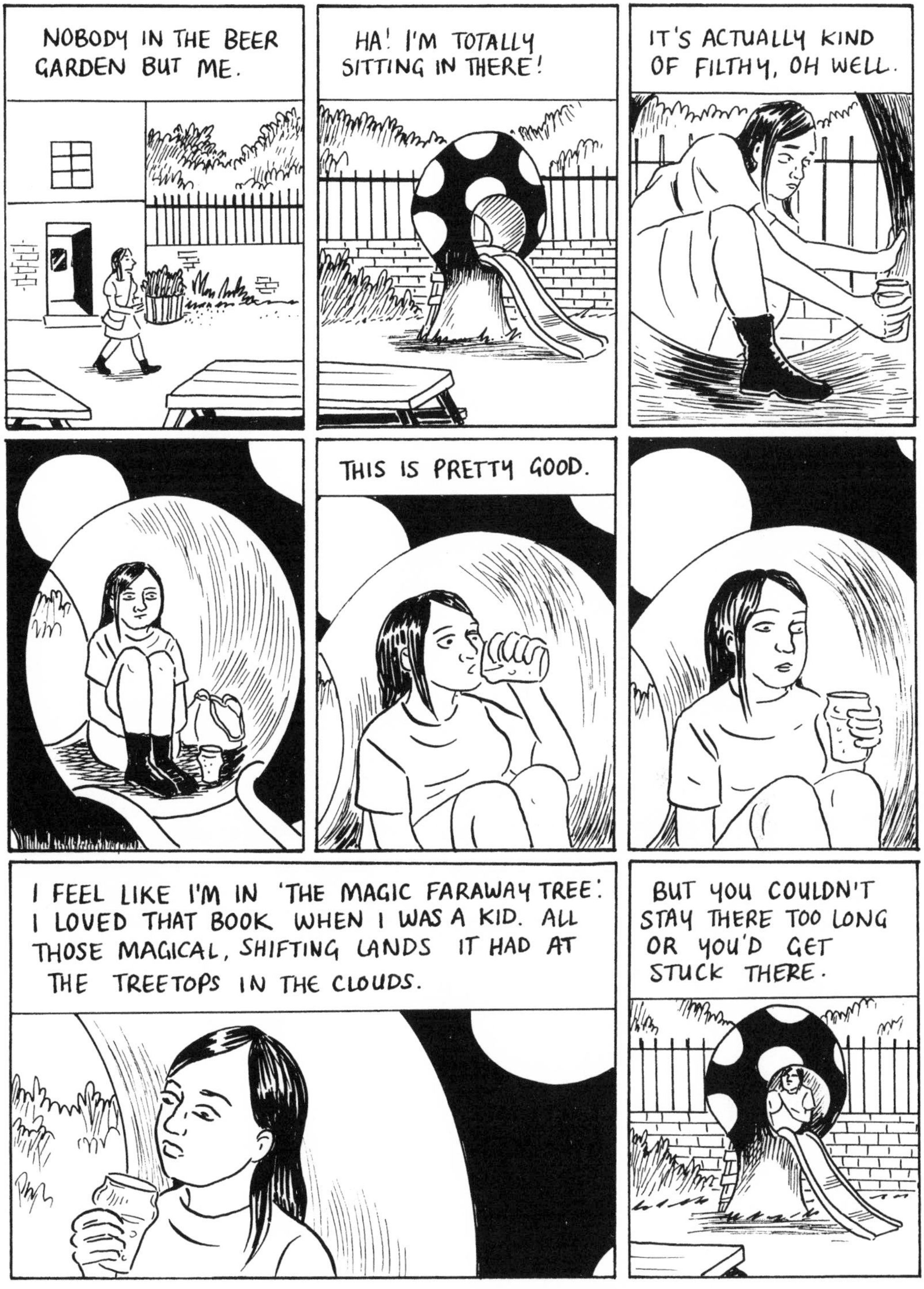
NOBODY IN THE BEER GARDEN BUT ME.
HA! I'M TOTALLY SITTING IN THERE!
IT'S ACTUALLY KIND OF FILTHY, OH WELL.
THIS IS PRETTY GOOD.
I FEEL LIKE I'M IN 'THE MAGIC FARAWAY TREE'. I LOVED THAT BOOK WHEN I WAS A KID. ALL THOSE MAGICAL, SHIFTING LANDS IT HAD AT THE TREETOPS IN THE CLOUDS.
BUT YOU COULDN'T STAY THERE TOO LONG OR YOU'D GET STUCK THERE.

ALL THE THINGS I'VE SEEN — I CAN'T GET THEM DOWN.

SCRITCH SCRATCH!

I'M STUCK IN THIS LIMBO. THE WORLD DOESN'T SEEM QUITE REAL ....

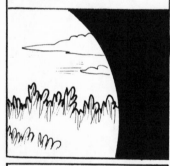

I SAW SOMETHING LIKE HEAVEN.

I WANT TO SEE IT AGAIN.

I WANT TO SEE IT WITH GLEN.

MAYBE IF I PLAY MY BOWIE TAPE HE'LL COME FIND ME.

" I'M IN THIS STUPID PLASTIC MUSHROOM, GLEN! "

HA HA!

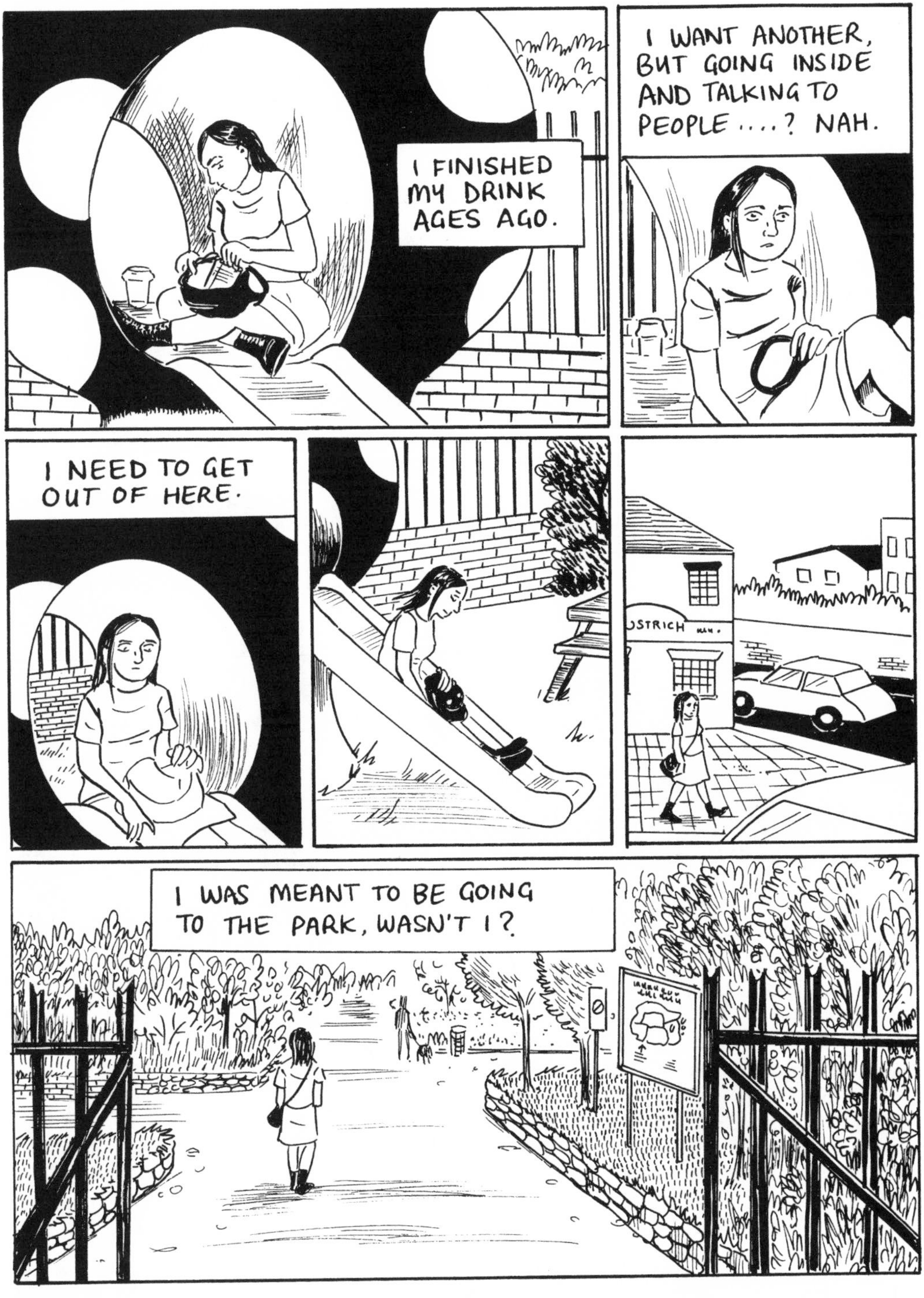
I FINISHED MY DRINK AGES AGO.
I WANT ANOTHER, BUT GOING INSIDE AND TALKING TO PEOPLE....? NAH.
I NEED TO GET OUT OF HERE.
STRICH
I WAS MEANT TO BE GOING TO THE PARK, WASN'T I?

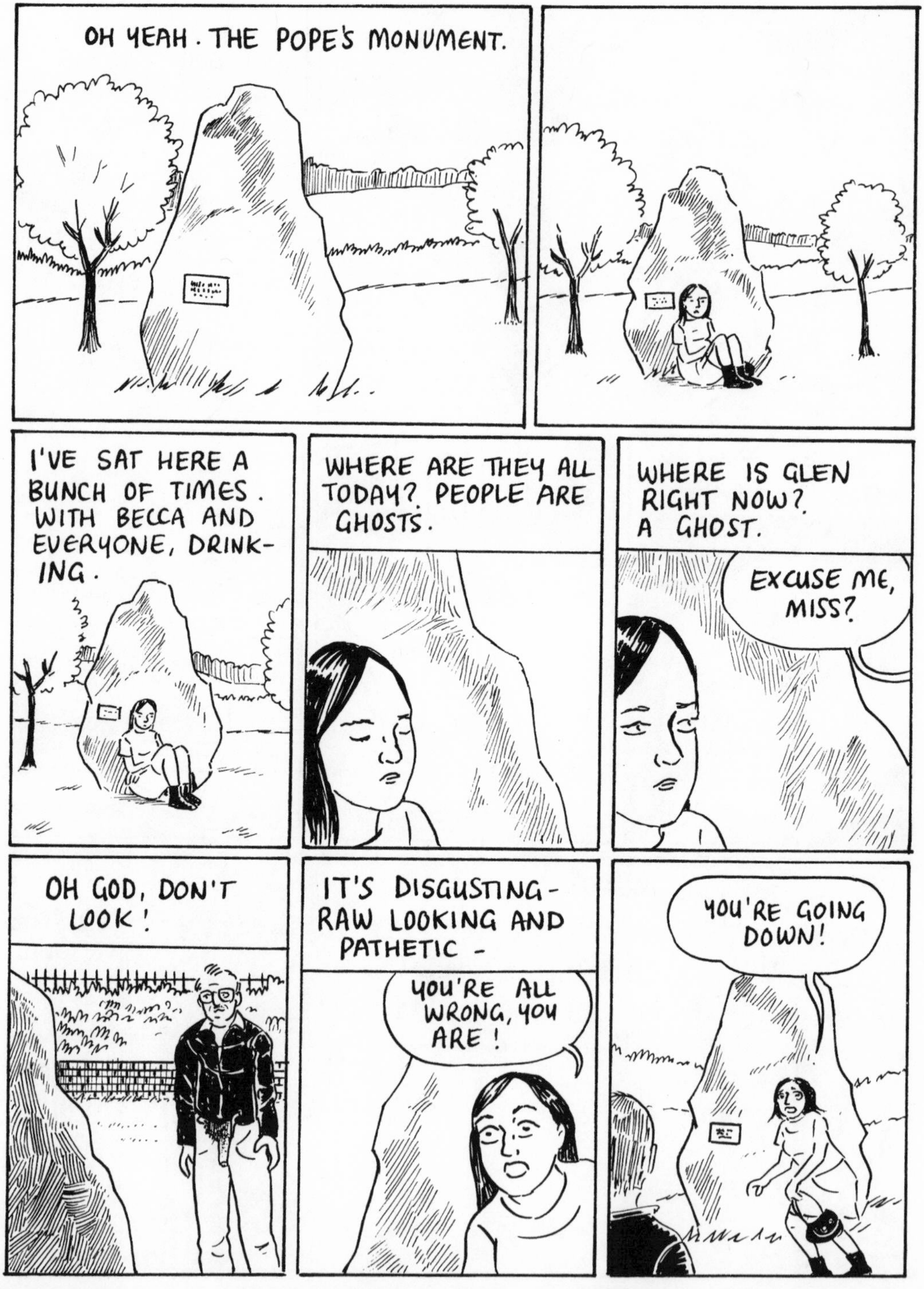
OH YEAH. THE POPE'S MONUMENT.
I'VE SAT HERE A BUNCH OF TIMES. WITH BECCA AND EVERYONE, DRINKING.
WHERE ARE THEY ALL TODAY? PEOPLE ARE GHOSTS.
WHERE IS GLEN RIGHT NOW? A GHOST.
EXCUSE ME, MISS?
OH GOD, DON'T LOOK!
IT'S DISGUSTING - RAW LOOKING AND PATHETIC -
YOU'RE ALL WRONG, YOU ARE!
YOU'RE GOING DOWN!

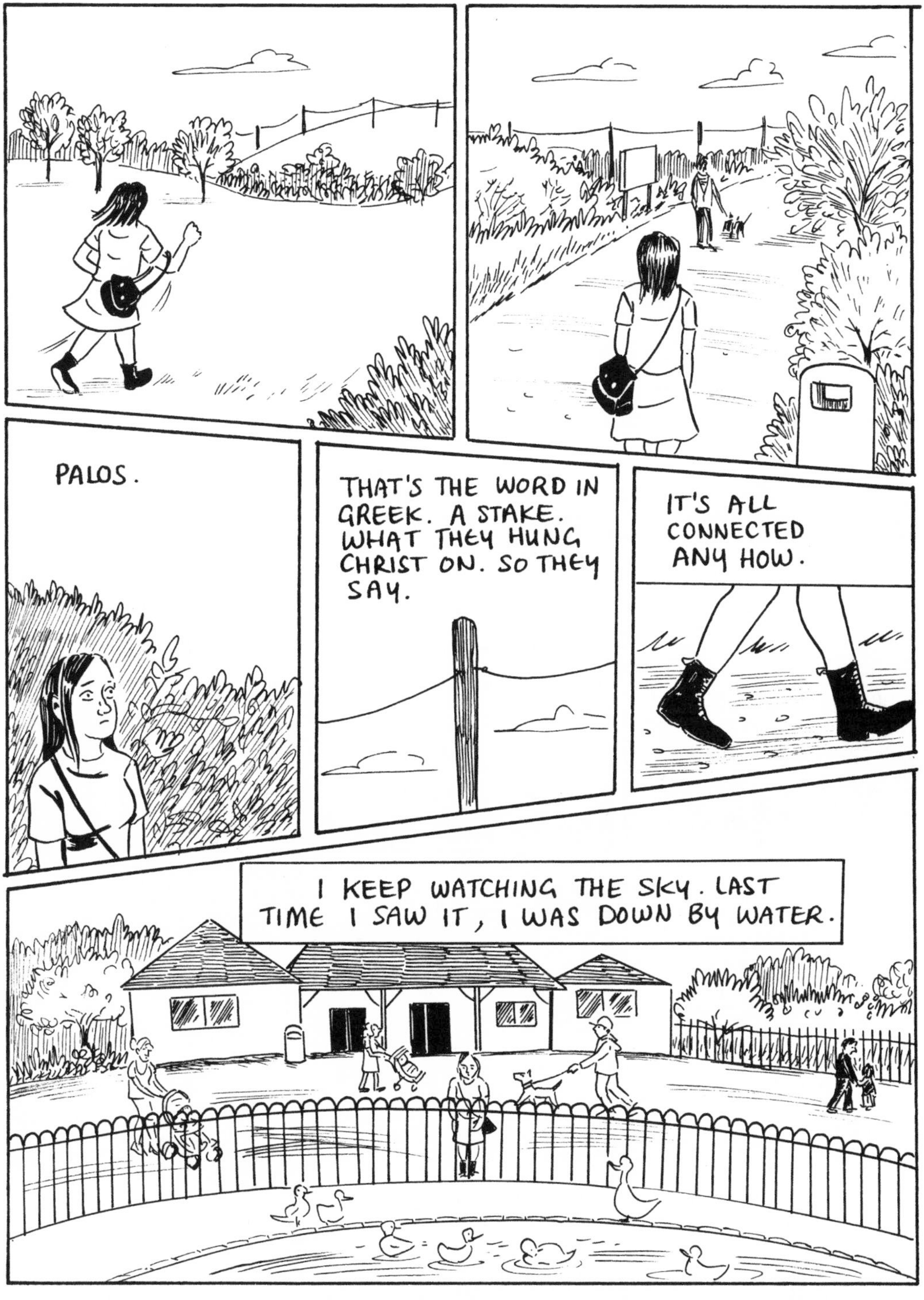
PALOS.
THAT'S THE WORD IN GREEK. A STAKE. WHAT THEY HUNG CHRIST ON. SO THEY SAY.
IT'S ALL CONNECTED ANY HOW.
I KEEP WATCHING THE SKY. LAST TIME I SAW IT, I WAS DOWN BY WATER.

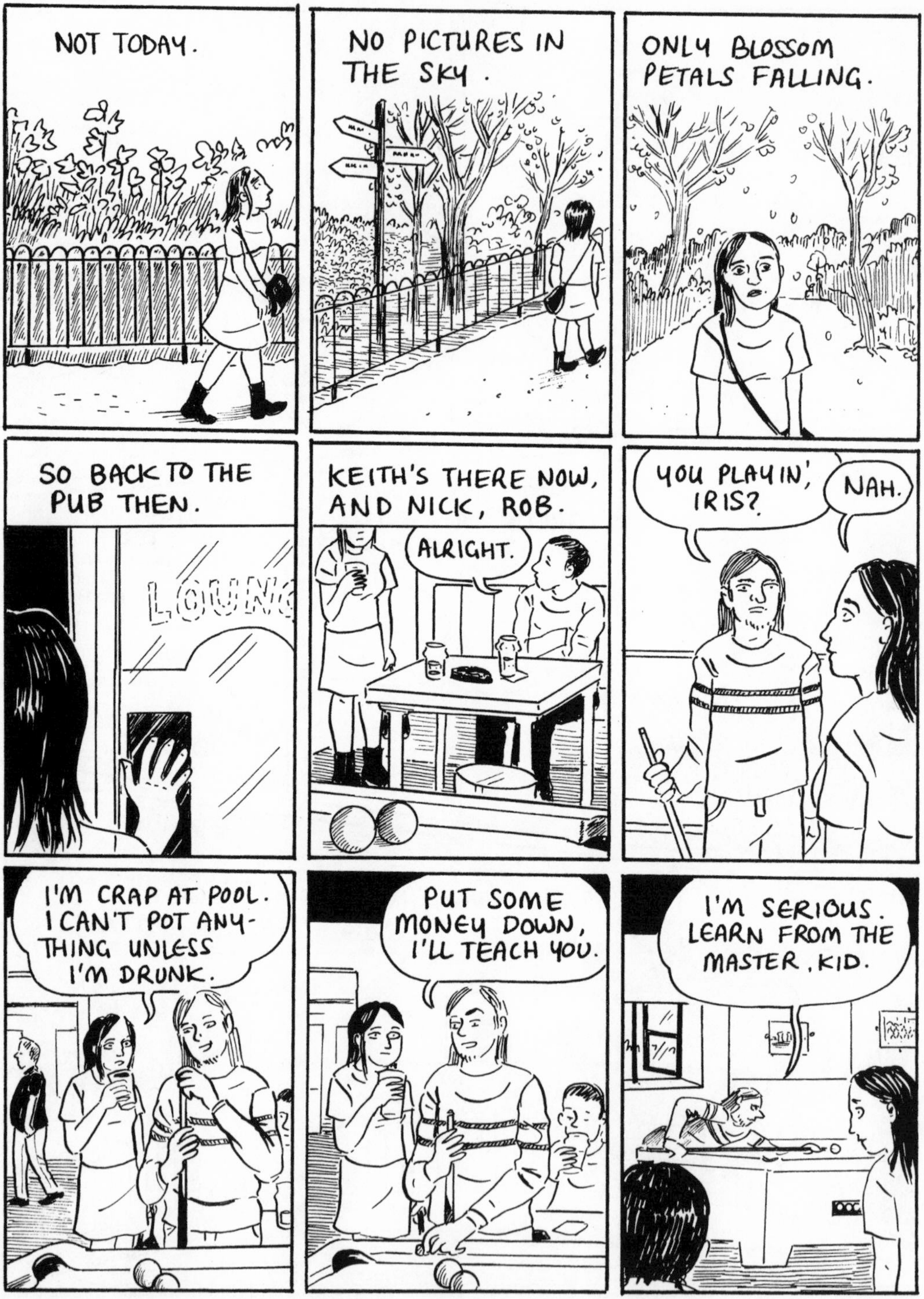
NOT TODAY.
NO PICTURES IN THE SKY.
ONLY BLOSSOM PETALS FALLING.
SO BACK TO THE PUB THEN.
LOUNG
KEITH'S THERE NOW, AND NICK, ROB.
ALRIGHT.
YOU PLAYIN', IRIS?
NAH.
I'M CRAP AT POOL. I CAN'T POT ANY-THING UNLESS I'M DRUNK.
PUT SOME MONEY DOWN, I'LL TEACH YOU.
I'M SERIOUS. LEARN FROM THE MASTER, KID.

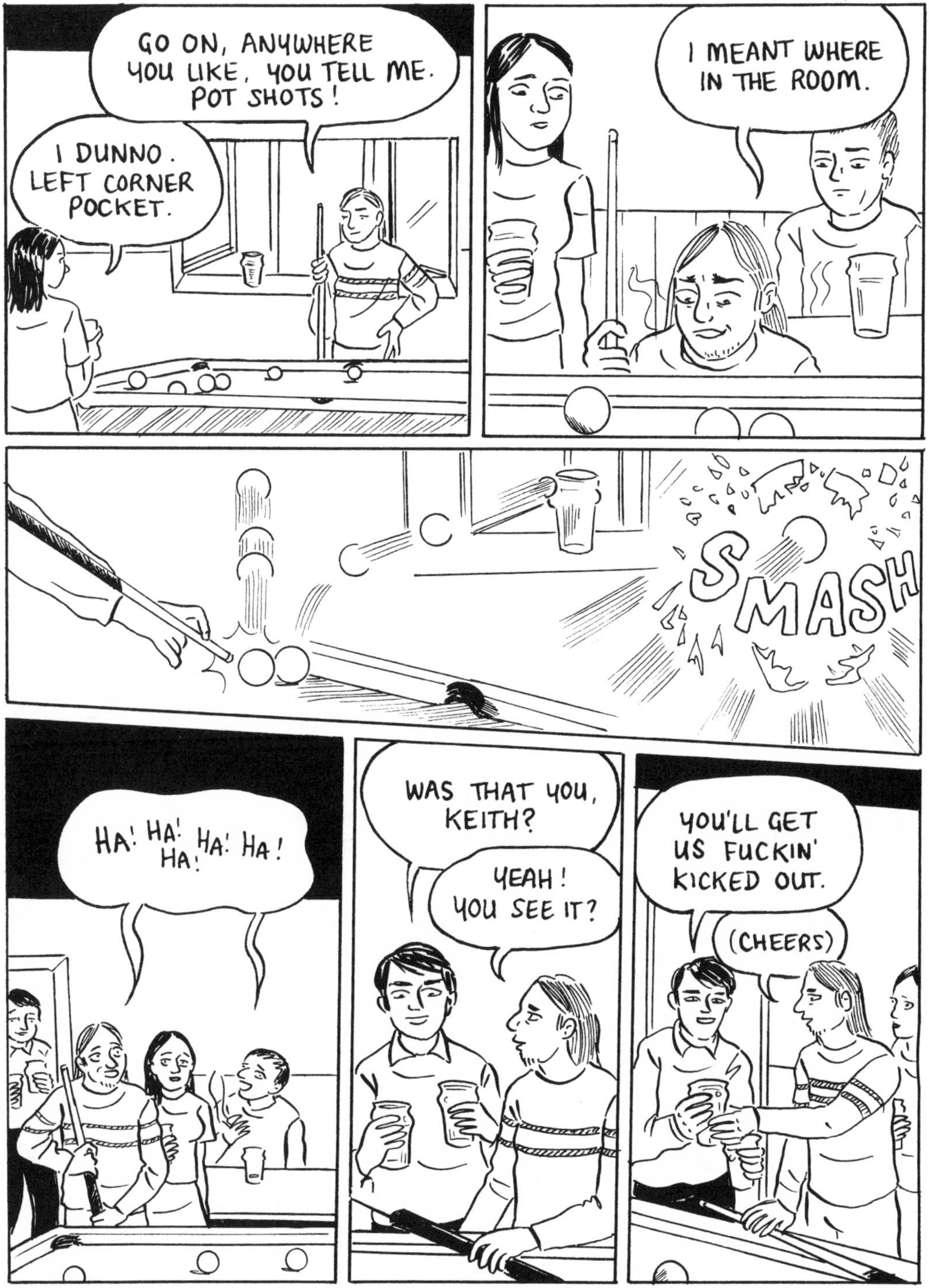
GO ON, ANYWHERE YOU LIKE, YOU TELL ME. POT SHOTS!
I DUNNO. LEFT CORNER POCKET.
I MEANT WHERE IN THE ROOM.
SMASH
HA! HA! HA! HA! HA!
WAS THAT YOU, KEITH?
YEAH! YOU SEE IT?
YOU'LL GET US FUCKIN' KICKED OUT.
(CHEERS)

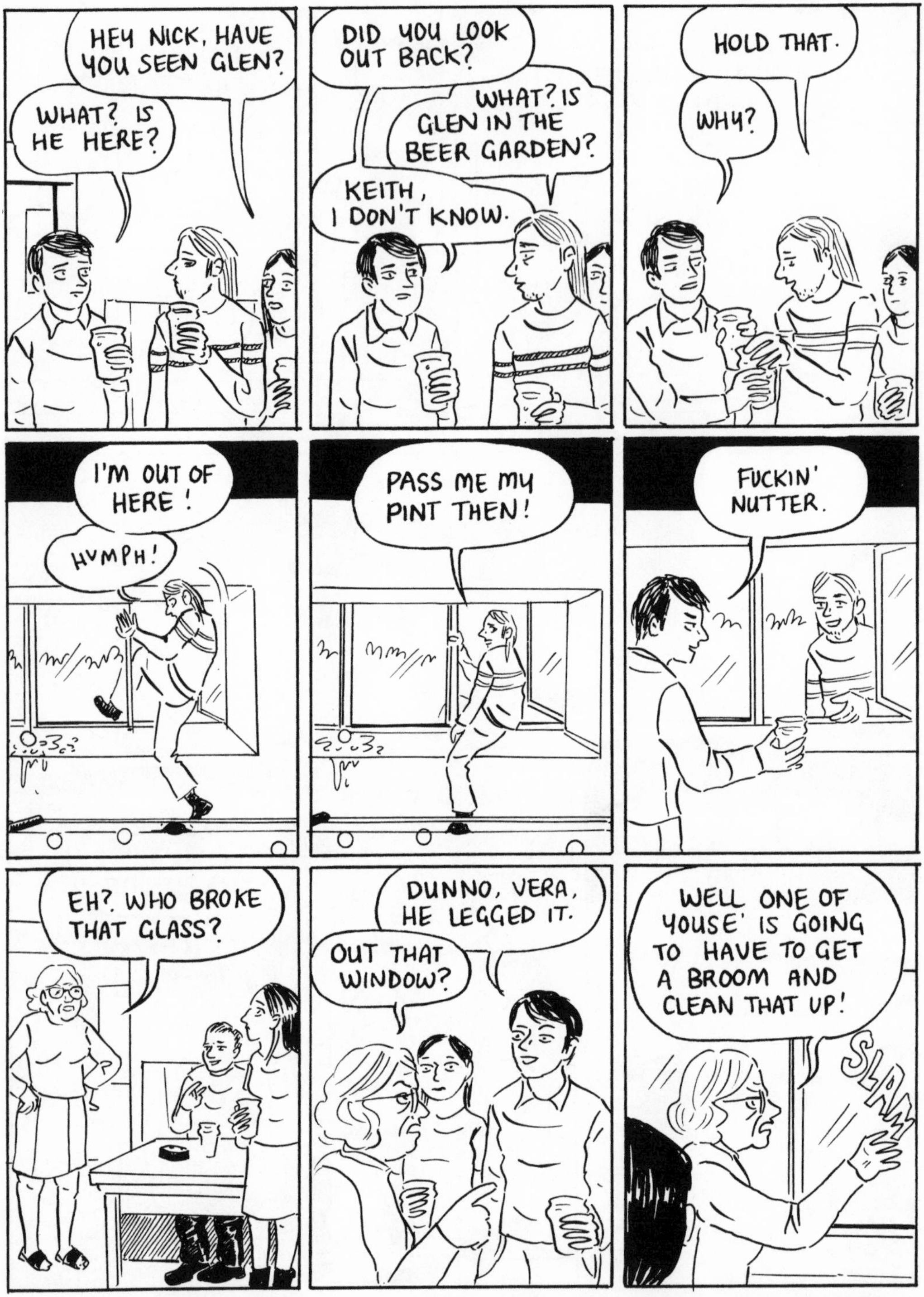
HEY NICK, HAVE YOU SEEN GLEN?
WHAT? IS HE HERE?
DID YOU LOOK OUT BACK?
WHAT? IS GLEN IN THE BEER GARDEN?
KEITH, I DON'T KNOW.
HOLD THAT.
WHY?
I'M OUT OF HERE!
HUMPH!
PASS ME MY PINT THEN!
FUCKIN' NUTTER.
EH?. WHO BROKE THAT GLASS?
DUNNO, VERA, HE LEGGED IT.
OUT THAT WINDOW?
WELL ONE OF YOUSE' IS GOING TO HAVE TO GET A BROOM AND CLEAN THAT UP!
SLAM

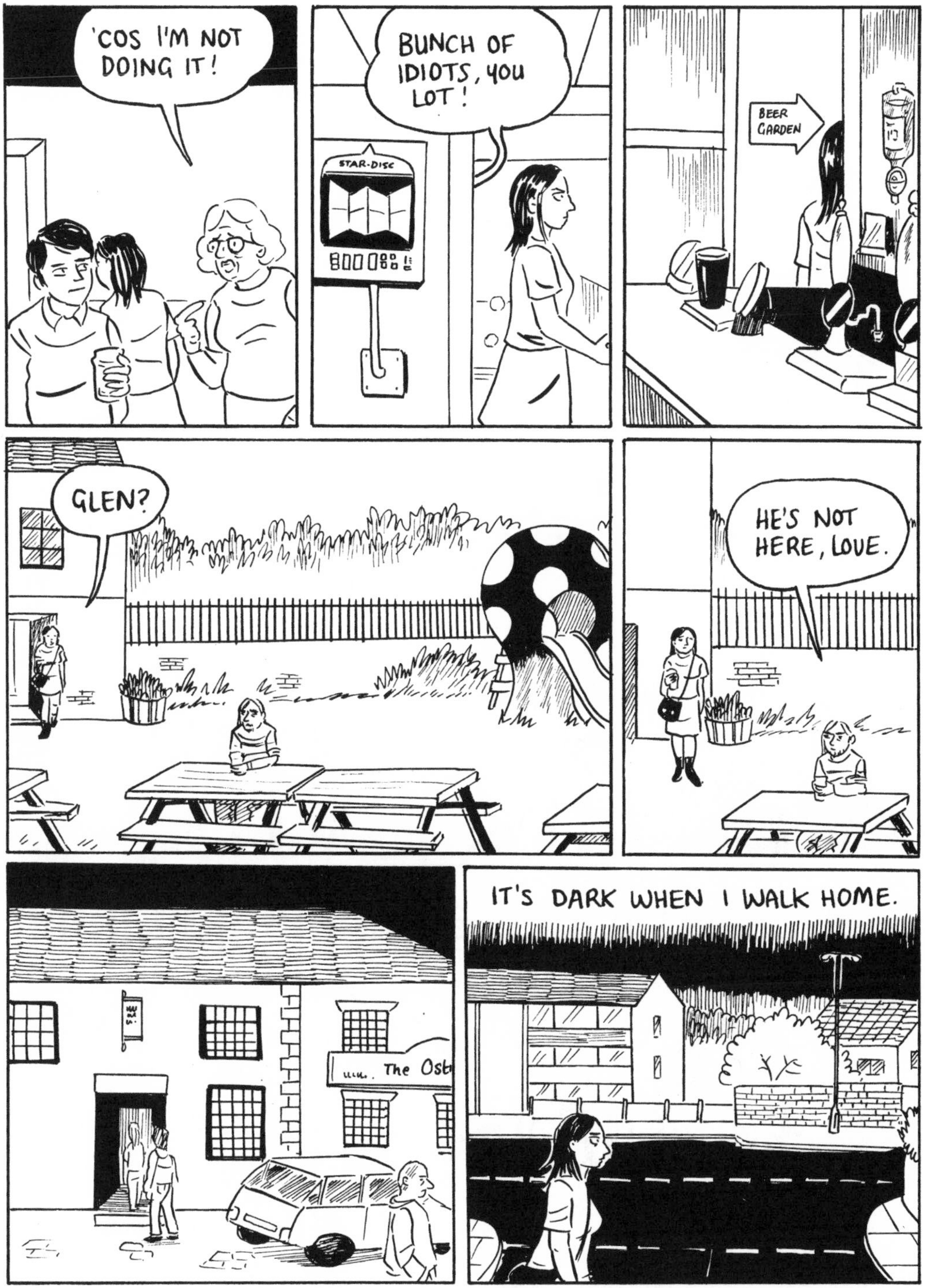
'COS I'M NOT DOING IT!
BUNCH OF IDIOTS, YOU LOT!
STAR-DISC
BEER GARDEN
GLEN?
HE'S NOT HERE, LOVE.
The Ost
IT'S DARK WHEN I WALK HOME.

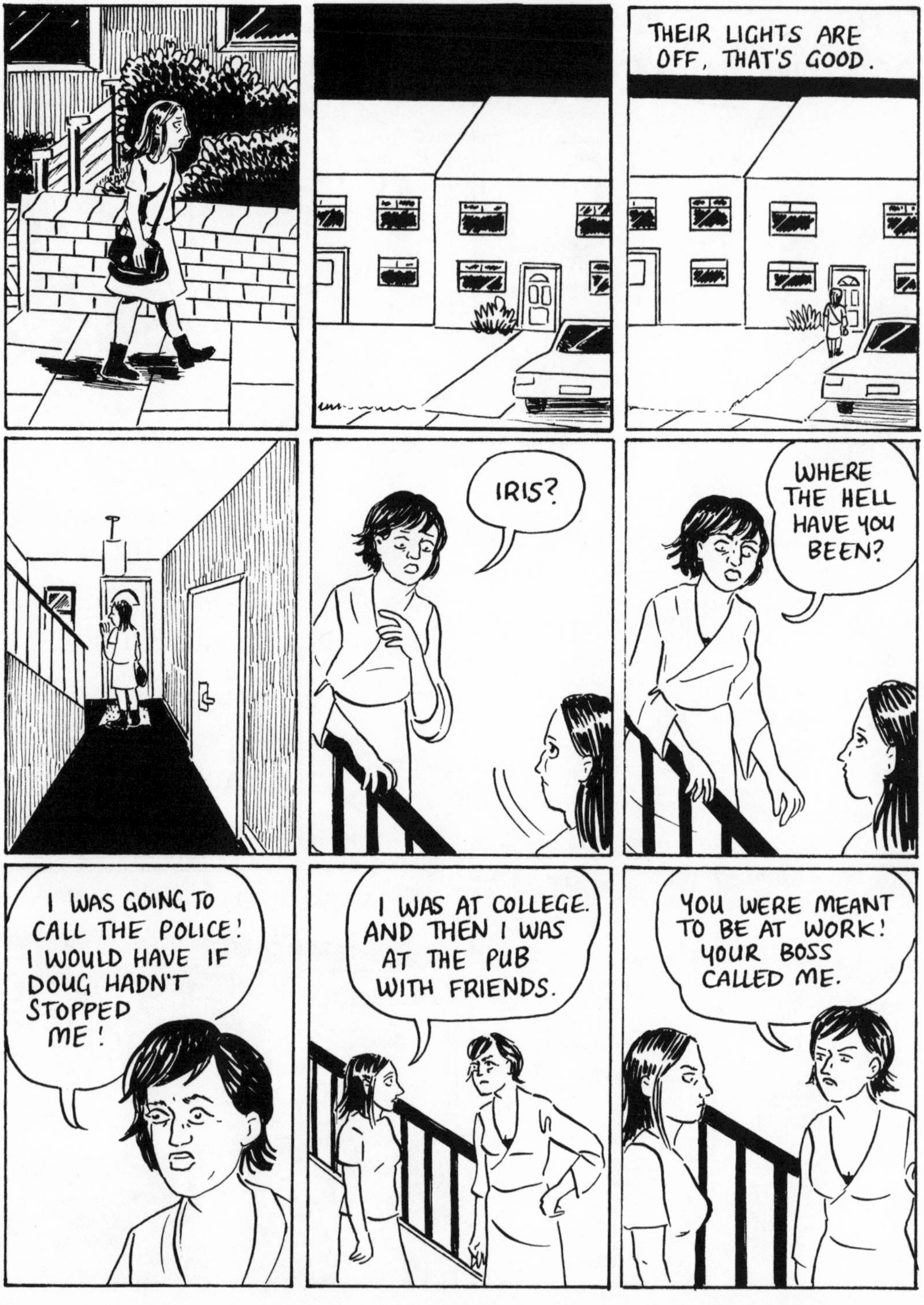
THEIR LIGHTS ARE OFF, THAT'S GOOD.
IRIS?
WHERE THE HELL HAVE YOU BEEN?
I WAS GOING TO CALL THE POLICE! I WOULD HAVE IF DOUG HADN'T STOPPED ME!
I WAS AT COLLEGE. AND THEN I WAS AT THE PUB WITH FRIENDS.
YOU WERE MEANT TO BE AT WORK! YOUR BOSS CALLED ME.

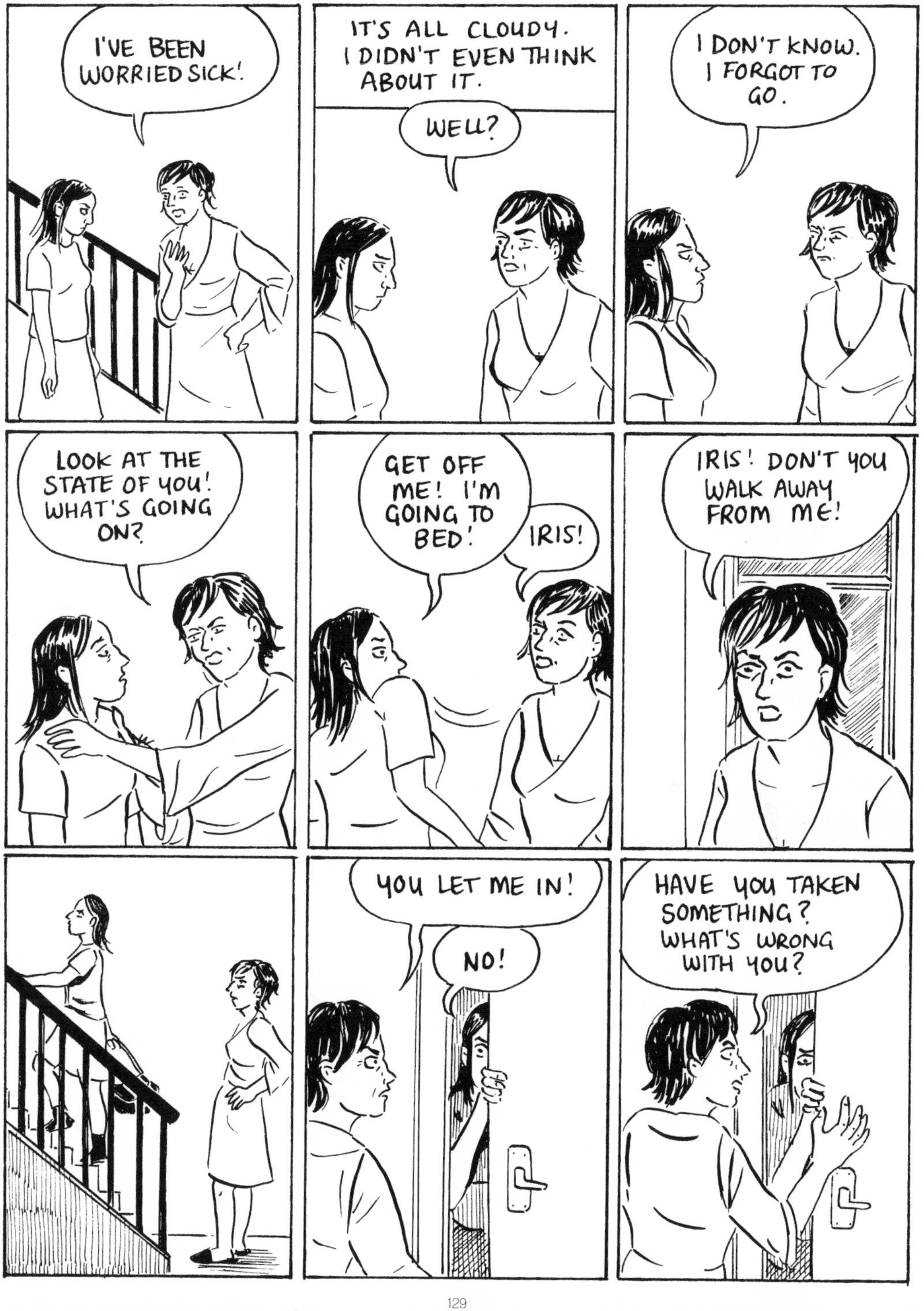
I'VE BEEN WORRIED SICK!
IT'S ALL CLOUDY. I DIDN'T EVEN THINK ABOUT IT.
WELL?
I DON'T KNOW. I FORGOT TO GO.
LOOK AT THE STATE OF YOU! WHAT'S GOING ON?
GET OFF ME! I'M GOING TO BED!
IRIS!
IRIS! DON'T YOU WALK AWAY FROM ME!
YOU LET ME IN!
NO!
HAVE YOU TAKEN SOMETHING? WHAT'S WRONG WITH YOU?

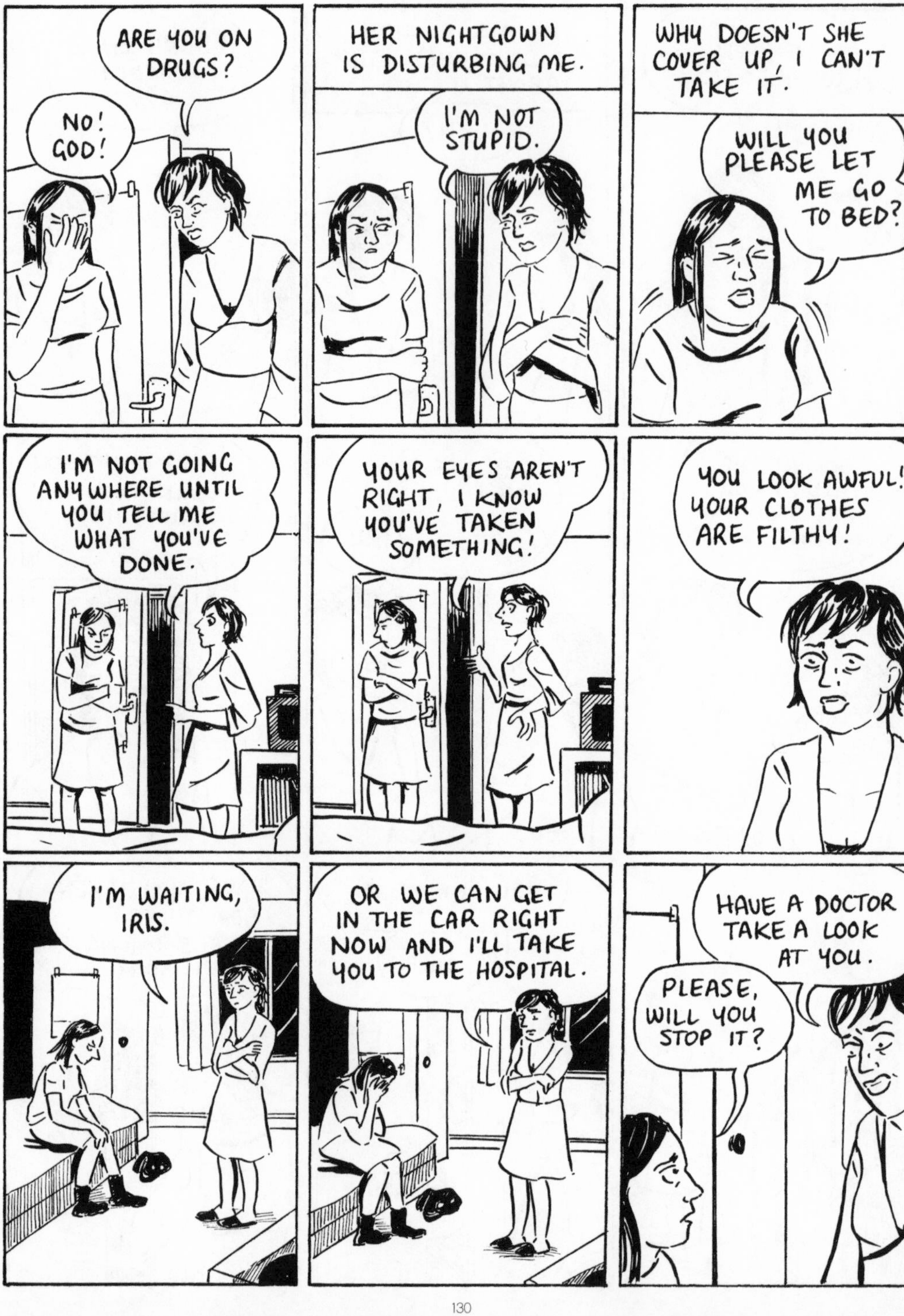
ARE YOU ON DRUGS?
NO! GOD!
HER NIGHTGOWN IS DISTURBING ME.
I'M NOT STUPID.
WHY DOESN'T SHE COVER UP, I CAN'T TAKE IT.
WILL YOU PLEASE LET ME GO TO BED?
I'M NOT GOING ANYWHERE UNTIL YOU TELL ME WHAT YOU'VE DONE.
YOUR EYES AREN'T RIGHT, I KNOW YOU'VE TAKEN SOMETHING!
YOU LOOK AWFUL! YOUR CLOTHES ARE FILTHY!
I'M WAITING, IRIS.
OR WE CAN GET IN THE CAR RIGHT NOW AND I'LL TAKE YOU TO THE HOSPITAL.
HAVE A DOCTOR TAKE A LOOK AT YOU.
PLEASE, WILL YOU STOP IT?

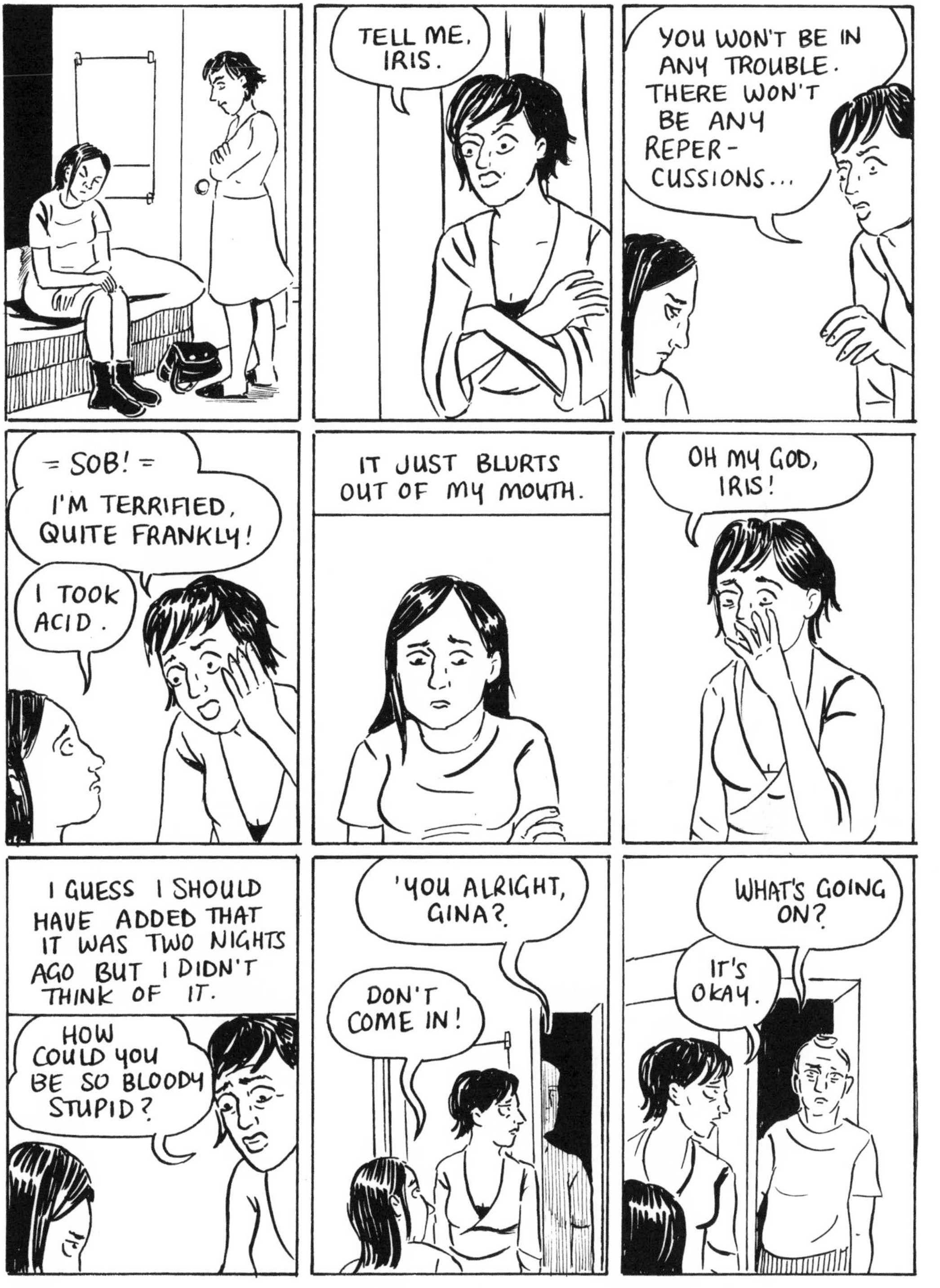
TELL ME, IRIS.
YOU WON'T BE IN ANY TROUBLE. THERE WON'T BE ANY REPERCUSSIONS...
= SOB! =
I'M TERRIFIED, QUITE FRANKLY!
I TOOK ACID.
IT JUST BLURTS OUT OF MY MOUTH.
OH MY GOD, IRIS!
I GUESS I SHOULD HAVE ADDED THAT IT WAS TWO NIGHTS AGO BUT I DIDN'T THINK OF IT.
HOW COULD YOU BE SO BLOODY STUPID?
'YOU ALRIGHT, GINA?
DON'T COME IN!
WHAT'S GOING ON?
IT'S OKAY.

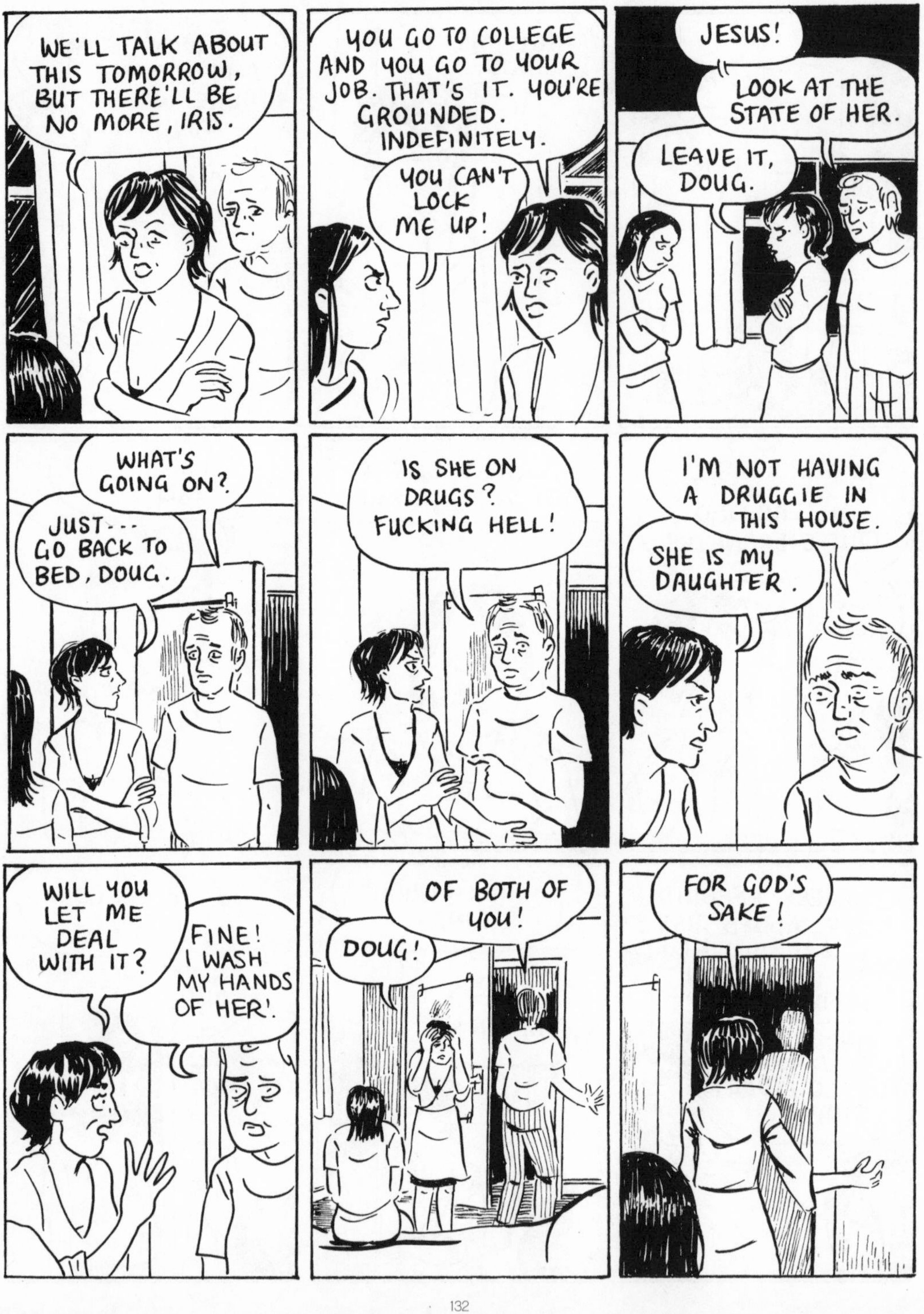
WE'LL TALK ABOUT THIS TOMORROW, BUT THERE'LL BE NO MORE, IRIS.
YOU GO TO COLLEGE AND YOU GO TO YOUR JOB. THAT'S IT. YOU'RE GROUNDED. INDEFINITELY.
YOU CAN'T LOCK ME UP!
JESUS!
LOOK AT THE STATE OF HER.
LEAVE IT, DOUG.
WHAT'S GOING ON?
JUST... GO BACK TO BED, DOUG.
IS SHE ON DRUGS? FUCKING HELL!
I'M NOT HAVING A DRUGGIE IN THIS HOUSE.
SHE IS MY DAUGHTER.
WILL YOU LET ME DEAL WITH IT?
FINE! I WASH MY HANDS OF HER!
DOUG!
OF BOTH OF YOU!
FOR GOD'S SAKE!

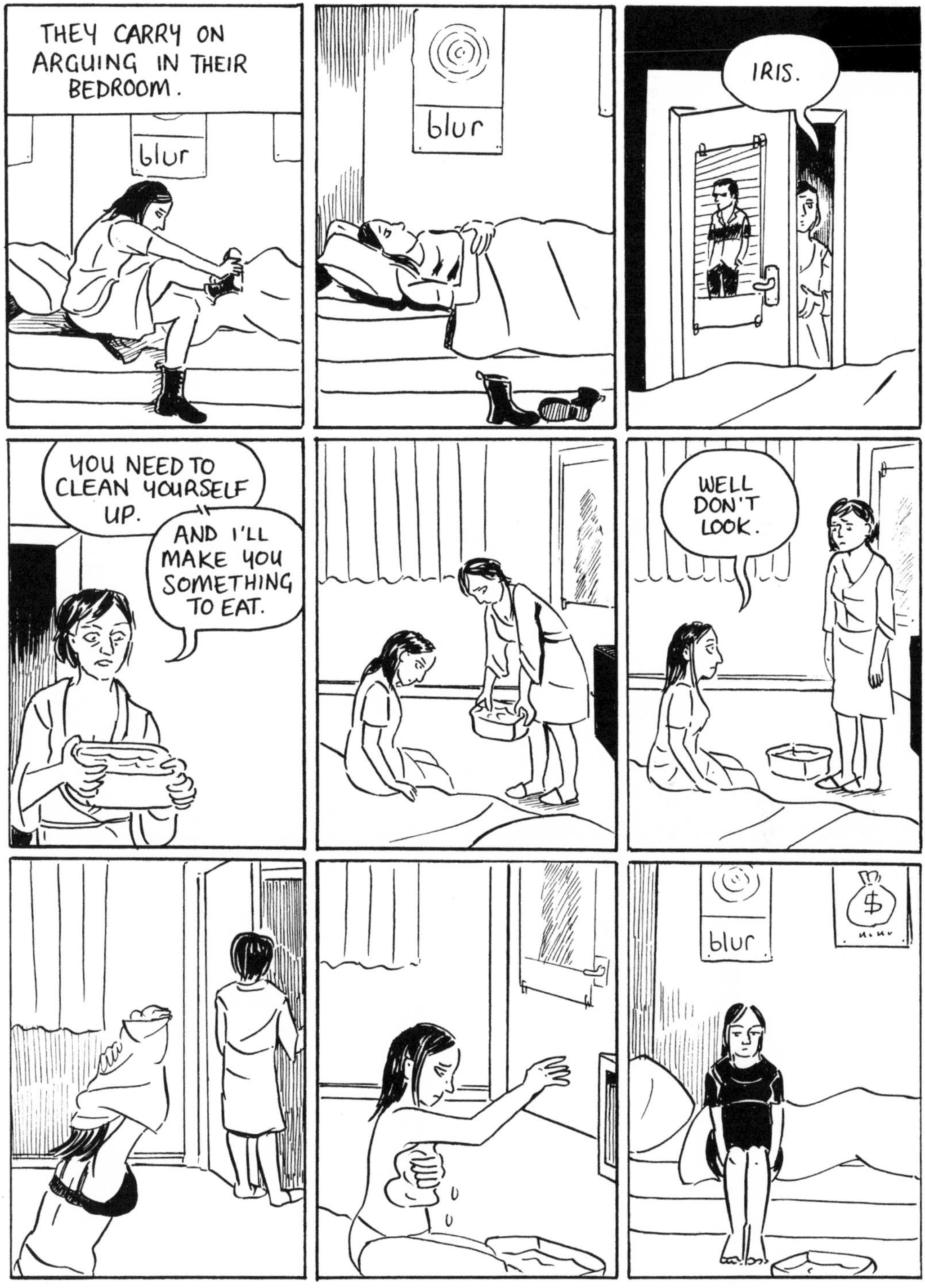
THEY CARRY ON ARGUING IN THEIR BEDROOM.
blur
blur
IRIS.
YOU NEED TO CLEAN YOURSELF UP.
AND I'LL MAKE YOU SOMETHING TO EAT.
WELL DON'T LOOK.
blur
$

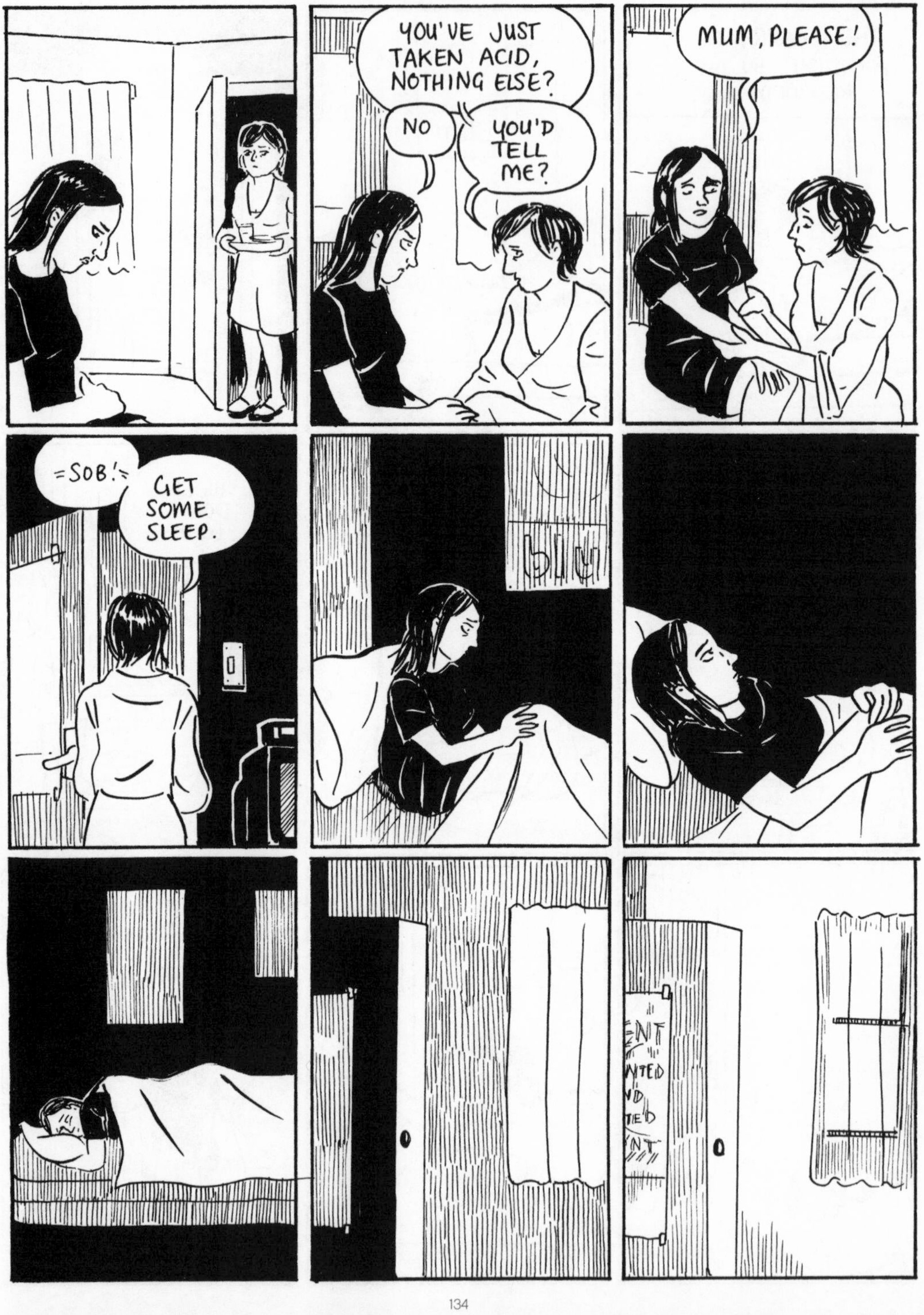
YOU'VE JUST TAKEN ACID, NOTHING ELSE?
NO
YOU'D TELL ME?
MUM, PLEASE!
=SOB!=
GET SOME SLEEP.

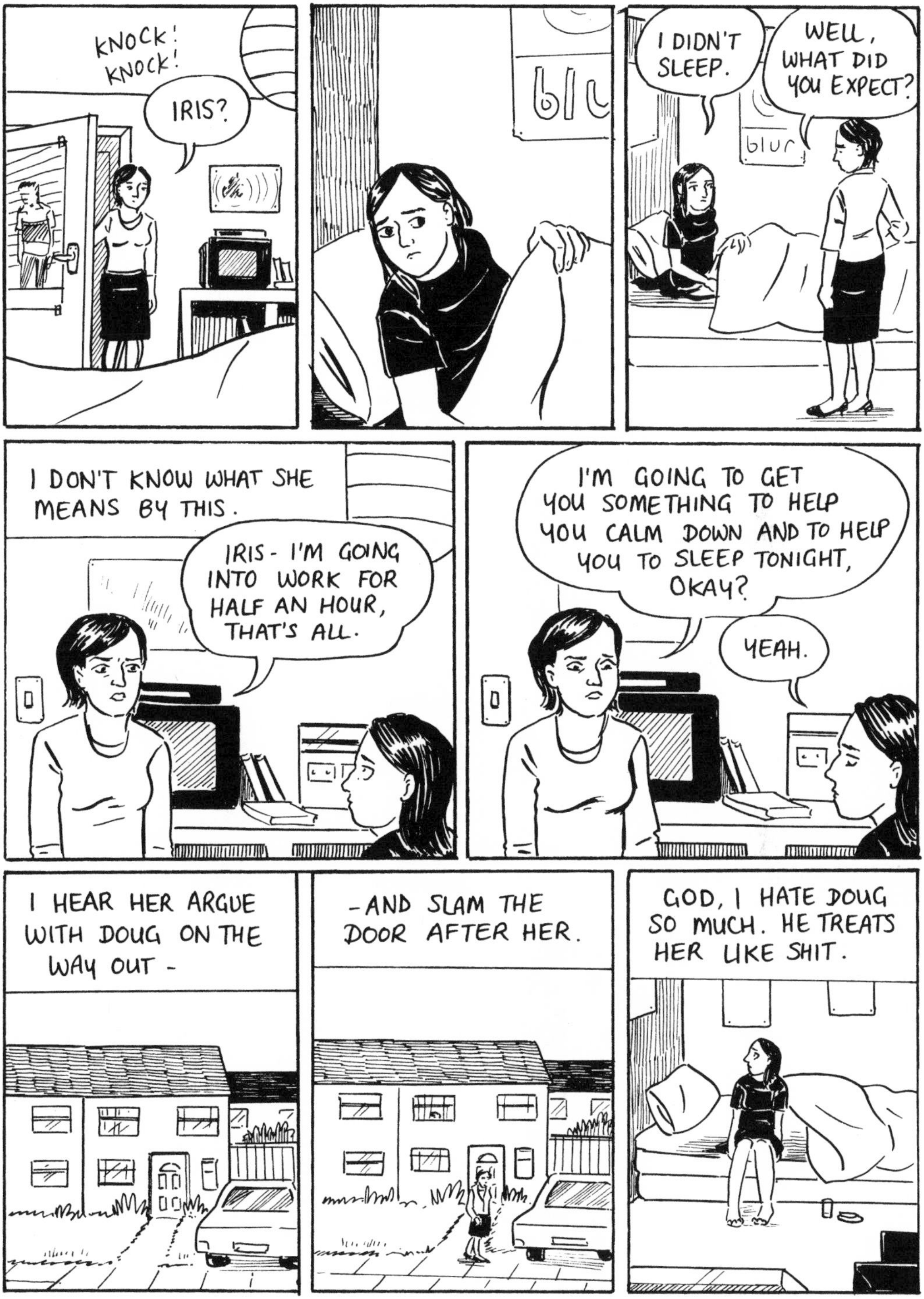
KNOCK! KNOCK!
IRIS?
blu
I DIDN'T SLEEP.
WELL, WHAT DID YOU EXPECT?
blur
I DON'T KNOW WHAT SHE MEANS BY THIS.
IRIS- I'M GOING INTO WORK FOR HALF AN HOUR, THAT'S ALL.
I'M GOING TO GET YOU SOMETHING TO HELP YOU CALM DOWN AND TO HELP YOU TO SLEEP TONIGHT, OKAY?
YEAH.
I HEAR HER ARGUE WITH DOUG ON THE WAY OUT -
-AND SLAM THE DOOR AFTER HER.
GOD, I HATE DOUG SO MUCH. HE TREATS HER LIKE SHIT.

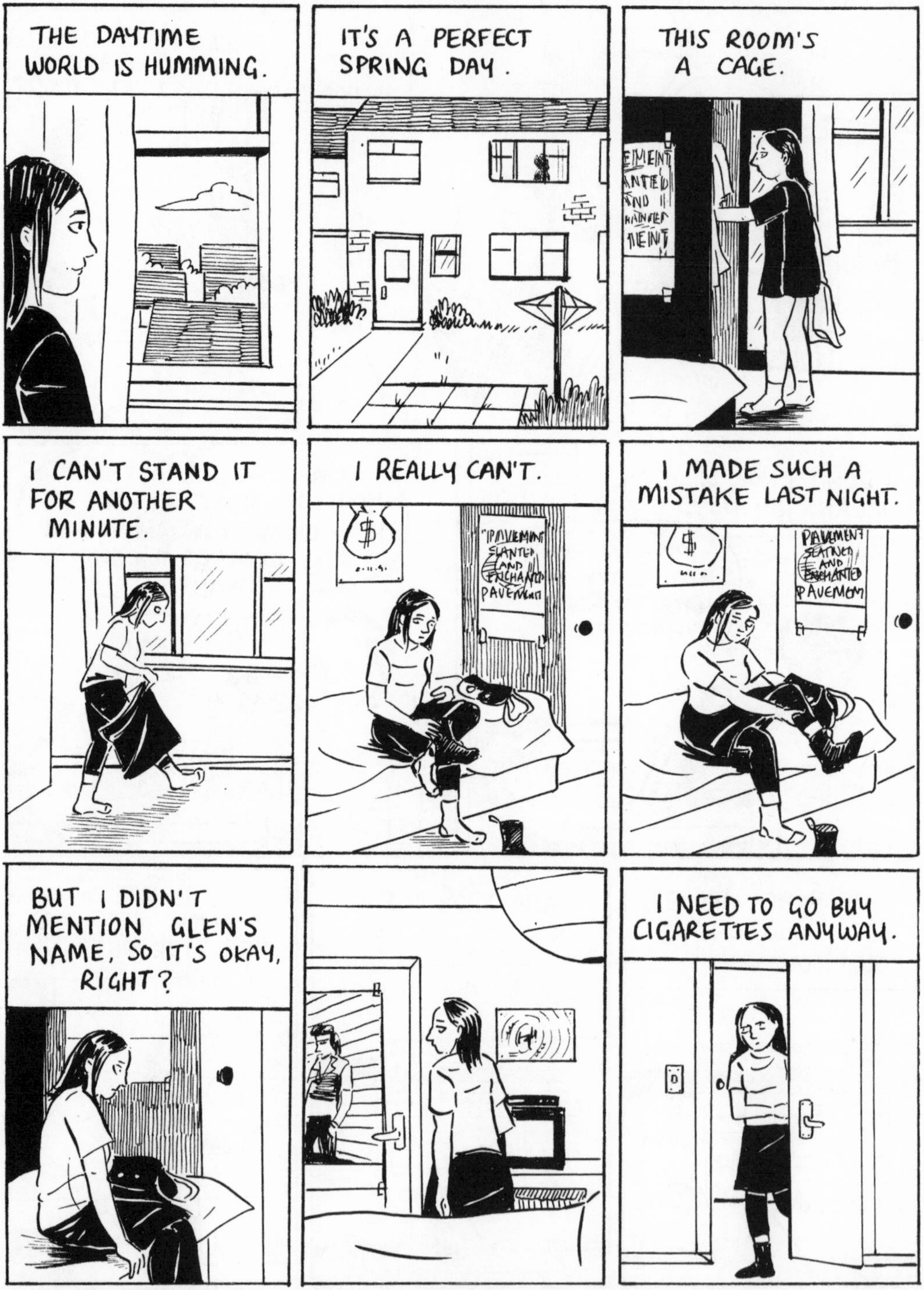
THE DAYTIME WORLD IS HUMMING.
IT'S A PERFECT SPRING DAY.
THIS ROOM'S A CAGE.
I CAN'T STAND IT FOR ANOTHER MINUTE.
I REALLY CAN'T.
I MADE SUCH A MISTAKE LAST NIGHT.
BUT I DIDN'T MENTION GLEN'S NAME, SO IT'S OKAY, RIGHT?
I NEED TO GO BUY CIGARETTES ANYWAY.

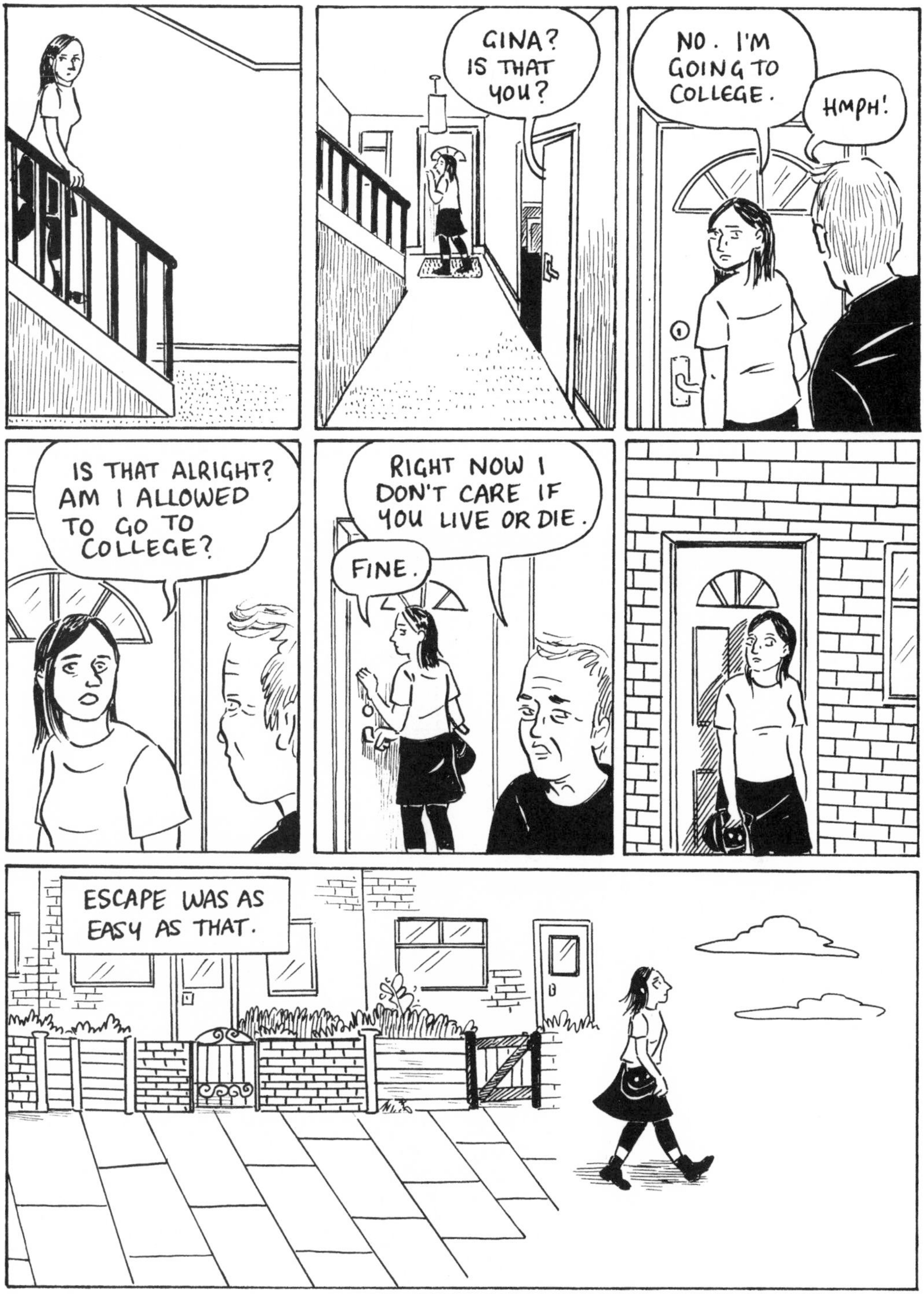
GINA? IS THAT YOU?
NO. I'M GOING TO COLLEGE.
HMPH!
IS THAT ALRIGHT? AM I ALLOWED TO GO TO COLLEGE?
RIGHT NOW I DON'T CARE IF YOU LIVE OR DIE.
FINE.
ESCAPE WAS AS EASY AS THAT.

chapter four

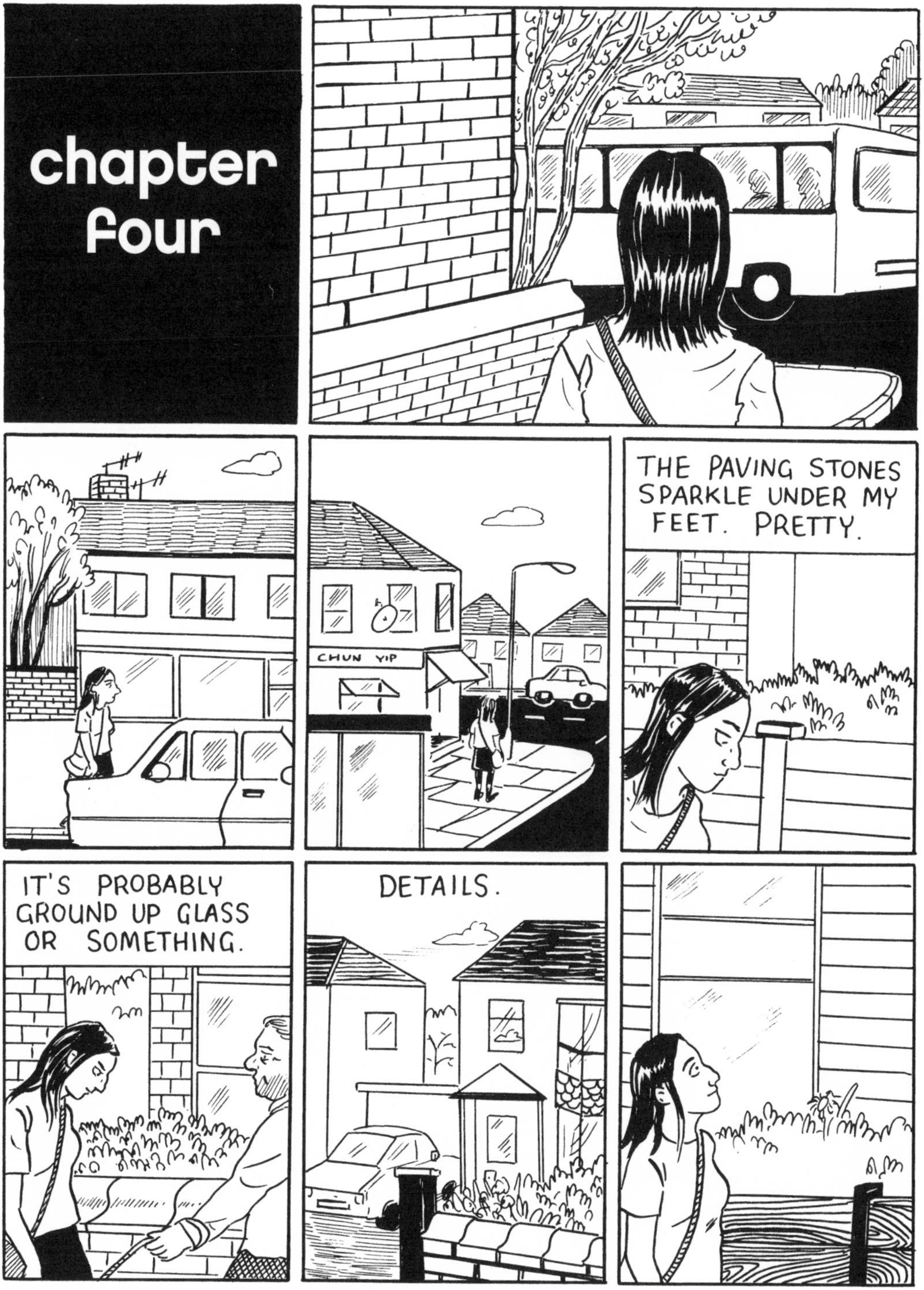
CHUN YIP
THE PAVING STONES SPARKLE UNDER MY FEET. PRETTY.
IT'S PROBABLY GROUND UP GLASS OR SOMETHING.
DETAILS.

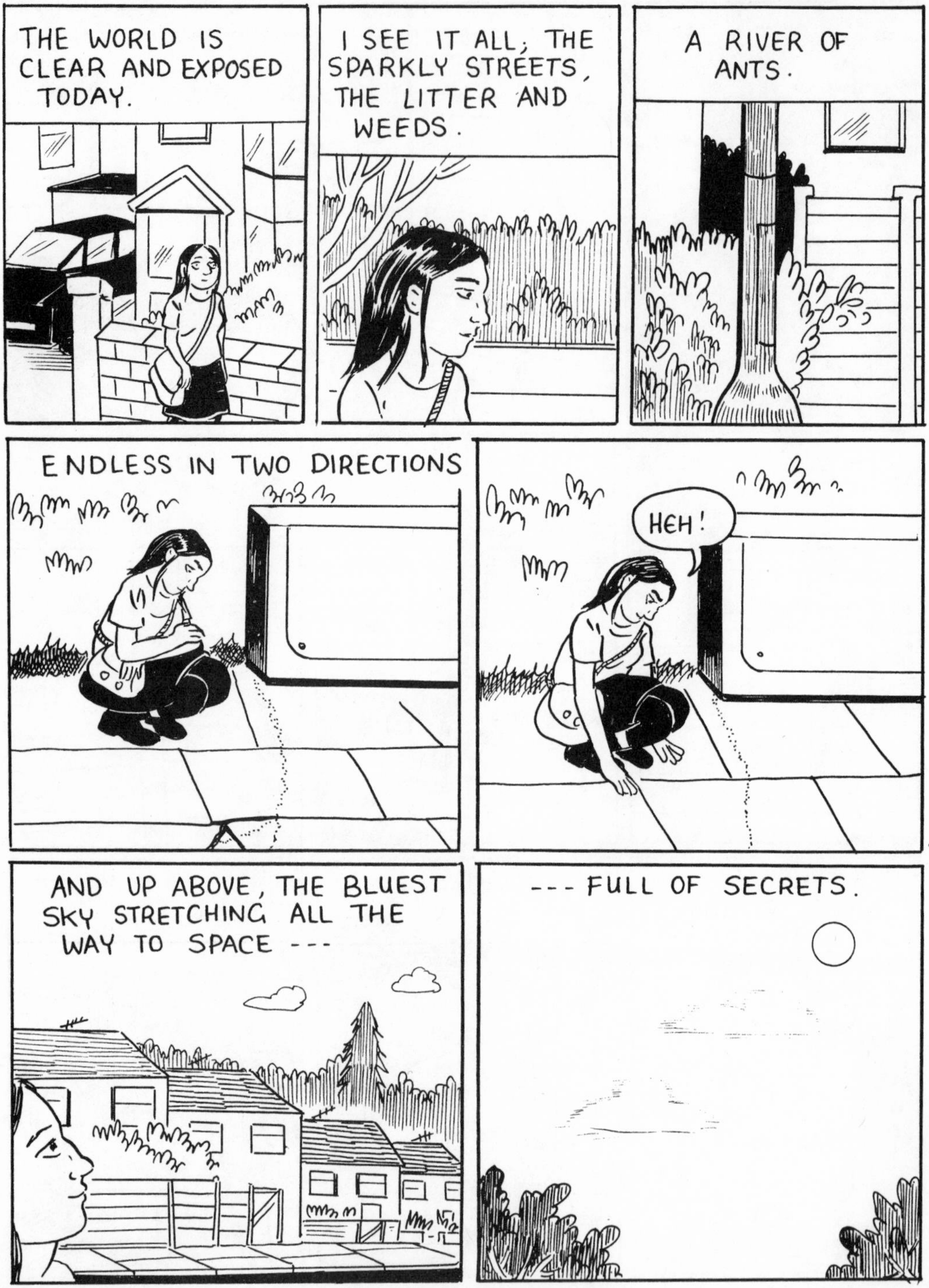
THE WORLD IS CLEAR AND EXPOSED TODAY.
I SEE IT ALL; THE SPARKLY STREETS, THE LITTER AND WEEDS.
A RIVER OF ANTS.
ENDLESS IN TWO DIRECTIONS
HEH!
AND UP ABOVE, THE BLUEST SKY STRETCHING ALL THE WAY TO SPACE ---
--- FULL OF SECRETS.

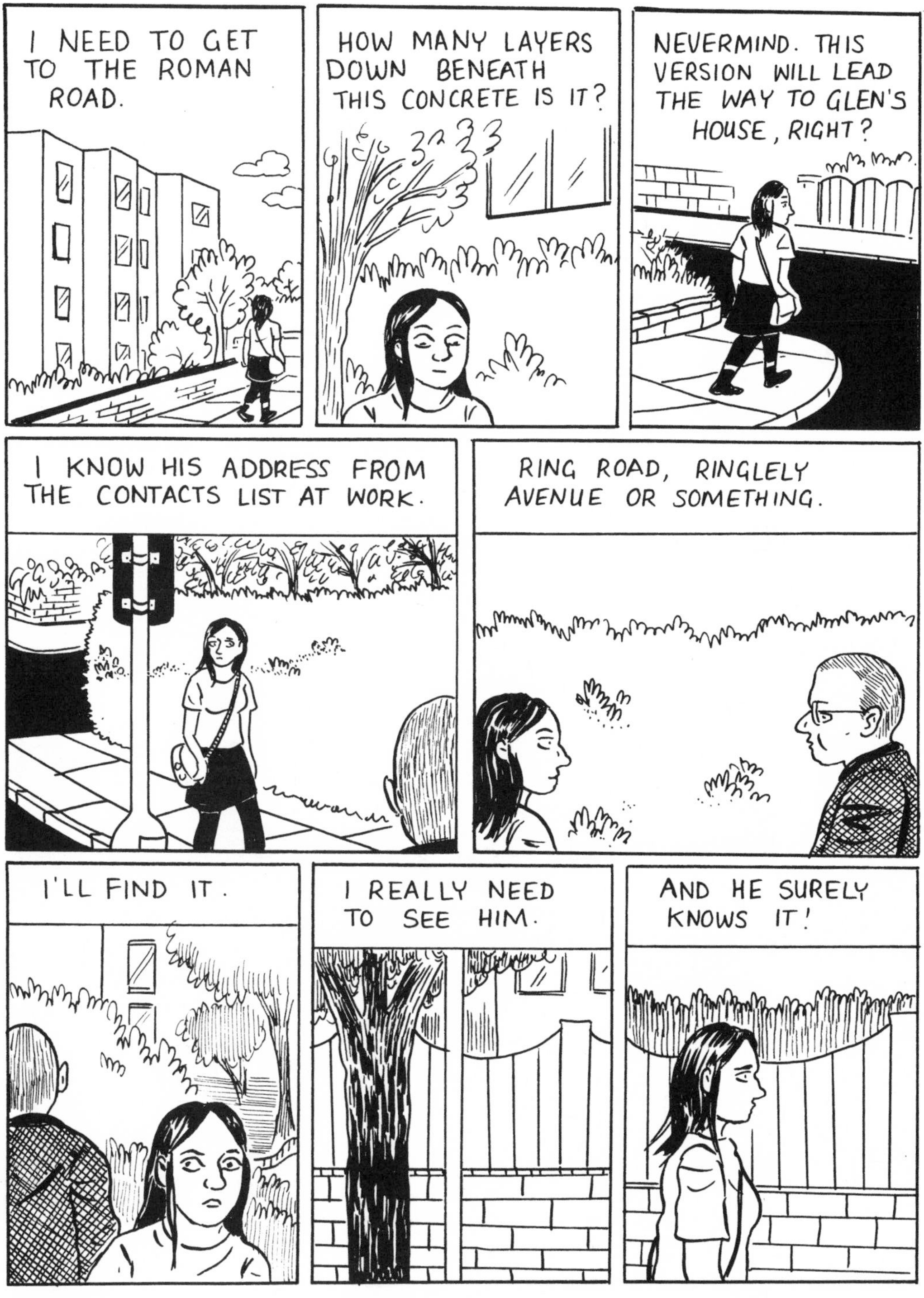
I NEED TO GET TO THE ROMAN ROAD.
HOW MANY LAYERS DOWN BENEATH THIS CONCRETE IS IT?
NEVERMIND. THIS VERSION WILL LEAD THE WAY TO GLEN'S HOUSE, RIGHT?
I KNOW HIS ADDRESS FROM THE CONTACTS LIST AT WORK.
RING ROAD, RINGLELY AVENUE OR SOMETHING.
I'LL FIND IT.
I REALLY NEED TO SEE HIM.
AND HE SURELY KNOWS IT!

SIGNS POINT THE WAY.

I START TO NOTICE THEM. LITTLE, SUBTLE SIGNS. NOT STREET SIGNS, BUT SMALL STUFF.

LIKE THESE LITTLE BLUE PENS.

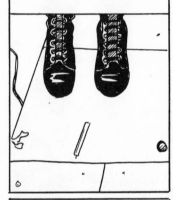

THE ONES MEN TAKE FROM BETTING SHOPS.

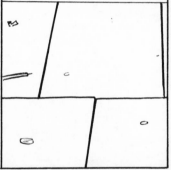

THERE ARE TWO MORE NOW. LIKE LITTLE ARROWS.

I KNOW ABOUT THIS! I'VE READ ABOUT IT!

HOW GYPSIES, ON MOORS WOULD LEAVE MARKERS FOR THOSE FOLLOW- ING BEHIND.

SIGNS ON THE TURF, LIKE A ROCK, A FEATHER, A LEAF. ARRANGED JUST SO!

DELIBERATE SIGNS PLACED BY FRIENDLY HANDS.

SO THEN..... BLUE?

BLUE THINGS ARE POINTERS.

THE RULES OF THE GAME EMERGE QUICKLY, BUT I'M A FAST LEARNER.

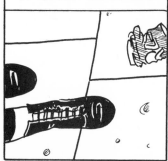

SEE - 7 UP ALREADY!

RED - IS THAT GLEN'S COLOUR? OR JUST 'STOP'?

WHAT COLOUR ARE **YOU**, GLEN? I WONDER!

THESE LITTLE BLUE DRINK TOPS. I KEEP SEEING THEM.

SOME HAVE LITTLE STARS MOULDED INSIDE. POINTS MAKE PRIZES!

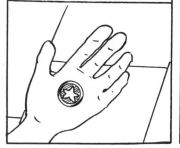

HA HA

TOSS!

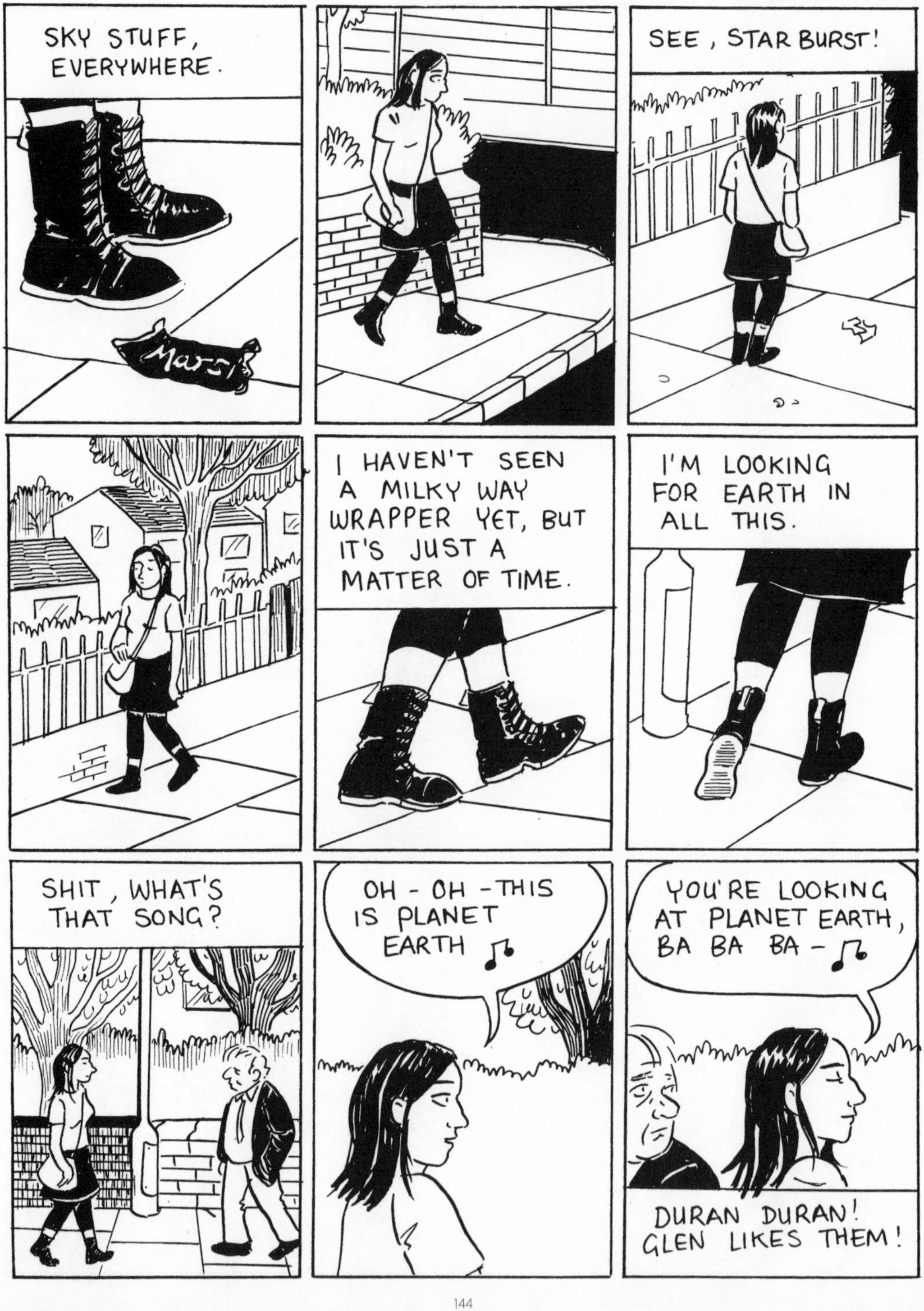
SKY STUFF, EVERYWHERE.
Mars
SEE, STAR BURST!
I HAVEN'T SEEN A MILKY WAY WRAPPER YET, BUT IT'S JUST A MATTER OF TIME.
I'M LOOKING FOR EARTH IN ALL THIS.
SHIT, WHAT'S THAT SONG?
OH - OH - THIS IS PLANET EARTH
YOU'RE LOOKING AT PLANET EARTH, BA BA BA -
DURAN DURAN! GLEN LIKES THEM!

HE SAID THAT SIMON LE BON IS A TRUE POET.

HA HA!

HE IS!

I'VE WALKED THIS WAY BEFORE.

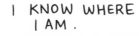

I KNOW WHERE I AM.

IT'S JUST THAT TODAY IS DIFFERENT.

EVERY HOUSE SEEMS SPECIAL IN ITS OWN WAY. LOOK, A LITTLE BOY MUST LIVE THERE.

DON'T GET DISTRACTED, IRIS.

BUT I DO, I DO.

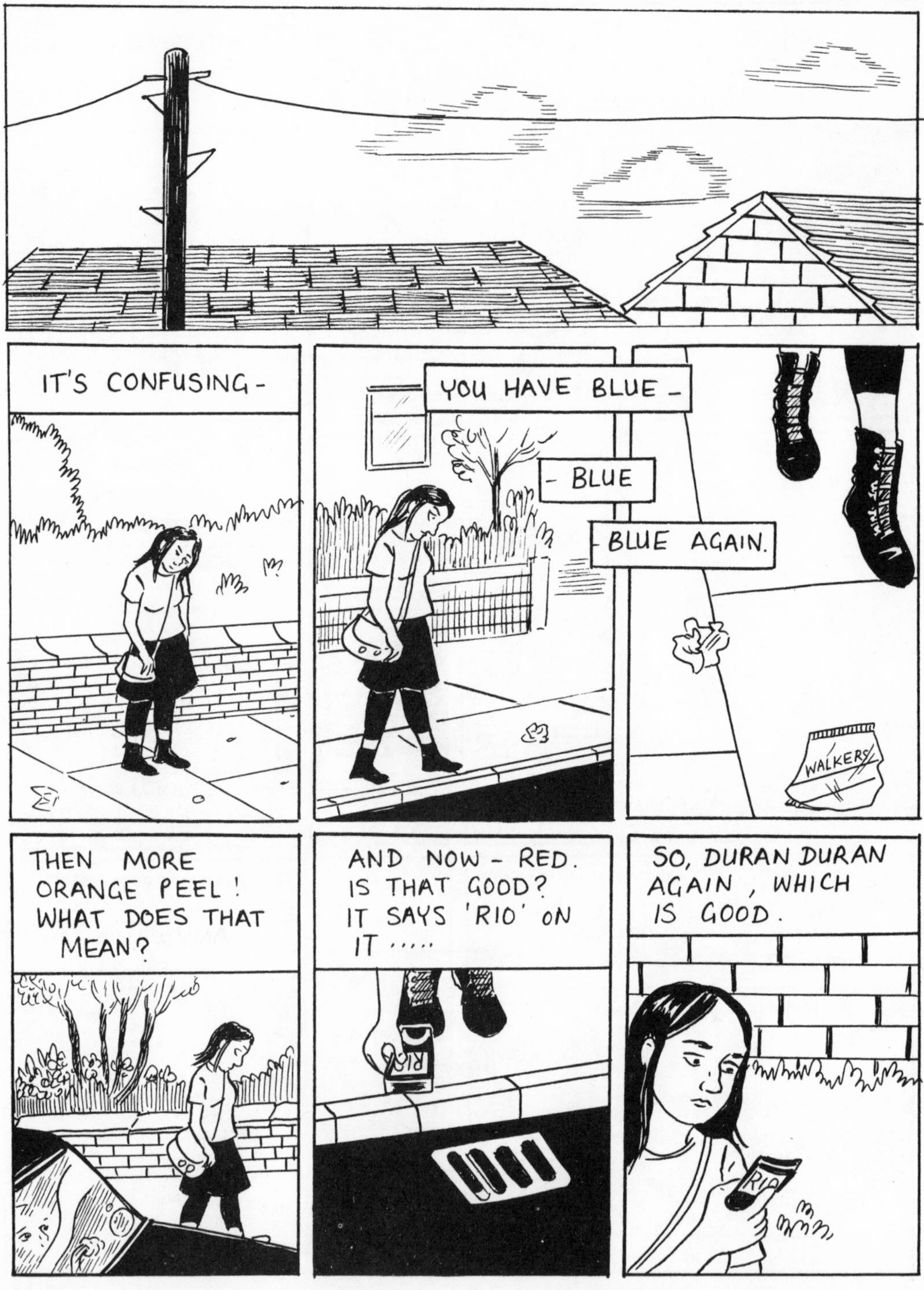
IT'S CONFUSING -
YOU HAVE BLUE -
- BLUE
- BLUE AGAIN.
WALKERS
THEN MORE ORANGE PEEL! WHAT DOES THAT MEAN?
AND NOW - RED. IS THAT GOOD? IT SAYS 'RIO' ON IT .....
RIO
SO, DURAN DURAN AGAIN, WHICH IS GOOD.
RIO

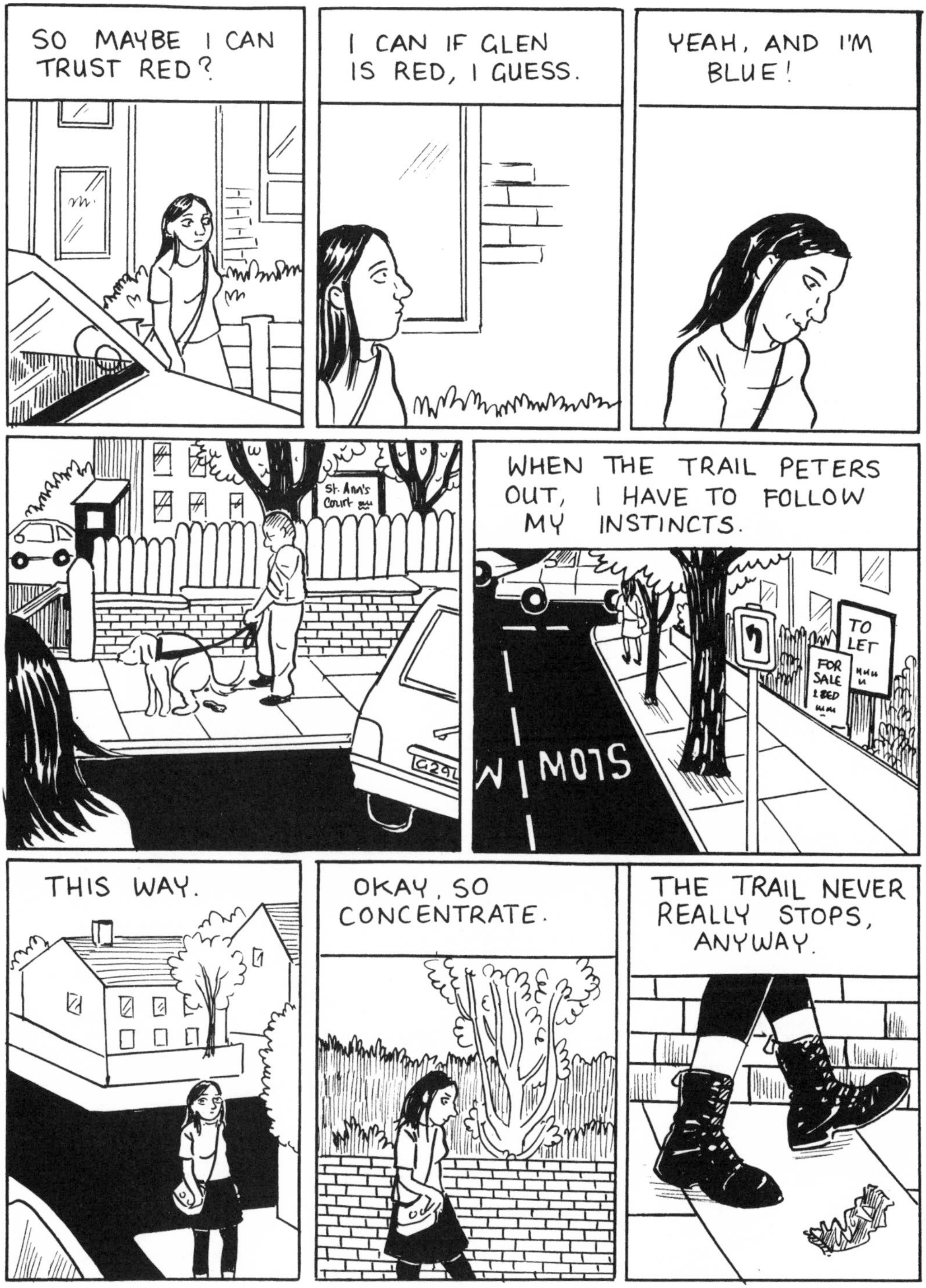
SO MAYBE I CAN TRUST RED?
I CAN IF GLEN IS RED, I GUESS.
YEAH, AND I'M BLUE!
St. Ann's Court
WHEN THE TRAIL PETERS OUT, I HAVE TO FOLLOW MY INSTINCTS.
TO LET
FOR SALE 2 BED
SLOW
THIS WAY.
OKAY, SO CONCENTRATE.
THE TRAIL NEVER REALLY STOPS, ANYWAY.

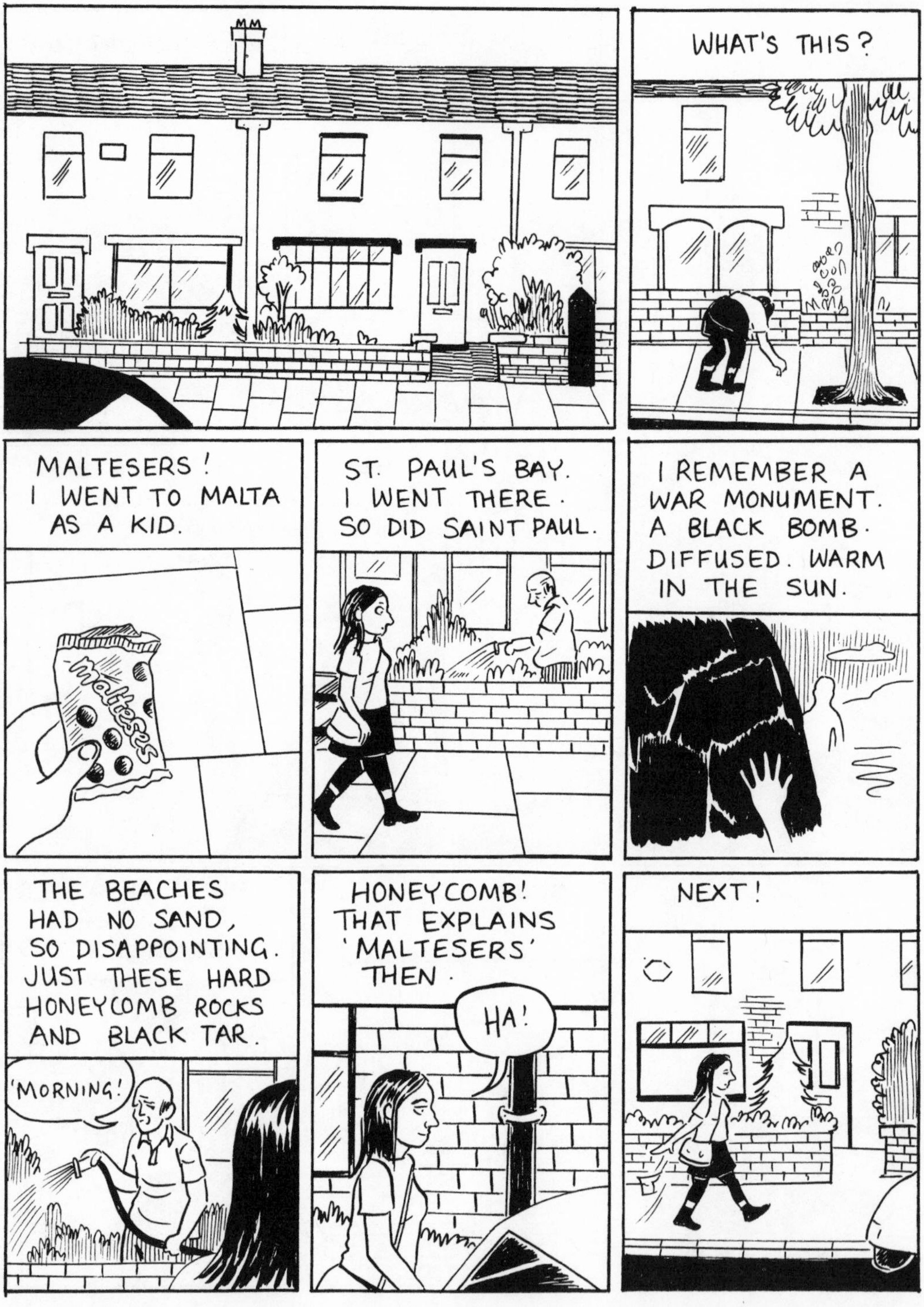
WHAT'S THIS?
MALTESERS! I WENT TO MALTA AS A KID.
maltesers
ST. PAUL'S BAY. I WENT THERE. SO DID SAINT PAUL.
I REMEMBER A WAR MONUMENT. A BLACK BOMB. DIFFUSED. WARM IN THE SUN.
THE BEACHES HAD NO SAND, SO DISAPPOINTING. JUST THESE HARD HONEYCOMB ROCKS AND BLACK TAR.
'MORNING!
HONEYCOMB! THAT EXPLAINS 'MALTESERS' THEN.
HA!
NEXT!

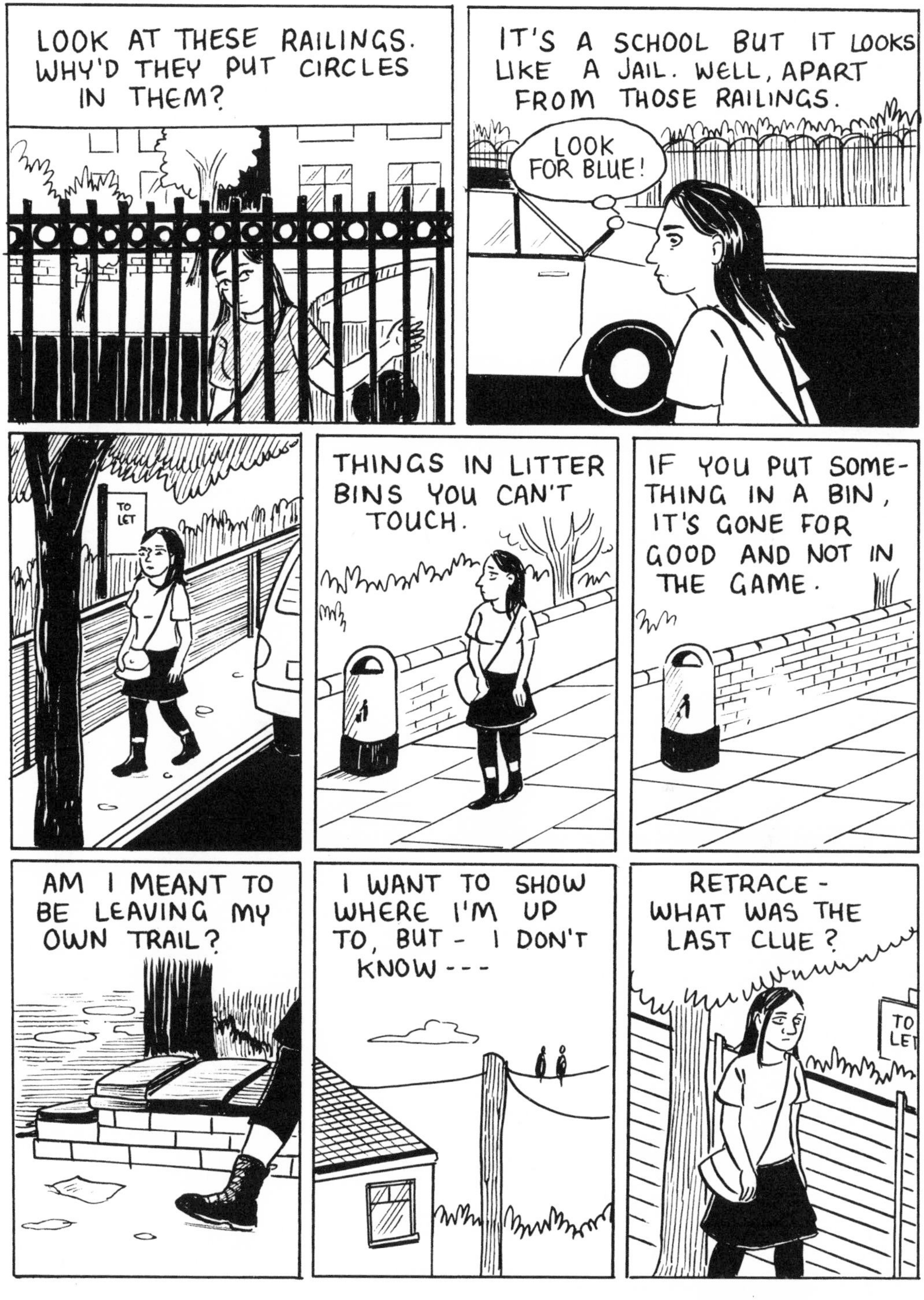
LOOK AT THESE RAILINGS. WHY'D THEY PUT CIRCLES IN THEM?
IT'S A SCHOOL BUT IT LOOKS LIKE A JAIL. WELL, APART FROM THOSE RAILINGS.
LOOK FOR BLUE!
TO LET
THINGS IN LITTER BINS YOU CAN'T TOUCH.
IF YOU PUT SOMETHING IN A BIN, IT'S GONE FOR GOOD AND NOT IN THE GAME.
AM I MEANT TO BE LEAVING MY OWN TRAIL?
I WANT TO SHOW WHERE I'M UP TO, BUT - I DON'T KNOW ---
RETRACE - WHAT WAS THE LAST CLUE?
TO LET

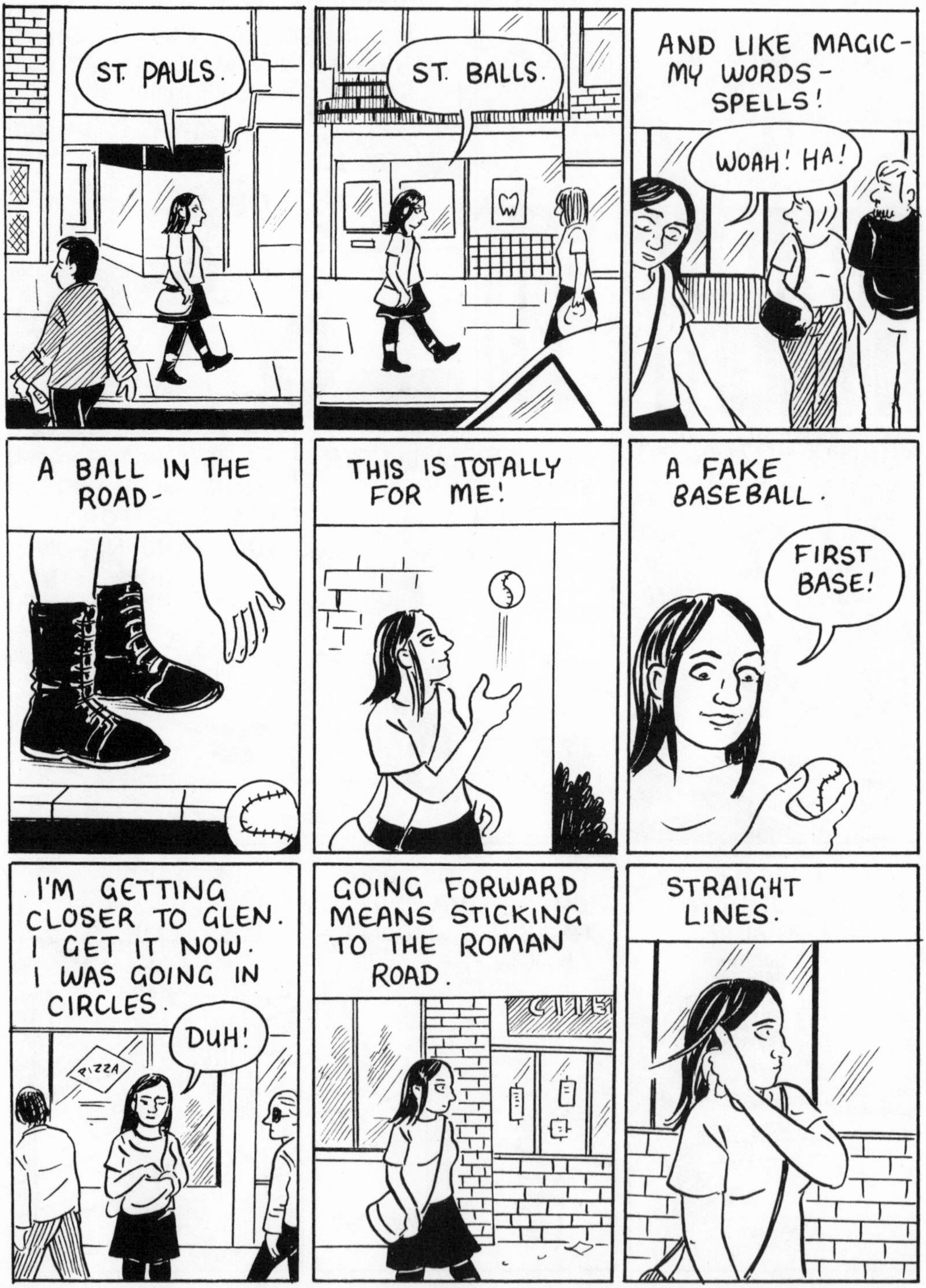
ST. PAULS.
ST. BALLS.
AND LIKE MAGIC- MY WORDS- SPELLS!
WOAH! HA!
A BALL IN THE ROAD-
THIS IS TOTALLY FOR ME!
A FAKE BASEBALL.
FIRST BASE!
I'M GETTING CLOSER TO GLEN. I GET IT NOW. I WAS GOING IN CIRCLES.
PIZZA
DUH!
GOING FORWARD MEANS STICKING TO THE ROMAN ROAD.
STRAIGHT LINES.

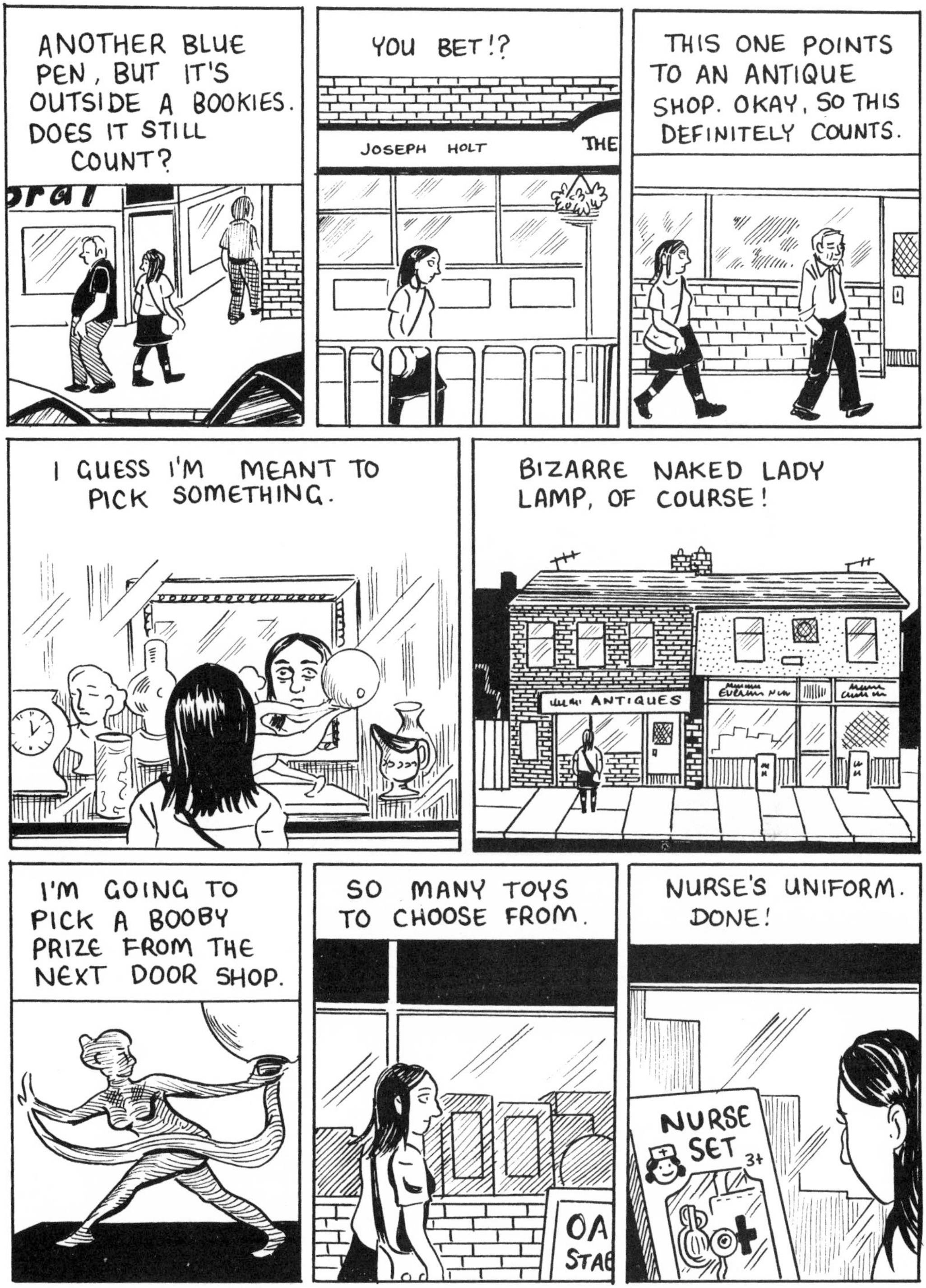

ANOTHER BLUE PEN, BUT IT'S OUTSIDE A BOOKIES. DOES IT STILL COUNT?
YOU BET!?
JOSEPH HOLT
THE
THIS ONE POINTS TO AN ANTIQUE SHOP. OKAY, SO THIS DEFINITELY COUNTS.
I GUESS I'M MEANT TO PICK SOMETHING.
BIZARRE NAKED LADY LAMP, OF COURSE!
ANTIQUES
I'M GOING TO PICK A BOOBY PRIZE FROM THE NEXT DOOR SHOP.
SO MANY TOYS TO CHOOSE FROM.
NURSE'S UNIFORM. DONE!
NURSE SET
3+

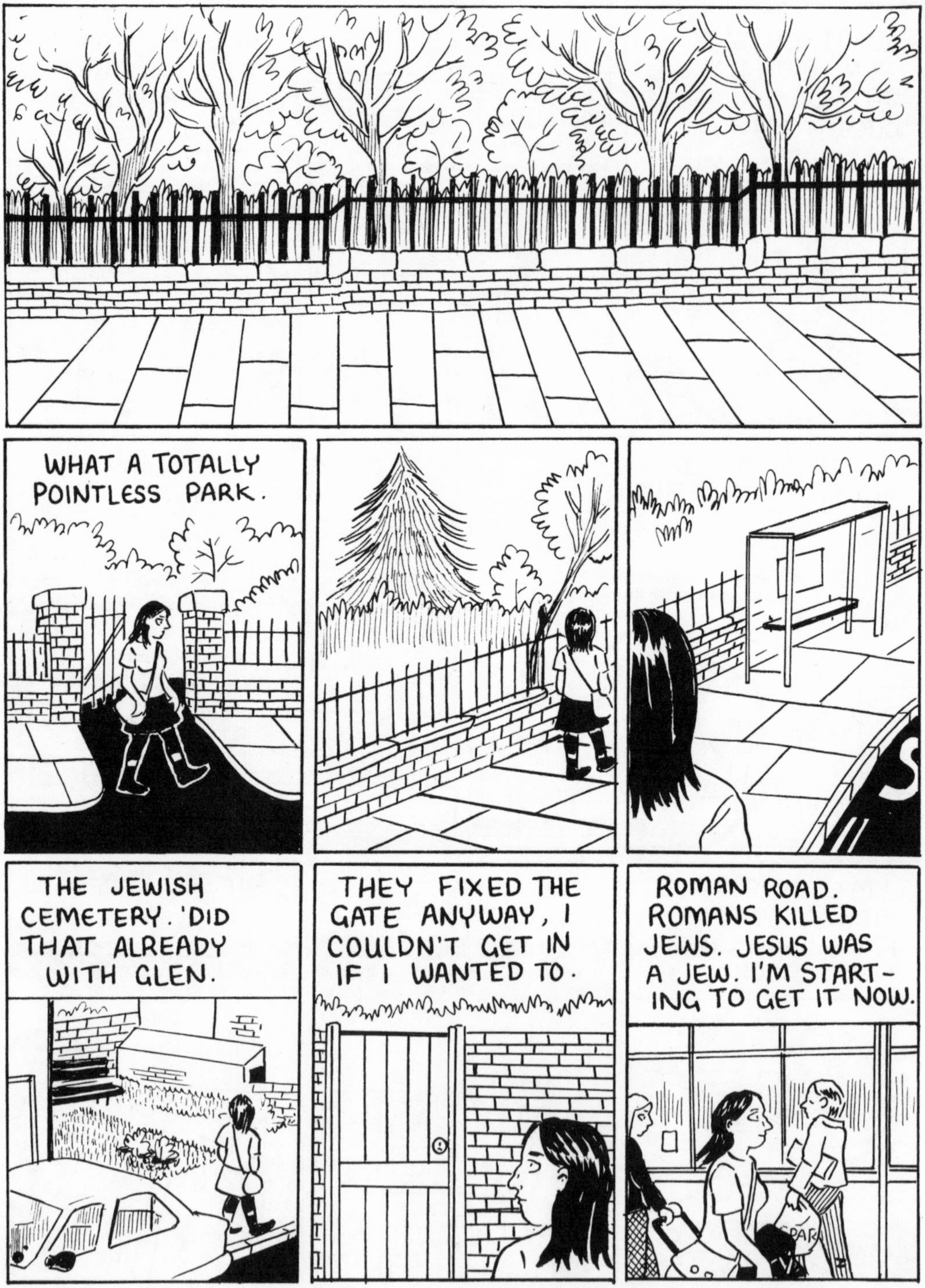
WHAT A TOTALLY POINTLESS PARK.
S
THE JEWISH CEMETERY. 'DID THAT ALREADY WITH GLEN.
THEY FIXED THE GATE ANYWAY, I COULDN'T GET IN IF I WANTED TO.
ROMAN ROAD. ROMANS KILLED JEWS. JESUS WAS A JEW. I'M STARTING TO GET IT NOW.

THIS WHOLE TOWN IS STARTING TO MAKE SENSE.

THE CIRCLE OF THIS MOTORWAY, A REVOLVING DOOR.

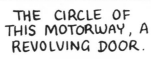

WHERE DID THE ROMAN ROAD CRUMBLE AND END?

THIS CIRCLE OF EARTH, ONCE EATEN BY BULLDOZERS?

WHAT WAS MISSED TO MAKE THIS?

COINS? A LOST SANDAL? GOUGED AWAY.

CARS CIRCLE ABOVE ME NOW, AND BELOW ME.

IT'S ALL TOO MUCH TO THINK ABOUT.

I SHOULD HAVE A CIGARETTE.

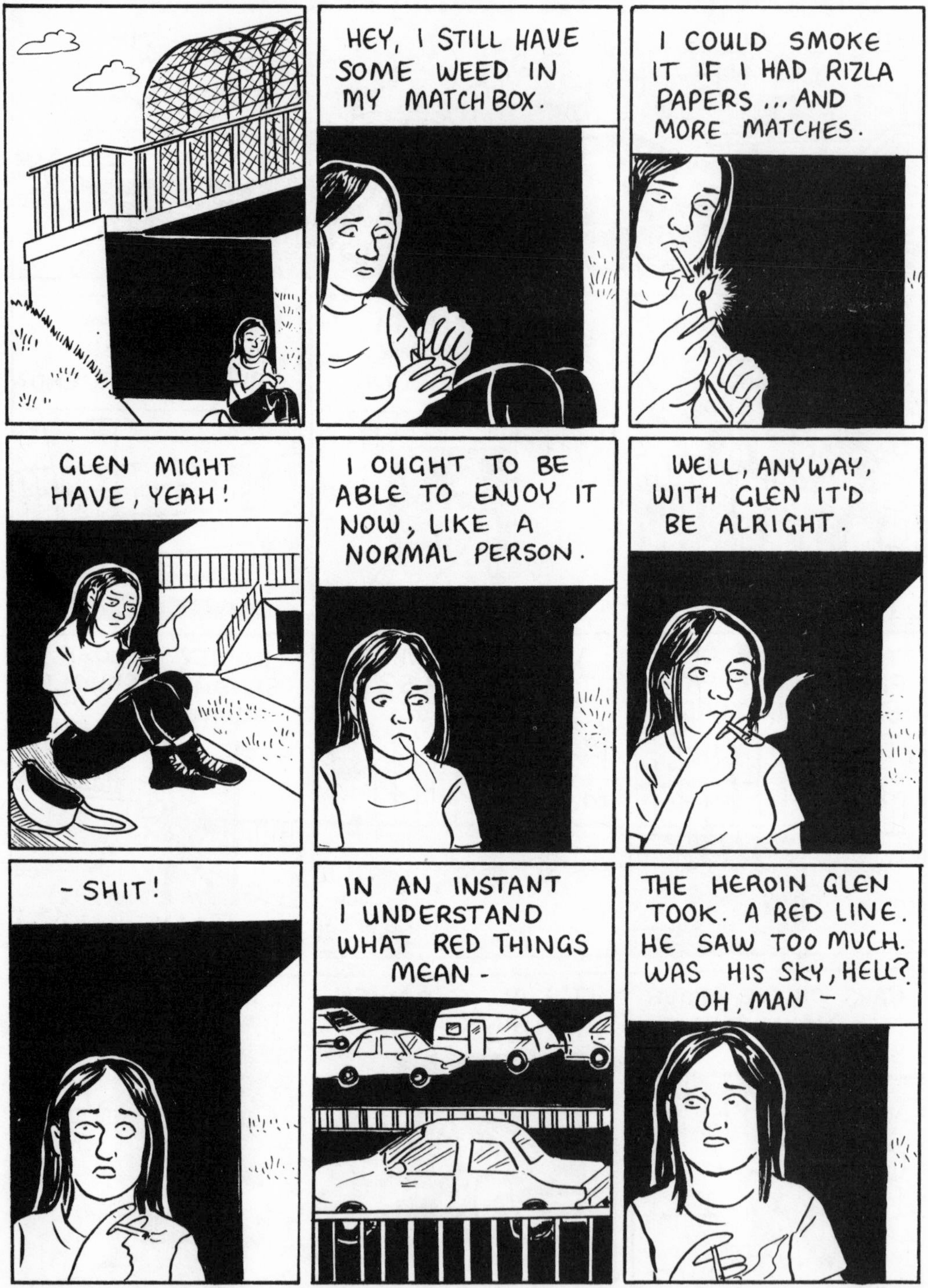
HEY, I STILL HAVE SOME WEED IN MY MATCHBOX.
I COULD SMOKE IT IF I HAD RIZLA PAPERS ... AND MORE MATCHES.
GLEN MIGHT HAVE, YEAH!
I OUGHT TO BE ABLE TO ENJOY IT NOW, LIKE A NORMAL PERSON.
WELL, ANYWAY, WITH GLEN IT'D BE ALRIGHT.
- SHIT!
IN AN INSTANT I UNDERSTAND WHAT RED THINGS MEAN -
THE HEROIN GLEN TOOK. A RED LINE. HE SAW TOO MUCH. WAS HIS SKY, HELL? OH, MAN -

I'M JUST GOING TO TOSS THIS.

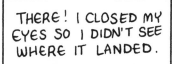

THERE! I CLOSED MY EYES SO I DIDN'T SEE WHERE IT LANDED.

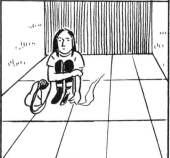

OH GOD!

DID THEY SEE ME? YUP.

SCALLIES.

LADY UNDER THE BRIDGE!

HAVE YOU GOT A SPARE CIGGIES?

(SIGH). YEAH. NO MATCHES THOUGH.

OH, I GOT A LIGHT.

SO, HAVE YOU GOT ANY DRAW,* YEAH?

(* WEED)

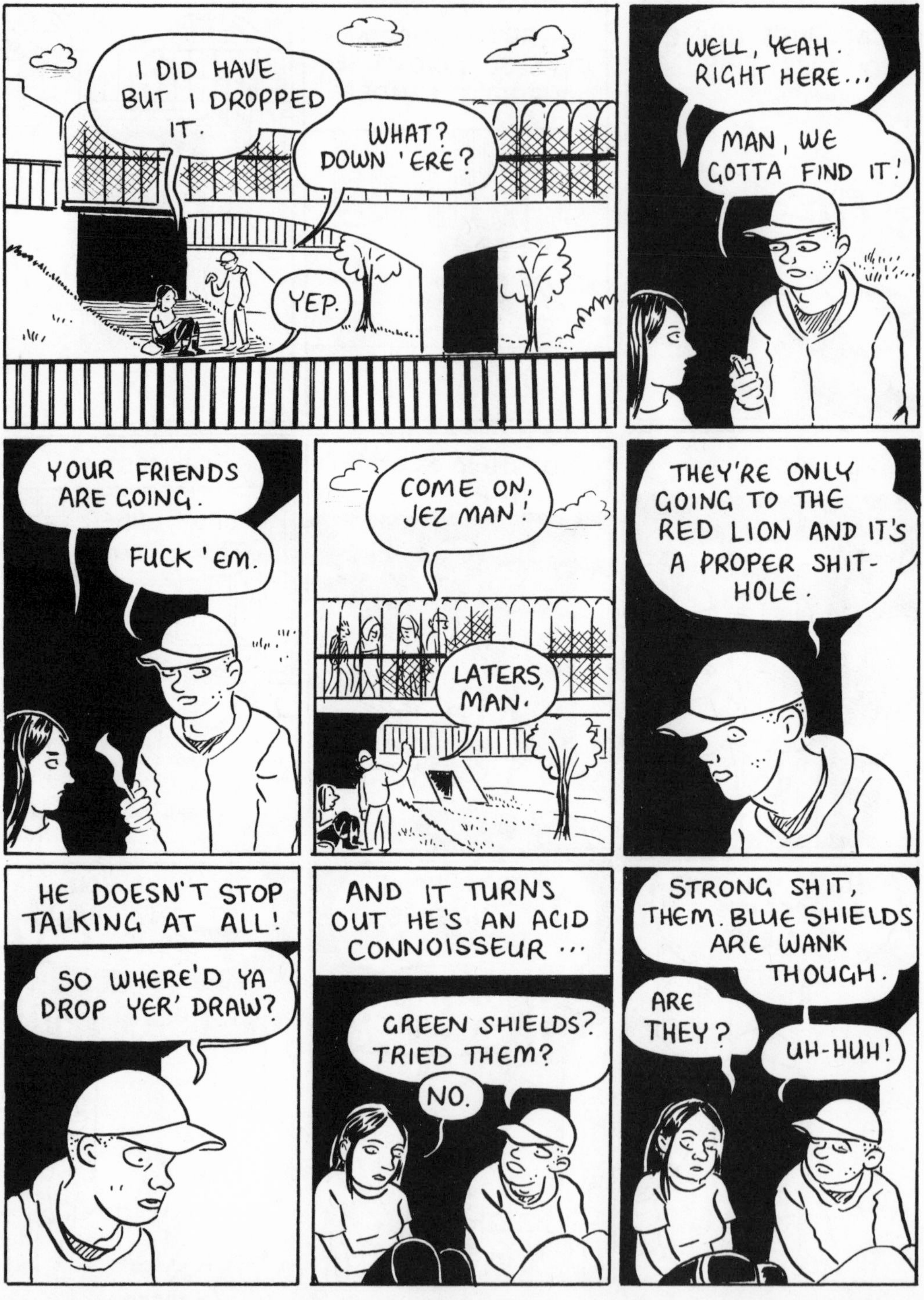
I DID HAVE BUT I DROPPED IT.
WHAT? DOWN 'ERE?
YEP.
WELL, YEAH. RIGHT HERE...
MAN, WE GOTTA FIND IT!
YOUR FRIENDS ARE GOING.
FUCK 'EM.
COME ON, JEZ MAN!
LATERS, MAN.
THEY'RE ONLY GOING TO THE RED LION AND IT'S A PROPER SHIT-HOLE.
HE DOESN'T STOP TALKING AT ALL!
SO WHERE'D YA DROP YER' DRAW?
AND IT TURNS OUT HE'S AN ACID CONNOISSEUR...
GREEN SHIELDS? TRIED THEM?
NO.
STRONG SHIT, THEM. BLUE SHIELDS ARE WANK THOUGH.
ARE THEY?
UH-HUH!

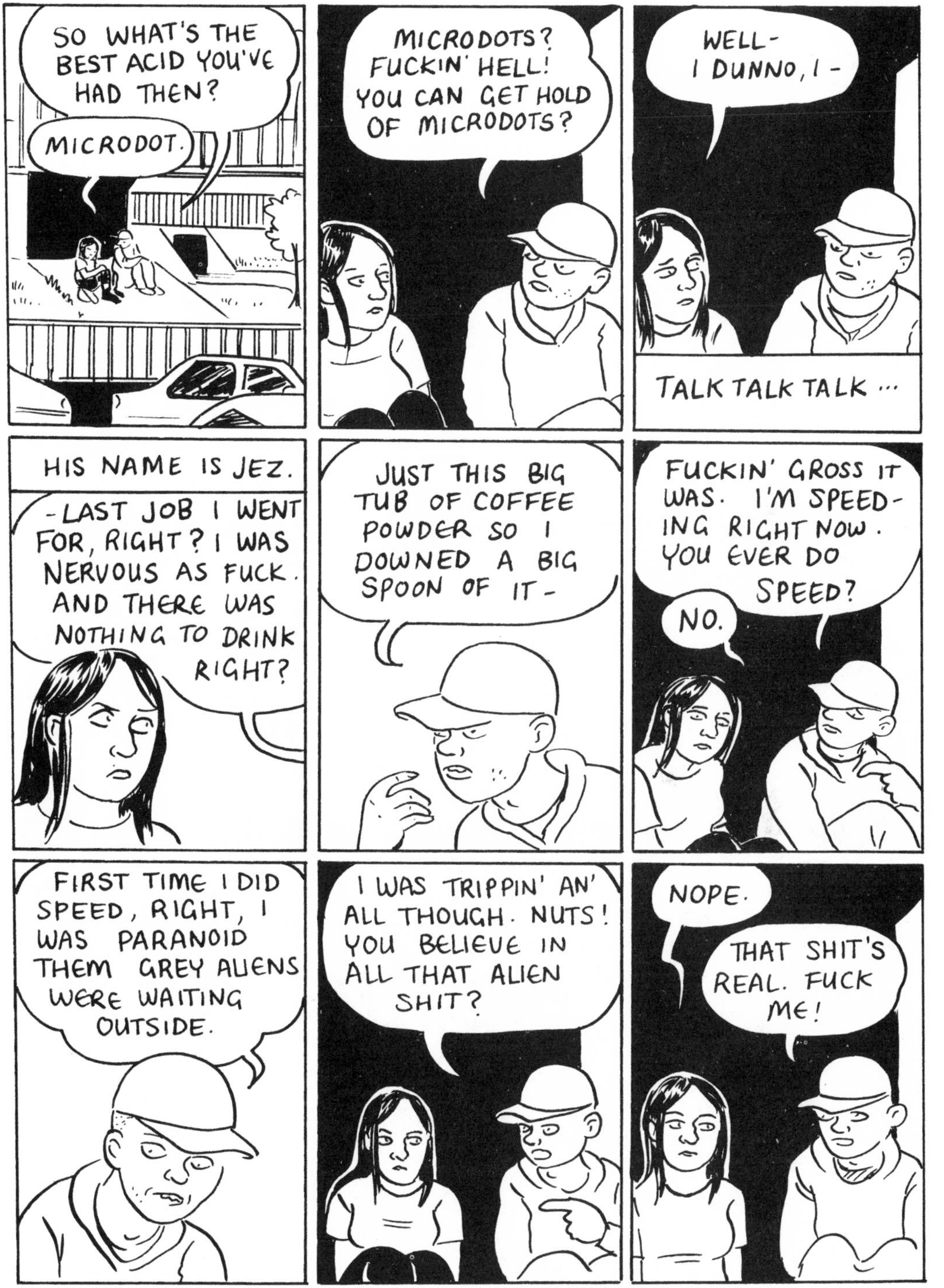
SO WHAT'S THE BEST ACID YOU'VE HAD THEN?
MICRODOT.
MICRODOTS? FUCKIN' HELL! YOU CAN GET HOLD OF MICRODOTS?
WELL- I DUNNO, I -
TALK TALK TALK ...
HIS NAME IS JEZ.
-LAST JOB I WENT FOR, RIGHT? I WAS NERVOUS AS FUCK. AND THERE WAS NOTHING TO DRINK RIGHT?
JUST THIS BIG TUB OF COFFEE POWDER SO I DOWNED A BIG SPOON OF IT -
FUCKIN' GROSS IT WAS. I'M SPEEDING RIGHT NOW. YOU EVER DO SPEED?
NO.
FIRST TIME I DID SPEED, RIGHT, I WAS PARANOID THEM GREY ALIENS WERE WAITING OUTSIDE.
I WAS TRIPPIN' AN' ALL THOUGH. NUTS! YOU BELIEVE IN ALL THAT ALIEN SHIT?
NOPE.
THAT SHIT'S REAL. FUCK ME!

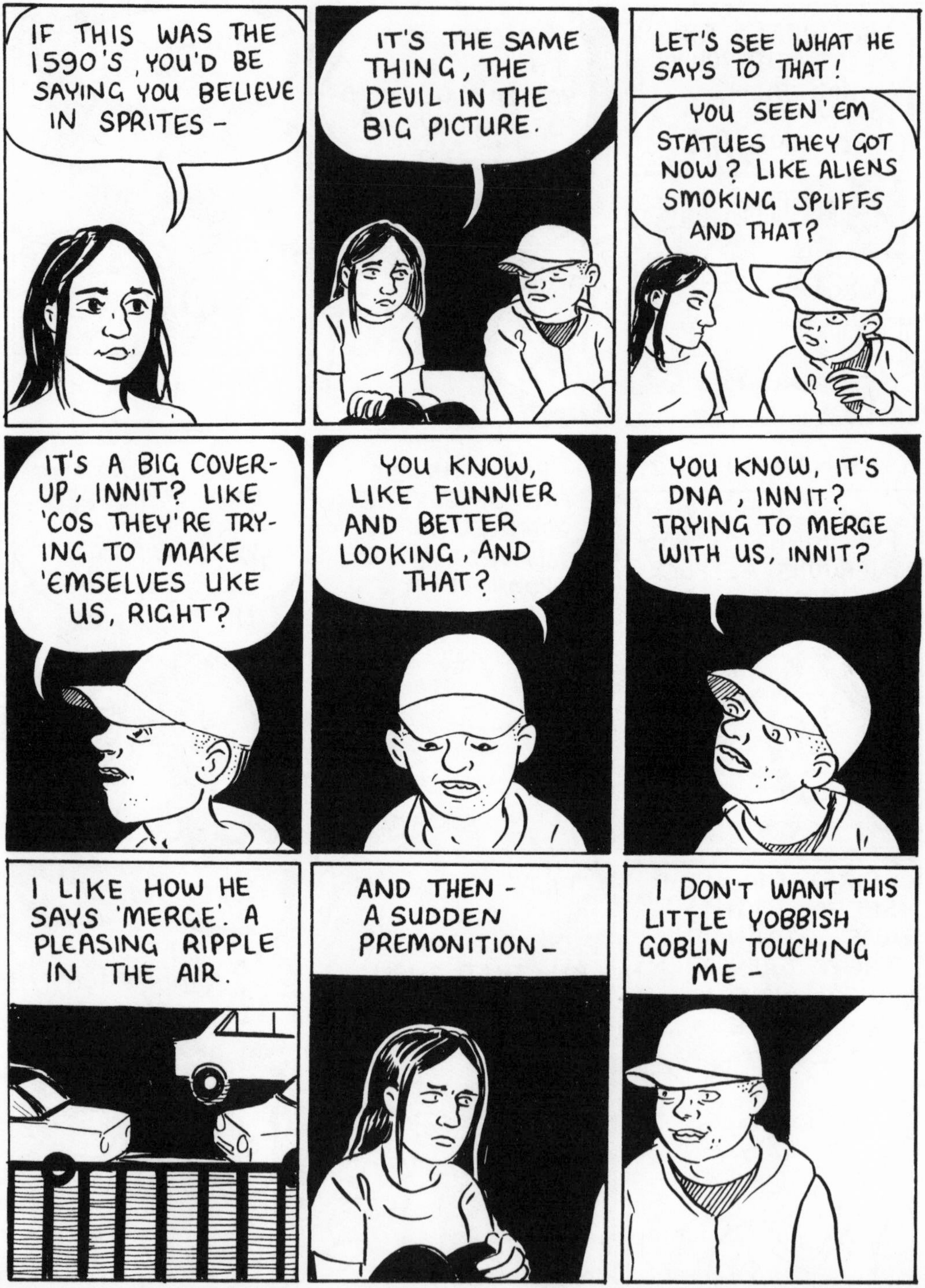
IF THIS WAS THE 1590'S, YOU'D BE SAYING YOU BELIEVE IN SPRITES -
IT'S THE SAME THING, THE DEVIL IN THE BIG PICTURE.
LET'S SEE WHAT HE SAYS TO THAT!
YOU SEEN 'EM STATUES THEY GOT NOW? LIKE ALIENS SMOKING SPLIFFS AND THAT?
IT'S A BIG COVER-UP, INNIT? LIKE 'COS THEY'RE TRYING TO MAKE 'EMSELVES LIKE US, RIGHT?
YOU KNOW, LIKE FUNNIER AND BETTER LOOKING, AND THAT?
YOU KNOW, IT'S DNA, INNIT? TRYING TO MERGE WITH US, INNIT?
I LIKE HOW HE SAYS 'MERGE'. A PLEASING RIPPLE IN THE AIR.
AND THEN - A SUDDEN PREMONITION -
I DON'T WANT THIS LITTLE YOBBISH GOBLIN TOUCHING ME -

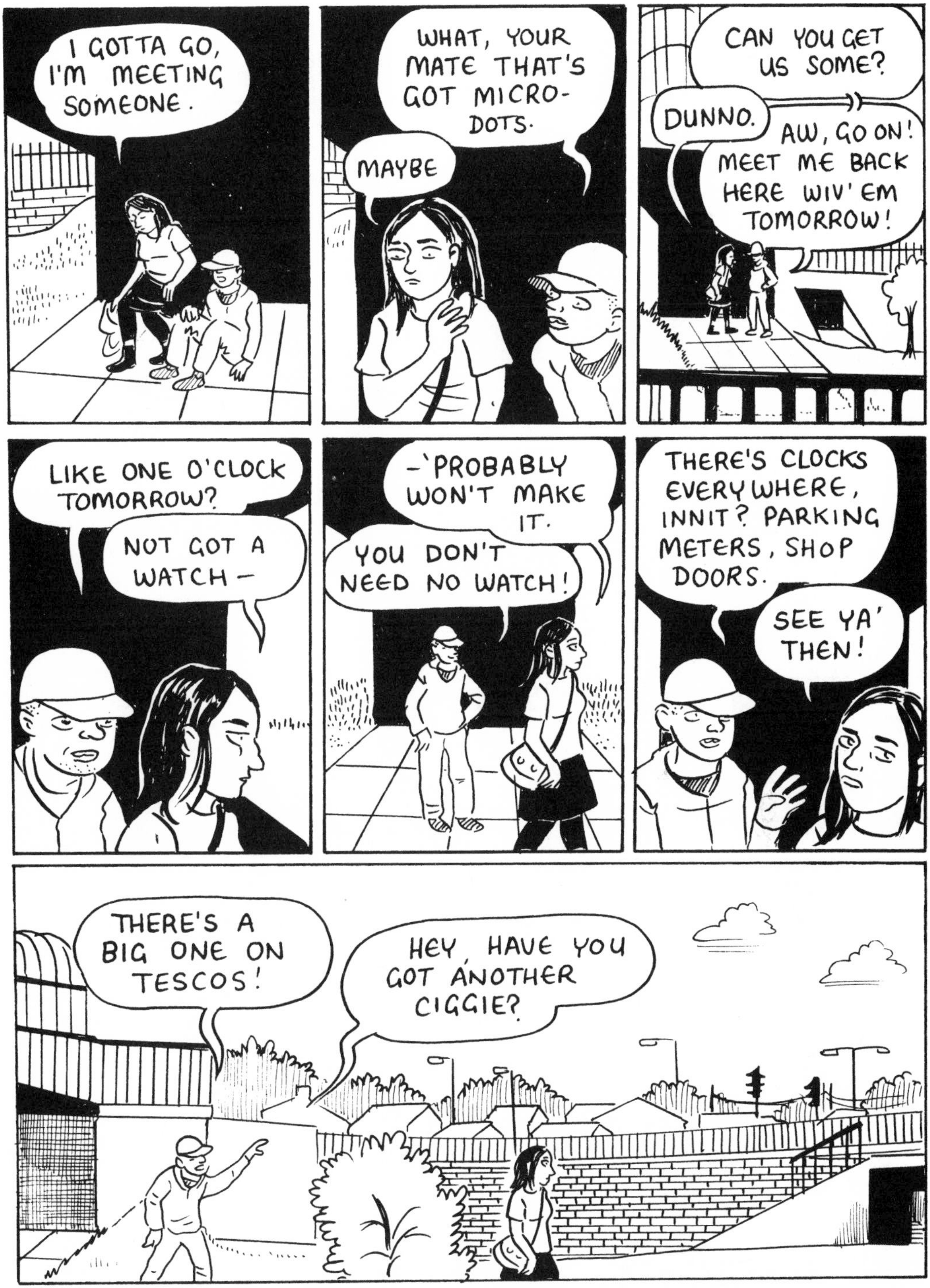
I GOTTA GO, I'M MEETING SOMEONE.
WHAT, YOUR MATE THAT'S GOT MICRO-DOTS.
MAYBE
CAN YOU GET US SOME?
DUNNO.
AW, GO ON! MEET ME BACK HERE WIV' EM TOMORROW!
LIKE ONE O'CLOCK TOMORROW?
NOT GOT A WATCH –
–'PROBABLY WON'T MAKE IT.
YOU DON'T NEED NO WATCH!
THERE'S CLOCKS EVERYWHERE, INNIT? PARKING METERS, SHOP DOORS.
SEE YA' THEN!
THERE'S A BIG ONE ON TESCOS!
HEY, HAVE YOU GOT ANOTHER CIGGIE?

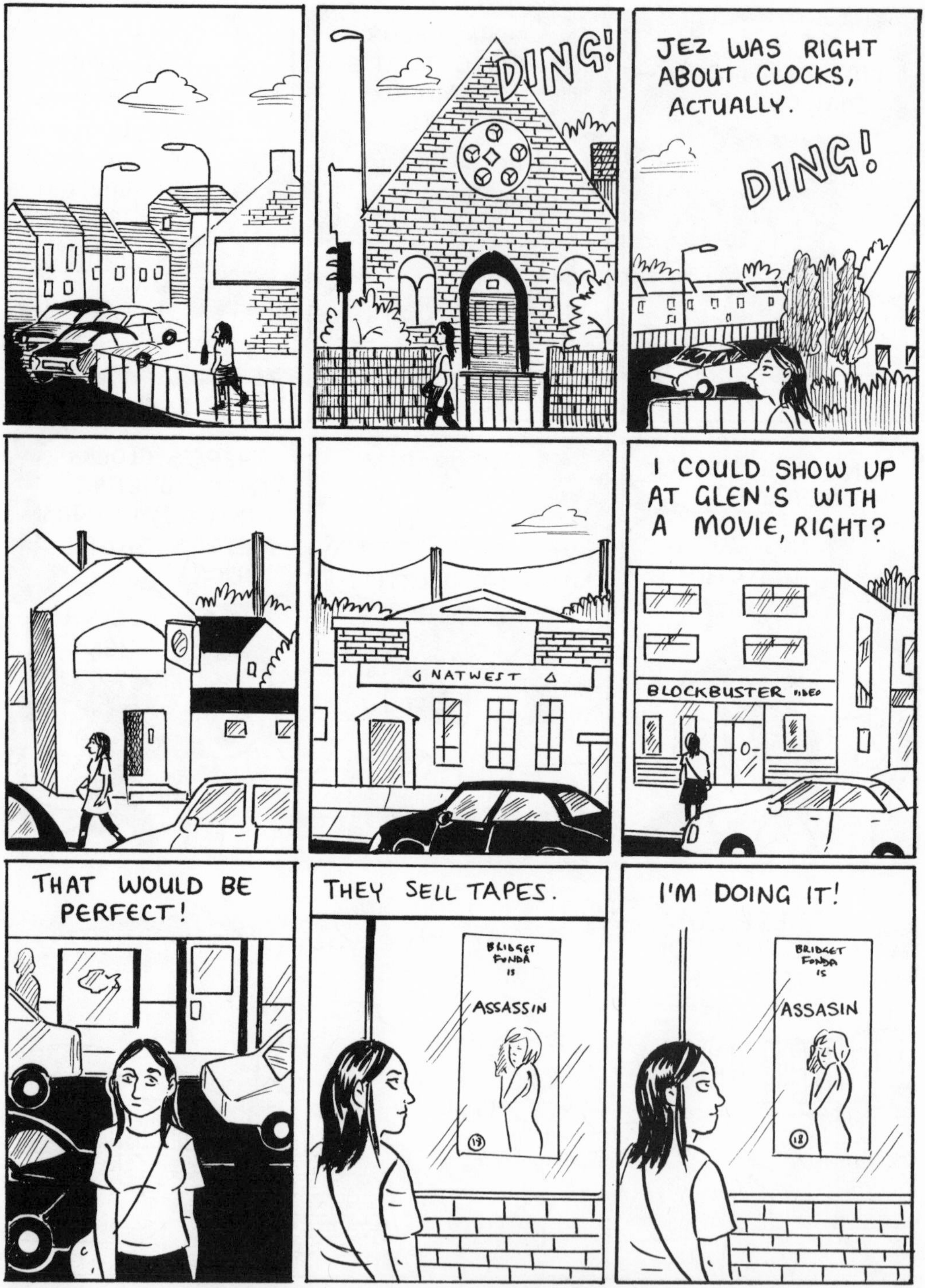
DING!
JEZ WAS RIGHT ABOUT CLOCKS, ACTUALLY.
DING!
NATWEST
I COULD SHOW UP AT GLEN'S WITH A MOVIE, RIGHT?
BLOCKBUSTER VIDEO
THAT WOULD BE PERFECT!
THEY SELL TAPES.
BRIDGET FONDA IS
ASSASSIN
18
I'M DOING IT!
BRIDGET FONDA IS
ASSASIN
18

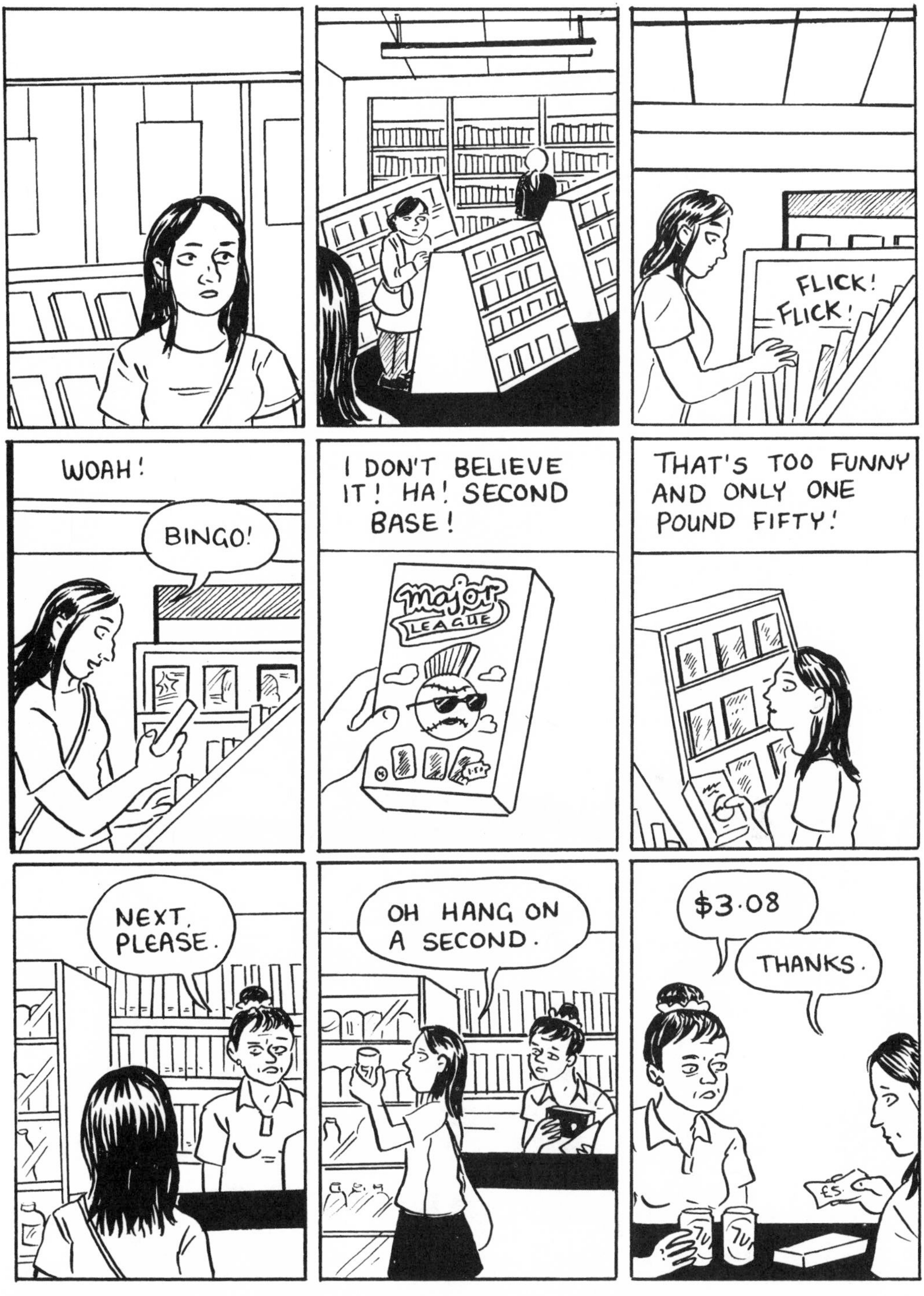
FLICK! FLICK!
WOAH!
BINGO!
I DON'T BELIEVE IT! HA! SECOND BASE!
major LEAGUE
THAT'S TOO FUNNY AND ONLY ONE POUND FIFTY!
NEXT. PLEASE.
OH HANG ON A SECOND.
$3.08
THANKS.
£5

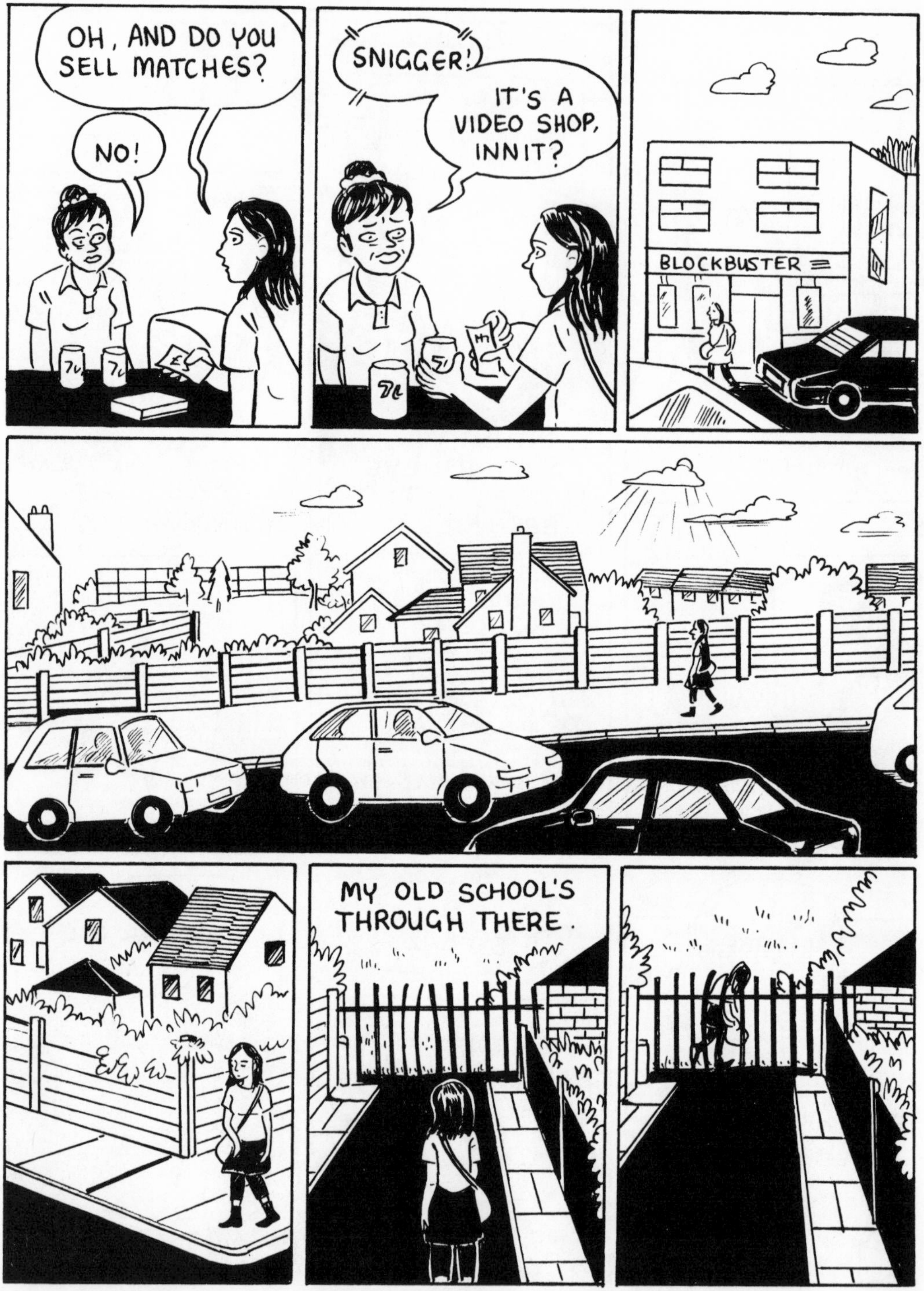
OH, AND DO YOU SELL MATCHES?
NO!
SNIGGER!
IT'S A VIDEO SHOP, INNIT?
BLOCKBUSTER
MY OLD SCHOOL'S THROUGH THERE.

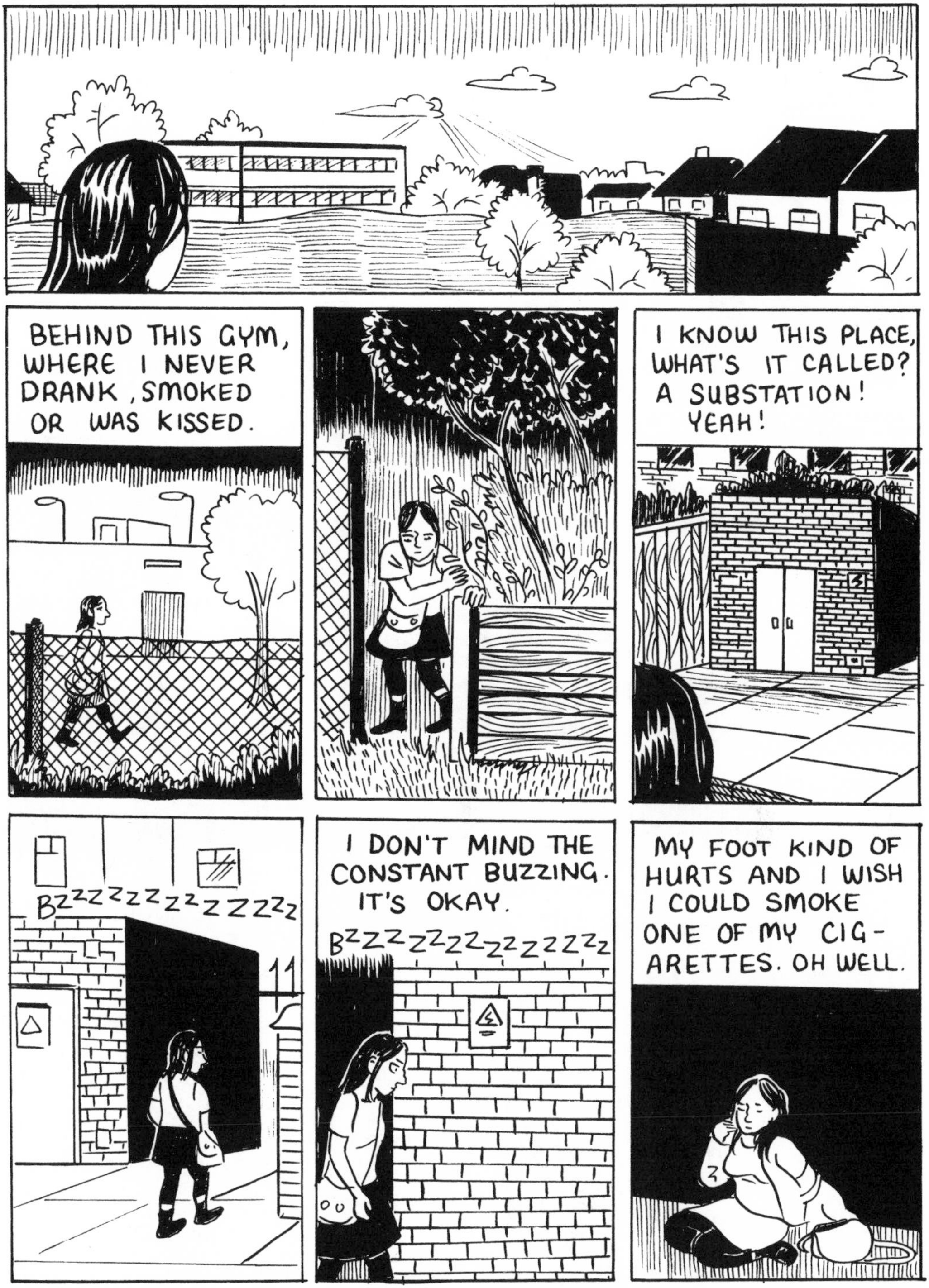
BEHIND THIS GYM, WHERE I NEVER DRANK, SMOKED OR WAS KISSED.
I KNOW THIS PLACE, WHAT'S IT CALLED? A SUBSTATION! YEAH!
BZZZZZZZZZZZZZ
I DON'T MIND THE CONSTANT BUZZING. IT'S OKAY.
BZZZZZZZZZZZZZ
MY FOOT KIND OF HURTS AND I WISH I COULD SMOKE ONE OF MY CIG-ARETTES. OH WELL.

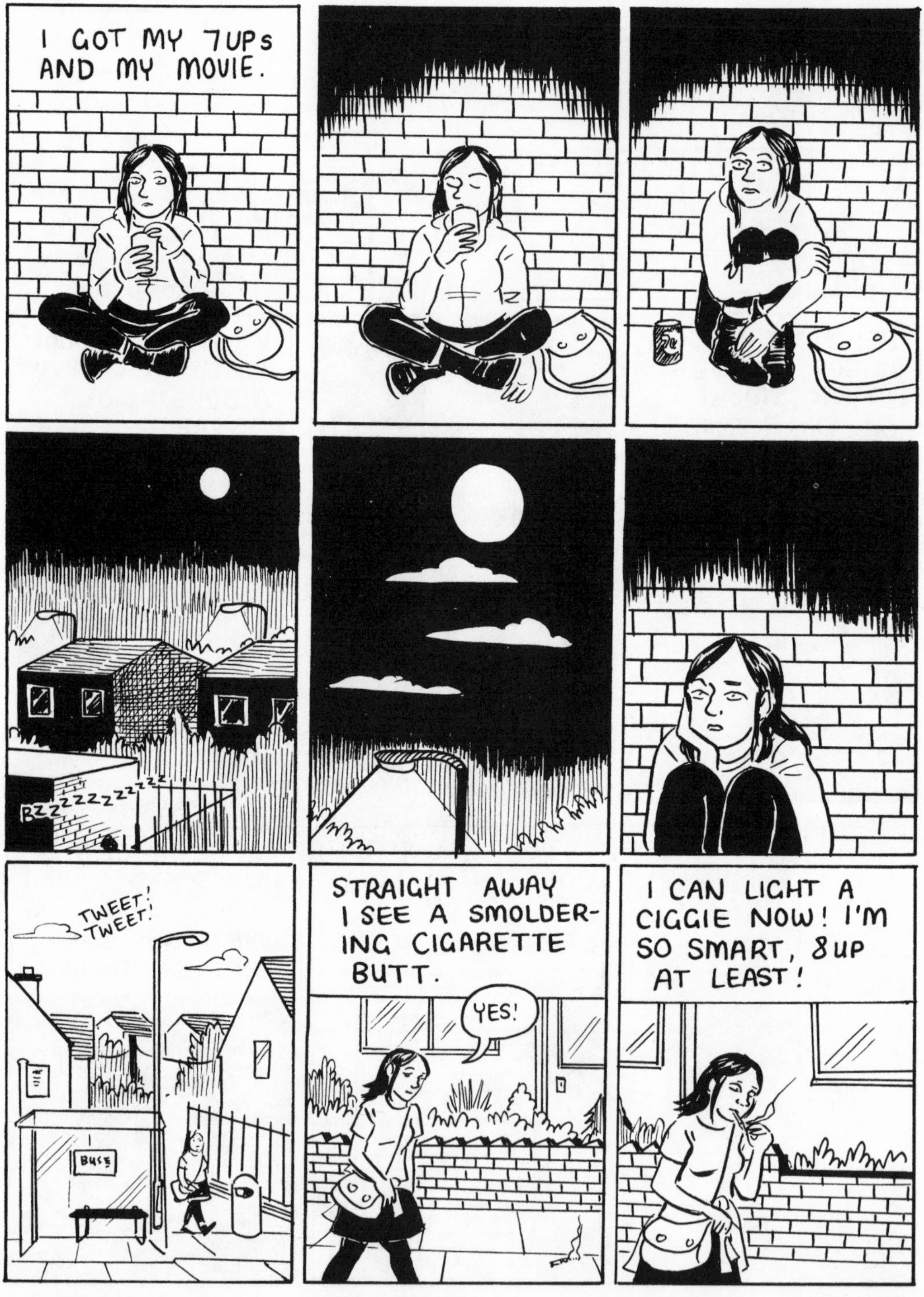
I GOT MY 7UPS AND MY MOVIE.
BZZZZZZZZZZZZ
TWEET! TWEET!
BUS
STRAIGHT AWAY I SEE A SMOLDERING CIGARETTE BUTT.
YES!
I CAN LIGHT A CIGGIE NOW! I'M SO SMART, 8UP AT LEAST!

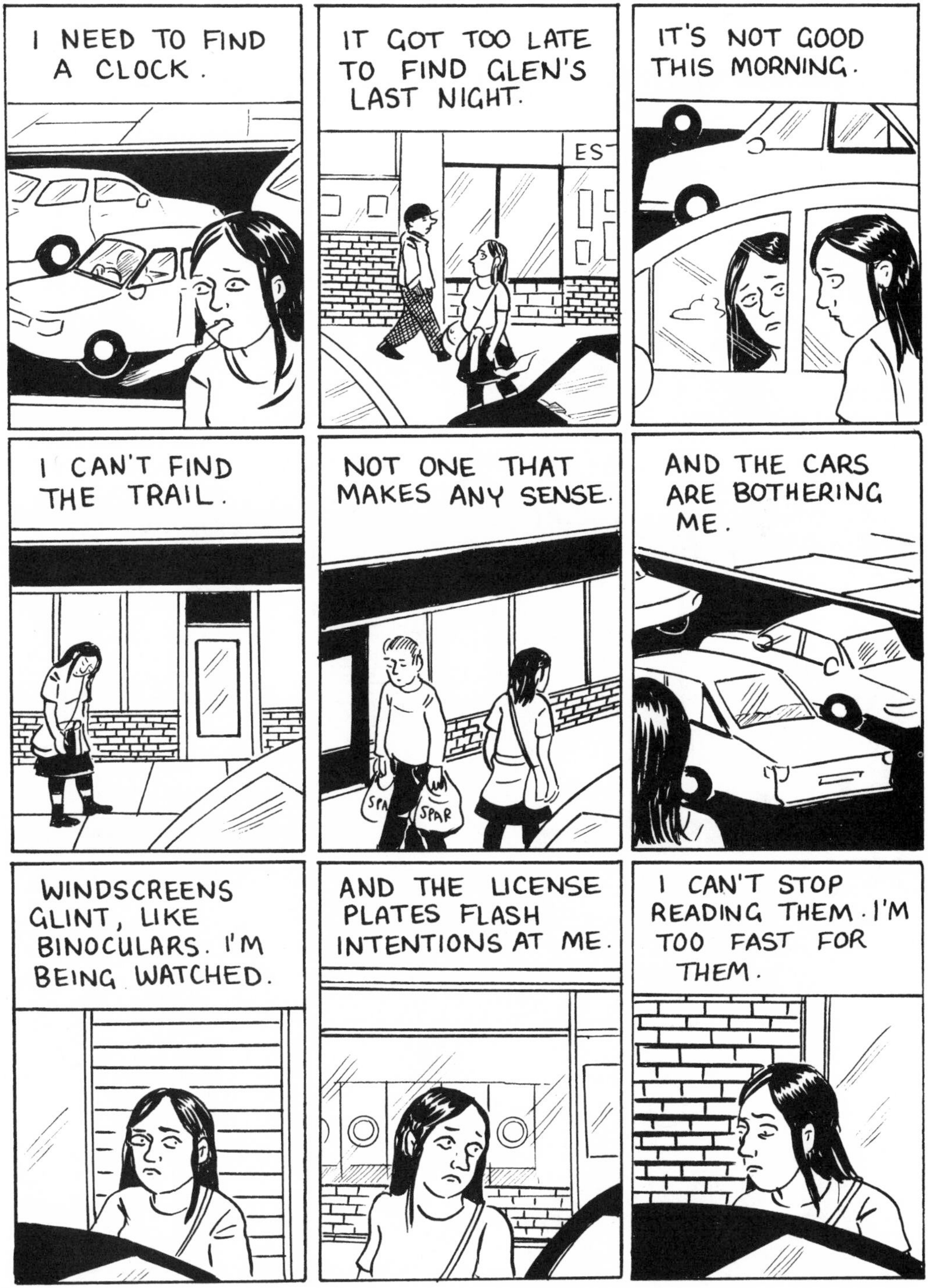
I NEED TO FIND A CLOCK.
IT GOT TOO LATE TO FIND GLEN'S LAST NIGHT.
ES
IT'S NOT GOOD THIS MORNING.
I CAN'T FIND THE TRAIL.
NOT ONE THAT MAKES ANY SENSE.
SPAR
SPAR
AND THE CARS ARE BOTHERING ME.
WINDSCREENS GLINT, LIKE BINOCULARS. I'M BEING WATCHED.
AND THE LICENSE PLATES FLASH INTENTIONS AT ME.
I CAN'T STOP READING THEM. I'M TOO FAST FOR THEM.

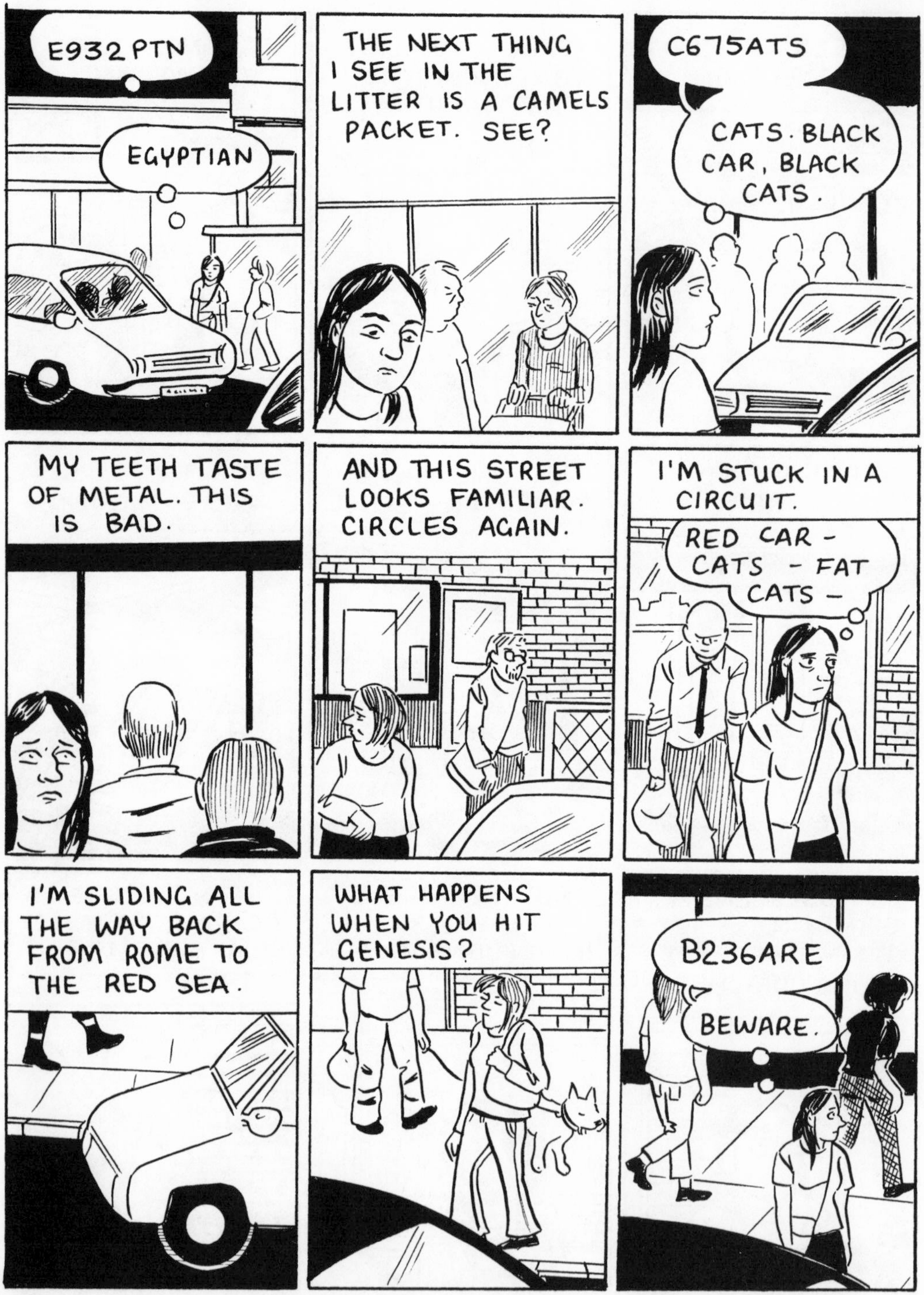
E932 PTN
EGYPTIAN
THE NEXT THING I SEE IN THE LITTER IS A CAMELS PACKET. SEE?
C675ATS
CATS. BLACK CAR, BLACK CATS.
MY TEETH TASTE OF METAL. THIS IS BAD.
AND THIS STREET LOOKS FAMILIAR. CIRCLES AGAIN.
I'M STUCK IN A CIRCUIT.
RED CAR - CATS - FAT CATS -
I'M SLIDING ALL THE WAY BACK FROM ROME TO THE RED SEA.
WHAT HAPPENS WHEN YOU HIT GENESIS?
B236ARE
BEWARE.

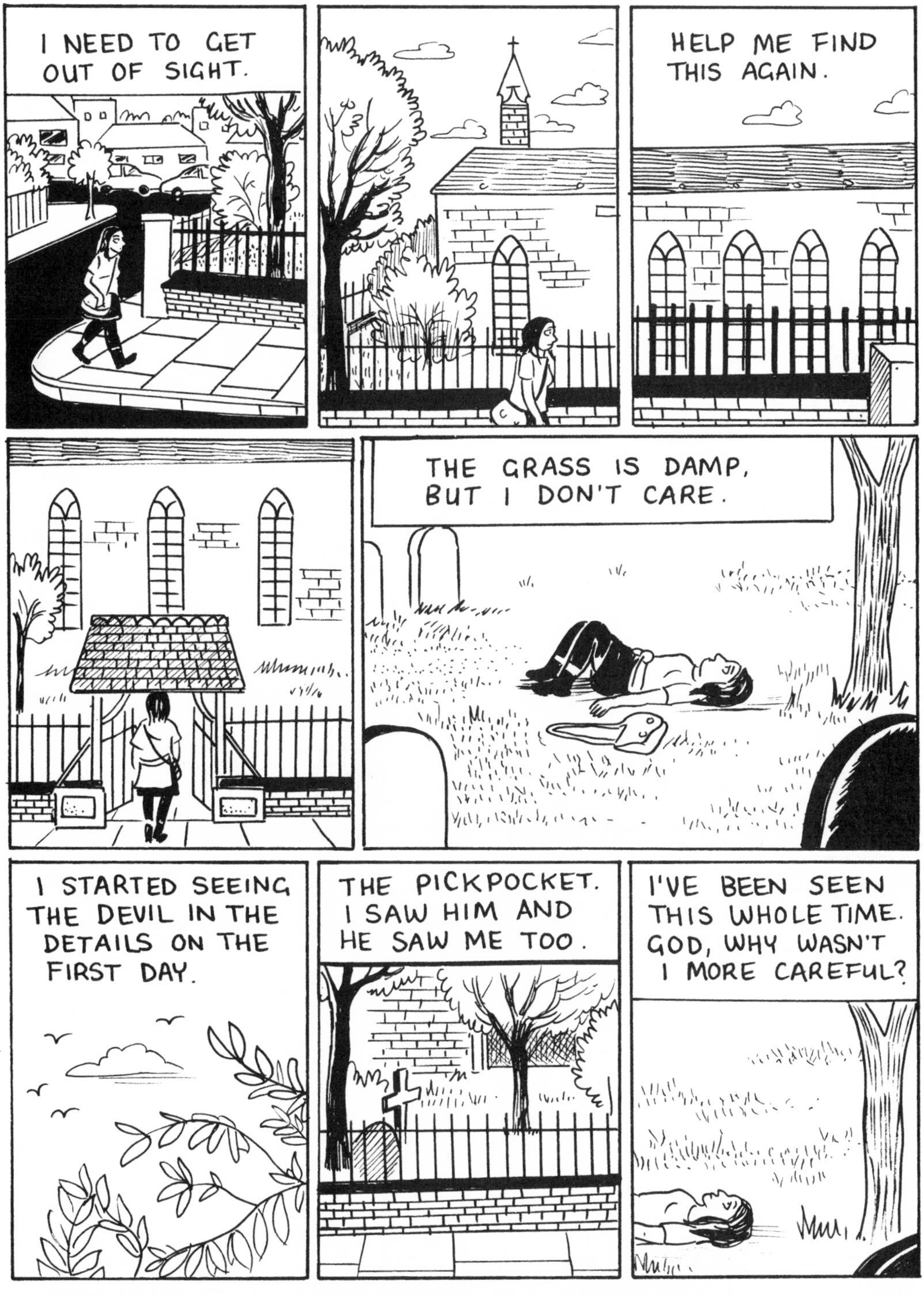
I NEED TO GET OUT OF SIGHT.
HELP ME FIND THIS AGAIN.
THE GRASS IS DAMP, BUT I DON'T CARE.
I STARTED SEEING THE DEVIL IN THE DETAILS ON THE FIRST DAY.
THE PICKPOCKET. I SAW HIM AND HE SAW ME TOO.
I'VE BEEN SEEN THIS WHOLE TIME. GOD, WHY WASN'T I MORE CAREFUL?

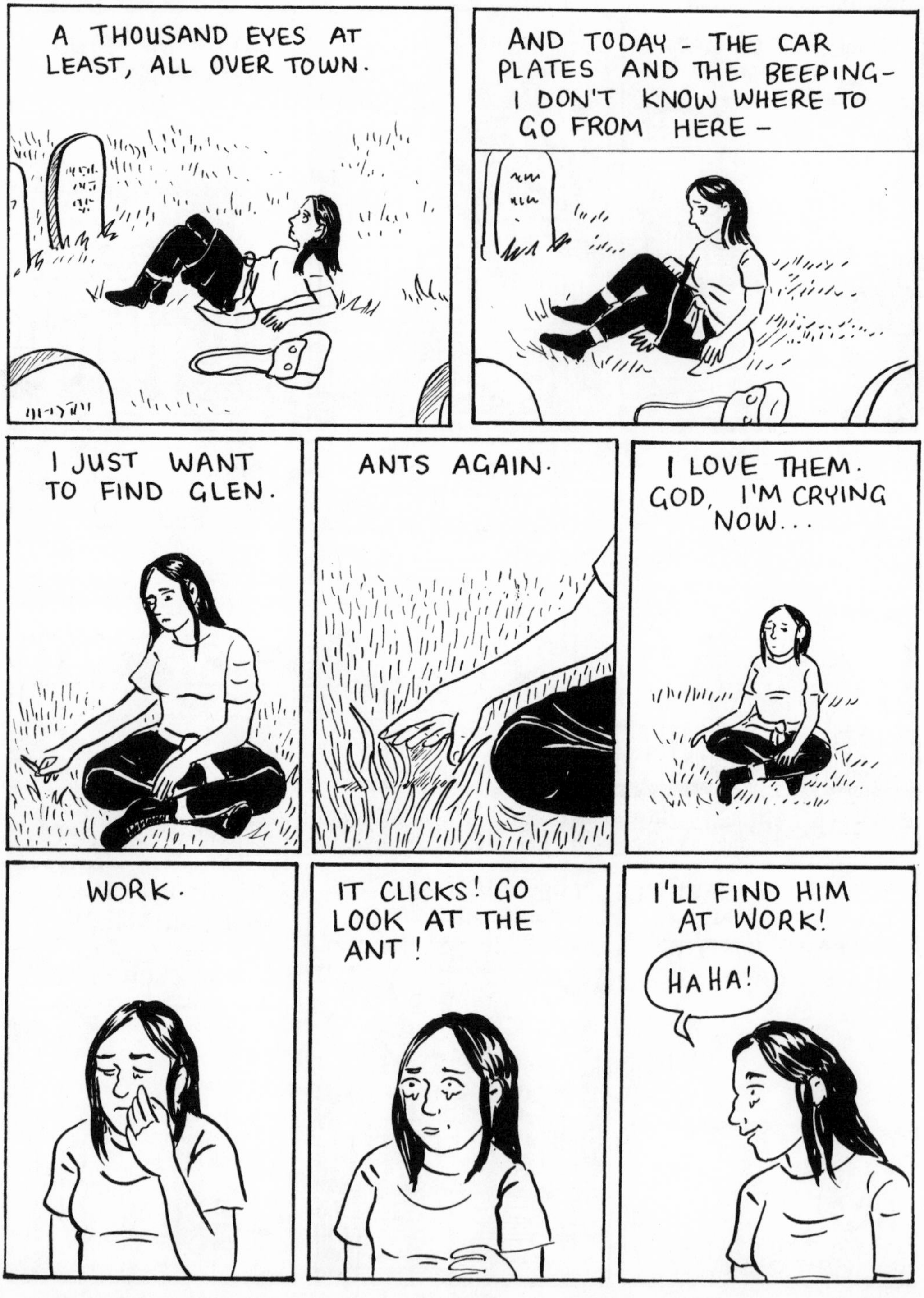
A THOUSAND EYES AT LEAST, ALL OVER TOWN.
AND TODAY - THE CAR PLATES AND THE BEEPING - I DON'T KNOW WHERE TO GO FROM HERE -
I JUST WANT TO FIND GLEN.
ANTS AGAIN.
I LOVE THEM. GOD, I'M CRYING NOW...
WORK.
IT CLICKS! GO LOOK AT THE ANT!
I'LL FIND HIM AT WORK!
HAHA!

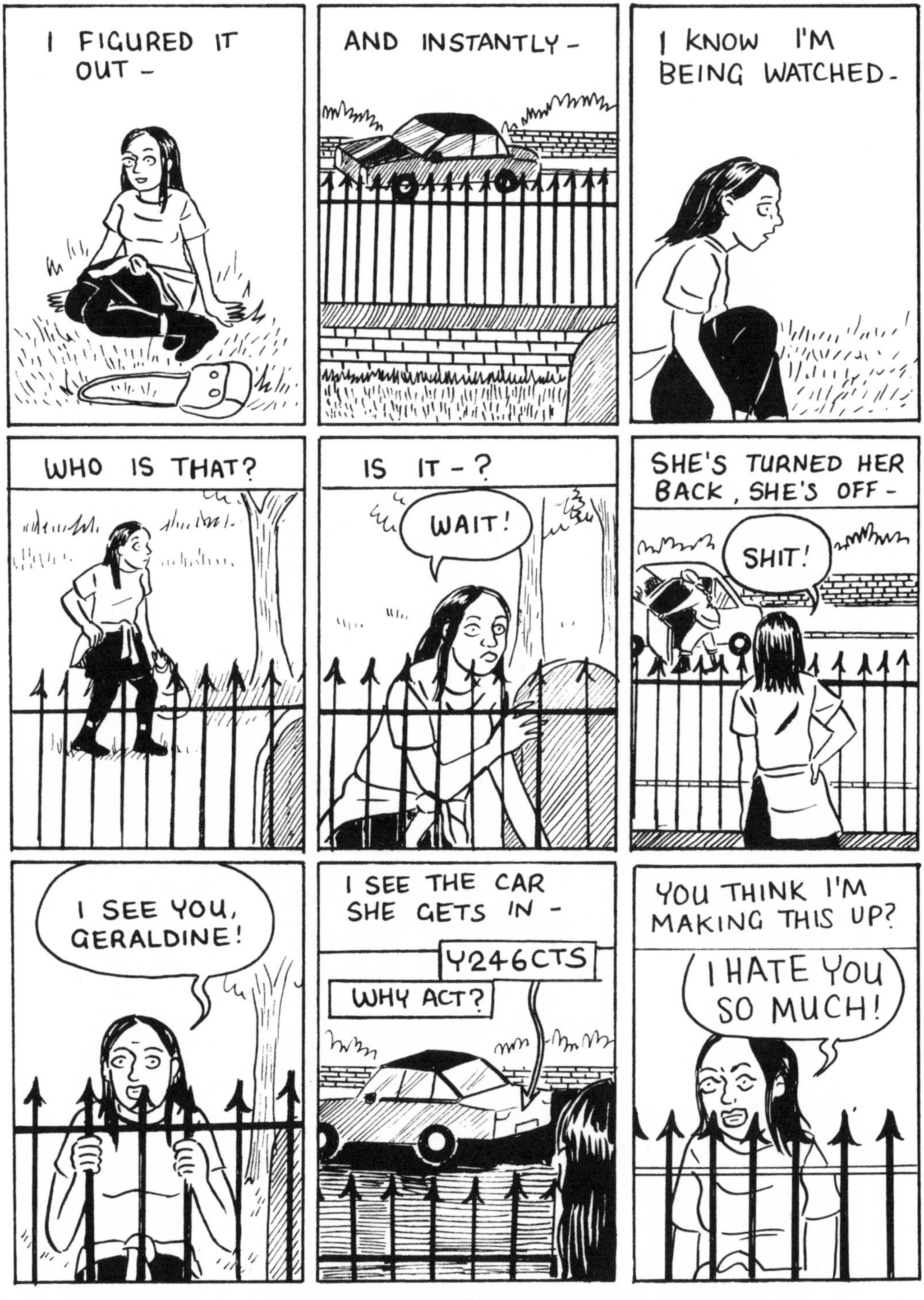
I FIGURED IT OUT -
AND INSTANTLY -
I KNOW I'M BEING WATCHED -
WHO IS THAT?
IS IT - ?
WAIT!
SHE'S TURNED HER BACK, SHE'S OFF -
SHIT!
I SEE YOU, GERALDINE!
I SEE THE CAR SHE GETS IN -
Y246CTS
WHY ACT?
YOU THINK I'M MAKING THIS UP?
I HATE YOU SO MUCH!

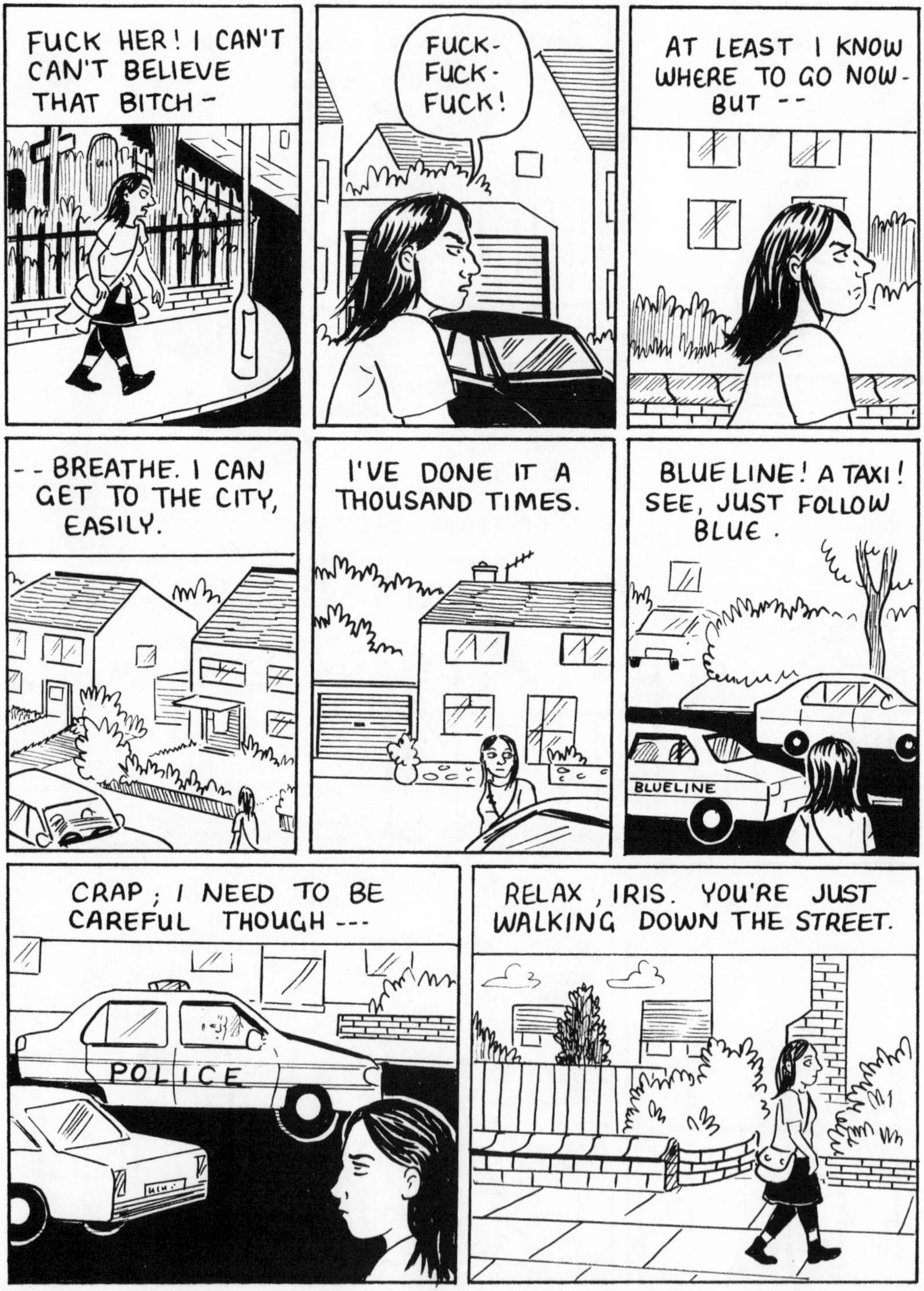
FUCK HER! I CAN'T CAN'T BELIEVE THAT BITCH -
FUCK-FUCK-FUCK!
AT LEAST I KNOW WHERE TO GO NOW- BUT --
-- BREATHE. I CAN GET TO THE CITY, EASILY.
I'VE DONE IT A THOUSAND TIMES.
BLUE LINE! A TAXI! SEE, JUST FOLLOW BLUE.
BLUELINE
CRAP; I NEED TO BE CAREFUL THOUGH ---
POLICE
RELAX, IRIS. YOU'RE JUST WALKING DOWN THE STREET.

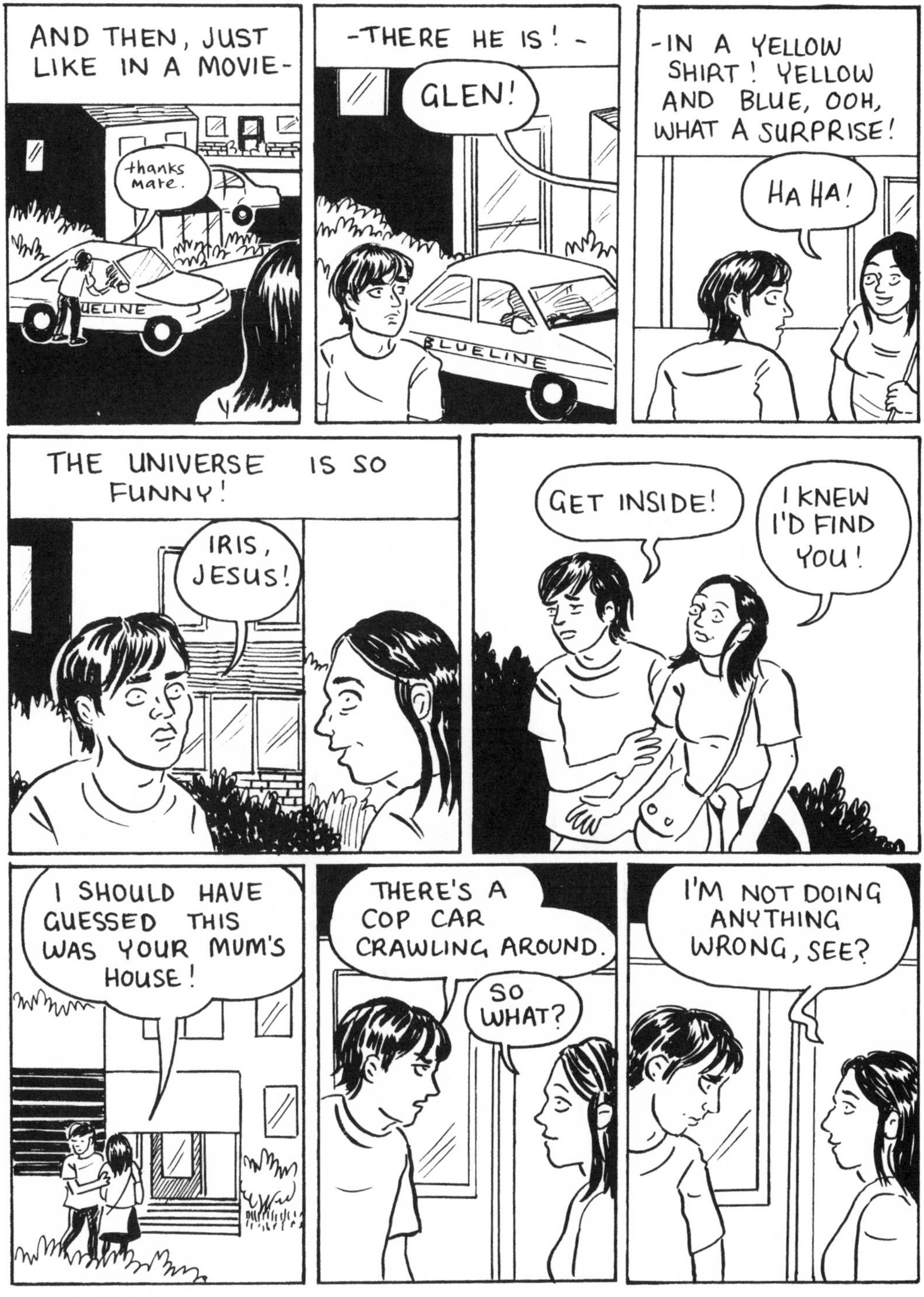
AND THEN, JUST LIKE IN A MOVIE-
thanks mate.
UELINE
-THERE HE IS! -
GLEN!
BLUELINE
-IN A YELLOW SHIRT! YELLOW AND BLUE, OOH, WHAT A SURPRISE!
HA HA!
THE UNIVERSE IS SO FUNNY!
IRIS, JESUS!
GET INSIDE!
I KNEW I'D FIND YOU!
I SHOULD HAVE GUESSED THIS WAS YOUR MUM'S HOUSE!
THERE'S A COP CAR CRAWLING AROUND.
SO WHAT?
I'M NOT DOING ANYTHING WRONG, SEE?

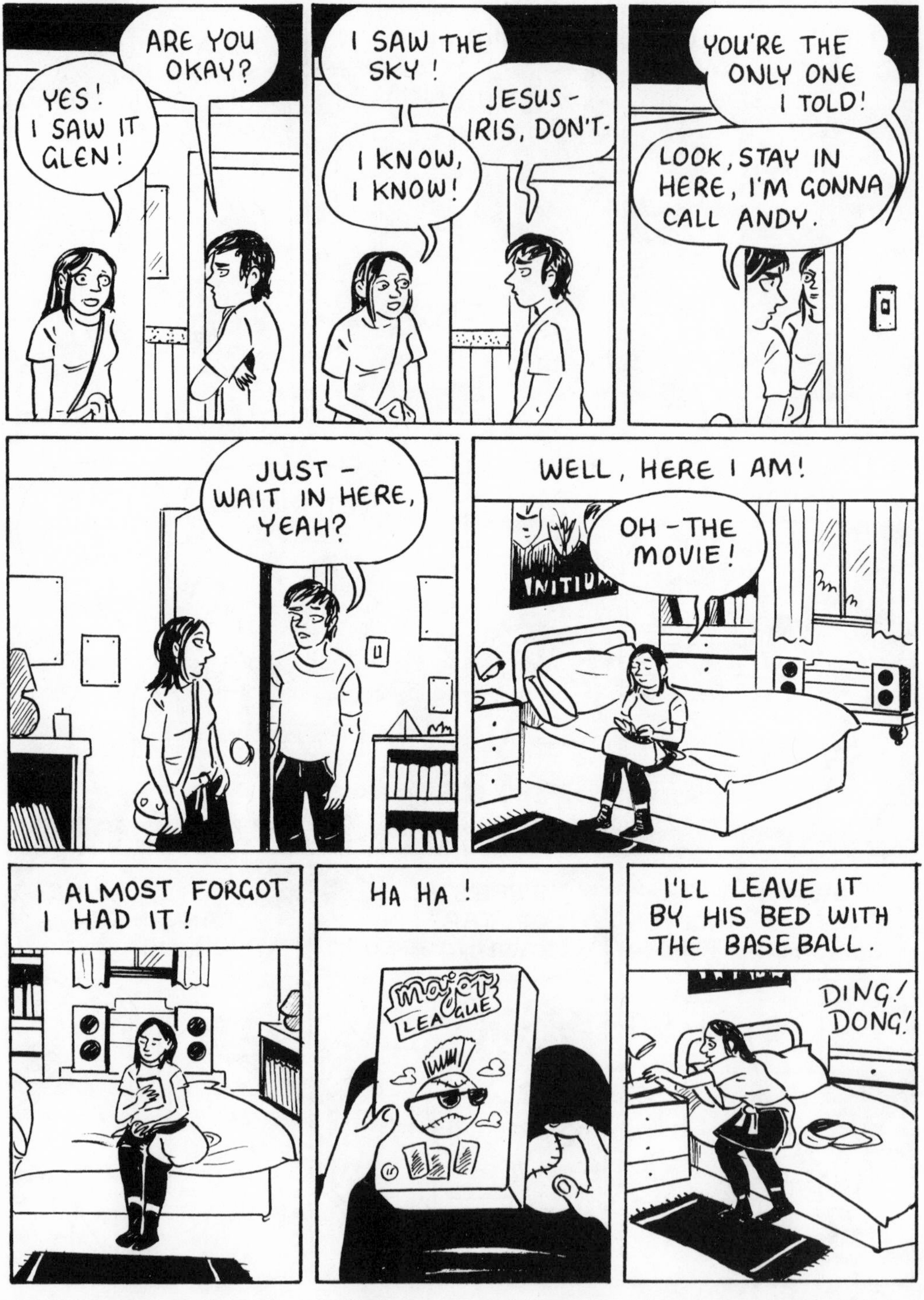
ARE YOU OKAY?
YES! I SAW IT GLEN!
I SAW THE SKY!
JESUS - IRIS, DON'T-
I KNOW, I KNOW!
YOU'RE THE ONLY ONE I TOLD!
LOOK, STAY IN HERE, I'M GONNA CALL ANDY.
JUST - WAIT IN HERE, YEAH?
WELL, HERE I AM!
INITIUM
OH - THE MOVIE!
I ALMOST FORGOT I HAD IT!
HA HA!
I'LL LEAVE IT BY HIS BED WITH THE BASEBALL.
DING! DONG!

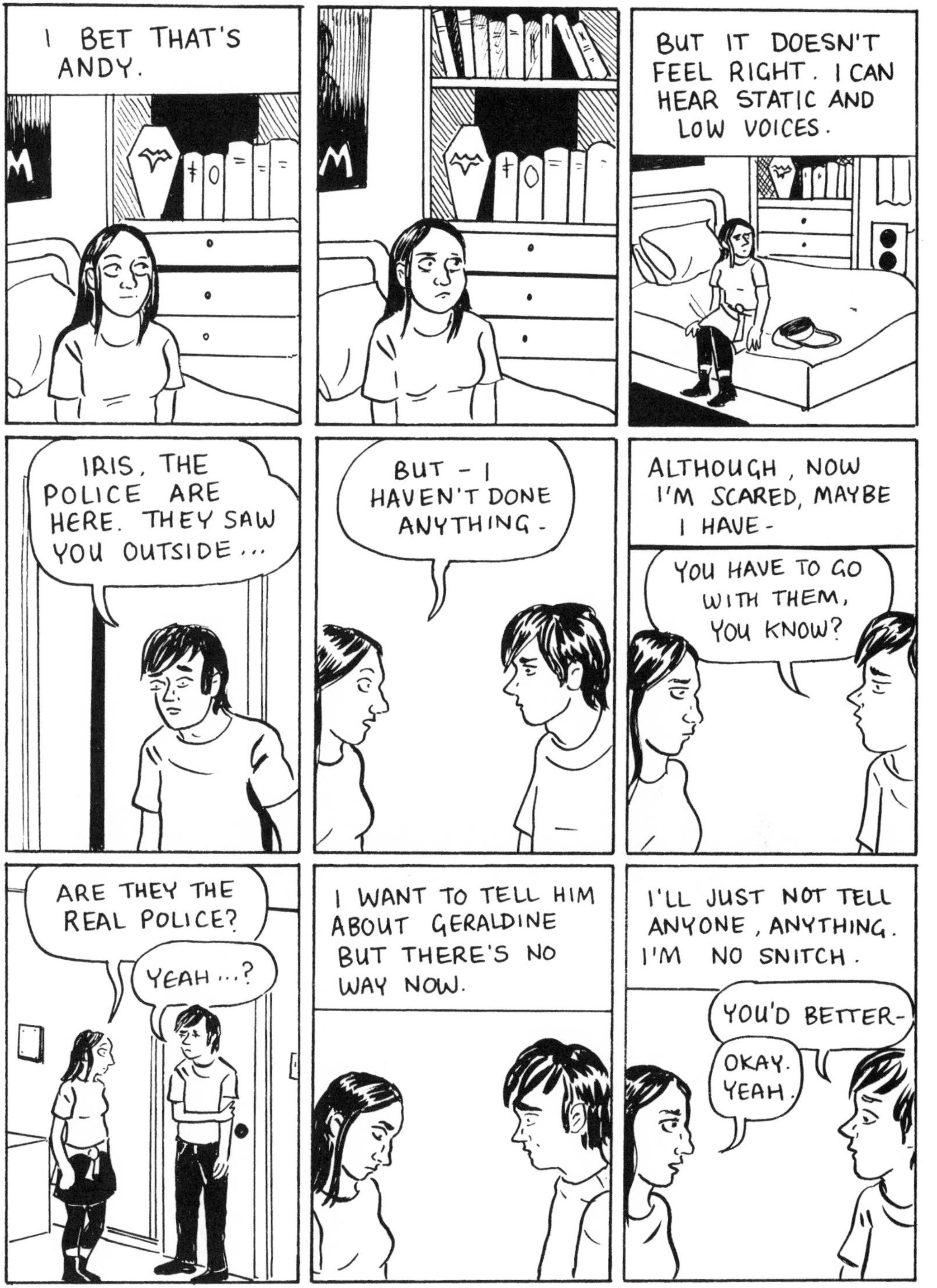
I BET THAT'S ANDY.
BUT IT DOESN'T FEEL RIGHT. I CAN HEAR STATIC AND LOW VOICES.
IRIS, THE POLICE ARE HERE. THEY SAW YOU OUTSIDE...
BUT - I HAVEN'T DONE ANYTHING -
ALTHOUGH, NOW I'M SCARED, MAYBE I HAVE -
YOU HAVE TO GO WITH THEM, YOU KNOW?
ARE THEY THE REAL POLICE?
YEAH...?
I WANT TO TELL HIM ABOUT GERALDINE BUT THERE'S NO WAY NOW.
I'LL JUST NOT TELL ANYONE, ANYTHING. I'M NO SNITCH.
YOU'D BETTER-
OKAY. YEAH.

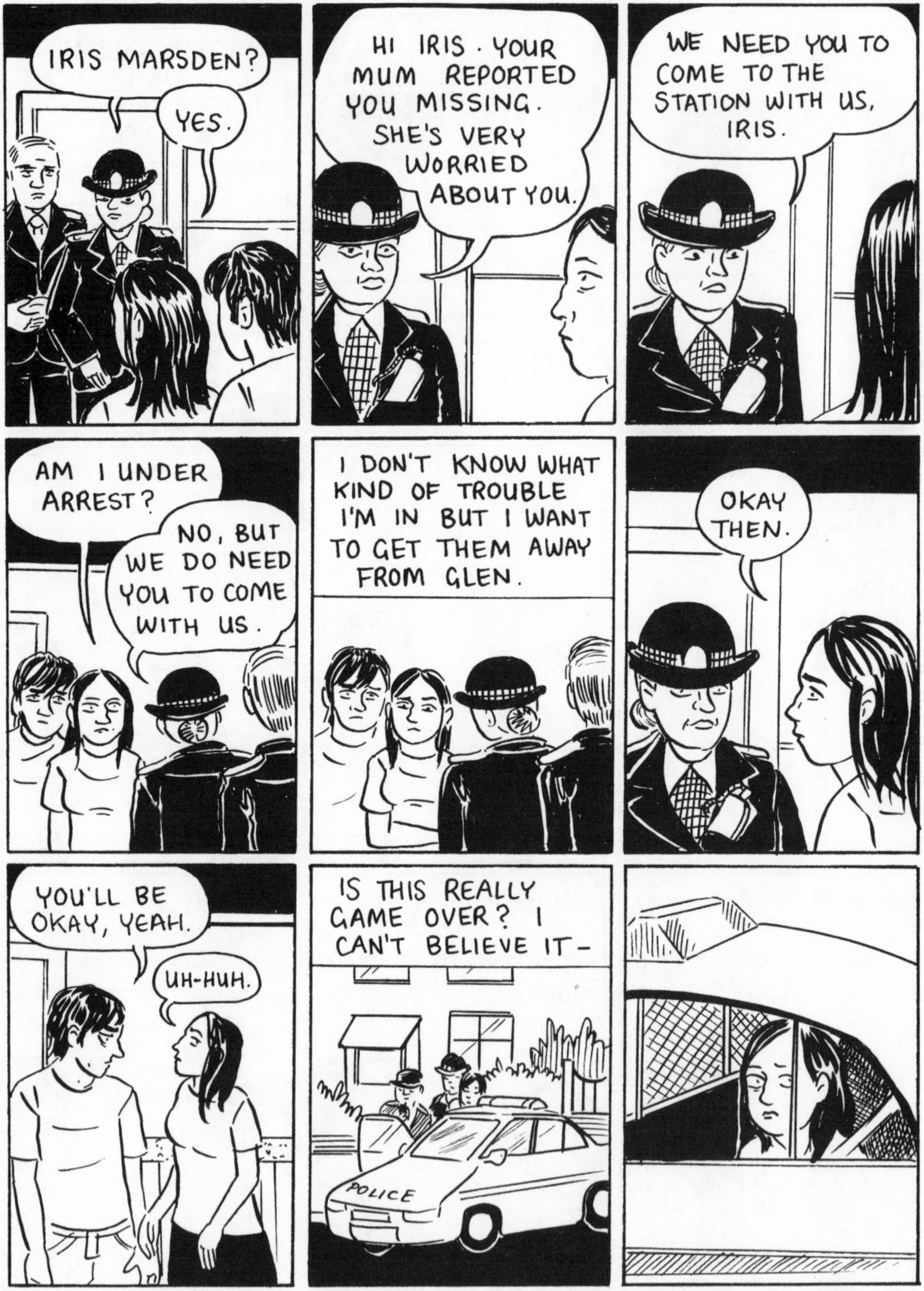
IRIS MARSDEN?
YES.
HI IRIS. YOUR MUM REPORTED YOU MISSING. SHE'S VERY WORRIED ABOUT YOU.
WE NEED YOU TO COME TO THE STATION WITH US, IRIS.
AM I UNDER ARREST?
NO, BUT WE DO NEED YOU TO COME WITH US.
I DON'T KNOW WHAT KIND OF TROUBLE I'M IN BUT I WANT TO GET THEM AWAY FROM GLEN.
OKAY THEN.
YOU'LL BE OKAY, YEAH.
UH-HUH.
IS THIS REALLY GAME OVER? I CAN'T BELIEVE IT-
POLICE

TO BE CONTINUED.

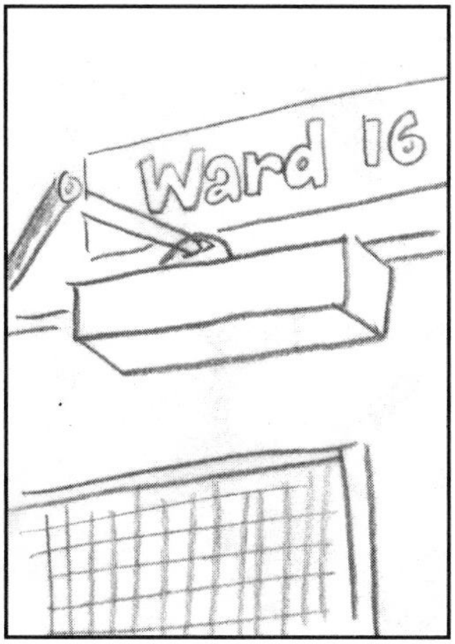
Ward 16

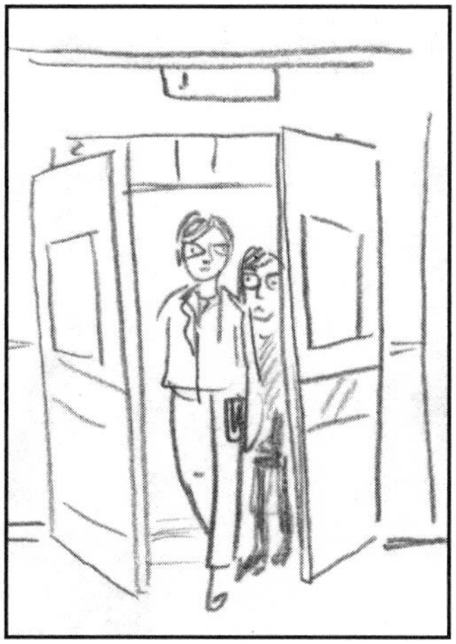

The following is an excerpt from *Sky in Stereo* book two.

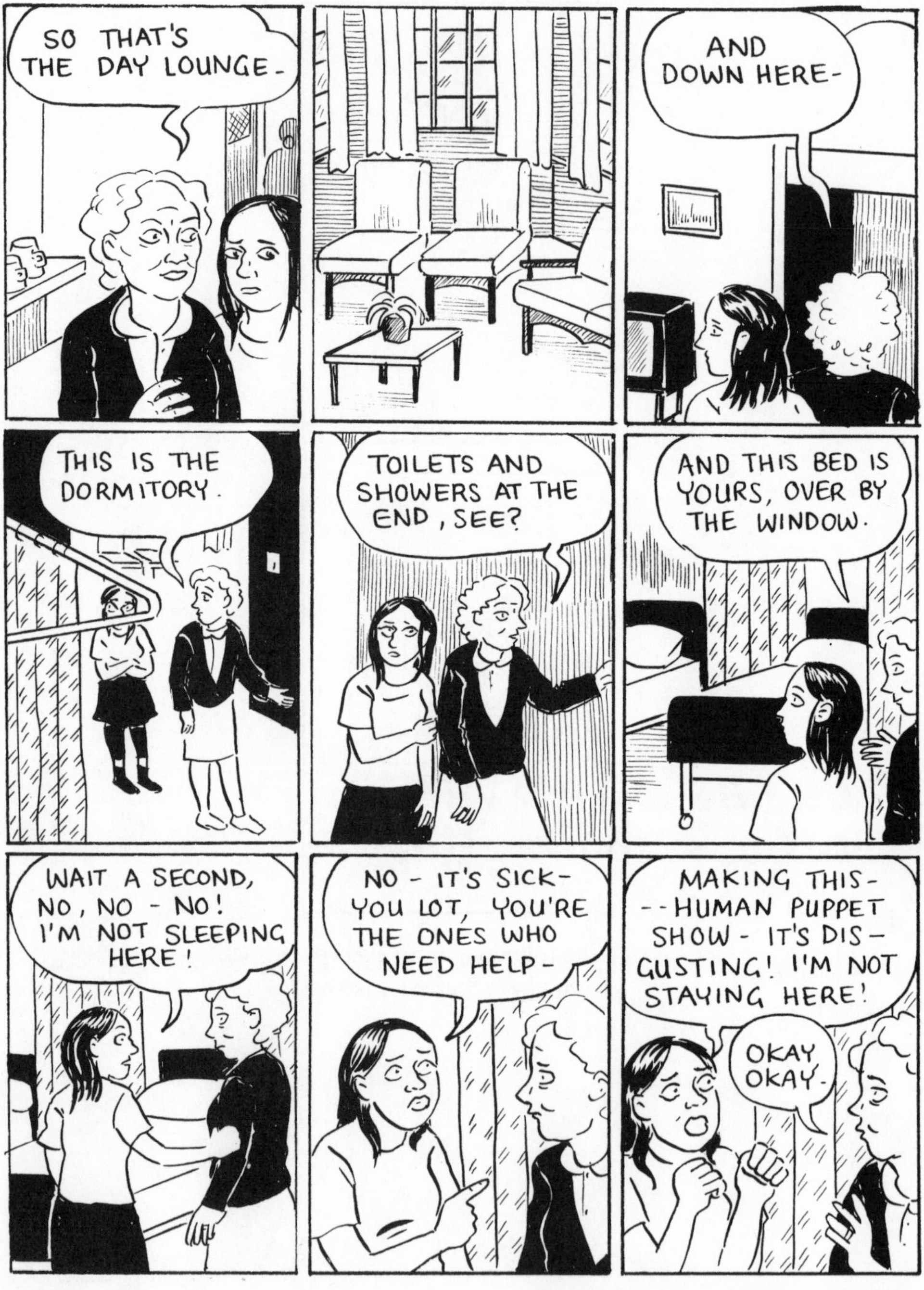
SO THAT'S THE DAY LOUNGE -
AND DOWN HERE -
THIS IS THE DORMITORY.
TOILETS AND SHOWERS AT THE END, SEE?
AND THIS BED IS YOURS, OVER BY THE WINDOW.
WAIT A SECOND, NO, NO - NO! I'M NOT SLEEPING HERE!
NO - IT'S SICK - YOU LOT, YOU'RE THE ONES WHO NEED HELP -
MAKING THIS - - HUMAN PUPPET SHOW - IT'S DIS - GUSTING! I'M NOT STAYING HERE!
OKAY OKAY -

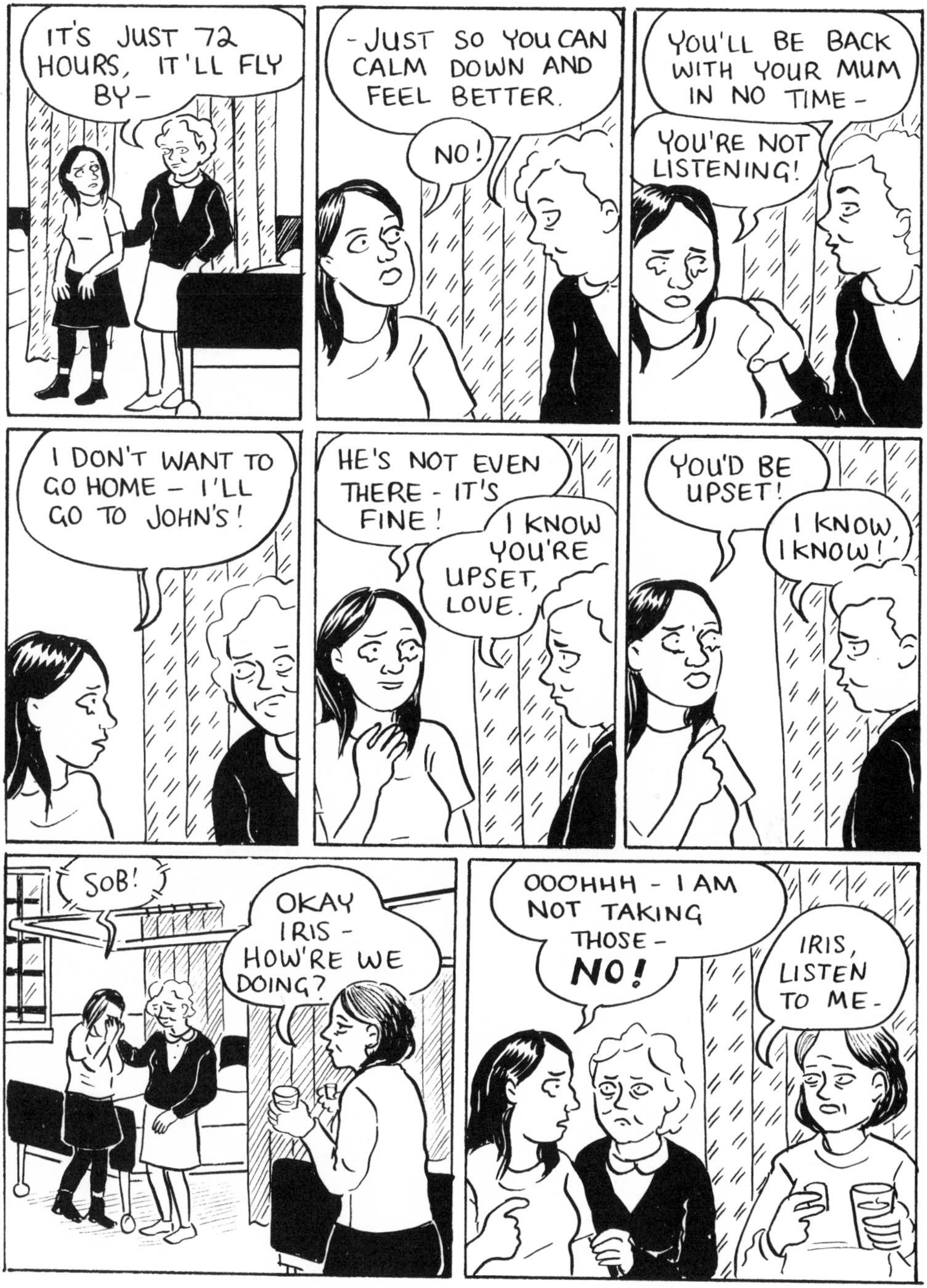
IT'S JUST 72 HOURS, IT'LL FLY BY-
-JUST SO YOU CAN CALM DOWN AND FEEL BETTER.
NO!
YOU'LL BE BACK WITH YOUR MUM IN NO TIME-
YOU'RE NOT LISTENING!
I DON'T WANT TO GO HOME - I'LL GO TO JOHN'S!
HE'S NOT EVEN THERE - IT'S FINE!
I KNOW YOU'RE UPSET, LOVE.
YOU'D BE UPSET!
I KNOW, I KNOW!
SOB!
OKAY IRIS - HOW'RE WE DOING?
OOOHHH - I AM NOT TAKING THOSE - NO!
IRIS, LISTEN TO ME-

NO!
TUG! TUG!
IRIS!
LET ME OUT!
NO!
AND LIKE I'M IN A ZOMBIE MOVIE, HANDS GRAB ME! –
I GOT HER
OKAY-
DOORS FLY OPEN, WHITE COATED ARMS APPROACH –
TO BE CONCLUDED IN BOOK 2.

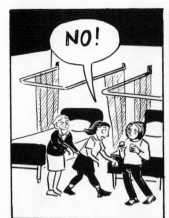

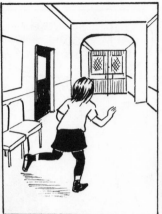

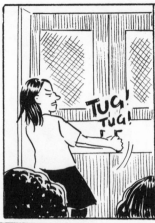

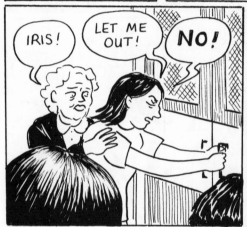

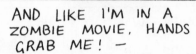

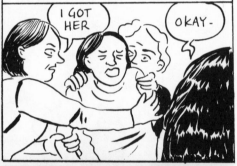

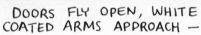

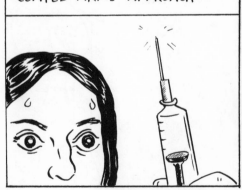

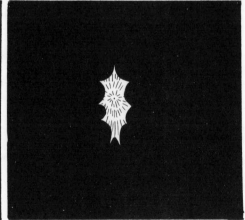

Mardou is from Manchester, England . She now lives in St. Louis, Missouri with her husband - the cartoonist Ted May - and their kid. Since 2001, she has made mini-comics such as *Manhole* and *Anais in Paris* and founded the all-girl anthology, *Whores of Mensa*. Her comics have more recently featured in the British Library's retrospective *Comics Unmasked* (2014) and in the forthcoming movie, *The Missing Girl* (2015). The Ignatz nominated series, *Sky in Stereo* began life as a mini-comic and is her first graphic novel.

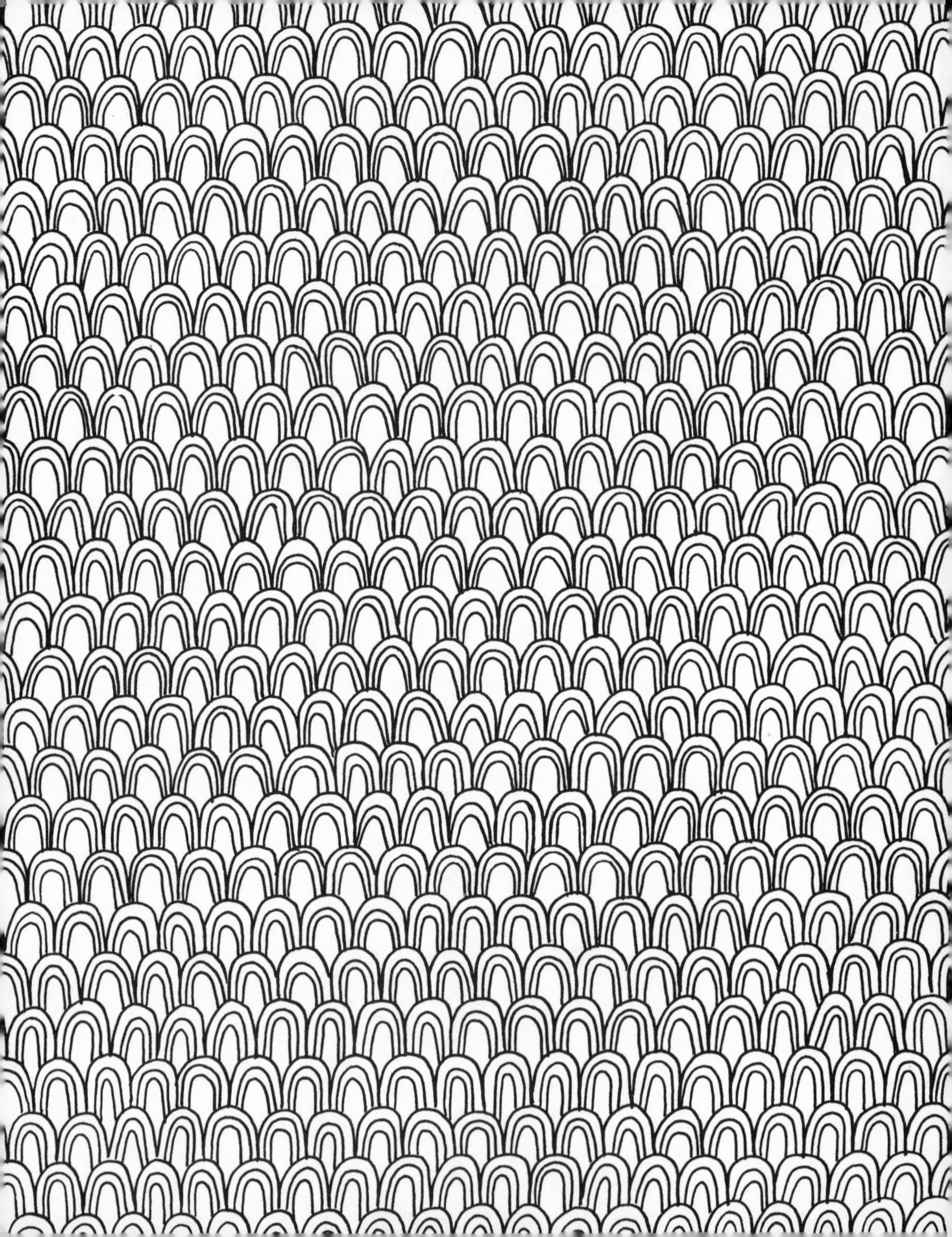